GRAND FINAL

100 Years of Rugby League Championship Finals

Graham Morris

VERTICAL EDITIONS

www.verticaleditions.com

First published in the United Kingdom in 2007 by Vertical Editions, 7 Bell Busk, Skipton, North Yorkshire BD23 4DT

www.verticaleditions.com

ISBN 978-1-904091-22-6

Cover design and typeset by HBA, York

Printed and bound by the Cromwell Press, Trowbridge

CONTENTS

ACKNOWLEDGEMENTS

No publication of this type is ever compiled without the generous support of others and I would particularly like to thank Ron Bailey, Tony Collins, Stuart Duffy, Harry Edgar, Mike Flynn, Simon Foster, Steve Fox, Eddie Fuller, Robert Gate (whose assistance was especially helpful), David Gronow, Derek Hallas, Andrew Hardcastle, Mick Harrop, Phil Hodgson, Sig Kasatkin and Dave Williams (www.RLphotos.com), Stan Lewandowski, Phil Oakes (Micron Video Production Ltd), John Riding, Alex Service, Michael Turner, Brian Walker and Harry Waring for their kind and much appreciated help.

During my research I have referred to many periodicals and books including: *Eddie Waring Rugby League Annual* (1959/60 to 1968/69), *Windsor's Rugby League Annual* (1961/62 to 1963/64), *John Player Rugby League Yearbooks* (1973/74 to 1976/77), *Rothmans Rugby League Yearbooks* (1981-82 to 1999), *League Publications Limited Yearbooks* (1996 to 2006/07), *Rugby League Record Keepers' Club publications* (Irvin Saxton), *50 Greats: Castleford RL Club* by David Smart and Andy Howard (2002), *100 Greats: Cumberland Rugby League* by Robert Gate (2002), *100 Greats: Featherstone Rovers RLFC* by Ron Bailey (2002), 1*00 Greats: Hull RL Club* by Raymond Fletcher (2002), *100 Greats: St Helens RLFC* by Alex Service (2006), *100 Greats: Thrum Hallers 1945-1998* by Robert Gate (2004), *100 Greats: Warrington RLFC* by Eddie Fuller and Gary Slater (2002), *100 Years of Featherstone* Rugby by Ian Clayton (1984), The *All Leeds Final* by Les Hoole (1988), *Bradford Northern: The History 1863-1989* by Nigel Williams (1989), *Castleford RLFC: A Sixty Year History* by Len Garbett (1986), *Challenge for the Championship* by John C. Lindley (1968), *Champions* by Robert Gate (1987), *Claret and Gold* by Stanley Chadwick (1946), *Classics: Hunslet RLFC* by Phil Hodgson (2006), *The Complete History of Bradford Northern* by Cedric H. Ludlam (1969), *Trevor Foster: The Life of a Rugby League Legend* by Simon Foster, Robert Gate and Peter Lush (2005), *Neil Fox: Rugby League's Greatest Points Scorer* by Robert Gate (2005), *Headingley Heroes* by Phil Hodgson (2004), *The Headingley Story 1890-1955* by Ken Dalby (1955), *Hull Centenary Brochure* by R.E. Lee and J.A. Saville (1965), *Hull FC: An Illustrated History* by Les Hoole (2001), *Odsal Odyssey's* by Phil Hodgson (2006), *The Official History of Dewsbury RLFC* by Tony Scargill, Bob Fox and Ken Crabtree (1989), *Oldham RLFC: The Complete History* by Michael Turner (1997), *Rivals Across the River* by David Bond (1999), *Rugby League Hall of Fame* by Robert Gate (2003), *Rugby League in the Twentieth Century* by Tony Collins (2006), *There Were a Lot More Than That* by Robert Gate (1994), *Thrum Hall Greats* by Andrew Hardcastle (1994), *The Thrum Hall Story* by Andrew Hardcastle (1986), *We've Swept the Seas Before Boys* by Les Hoole (1991).

I would also like to thank the always helpful staff of the following main/central libraries: Batley, Bradford, Castleford, Dewsbury, Halifax, Huddersfield, Hull, Leeds, Manchester, Oldham, St Helens, Salford, Wakefield, Warrington, Widnes, Wigan and Workington. There are also a great number of newspapers that I have consulted along the way, mostly at the aforementioned libraries, too numerous to list here, although I have endeavoured to give due acknowledgement within the main text where appropriate.

Graham Morris, October 2007

INTRODUCTION

The Super League Grand Final is one of the highlights in the British sporting calendar, a thrilling, incident-packed event that continues the rugby league tradition of deciding its champion team through the drama of an end-of-season play-off. The 2007 Grand Final marks the 100th anniversary of the first such contest when, in 1907, the Northern Union code, as it was then known, pioneered the sudden-death concept for its championship finale. An idea conceived in only its 12th season of existence following the breakaway from rugby union in 1895, it was an innovation that has since been emulated by many other sports in Great Britain; the English rugby union now use a play-off system in establishing their champion side, whilst, in Association Football, a knock-out series is used in determining promotion from the lower divisions. In the United States, post-season activity is a staple diet for all their major professional sports although only baseball can claim to pre-date the Northern Union idea, having its inaugural 'World Series' in 1903. Interestingly, considering Australia's influence on rugby league, the Australian Football League (Australian Rules) held their first play-off in 1898.

After the inaugural Northern Rugby League Championship Final in 1907, the formula was continued – excepting the unfortunate but necessary disruption of two world wars, plus a two-season break during the 1960s when two divisions were experimented with – until 1973. During that initial 67-year period, the final produced many memorable matches and sensational incidents. In 1920, a thrilling late try by the legendary Billy Batten of Hull denied Huddersfield a second 'All Four Cups' triumph, whilst, in 1938, Leeds United Football Club famously hosted the 'All-Leeds Final.' Following the Second World War, Manchester City Football Club's Maine Road enclosure became established as the venue for the showpiece occasion, including Wigan's 'Finest Hour' in 1950. Bradford's vast Odsal Stadium complex then became a regular host, providing the setting for Tom van Vollenhoven's incredible try for St Helens in 1959 and the Championship Final record crowd of 83,190 the following year to witness the Wakefield-Wigan clash. Odsal also staged the last Championship Final in 1973 when Sky Television commentator Mike (Mick) Sullivan was so influential in his Dewsbury team's mighty upset against Leeds.

Two divisions were revived for the 1973/74 campaign (a divisional system continuing in rugby league until the present day), the team heading the First Division table being awarded the Championship trophy. It was, however, decided to retain the play-off tradition as the season's climax through the introduction of the Club Championship. Although well intentioned, its complex formula for deciding the contesting teams ensured it would survive for just one campaign. The more straight-forward Premiership Trophy was conceived and launched the following year in 1975 and, after an uncertain beginning, proved extremely popular. It drew large crowds to its final, particularly after its transference in 1987 to Manchester United's famous Old Trafford ground. It paved the way for the introduction of the Super League Grand Final in 1998, which, after a 25-year gap, reverted to the play-off principle in determining the champion team. It is an event that has blossomed into an unprecedented success as it continues the modern tradition of staging Rugby League's big finale at 'The Theatre of Dreams.'

Graham Morris, October 2007

NOTES ON FACTS & FIGURES

The 'Champion Captain' profiles are correct up to 15 October 2007.

Under the match 'Stats' where 'dnp' appears in parentheses after a players name it indicates he did not play.

NORTHERN RUGBY LEAGUE CHAMPIONSHIP FINAL

The opening round of matches in the first Northern Rugby League Championship took place on Saturday 7 September 1895, nine days after the historic meeting at the George Hotel, Huddersfield, at which 22 of the north's senior clubs (11 from Yorkshire, nine from Lancashire, two from Cheshire) elected to leave the Rugby Football Union. They arranged a full programme of League fixtures, a total of 42 games each, to determine their first champion club, destined to be Bradford-based Manningham.

After such a heavy list, requiring plenty of cross-Pennine travel, plus a subsequent increase in senior clubs to 30, the Championship was shelved after one season. For the following five terms, separate county leagues operated; a Lancashire Senior Competition (incorporating the Cheshire clubs) and a Yorkshire Senior Competition.

In 1901/02, the leading 14 clubs across the two competitions pre-empted the creation of a Super League by some 95 years when they controversially broke away to resurrect the Northern Rugby League Championship. Their ambition was based on a desire to stimulate gate receipts, reducing fixtures against so-called weaker clubs that did not entice crowds. The inaugural winners were Broughton Rangers, who completed the sports first double by capturing the Northern Union (now 'Rugby League') Challenge Cup. The competition was expanded to 18 clubs a year later, a second tier also being introduced containing a further 18 clubs.

The two-division system lasted three seasons but, with the loss of several Second Division sides due to the poor finances generated in the lower league, an all-embracing competition containing 31 clubs was introduced for 1905/06. Within certain guidelines, the clubs arranged their own fixtures, the champions being calculated on a percentage basis, Leigh finishing top.

Because of the uneven nature of the fixtures, with not all the clubs meeting each other, a further adjustment came about for the 1906/07 term when a top-four play-off was introduced to decide the winners. The first Championship Final took place at Huddersfield's Fartown ground, contested by Halifax and Oldham. Although quite radical at the time, it was a decision typical of a sport that, over the years, has been unafraid to implement changes.

Strictly speaking the 1907 Championship Final was not the first where a one-off match settled the issue. The climax to 1903/04 saw Bradford and Salford involved in a 'shoot-out' after the two finished level at the head of the First Division table. With for-and-against scoring records not then being taken into account, a hastily arranged decider took place at Thrum Hall, Halifax, on Thursday 28 April, less than a week after the regular League programme finished. Bradford won 5-0 in front of 12,000 spectators.

The top-four play-off was a simple and, on the face of it, fair formula given the circumstances; the top team hosted the fourth side in the table, the second entertained the third, the winners' meeting in the final tie at a neutral venue. It was an idea, though, that did not 'sit well' with a lot of people – officials, supporters and press – who found it hard to come to terms with the top team not being declared champions. Comments, both for and against, reappeared annually at the time the final was taking place and it was amazing how consistent local journalists were in their condemnation of the system if their side, having finished 'top' did not ultimately take the trophy!

The secretary of the Northern Union, Joseph Platt, speaking after the first trophy presentation in 1907, made by his wife, said: 'The alteration in the League system for the present season, which had brought about the playing of semi-final and final ties, had, it had been said, not been successful in Yorkshire, but if they looked at the gate at that match (the Halifax v Keighley semi-final) opinions would change considerably. They would become of the opinion that the system was the best that could be devised under the circumstances.'

Throughout the 1920s, when the 'anti-brigade' was at their most vociferous, the team finishing top was usually referred to as the 'champion side' by the press, the play-off being consistently called a 'supplementary competition' rather than a Championship decider. Part of the reason for this disdain was that, following the First World War, none of the first six finals (1920 to 1925) were won by the leading team. *The Huddersfield Examiner* said in 1920 that the play-off served 'to imitate a position we usually look for in a comic opera' whilst, in 1925 after League leaders Swinton lost to Hull Kingston Rovers in the final, the local paper, *The Journal*, called it 'another illustration of the farcical method of deciding the Rugby League Championship.'

The respected sports newspaper, the *Athletic News*, commented in 1922: 'It is felt and suggested that the club completing its League programme (at the top of the table) should be given some tangible reward, and not compelled to risk all the season's honours on the result of one particular game in an additional competition. If it is necessary for the League to promote this supplementary tournament, then it is suggested that the actual League champions should receive a fitting reward for their consistency and skill during the season.' The writer's sound suggestion of rewarding the leading club did come about, although not until 1964/65 when St Helens, who lost in the Championship Final, became the first recipient of the League Leaders' Trophy.

But the play-offs survived and, by the late 1930s, huge audiences were attracted to the event. The last two pre-Second World War Championship Finals in 1938 in 1939, and the first peacetime decider in 1946, drew larger attendances than the Challenge Cup Final, the first time that had happened since before the First World War. It was stimulated, in part, by the interest generated through staging the games at soccer grounds for the first time. After the Second World War attitudes towards the event had changed dramatically and there were suggestions the final should be taken to Wembley as it often provided more entertainment than the Challenge Cup Final! In 1949 the *Warrington Guardian* said: 'The latest meeting (between Huddersfield and Warrington) had more thrills and more brilliant rugby than had been packed into half-a-dozen Empire Stadium games.'

Big crowds continued, a massive 83,100 watching Wakefield and Wigan in 1960, the first time since 1946 that the attendance outnumbered the Wembley showpiece. By the mid-1960s though, the crowds began to drop, partly blamed on changing social habits, partly on live televising of the games. After a brief two-season interlude where two divisions were experimented with, it resumed with an expanded top-16 play-off (an attempt to spread interest amongst the clubs) until 1973 when it was again decided a change was needed.

EARLY CHAMPIONS

Championship winners prior to the first Championship Final in 1906/07

(NRL – Northern Rugby League, LSC – Lancashire Senior Competition, YSC – Yorkshire Senior Competition, FD – Northern Rugby League First Division)

1895/96 Manningham (NRL)

1896/97 Broughton Rangers (LSC), Brighouse Rangers (YSC)

1897/98 Oldham (LSC), Hunslet (YSC)

1898/99 Broughton Rangers (LSC), Batley (YSC)

1899/1900 Runcorn (LSC), Bradford (YSC)

1900/01 Oldham (LSC), Bradford (YSC)

1901/02 Broughton Rangers (NRL)

1902/03 Halifax (FD)

1903/04 Bradford (FD)

1904/05 Oldham (FD)

1905/06 Leigh (NRL)

1907 Northern Rugby League Championship Final
HALIFAX V OLDHAM

The revolutionary idea by the Northern Union to introduce a play-off to settle the Championship was, despite misgivings in other quarters, greeted enthusiastically by the two towns involved in the inaugural final. The *Halifax Evening Courier* declared: 'We are on the eve of a great day. Tomorrow holds the great secret as to whether Halifax or Oldham is to hold the Northern Union Cup during the next twelve months. Seldom has a cup final in Yorkshire or Lancashire aroused so much interest as tomorrow's encounter at Fartown and given decent weather conditions there should be a huge gate, despite the fact that there will be the Association Cup Final (Everton versus Sheffield Wednesday) in progress at the Crystal Palace.' The anticipation was shared by the *Oldham Evening Chronicle*: 'The interest in today's Oldham v Halifax match has been enormous and we do not think there was ever more interest and excitement about a rugby match in the local annals of the game.'

BRAVO, HALIFAX !

CHAMPIONS OF THE LEAGUE.

OLDHAM BADLY BEATEN.

BLUE AND WHITES SUPERIOR IN ALL DEPARTMENTS.

[BY "ROCKET."]

My congratulations are due to the Halifax premier team for their splendid victory on Saturday, a victory which enabled them to claim out and out the championship of the Northern Union League. My lads, you did well. You covered yourselves with glory. You undoubtedly stood head and shoulders above your opponents on the day's play, and had sweet revenge for the three defeats you have sustained at the hands of Oldham this season. It is not as though you won by the matter of a couple of tries to one. You were not content with that. You ran out in fine style, and the score of 18 points to three is not an unfair reflex of the run of play. Moreover, you came off the field of play capable—as one of the musical forwards said—of each singing a song and playing another forty minutes ! Every man Jack of you was a trier, and all equally share in the spoils.

So much for the personal side. In expectation of a

The Halifax Evening Courier acclaims its local heroes!

The decision taken at the Northern Union meeting on Thursday 9/4/1907 in Huddersfield's George Hotel to stage the first ever final at the Huddersfield club's Fartown ground was well received, both camps agreeing it was an excellent choice for both sets of fans who wished to travel. Although Halifax had led the League table, many felt that Oldham, having beaten their rivals in all three meetings during the season, would have the edge. Both teams, though, were hampered by injury woes, each including a forward in their three-quarter line; Halifax placing Harry Morley on the wing for W.J. 'Billy' Williams (knee injury despite a week of treatment at Allerton's Hydro in Manchester), Oldham – already missing Tommy Cash on the left wing – relocating Bert Avery to the centre for influential 'Birdie' Dixon (leg injury).

Before kick-off a gymnast, who went under the name of The Dutchman attempted to get onto the field to entertain the crowd but was removed by the police, who were jeered for their spoilsport efforts. Apparently, the norm was that performers paid the club for the privilege and were then allowed to make a collection afterwards. Apparently he had refused to pay, although he still made his collection!

Arthur Lees led Oldham out closely followed by Joe Riley and 'his blue and white brigade' to the strains of 'Auld Lang Syne' and 'prolonged cheering' by the crowd. Referee Joseph Priestley then 'gave a few words of advice' to the two captains before the coin toss. Oldham won and decided to begin with the wind at their backs. Halifax's Billy Little kicked off and the first Championship Final was underway!

Unfortunately, earlier heavy rain quickly made playing conditions difficult, the *Athletic News* describing the pitch as 'a mass of slime.' Oldham threatened first; Joe Ferguson missing an 'easy' penalty kick in the opening minute and winger Tom White being denied a try when Billy

Billy Little – the Halifax full-back kicked off the first ever Championship Final

Dixon's pass was intercepted by Percy Eccles. Halifax, though, was generally on top in the opening half and soon claimed the first score. It came when Avery was slow in dealing with a long downfield kick from Halifax, his eventual attempted clearance bouncing off Asa Robinson, who caught it and ran for the try line. Held up by Lees, Robinson sent an inside pass to Ike Bartle who 'smiled all over his face when he took the ball' before a simple run in. Little added the goal. Oldham replied when they found touch near the Halifax line, their pack winning the scrum and 'rushing' over for Ferguson to touch down underneath a pile of bodies. Ferguson failed to augment and later missed with a penalty during a barren afternoon for the normally reliable marksman. Billy Bulmer grabbed a second Halifax touchdown following a 'scramble for possession' after Joe Riley had initially lost the ball over the line following a Jimmy Hilton pass. Little missed the goal, Halifax leading 8–3 at the break.

Oldham, reportedly, 'fell apart completely' in the second half as their forwards were 'rushed off the ball.' Little provided the pivotal moment of the match when, having missed an earlier penalty, he landed one from a foot inside his own half and five yards in from touch following a 'deliberate' knock-on. At 10–3, most observers already believed the day belonged to the Yorkshiremen. Little was on target again with a brilliant touchline effort, converting the Thrum Haller's third try after they had won a scrum in the Oldham 25 area, Hilton transferring to Morley who charged through a fragile defence to score. Two minutes later Riley produced a wonderful solo effort following his dummy pass to grab another try, despite Billy Dixon's attempt to overhaul him. Little just missed the goal. There was no further scoring, Little gallantly failing with a drop-goal effort from halfway and

STATS

Halifax 18 Oldham 3

Saturday 20 April at Fartown, Huddersfield (3.30 pm)

Halifax: (blue and white hoops): Little, Eccles, Atkins, Joe Riley (captain), Morley, Hilton, Grey, Bartle, Bulmer, Brearley, Littlewood, Robinson, Langhorn. Trainer: J. Midgley

Oldham: (red and white hoops): Thomas, White, Avery, Billy Dixon, Tyson, A. Lees (captain), Yewlett, Ferguson, Topham, A. Smith, Vowles, Longworth, Wilkinson. Trainer: unknown

Half-time: 8–3 **Referee:** J. Priestley
Attendance: 13,325 **Receipts:** £772

Weather: overcast and windy, drizzle at start then sunny; slippery conditions

Progressive score:

Halifax	score (min)	Oldham
Bartle try, Little goal	5–0 (7)	
	5–3 (15)	Ferguson try
Bulmer try	8–3 (38)	
Little penalty	10–3 (-)	
Morley try, Little goal	15–3 (-)	
Joe Riley try	18–3 (-)	

League leaders	P	W	D	L	For	Agst	Pts	Percent
1 Halifax	34	27	2	5	64	229	56	82.35
2 Oldham	34	26	1	7	457	227	53	77.94
3 Runcorn	30	23	0	7	546	216	46	76.66
4 Keighley	24	17	1	6	431	231	35	72.91

Semi-finals:
Halifax 9 Keighley 4
Oldham 11 Runcorn 3

Head-to-head form guide:
Halifax 6 Oldham 12 (League)
Oldham 10 Halifax 5 (League)
Halifax 5 Oldham 10 (Challenge Cup)

Morley being brought down just short of the line. For the final five minutes touch judge Jimmy Lumley of Leeds, who was to take charge of the 1909 Championship Final, took over from Priestley following an attack of cramp.

The *Sporting Chronicle* had no doubt about who had been the better side, saying: 'At every point of the game Halifax proved much superior. The Yorkshire forwards played a typical, bustling game, which rarely allowed the Oldham half-backs to secure the ball.' The paying attendance was given as 13,325, although it was estimated that, with ticket admissions, the total would have reached 15,000.

Halifax captain Joe Riley scored the last try

CHAMPION CAPTAIN

Joe Riley (Halifax 1907)

Joe Riley joined Halifax in 1901 from his hometown Northern Union club, Sowerby Bridge. He went on to make 419 appearances for Halifax until a broken leg during a match at Bradford Northern in January 1915 forced his retirement. His honours with Halifax include the Championship (1902/03, 1906/07), Northern Union Challenge Cup (1903, 1904), Yorkshire Cup (1908) and Yorkshire League (1908/09). A centre or stand-off, described as a reliable defender and 'dangerous attacker', he could kick with either foot. He held the club captaincy on three occasions, the first being in 1906. In 1910, he was the first player from the club to tour 'Down Under', appearing in the series-clinching second Test win against Australia, played in Brisbane, and the second of two matches versus Australasia, in Sydney. He represented England (twice) and Yorkshire (6 times).

The Halifax squad pose with their trophy. Standing: Midgley (trainer), W.W. Williams, Wedgewood, J. Dodd (president), Bulmer, A. Ricketts (secretary), Robinson, Bartle, Brearley, Colonel Foster, Morris (asst. trainer). Seated: Swinbank, Atkins, Littlewood, Joe Riley, Langhorn, W.J. Williams, Ward, Morley. On ground: Grey, Hilton, Eccles

1908 Northern Rugby League Championship Final HUNSLET V OLDHAM

Hunslet was the first to complete an 'All Four Cups' season when they took the 1907/08 Championship title in the first-ever replayed final, having secured the Challenge Cup, Yorkshire Championship and Yorkshire Cup. They owed much to a pack famed as 'The Terrible Six', their relentless industry laying the platform for legendary skipper Albert Goldthorpe to dictate matters in the middle of the field. Their Championship decider opposition was Oldham, who had led the table with only two defeats in 32 matches, Hunslet finishing second.

Their first attempt to settle the matters was at The Willows, Salford. Hunslet was deprived of winger Fred Farrar, his heavy cold being blamed on listening to overlong speeches from officials during a snowstorm at the conclusion of the previous weekend's Challenge Cup Final! He recovered sufficiently for the replay, his place meantime going to Charlie Ward. In contrast to the previous week, The Willows was bathed in glorious sunshine.

Hunslet's pack was too keen in the early stages and penalised several times for offside, a penalty goal from one offence enabling Oldham's Tom White to put his side ahead. Albert Goldthorpe equalised with a similar effort following obstruction on Billy Batten, White restoring Oldham's advantage with his second, a magnificent effort from near halfway. After brother Walter had missed with a penalty shot, Albert Goldthorpe's failed drop-goal attempt led to the first try. Oldham centre Billy Dixon fielded the ball but, having been tackled, his play-the-ball effort saw Albert Goldthorpe put a boot to it, following it across the try-line to score with ease. His simple conversion brought up a 7–4 half-time lead.

Hunslet should have sealed victory 25 minutes from time when Fred Smith broke, but supporting Billy Eagers failed to take the pass

Photo by Parkinson & Roy.
HUNSLET R, F, C,
Published by J. Booth.
W. H. Cockeram. Sec. Smales, Farrar, Higson. W, Hannah, Trainer. Wilson, Wray, Cappleman, J Lewthwaite, Chairman.
Eagers, Randall, W. Ward, A. F. Goldthorpe, Captain, Jukes, Brookes, W. Goldthorpe.
C. Ward, Place, Smith, Batten, Walsh

Hunslet with the Yorkshire Cup - their first trophy of 1907/08

Impressions of the first meeting from the Athletic News' caricaturist

with an open line. A minute later, Eagers tried to make amends with a long-range drop-goal, the ball going under the bar. A relieved Oldham lifted their game and, eventually, from a scrum close to the Yorkshire side's line, skilful handling by George Tyson created the chance for Jim 'Bumper' Wright to force his way over. White missed the difficult conversion, the score being tied at 7–7. As the match drew to a close, both teams raised the tempo in searched of the winner; Walter Goldthorpe almost scoring a try, White missing two drop goals. The deadlock, though, could not be broken.

It was an anti-climax for the spectators, the *Leeds Mercury* saying: 'When the referee sounded his whistle for time, amid almost perfect silence, so different from the wild cheering that might have been anticipated had either side proved victorious, no one appeared to know exactly what to do.' Fans called for the teams to 'play it out' but, as the report went on to say: 'The players had had quite enough of strenuous football on what was an almost perfect cricket afternoon, and it would have been positive cruelty to have asked them to play extra time.' It was an unexpected outcome, certainly by the officials who, apparently, had made no provision for a replay. Consequently, a special Northern League Committee meeting was held that evening at Manchester's Grand Hotel, resulting in a replay being scheduled for Wakefield Trinity's Belle Vue ground seven days later.

The fine, sunny weather of the first meeting was repeated, and it was reported 'there were wagonettes and cycles galore and in addition to this, heavily laden tram-cars were run from Hunslet.' The swelling numbers outside the turnstiles pushed the scheduled 3.30 pm kick-off back 20 minutes, although the 14,000 attendances for both ties was considered disappointing, blamed on the 'excessive' one shilling (5p) ground admission.

Again, Hunslet's over-zealous forwards, now including 16-stone Billy Brookes instead of the lighter, more mobile John Smales, incurred early penalties for offside. But Oldham, who replaced out of form George Smith with Arthur Oldershaw, failed to convert them into points, Joe Ferguson uncharacteristically missing four goal attempts. Instead, Albert Goldthorpe got the afternoon's opening scores, succeeding with two penalties (a scrum offence and obstruction, respectively), the first being a magnificent long distance effort, the second sneaking over off the crossbar. As half-time approached, Hunslet virtually clinched the match after Tyson lost the

CHAMPION CAPTAIN

Albert Goldthorpe (Hunslet 1908)

Albert Edward Goldthorpe is, arguably, the most famous name in Hunslet's proud history. Raised in Stourton, on the outskirts of Leeds, and one of five brothers who played for the club, he made his debut aged 16 during 1888. A model sportsman, he turned out for the Parkside club until 1910. Initially a centre, he moved to stand-off in 1901, where his skilful ball handling and awareness made him a pivotal figure. An excellent tactical kicker, he reportedly scored well over 800 goals including in excess of 200 drop-goals. During Hunslet's successful 1907/08 'Four Cups' campaign, he set a, then, club record of 101 goals in a season, the first Northern Union player to claim a century. Affectionately known as 'Ahr Albert', his first club honour was under rugby union rules, defeating Huddersfield in the 1892 Yorkshire Cup Final. After Hunslet left the RU in 1895, Goldthorpe gained further successes in Northern Union, winning the Championship ((1907/08), Northern Union Challenge Cup (1908), Yorkshire Cup (1905, 1907) and Yorkshire League (1897/98, 1907/08). He represented Yorkshire six times, incorporating the 1898/99 county championship, adding to three previous titles with the white rose (1891/92, 1892/93, 1893/94) under RU rules.

ball when tackled near his line. Walter Goldthorpe hacked it towards the Lancastrian's in-goal area, following up virtually unopposed to score close to the goals. Albert Goldthorpe surprisingly missed the easy conversion, Hunslet turning around 7–0 ahead.

Three minutes after the restart, White cut the arrears with a penalty, spurring Oldham to greater effort, David Beynon appearing to score in the corner but judged to have put a foot in touch. As in the opening half, Oldham continued to press hard, but was resisted, not least by Hunslet full-back Harold Place whose long relieving kicks were a feature of both matches. The Parksider's eventually got on top, Fred Smith and Eagers both having try chances repelled. Place and then Eagers made a 'mark' (a practice allowing a 'free kick' if a player caught an opponent's kick on the full), both times from the boot of Beynon. The resultant goal attempts by Walter and Albert Goldthorpe (who hit the post) failed. In between their efforts White missed a penalty for Oldham. Place eventually dropped a goal after fielding a clearance from Ferguson, making it 9–2, and Jack Randall almost added a second try. In the final minutes, Hunslet rounded off an historic day with a spectacular touchdown instigated by their celebrated winger Billy Batten whose break drew the cover before Eagers, Fred Smith and Walter Goldthorpe combined for the latter to score. Albert Goldthorpe missed the goal.

Apart from the closing stages, the match was not considered to have reached great heights, the *Leeds Mercury* noting that 'interesting running and passing was as rare as the visits of angels. It was a case of kicking and trusting to Providence.' One exception to criticism was victorious skipper Albert Goldthorpe, the 'only one man who kicked with judgement' who said the occasion was 'without doubt the proudest of my life.'

STATS

Hunslet 7 Oldham 7

Saturday 2 May at The Willows, Salford (3.30 pm)

Hunslet (white): Place, Ward, W. Goldthorpe, Eagers, Batten, A. Goldthorpe (captain), F. Smith, Wilson, Brookes, Jukes, Randall, Higson, Walsh. Trainer: W. Hannah

Oldham (red and white hoops): Thomas, G. Smith, Billy Dixon, Llewellyn, Tyson, Beynon, White, Ferguson (captain), A. Smith, Avery, Wilkinson, Wright, Longworth. Trainer: unknown

Half-time: 7–4 **Referee:** R. Robinson
Attendance: 14,000 **Receipts**: £690

Weather: very hot and humid

Progressive score:

Hunslet	score (min)	Oldham
	0–2 (11)	White penalty
A. Goldthorpe penalty	2–2 (15)	
	2–4 (25)	White penalty
A. Goldthorpe try, A. Goldthorpe goal	7–4 (35)	
	7–7 (68)	Wright try

Replay: Hunslet 12 Oldham 2

Saturday 9 May at Belle Vue, Wakefield (3.30 pm)

Hunslet (white): unchanged except Farrar for Ward, Smales for Brookes

Oldham (red and white hoops): unchanged except Oldershaw for G. Smith

Half-time: 7–0 **Referee:** E. Tonge
Attendance: 14,054 **Receipts**: £800

Weather: fine and warm, slight breeze

Progressive score:

Hunslet	score (min)	Oldham
A. Goldthorpe penalty	2–0 (30)	
A. Goldthorpe penalty	4–0 (35)	
W. Goldthorpe try	7–0 (38)	
	7–2 (43)	White penalty
Place drop-goal	9–2 (65)	
W Goldthorpe try	12–2 (75)	

League leaders	P	W	D	L	For	Agst	Pts	Percent
1 Oldham	32	28	2	2	396	121	58	90.62
2 Hunslet	32	25	1	6	389	248	51	79.28
3 Broughton Rangers	30	23	1	6	421	191	47	78.33
4 Wigan	32	23	1	8	501	181	47	73.43

Semi-finals:
Oldham 12 Wigan 5
Hunslet 28 Broughton Rangers 3

Head-to-head form guide:
Hunslet 15 Oldham 8 (Challenge Cup)

1909 Northern Rugby League Championship Final
WIGAN V OLDHAM

Wigan won their first Championship after overcoming their keenest Lancashire rivals of that period, Oldham, in wretched weather at The Willows. It completed a four-match clean sweep for the season over the Roughyeds – including a 10–9 Lancashire Cup Final success at Broughton during December – as Wigan gained the upper hand after succeeding just once in eight clashes over the preceding three campaigns.

The third Championship decider staged, the occasion had taken on a carnival-like atmosphere with the gathering crowd treated to pre-match entertainment from a trick cyclist, albeit unauthorised. Although allowed to perform in the past, officials of host club, Salford, denied consent this time due to the poor state of the pitch, fearing further damage. He was, however, every bit as determined to succeed as the players that followed and, complete with bicycle, climbed over the fence regardless. The police pursued him around the pitch unable to lay a hand on him until one inventive officer picked up a flagpole and propelled it through the spokes of his front wheel. More ignominy followed when he was led away in handcuffs!

Once the match was underway, all the scoring occurred during the opening half. Wigan took an early lead through skipper Jimmy Leytham's penalty after a foul on New Zealand centre Lance Todd. Following a missed penalty apiece from Leytham and Oldham's Alf Wood, the Roughyeds, benefiting from a strong first half wind, replied. A Billy Jardine try in the corner, following some frantic play on Wigan's line put them 3–2 ahead, Wood missing the goal. The Cherry and Whites went down to 12 men after full-back Jim Sharrock sustained a kick to his neck trying to recover a ball dribbled his way by Oldham's marauding pack. During his absence Oldham almost scored, Joe Ferguson's touchdown being vetoed by referee Jimmy Lumley who ruled the ball had gone dead. Wigan regained the initiative on the half-hour after Johnny Thomas, Leytham and Walter Cheetham created space for powerfully built forward Dick Ramsdale to charge in under the posts. Leytham augmented for a 7–3 interval lead.

WIGAN FOOTBALL CLUB.
PLAYERS and COMMITTEE. Season 1908-1909.
Top Row: S. Wood, W. Hargreaves, H. Bouchier, (Vice-Chairman), A. Laing, J. H. Prescott, W. Counsell.
Middle Row: J. Hesketh, (Trainer), S. Latham, (Treasurer), J. Brown, T. Whittaker, H. Francis, W. Johnston, R. Ramsdale, J. Blears, W. Cheetham, J. Barton, J. Henderson, G. Taylor, (Secretary.)
Sitting: N. Jones, J. Thomas, J. Miller, L. B. Todd, (Vice-Captain). J. Counsell, (Chairman), J. Leytham, (Captain), B. Jenkins, F. Gleave, J. Sharrock, Dr. Monks, (Hon. Surgeon.
Cups: Lancashire Cup, Northern Rugby League, Lancashire Rugby League, West Lancashire League.

Wigan with their 1908/09 trophy haul

CHAMPION CAPTAIN

Jimmy Leytham (Wigan 1909)

Jimmy Leytham was a flying, graceful winger, dubbed 'Gentleman Jim' due to his sportsmanship. He was the Northern Union's top try scorer in three campaigns, the last – in 1909/10 – incorporating a club record-equalling 47 for Wigan, six being in a match against Merthyr Tydfil, another club record. He joined Wigan from hometown club, Lancaster, in 1903, reportedly for £80. Honours with the 'Cherry and Whites' include the Championship (1908/09), Lancashire Cup (1905, 1908, 1909), and Lancashire League (1908/09, 1910/11, 1911/12). A member of the first touring side to the Antipodes in 1910, his representative career covers appearances for Great Britain (7 – five Test matches plus two games versus Australasia), England (5) and Lancashire (11).

Oldham's best spell of the afternoon occurred during the opening stages of the second half. Raising the tempo as their pack began to dominate, they came close to scoring several times despite Sharrock's reappearance. Joe Owens lost possession when he looked a certain scorer and Wigan's Bert Jenkins was forced to boot the ball dead when their forwards, led by Arthur Smith and Jardine dribbled the ball across the Wigan try-line. As the tension mounted, several altercations occurred, the referee cautioning Sid Deane and Cheetham for fighting. Wigan's line held and, as conditions deteriorated, the last quarter of the game developed into a virtual stalemate, although Joe Miller had a 'try' ruled out for a forward pass and Leytham missed a penalty. With minutes left to play, the occasion was sullied by the dismissal – the first in a Championship Final – of opposing forwards Cheetham and Arthur Smith. The *Manchester Guardian* noted that the pair, who had both, apparently, played 'roughly' during the match, 'might, with advantage to the game, have left the field earlier.'

Wigan winger Joe Miller had a second half try disallowed

Reportedly, Oldham's forwards generally held sway over the Central Park side's sextet, a fact that should have worked to their advantage considering the heavy going. Instead, it was Wigan's classier backs that were feted as the day's heroes, particularly Leytham and centre partner, Jenkins. Less fortunate was their regular scrum half, Fred Gleave. He missed out on the glory – and all of the following season – after a leg injury sidelined him, his place going to Neddy Jones. He eventually appeared in three Championship Finals with the Cherry and Whites, but lost each time.

STATS

Wigan 7 Oldham 3

Saturday 1 May at The Willows, Salford (3.30 pm)

Wigan (white): Sharrock, Leytham (captain), Jenkins, Todd, Miller, Thomas, Jones, Barton, Cheetham, de Francis, Ramsdale, Silcock, Whittaker. Trainer: J. Hesketh

Oldham (blue): Wood, Tyson, Deane, Llewellyn, G. Smith, Billy Dixon, Anlezark, Avery, Ferguson (captain), Jardine, Owens, A. Smith, Topham. Trainer: unknown

Half-time: 7–3 **Referee:** J.C. Lumley
Attendance: 12,000 **Receipts**: £630

Weather: heavy rain and gale force wind; muddy conditions

Progressive score:

Wigan	score (min)	Oldham
Leytham penalty	2–0 (3)	
	2–3 (15)	Jardine try
Ramsdale try, Leytham goal	7–3 (30)	

League leaders	P	W	D	L	For	Agst	Pts	Percent
1 Wigan	32	28	0	4	706	207	56	87.50
2 Halifax	34	28	1	5	526	174	57	83.82
3 Oldham	32	26	0	6	488	176	52	81.25
4 Batley	32	23	3	6	412	176	49	76.56

Semi-finals:
Wigan 18 Batley 2
Halifax 3 Oldham 3
Replay: Oldham 8 Halifax 2

Head-to-head form guide:
Wigan 10 Oldham 9
(Lancashire Cup at Wheater's Field, Broughton)
Wigan 23 Oldham 10 (League)
Oldham 2 Wigan 8 (League)

1910 Northern Rugby League Championship Final
OLDHAM V WIGAN

Oldham exacted revenge on Wigan in the 1910 Championship re-match, their 13–7 victory tasting particularly sweet after taking part, and losing, in all three Championship Finals to date. Oldham's selectors produced a pre-match surprise, preferring the bulkier frames of Billy Dixon and Jim Wright to centre Tom Llewellyn and forward Billy Jardine. They made their decision during a meeting at Broughton Baths where both teams changed before and after the match, being conveyed to the ground by wagonette. The inaugural Northern Union tour to Australia and New Zealand affected both line-ups, forwards Tom Helm (Oldham) and Dick Ramsdale (Wigan) having set sail. Five other tourists – Bert Avery (Oldham), Bert Jenkins, Jimmy Leytham, Johnny Thomas and Jimmy Sharrock (all Wigan) – remained for the final, travelling later, although Sharrock missed the clash, unable to recover from a mid-March injury. His place went to Harry Price.

Oldham threatened from the kick-off, a forward rush setting up a position on halfway for George Anlezark to kick into space on the right, the ball bouncing over Leytham, allowing Tom McLean to race clear. Jenkins managed to detain him, averting the danger. Anlezark also instigated the next raid, his thrilling break, continued by Sid Deane, ending when George Smith spilled the ball with the line beckoning. Oldham, though, could not be denied and from the next scrum Dixon received from Tom White, outwitting Wigan's defence with his 'quick and strong dash' to place the ball behind the posts. Alf Wood converted and Oldham was five points up in as many minutes.

Wigan responded, a brilliant kick from Lance Todd sending the ball halfway down the field into touch. A subsequent penalty for a scrum indiscretion allowed Leytham, despite a difficult angle and strong wind, to boot over his side's first points. Encouraged by the score, they applied sustained pressure on Oldham's line, Todd being tackled from behind when a try looked certain, Wood standing out in defence to keep his line intact. Leytham missed a chance to close the deficit, failing with a touchline penalty from the Oldham 25 line. Wigan's Neddy Jones left the field briefly for treatment but, despite their numerical disadvantage, his side drew level. Tom Whittaker scooped up a loose ball near Oldham's posts and, although held,

STATS

Oldham 13 Wigan 7

Saturday 23 April at Wheater's Field, Broughton (3.30 pm)

Oldham (red): Wood, G. Smith, Billy Dixon, Deane, McLean, Anlezark, White, Ferguson (captain), Avery, A. Smith, Wright, McCabe, Owens. Trainer: unknown

Wigan (blue): Price, Leytham (captain), Jenkins, Todd, Miller, Jones, Thomas, Barton, de Francis, Topping, Seeling, Silcock, Whittaker. Trainer: J. Hesketh

Half-time: 5–5 **Referee:** J.H. Smith
Attendance: 10,850 **Receipts**: £520

Weather: periodic heavy rain, strong cross wind

Progressive score:

Oldham	score (min)	Wigan
Dixon try, Wood goal	5–0 (5)	
	5–2 (10)	Leytham penalty
	5–5 (30)	Todd try
Ferguson goal from mark	7–5 (45)	
	7–7 (49)	Leytham penalty
McCabe try	10–7 (67)	
G. Smith try	13–7 (80)	

League leaders	P	W	D	L	For	Agst	Pts	Percent
1 Oldham	34	29	2	3	604	184	60	88.23
2 Salford	31	24	1	6	387	210	49	79.03
3 Wigan	30	23	1	6	545	169	47	78.33
4 Wakefield Trinity	32	24	0	8	435	242	48	75.00

Semi-finals:

Oldham 12 Wakefield Trinity 6
Salford 6 Wigan 17

Head-to-head form guide:

Oldham 8 Wigan 2 (League)
Wigan 7 Oldham 15 (League)

A postcard featuring the 1909/10 Oldham team with skipper Joe Ferguson, centre with ball

transferred it to Todd who just squeezed through. Leytham missed the goal. Thomas became another Wigan casualty and Oldham almost scored during his temporary absence, but the teams remained all square at half-time.

The first chance to score after the break went to Oldham's Joe Ferguson whose goal attempt from halfway, after Wood made a 'mark', went under the bar. A few minutes later he was more successful, landing a brilliant touchline effort having made a mark himself. Leytham equalised with another penalty, again not from the easiest position, having received a late tackle from McLean. But Oldham's forwards began to take a grip, dominating scrum possession, enabling halves Anlezark and White – who was unsuccessful with a drop-goal effort – to dictate. Wigan defended well, repelling several potential scoring threats, but the breakthrough came 13 minutes from full time. Anlezark fed a scrum near Wigan's line and, as his front row wheeled the scrum round, Tom McCabe – despite struggling with a painful first half rib injury – peeled away to pounce for the touchdown as the ball emerged. The goal was missed by Ferguson but Oldham led 10–7.

Then it was White's turn to leave the field, limping off through injury, Avery moving to half-back. After Wood failed to increase Oldham's lead with a penalty, White returned but was a virtual passenger and Avery continued to partner Anlezark. For the remaining minutes Oldham was on a roll, Wigan's Charlie Seeling thwarting George Smith's effort to score, Ferguson having several goal attempts from marks. One hit the post from halfway and, following up quickly, Ferguson almost scored, Jones, after missing the rebound, recovering to claim the first touch. Eventually, George Smith sidestepped his way over near the posts to seal victory, Wood surprisingly missing the goal.

The *Wigan Examiner* gave due credit to victors Oldham, stating 'no one could deny their superiority.' The 'disappointing' 10,850 turnout was blamed on the strong wind and frequent bouts of rain.

New Zealander Lance Todd – scorer of Wigan's only try

1911 Northern Rugby League Championship Final
OLDHAM V WIGAN

Oldham retained their title in 1911, their fifth consecutive Championship Final and third in a row against Wigan. In contrast to the previous year's low turnout, the keen rivals attracted 15,543, a record for the occasion. Oldham, in winning 20–7, were again superior throughout much of the match, Wigan's display being rated as low beat as in their shock Challenge Cup Final defeat to Broughton Rangers seven days earlier. Whilst Wigan's passing was noted as 'poor', Oldham's was described as 'delightfully clever', centres James Lomas, judged by most as the final's outstanding player, and Sid Deane leading the way.

The Roughyeds took a three-minute lead following a high kick into the corner by Lomas. Johnny Thomas' clearance kick for Wigan was not good, Arthur Smith catching cleanly and making a mark from which Lomas put Oldham 2–0 up. They increased the margin after Billy Dixon recovered Lance Todd's fumble to race downfield, his inter-passing with a colleague setting up Tom White who rounded Jimmy Sharrock to score. Lomas missed the 'easy' conversion and then, after White was just off target with a drop-goal attempt from halfway, struck the post with a penalty attempt.

James Lomas – who scored 12 points for Oldham – was considered in some quarters to be the finals top performer

Sharrock gave Wigan hope with an excellent goal after Thomas was obstructed, reaching the target from near midfield, 12 yards from touch. At 5–2 both sides pushed for the vital next try; Oldham's Deane being forced into touch by Todd, Wigan's Jimmy Leytham denied by an excellent Birdie Dixon tackle. Seven minutes from the break, Lomas crossed at the corner off a return Billy Dixon pass, skipper Joe Ferguson's excellent goal setting up a 10–2 interval lead.

The second half opened with Sharrock making a disappointing stab at a penalty attempt and, when Fred Gleave was not allowed to play the ball, Thomas proved more successful. But

CHAMPION CAPTAIN

Joe Ferguson (Oldham 1910, 1911)

Joe Ferguson is considered by many to be the greatest player in the history of the Oldham club. A Cumbrian, born in Maryport, he was signed in 1899 from Brookland Rovers, his last match being in 1923, when he was 44 years old. His career covered 682 first class games, including 677 in the pack – a rugby league record for a forward. A prolific goal-scorer with a career aggregate of 582, he was considered an 'industrious' forward who – at a time when pack roles were less defined – usually played in the 'hooking' role. With Oldham, he won the Championship (1904/05, 1909/10, 1910/11), Lancashire Cup (1907, 1910, 1913, 1919) and Lancashire League (1900/01, 1907/08, 1909/10). He represented England (4 times), Cumberland (31) and Lancashire (16), 'business reasons' causing him to turn down the opportunity to join the 1910 tour of Australia and New Zealand.

any thoughts of a Wigan comeback evaporated as Oldham scored minutes later. Lomas, receiving the ball from Avery on halfway, raced down the flank and, confronted by Sharrock, passing to White who just got over. Ferguson missed the kick, the score standing at 13–4. Another powerful Lomas break, in which he beat several opponents, almost led to a Joe Owens try. White tried to capitalise on the good field position but his drop-goal failed, Lomas

Oldham captain Joe Ferguson

then notching a penalty for obstruction.

Wigan's only try went to Leytham, following an excellent passing movement after Gleave broke from a scrum, claimed the touchdown despite the pass from Price first ricocheting off his knee to cross the whitewash. Sharrock missed the goal. Oldham had the last word, Lomas 'stealing' from Todd and diving over Sharrock to score behind the posts, adding the extras himself.

The two clubs had already met in the play-offs after tying at the top of the table with an average of 83.82 each. They were required to meet at Wakefield Trinity's ground on the Wednesday evening to decide first place prior to the semi-finals in a 'preliminary' match that would be deemed unnecessary by today's standards. Both clubs clearly thought so at the time. Just five of Oldham's line-up survived for the final (it would have been six had full-back Alf Wood not cried off, Birdie Dixon replacing him), whilst Wigan had only two appearing in both games, one of them, Harry Price, making the final due to an injury to Bert Jenkins. Wigan, who had the superior scoring record over the campaign, claimed 'first' place and a home tie with fourth club Widnes after an 11–3 win, although subsequently fined £25 for fielding a virtual 'A' (reserve) team.

STATS

Oldham 20 Wigan 7

Saturday 6 May at Wheater's Field, Broughton (3.30 pm)

Oldham: (red): Birdie Dixon, G. Smith, Deane, Lomas, Billy Dixon, Anlezark, White, Ferguson (captain), Avery, A. Smith, J. Wright, McCabe, Owens. Trainer: J. Mallalieu

Wigan: (blue): Sharrock, Leytham (captain), Price, Todd, Miller, Gleave, Thomas, de Francis, Ramsdale, Whittaker, Williams, Shallcross, Seeling. Trainer: J. Hesketh

Half-time: 10–2 **Referee:** J.W. Whiteley
Attendance: 15,543 **Receipts**: £717

Weather: sunny and very hot

Progressive score:

Oldham	score (min)	Wigan
Lomas goal from mark	2–0 (3)	
White try	5–0 (15)	
	5–2 (19)	Sharrock penalty
Lomas try, Ferguson goal	10–2 (33)	
	10–4 (47)	Thomas penalty
White try	13–4 (50)	
Lomas penalty	15–4 (-)	
	15–7 (65)	Leytham try
Lomas try, Lomas goal	20–7 (70)	

League leaders	P	W	D	L	For	Agst	Pts	Percent
1 Wigan	34	28	1	5	650	205	57	83.82
2 Oldham	34	28	1	5	441	210	57	83.82
3 Wakefield Trinity	33	24	1	8	493	264	49	74.24
4 Widnes	30	19	3	8	310	137	41	68.33

First place play-off:
Wigan 11 Oldham 3 (at Belle Vue, Wakefield)

Semi-finals:
Wigan 16 Widnes 0
Oldham 15 Wakefield Trinity 12

Head-to-head form guide:
Oldham 16 Wigan 2 (League)
Wigan 11 Oldham 5 (League)
Wigan 11 Oldham 3 (play-off at Wakefield)

1912 Northern Rugby League Championship Final
HUDDERSFIELD V WIGAN

Huddersfield's 'Team of All the Talents' is acclaimed as one of the greatest in the history of the 13-man code. Their 1912 Championship Final victory catapulted them into a period of unprecedented success having previously claimed the Yorkshire Cup in 1909 and 1911. Their 13–5 win over Wigan at Thrum Hall, Halifax, was hailed as 'a brilliant exhibition' of rugby, one newspaper claiming 'since the formation of the (Northern) Union two such clever sides had never opposed each other for the final of the championship.' Whilst it was Huddersfield's debut in the final, it marked a fourth consecutive appearance for Wigan as the two sides trotted out to the strains of 'Auld Lang Syne.'

Wigan controlled the early stages thanks to a generous supply of scrum possession, but Huddersfield, minus centre Edgar Wrigley due to blood poisoning in his leg after being kicked, proved equal to the challenge. They placed the first points on the scoreboard after 17 minutes when brilliant handling saw winger Albert Rosenfeld shoot clear to score near the corner flag. Fred Gleave failed to halt him and had to leave the field for several minutes after injuring himself in the process. Fred Longstaff added a great touchline goal. Wigan's talented backs, though, were in mesmerising form for much of the first half despite lacking Lance Todd (a three-month old rib injury failing to heal) and Jimmy Leytham (his injury blighted season meant he had already played his last match). But they lacked finish and poor territorial kicking on the day yielded good field position to a Yorkshire side known to prefer a quick handling game to a kicking duel.

Bert Jenkins almost scored for Wigan, held up after excellent approach work from Joe Miller and Johnny Thomas. Their breakthrough came when Thomas, retrieving from a scrum,

Huddersfield 1911/12 (players/trainer only). Third row: Bennett (trainer), Clark, Trevarthen, Higson, Gronw, Longstaff, Brook, Sherwood, Walton. Seated: Wrigley, Moorhouse, Wagstaff, Davies, Grey, Kitchin. On ground: Rosenfeld, Holland

CHAMPION CAPTAIN

Harold Wagstaff (Huddersfield 1912, 1913, 1915)

Harold Wagstaff – dubbed 'The Prince of Centres' – is one of the most legendary names in Rugby League history. He joined Huddersfield from his local club Underbank Rangers in 1906, his 436th – and last – match for the club being in 1925. A hugely gifted player, he became captain of Huddersfield in 1911 when he was still only 19 years old, leading the Fartowners to success three times each in the Championship (1911/12, 1912/13, 1914/15) and Northern Union Challenge Cup (1913, 1915, 1920). Other club honours included the Yorkshire Cup (1911, 1914, 1919 – May, 1919 – November) and Yorkshire League (1911/12, 1912/13, 1913/14, 1914/15, 1919/20, 1921/22). A knee infection cost him his 1910 tour place, but he was included in the 1914 and 1920 squads, both times as captain. He made 12 Test appearances and represented England (9 times) and Yorkshire (15). He became player-coach of Huddersfield (1924-25), subsequently coaching Halifax (1925–26) and Broughton Rangers (1935–36). In 1988, he was inducted into the Rugby League Hall of Fame.

propelled a wide pass across the face of the Fartowner's posts. It connected with centre Jack Prescott who provided Lew Bradley with the scoring pass. Thomas was equal to the difficult kick, and the teams were level at 5–5. Thomas tried to push Wigan ahead with a drop-goal, but it was charged down. Just before half-time Prescott was forced to leave the field with an injury and, although returning, was unable to contribute meaningfully afterwards.

After the break Thomas again tried to give Wigan the lead, his penalty being off target. Huddersfield also sought the crucial go-ahead score, Tommy Grey (penalty) and Major Holland (drop-goal) both failing to hit the spot. Their legendary skipper, Harold Wagstaff, who threatened several times after the interval despite not being 100 percent due to influenza earlier in the week, eventually broke the deadlock. Bursting through a gap, he passed to Stanley Moorhouse who hugged the touchline before returning the ball inside. Duggie Clark ended the move, running in behind the posts. Grey appended the goal for a 10–5 lead with eight minutes remaining. Their triumph was completed just before full time, Wagstaff and Moorhouse combining again, to set up Jim Davies. Grey was wide with his kick as the final whistle was blown.

In addition to receiving the trophy (in Huddersfield's case) and medals from guest of honour, Lord St Oswald, the two sides were also presented with the respective county championship trophies and medals won during the season. Wagstaff, having been reported doubtful to play due to his illness, gave an outstanding display. At the post-match presentation in the grandstand he said: 'I am a proud man in receiving the cup for the Huddersfield, Cricket and Athletic Club. It has been a hard game, but I think we have been the better side.'

Huddersfield's flying Aussie winger Albert Rosenfeld grabbed the opening try

STATS

Huddersfield 13 Wigan 5

Saturday 4 May at Thrum Hall, Halifax (3.30 pm)

Huddersfield: Holland, Rosenfeld, Kitchin, Wagstaff (captain), Moorhouse, Davies, Grey, Byrne, Clark, Gronow, Higson, Longstaff, Sherwood. Trainer: A. Bennett

Wigan: Sharrock (captain), Bradley, Jenkins, Prescott, Miller, Thomas, Gleave, Ramsdale, Seeling, Silcock, Whittaker, Williams, Winstanley. Trainer: J. Hesketh

Half-time: 5–5 | **Referee:** J.F. May
Attendance: 15,000 | **Receipts**: £591

Weather: fine and dry; ground very uneven and bumpy

Progressive score:

Huddersfield	score (min)	Wigan
Rosenfeld try, Longstaff goal	5–0 (17)	
	5–5 (35)	Bradley try, Thomas goal
Clark try, Grey goal	10–5 (68)	
Davies try	13–5 (79)	

League leaders	P	W	D	L	For	Agst	Pts	Percent
1 Huddersfield	36	31	1	4	996	238	63	87.50
2 Wigan	34	27	1	6	483	215	55	80.00
3 Hull Kingston Rovers	34	25	0	9	597	294	50	73.52
4 Hunslet	34	24	1	9	554	286	49	72.05

Semi-finals:

Huddersfield 27 Hunslet 3

Wigan 41 Hull Kingston Rovers 3

Head-to-head form guide:

Wigan 3 Huddersfield 23 (League)

Huddersfield 24 Wigan 0 (League)

1913 Northern Rugby League Championship Final
HUDDERSFIELD V WIGAN

The 1913 Championship Final was the most one-sided so far, Huddersfield's 29–2 victory over luckless Wigan producing the highest score and winning margin to date. Over the past couple of seasons the two had emerged as the sport's top sides, referred to in one preview as 'without doubt the best in the Northern League.' Their meeting was eagerly anticipated, producing a new record attendance and receipts for the occasion. For Huddersfield, centre Edgar Wrigley was declared 'unfit', whilst Wigan were without star forward Charlie Seeling due to a broken bone above the ankle.

In view of the final margin, the first half was remarkably close, score-wise, much of the credit going to Wigan's Lance Todd, who raced across the field on three occasions to deny flying winger Albert Rosenfeld. The first two instances were each followed by abortive penalty attempts from Huddersfield's Fred Longstaff, the latter rebounding off the post. Major Holland had no better luck for the Fartowners after Jim Davies was obstructed. Points did go on the board after 23 minutes, however, but in Wigan's favour, Bert Jenkins fielding a clearance, making a mark from which Johnny Thomas kicked a goal. Goal efforts for Huddersfield followed, Longstaff (penalty) and Holland (from a mark by Jack Chilcott) failing to deliver. A poor clearance kick by Wigan's Fred Gleave enable Harold Wagstaff to mark in a 'good position' but Holland was wide. Minutes later, Wigan full-back Jim Sharrock had a clearance kick charged down by Duggie Clark, the rampaging forward being on it in a flash for an easy try. Holland missed the goal but it was 3–2 to Huddersfield. Sharrock, in

Three-try hero Duggie Clark

Triumphant captain Harold Wagstaff

his last match, tried to make amends, but his drop-goal effort was poor. As the interval approached, Percy Coldrick sent Arthur Francis on a long run to the Huddersfield line but Wagstaff overhauled him.

The second half was a complete contrast to the first, the Fartowners continually bombarding Wigan's defences. The signs were ominous when Rosenfeld almost scored in the opening seconds, losing the chance after kicking over Sharrock's head, the ball rolling dead. Within seven minutes of the restart, though, they had effectively won the match through posting two tries, courtesy of Tommy Grey and Clark, both converted by Holland for a 13–2 lead. Grey's came after he retrieved the ball from a scrum near Wigan's line, racing through a gap when his dummy pass to Davies bamboozled Wigan's halves before rounding Sharrock to go under the posts. Clark's touchdown was the result of following Longstaff's kick over the try-line, the latter having recovered a wickedly bouncing ball from Wagstaff's high punt. At this point Wigan's Todd (limping and suffering with a hand injury) and Percy Williams (damaged knee) both left for attention. Todd resumed but Williams could not, reducing his side to 12 for the last half-hour. Huddersfield was now 'flying high' and wonderful passing skills from Clark, Grey and Wagstaff saw Stanley Moorhouse cross in the corner, Holland hitting the post with his goal attempt. Wigan's best second-half moment came when winger Lew Bradley intercepted and raced away, Rosenfeld, chasing half a yard behind, eventually overhauling him after a 50-yard chase. A brilliant run from Grey ended with the intervention of Francis but Huddersfield closed their account with three more tries; Clark (completing his hat-trick to score near the posts after another supreme passing move triggered by Davies' break) and Rosenfeld with two (firstly, in the corner after Clark claimed the ball from Sharrock, the second off Gleeson's pass). Holland converted the first two efforts.

The *Yorkshire Post* said: 'It took the Fartowner's a long time to settle down to their real game, but once they felt confidence in themselves they demonstrated their transcendent qualities to the full. Their forwards have never played better than they did on Saturday.' Clark's three try haul set a Championship Final record that was replicated four times but never beaten. For Wigan, it was a disappointing fourth consecutive defeat in a record-equalling fifth successive final appearance.

STATS

Huddersfield 29 Wigan 2

Saturday 3 May at Belle Vue, Wakefield (3.30 pm)

Huddersfield: Holland, Rosenfeld, Wagstaff (captain), Gleeson, Moorhouse, Davies, Grey, Clark, Chilcott, Gronow, Higson, Lee, Longstaff. Trainer: A. Bennett

Wigan: Sharrock (captain), Bradley, Jenkins, Todd, Walford, Thomas, Gleave, Coldrick, Francis, Melling, Ramsdale, Silcock, Williams. Trainer: J. Hesketh

Half-time: 3–2 **Referee:** W. McCutcheon
Attendance: 17,000 **Receipts**: £914

Weather: heavy rain at intervals, strong wind

Progressive score:

Huddersfield	score (min)	Wigan
	0–2 (23)	Thomas goal from mark
Clark try	3–2 (30)	
Grey try, Holland goal	8–2 (43)	
Clark try, Holland goal	13–2 (47)	
Moorhouse try	16–2 (56)	
Clark try, Holland goal	21–2 (70)	
Rosenfeld try, Holland goal	26–2 (75)	
Rosenfeld try	29–2 (78)	

League leaders	P	W	D	L	For	Agst	Pts	Percent
1 Huddersfield	32	28	0	4	732	217	56	87.50
2 Wigan	34	28	0	6	702	251	56	82.35
3 Hull Kingston	32	23	1	8	479	273	47	73.43
4 Dewsbury	34	23	1	10	534	230	47	69.11

Semi-finals:
Huddersfield 30 Dewsbury 3
Wigan 16 Hull Kingston Rovers 3

Head-to-head form guide:
Huddersfield 11 Wigan 10 (League)
Wigan 5 Huddersfield 14 (Challenge Cup)
Wigan 31 Huddersfield 10 (League)

1914 Northern Rugby League Championship Final
SALFORD V HUDDERSFIELD

Salford pulled off the biggest Championship Final upset to date in overcoming Huddersfield's star-studded side in the 1914 decider. The Fartowners looked hot favourites to complete a third consecutive title and it was easy to see why. The comparative strengths of the two teams could be gauged from the Yorkshire side having six players departing the following Tuesday on the Northern Union tour to Australasia, including tour captain Harold Wagstaff, whilst Salford had none. Their brilliant attacking machine had amassed 830 points during the League campaign and they easily led the table, whereas second-placed Salford mustered just 320. Salford's strength, though, lay with a defence that had conceded a miserly 140 points in 32 League games. Huddersfield was at full strength, the Reds being without wingman George Callender (leg injury), his place going to reserve stand-off Walter Clegg.

The paid attendance of 8,091 was disappointing, although it was estimated that with ticket admissions, a crowd of over 10,000 was present. Reportedly, 4,000 Salford supporters travelled across the Pennines to Headingley by train, apparently in cramped conditions; 'Fifteen in a compartment and nearly a hundred in a carriage corridor.' They must have feared the worst when Huddersfield, having failed with a Jack Chilcott drop-kick and Major Holland penalty, scored through a

CHAMPION CAPTAIN

Willie Thomas (Salford 1914)

William Strother 'Willie' Thomas joined Salford in 1903 from Aberavon Rugby Union Club, being appointed captain in 1911. It was a position he retained until his 444th and final outing for the club in 1921, the highlight being when he led Salford to victory in the 1913/14 Championship – his only winners' medal. Born in Swansea, the elegant, elusive centre gained surprisingly few representative honours during his long career, being picked once each for Wales and Other Nationalities. He made a brief comeback with Broughton Rangers during the 1922/23 term when he played eight times. He later became a director at Salford.

Salford players and officials commemorate their first Championship

Tommy Gleeson try, set up by Wagstaff after a Johnny Rogers' break. Holland missed the conversion. It sparked Huddersfield into gear and, for a while, Salford struggled to contain them, regaining confidence through a length of field break by wingman Bernard Mesley. It boosted the Reds' morale, although Harry Launce was unsuccessful with a drop-goal attempt. Eventually, following several scrums on the Huddersfield line, Charlie Rees touched down in the corner to level the scores. Mesley became the hero of Salford when his difficult touchline conversion, taken against a strong wind, sailed between the posts, for a 5–3 interval lead.

After the interval Fred Longstaff tried to level the scores, missing with a goal effort from a mark by Rogers. Mesley too, was out of luck, a penalty being 'inches wide', another attempt, from inside his own half after he made a mark, also failing. But the men from Fartown pressed hard in the second half, one scribe noting: 'How Salford withstood and repelled that terrible attack in the last 20 minutes is known only to those who were the defenders.' The Reds' situation was compounded by full-back Launce leaving the field during this period with a rib injury. He returned for just one minute, made a tackle, and then went off permanently, Harry Goldsmith taking up his position. Stanley Moorhouse (who knocked over the corner flag) and Albert Rosenfeld (held on the line) almost got over towards the end but Salford's defence held out and, with no further score, they found themselves being crowned Champions, their fans 'cheering loud and long' after the match finished.

Salford captain Willie Thomas

Much of the success could be attributed to Salford captain Willie Thomas who developed a 'game plan' long before it was fashionable to do so! After Salford had defeated Wigan in the play-off the previous Saturday, their opposition for the final was still unknown, the Huddersfield-Hull semi-final that day being postponed through bad weather. Rearranged for Monday it enabled Thomas to travel over the Pennines to watch the tie, observing favourites Huddersfield in particular, who, as anticipated, won comfortably. Thomas came away with a defensive strategy to close down the free-scoring Fartown 13. In an era when clubs did not employ coaching staff, tactics usually rested on the shoulders of the senior players and Thomas did his job well, their hard-working pack dominating scrum possession to carry the day. As it was the club's first trophy since resigning from the Rugby Football Union, he could be forgiven the obvious post-match pun when he said 'It was a red letter day for us!'

STATS

Salford 5 Huddersfield 3

Saturday 25 April at Headingley, Leeds (3.30 pm)

Salford: (red): Launce, Clegg, W.S. Thomas (captain), Loveluck, Mesley, John, May, E.J. Thomas, Bevon, Ritchie, Woods, Rees, Goldsmith. Trainer: J. White

Huddersfield: (white): Holland, Rosenfeld, Gleeson, Wagstaff (captain), Moorhouse, Rogers, Davies, Clark, Chilcott, Gronow, Higson, Lee, Longstaff. Trainer: A. Bennett

Half-time: 5–3 **Referee:** W. McCutcheon
Attendance: 8,091 **Receipts**: £474

Weather: bright sunshine and strong wind

Progressive score:

Salford	score (min)	Huddersfield
	0–3 (20)	Gleeson try
Rees try, Mesley goal	5–3 (35)	

League leaders	P	W	D	L	For	Agst	Pts	Percent
1 Huddersfield	34	28	2	4	830	258	58	85.29
2 Salford	32	25	1	6	320	140	51	79.69
3 Wigan	34	25	2	7	676	252	52	76.47
4 Hull	34	24	1	9	507	264	49	72.06

Semi-finals:
Huddersfield 23 Hull 5
Salford 16 Wigan 5

Head-to-head form guide:
No previous meetings during season

1915 Northern Rugby League Championship Final
HUDDERSFIELD V LEEDS

Huddersfield set up a new Championship Final record score with their comprehensive 35–2 victory over Leeds, who qualified for the first time on the back of an unexpected semi-final win at Wigan. Having won the coin toss, Huddersfield looked confident from the moment Ben Gronow kicked off, scoring two tries in the opening 10 minutes. Huddersfield's Harold Wagstaff, set to be the first skipper to lead his side to three Championship Final wins, found touch just 20 yards from the Leeds try-line. At the resultant scrum, the Huddersfield pack wheeled round, breaking away with an irresistible dribbling 'rush' towards the line, Duggie Clark picking up a few yards out and shoving his way through near the posts. Immediately after the restart Leeds winger Albert Jenkinson threatened with a magnificent run but opposite number Albert Rosenfeld pulled off a superb tackle and, moments later, the Claret and Gold surged downfield where they again rotated a scrum near Leeds' line, Gronow claiming possession to score beneath the posts. His conversion of both tries established a quick 10–0 lead.

Welsh forward Ben Gronow led the way with two tries and seven goals

Showing character, Leeds tried to rally, George Rees making a telling break through Huddersfield's defence, but supporting winger, W.H. 'Hughie' Davies, was bustled into touch near the try-line. Johnny Rogers gave Huddersfield some relief from the resulting scrum with a great run to the opposite end but, after kicking over full-back Dan Lewis he was

Huddersfield, complete with 'All Four Cups'. Standing: A. Bennett (trainer), Lee, Higson, Banks, Jones, Heyes, Longstaff, Clark, Swinden, H. Bennett (asst. trainer). Seated: Habron, Holland, Moorhouse, Wagstaff, Gleeson, Todd, Gronow. On ground: Ganley, Rosenfeld, Rogers

obstructed following up. Gronow's resultant penalty just dipped below the crossbar. More Huddersfield pressure followed, Wagstaff cutting brilliantly through a sea of defenders to put Fred Longstaff under the posts, Gronow adding the goal. To their credit Leeds tried desperately hard to get back into the game and Ivor Jones almost got over the line, but they had to settle for a neat drop-goal from Lewis. Gronow missed his second penalty attempt but, shortly after, he picked up a loose ball beginning a move involving Rogers, Bert Ganley and Wagstaff that concluded with Stanley Moorhouse crossing the whitewash in the corner. Gronow was just wide with his kick, Huddersfield leading 18–2 at the break.

The second 40 minutes began with a bout of end-to-end kicking as both teams fought for territorial position. The first scoring threat came when Rosenfeld had his progress stopped near the line but, from the scrum that followed, Rogers managed to slip over for a try, Gronow converting. It was all Huddersfield now, Gronow being successful with the second of two further penalty awards, given for offside, and then scoring his second try. It began when Moorhouse attacked the line, kicking the ball over Lewis, Dinny Campbell's attempt to kick it dead being miscued. Moorhouse and Tommy Gleeson overran it but the supporting Gronow calmly picked up and walked across the line. He added the goal for a 30–2 lead. The scoring was completed when Gleeson recovered the ball after a Leeds passing move broke down, drawing Lewis before supplying Wagstaff, who ran under the posts, Gronow augmenting. Although more chances followed, particularly for Huddersfield, the scoreboard operator was not required again.

The Fartowners, in surpassing their own Championship Final score of two years earlier, won by a record 33-point margin, Gronow also setting new highs for the occasion with his seven goals and 20 points. A week later they added the Northern Union Cup thereby possessing all four major trophies open to them during the campaign, emulating Hunslet's 1907/08 feat. Forward John Higson was involved in both.

On a more sombre note, the 1914/15 season went ahead despite Britain having declared war on Germany during August 1914 as the First World War gained momentum. The Northern Union Committee, along with the Football League, had decided to continue providing competitive sport despite objections in many quarters. For the remainder of the war, though, teams only played friendly fixtures, without recompense to the players, excepting expenses. The next Championship Final was not staged until 1920 when Huddersfield would again grace the event. Sadly, one player who would not be there was 1914 tourist Fred Longstaff, who died at the Battle of the Somme during July 1916.

STATS

Huddersfield 35 Leeds 2

Saturday 24 April at Belle Vue, Wakefield (3.30 pm)

Huddersfield: (claret with narrow gold hoops): Holland, Rosenfeld, Gleeson, Wagstaff (captain), Moorhouse, Ganley, Rogers, Banks, Clark, Gronow, Higson, Lee, Longstaff. Trainer: A. Bennett

Leeds: (white): Lewis, W.H. Davies, W.A. Davies (captain), Campbell, Jenkinson, Jones, Sanders, Carter, Chilcott, Godward, Rees, Ward, Webster. Trainer: W. Morn

Half-time: 18–2 **Referee:** J.F. May
Attendance: 14,000 **Receipts**: £750

Weather: overcast and dry

Progressive score:

Huddersfield	score (min)	Leeds
Clark try, Gronow goal	5–0 (8)	
Gronow try, Gronow goal	10–0 (10)	
Longstaff try, Gronow goal	15–0 (25)	
	15–2 (-)	Lewis drop-goal
Moorhouse try	18–2 (38)	
Rogers try, Gronow goal	23–2 (-)	
Gronow penalty	25–2 (-)	
Gronow try, Gronow goal	30–2 (-)	
Wagstaff try, Gronow goal	35–2 (65)	

League leaders	P	W	D	L	For	Agst	Pts	Percent
1 Huddersfield	34	28	4	2	888	235	60	88.24
2 Wigan	32	25	1	6	679	206	51	79.69
3 Leeds	34	24	3	7	486	207	51	75.02
4 Rochdale Hornets	34	24	2	8	306	194	50	73.53

Semi-finals:

Huddersfield 33 Rochdale Hornets 2

Wigan 4 Leeds 15

Head-to-head form guide:

Huddersfield 27 Leeds 10 (League)

Leeds 5 Huddersfield 5 (League)

1920 Northern Rugby League Championship Final
HULL V HUDDERSFIELD

Hull won their first Championship with a dramatic late try against Huddersfield in the 1920 decider, a result that changed the course of rugby league history. Had the Fartowner's held on for the eight minutes remaining they could, today, claim to be the only club to secure the coveted 'All Four Cups' on two occasions following their 1914/15 achievement.

Hull's success against the side that beat them 34–10 in the last League fixture of the season looked unlikely when their forward Alf Grice was dismissed three minutes before half-time, but they clung on gamely before delivering their sucker punch. The man to thank was Billy Batten, diving through a crowded defence to cross the whitewash, described by the *Hull Daily Mail* as a 'superhuman effort.' It came after a surging charge by Hull's pack that dribbled menacingly towards the Huddersfield line before it was picked up and passed wide to John Markham, the winger turning it inside for Batten, who threw himself over the line. Billy Holder missed the goal, but Hull ran the clock down to win by the narrowest of margins, 3–2.

Both teams were badly depleted, the latest tour to the Antipodes claiming Billy Stone (Hull), and Harold Wagstaff, Duggie Clark, Ben Gronow, Johnny Rogers and Gwyn Thomas (all Huddersfield). Hull also lacked Jimmy Devereux, Eddie Caswell (both injured) and Ned Rogers (taken ill) amongst the backs, whilst their forwards Jack Beasty, Tom Herridge and Fred Newsome were all suspended, each sent off in consecutive games over a four-day period. Huddersfield three-quarter Stanley Moorhouse was also unfit.

The final was dominated by the two packs, 'deadly tackling' being a main feature, the backs struggling to get into the match, one scribe noting free kicks and penalties were 'the order of the day.' After their half-back Robert Habron failed with an earlier drop-goal attempt, Huddersfield took the lead when Major Holland landed a well-struck penalty on 27 minutes. Referee Albert Hestford gave the award because Batten was deemed offside during a scrum, although he vehemently disputed this with the official. The Fartowner's best try-scoring chance of the match followed when Tommy Gleeson made a glorious break but when he turned the ball inside for George Todd, the winger seemed to hesitate when a clear run beckoned, Alf Francis moving quickly to make the tackle. Hull skipper Jim Kennedy missed with a difficulty penalty before Grice was given his

The Hull team (including some players wearing suits). Back: Beasty, Devereux, Herridge, Caswell, Newsome, Oldham, Humphries. Third row: Wyburn, Garrett, Taylor, Shield, Grice, Holder, Melville (trainer). Seated: A.J. Boynton (chairman), Holdsworth, Batten, Kennedy, Milner, Markham, C.N. Lofthouse (secretary). On ground: Francis, Hulme

Billy Batten scored a sensational late winner for Hull

'marching orders' following a 'free for all' in the middle of the field. As half-time approached, Habron was off target with another drop-goal.

With their numerical disadvantage and the wind against them after the break, Hull had it all to do and could have fallen further behind had Holland not been short with another penalty attempt. But it was Hull that looked increasingly more threatening. Batten and Francis came close to scoring tries but both exerted too much pressure with boot on ball, causing it to disappear over the dead-ball line; Batten after a charge by his forwards had presented the opportunity, Francis in kicking over the head of remaining defender Holland, having made a searing break. In between those incidents Kennedy had two poor goal misses; firstly from a mark, then after a penalty award, subsequently hitting the post with another penalty. But it all came right for his colleagues and himself in the final minutes.

Played five years to the day since the last Championship decider due to the war, it was a date that presented sports minded people in Huddersfield with a dilemma as to where their loyalties lay. The Football Association Cup Final was also being staged at Chelsea's Stamford Bridge, Huddersfield Town being involved, although suffering a similar fate to the Claret and Gold's, losing 1–0 to Aston Villa in extra time.

CHAMPION CAPTAIN

Jim Kennedy (Hull 1920, 1921)

Locally-born Jim Kennedy made his Hull debut in 1915, managing five appearances before the First World War disrupted his playing career for over three years. A powerful centre – he occasionally played in the pack – he led Hull to two Championship successes (1919/20, 1920/21) and was in the side that won the Yorkshire Cup (1923) and Yorkshire League (1918/19, 1922/23). His goal-kicking prowess enabled him to set club records for a season of 108 goals and 264 points in 1920/21 (neither being surpassed until 1953/54) and match records of 14 goals in April 1921 (equalled in 1978) and 36 points in January 1921. He made his last appearance in 1926 and later became a club director. He made one representative appearance; for Yorkshire in 1919 when he lined up amongst the forwards.

STATS

Hull 3 Huddersfield 2

Saturday 24 April at Headingley, Leeds (3.30 pm)

Hull: (black and white irregular hoops): Holdsworth, Francis, Batten, Kennedy (captain), Markham, Milner, Hulme, Holder, Wyburn, Grice, Garrett, Shield, Taylor. Trainer: S. Melville

Huddersfield: (claret with narrow gold hoops): Holland, Todd, Gleeson, Rosenfeld (captain), Pogson, Marsden, Habron, Higson, Swinden, Sherwood, Fenwick, Naylor, Sutcliffe. Trainer: unknown

Half-time: 0–2 **Referee:** A. Hestford
Attendance: 12,900 **Receipts**: £1,615

Weather: cloudy and dry at first, started raining just before half-time, ground heavy

Progressive score:

Hull	score (min)	Huddersfield
	0-2 (27)	Holland penalty
Batten try	3–2 (72)	

League leaders	P	W	D	L	For	Agst	Pts	Percent
1 Huddersfield	34	29	0	5	759	215	58	85.29
2 Hull	34	25	1	8	587	276	51	75.00
3 Leeds	32	23	0	9	445	208	46	71.87
4 Widnes	30	21	1	8	250	115	43	71.67

Semi-finals:
Huddersfield 7 Widnes 5
Hull 11 Leeds 0

Head-to-head form guide:
Hull 24 Huddersfield 5 (League)
Huddersfield 33 Hull 8 (Yorkshire Cup)
Huddersfield 34 Hull 10 (League)

1921 Northern Rugby League Championship Final
HULL V HULL KINGSTON ROVERS

The all-Humberside 1921 Championship Final created immense anticipation, the *Hull Daily Mail* claiming 'never in the history of Hull rugby football has such enthusiasm and interest been shown in a local derby.' The problem for supporters of Hull and Hull Kingston Rovers was that the match was scheduled for Headingley. They had met there earlier that season in the Yorkshire Cup Final, but the 20,000 attendance that day was not expected to be repeated as 'labour troubles' limited rail travel. Only one train left Hull in time, arriving in Leeds at 10.00 am. The prediction was true; 10,000 saw the Championship decider, an estimated 500–600 travelling from Hull. Unhappily, fighting erupted amongst the crowd at the Town end before kick-off, order eventually being restored. Excepting injured Hull winger Alf Francis, both clubs had selected from a full squad.

The Rovers threatened almost from the start when their captain Arthur Moore raced towards the corner with winger Lou Harris in support, but was pulled up just short of the line. They did, however, take a 4th minute lead when Sandy Gibson landed a penalty for a scrum infringement. After that, the half mostly belonged to Hull, registering all three pre-interval tries. Billy Stone got the first after Eddie Caswell made an opening, the break continuing through Tommy Milner and Billy Batten, who delivered the final pass. After two near misses from Caswell and Jimmy Devereux, both just beaten in a chase for the ball near Rovers' line, Bob Taylor grabbed the second. Described as 'a scrambling state of affairs' he touched down after Robins' full-back Laurie Osbourne lost possession near his line. Gibson pulled two points back with a goal from a Gilbert Austin mark before Devereux completed his side's trio. Initially tackled a yard short, he went over off a sharp Caswell pass after play continued. Amidst claims he stepped out of play, the touch-judge confirmed the score. Jim Kennedy missed all

STATS

Hull 16 Hull Kingston Rovers 14

Saturday 7 May at Headingley, Leeds (3.30 pm)

Hull: (black and white irregular hoops): Rogers, Devereux, Kennedy (captain), Batten, Stone, Milner, Caswell, Newsome, Ellis, Beasty, Taylor, Wyburn, Garrett. Trainer: S. Melville

Hull Kingston Rovers: (white with red band): Osbourne, Harris, Cook, Austin, Mulvey, Clark, McGiever, Bob Wilkinson, Gibson, Jack Wilkinson, R. Boagey, Bielby, Moore (captain). Trainer: W. Jacques

Half-time: 9–4 **Referee:** A. Brown
Attendance: 10,000 **Receipts**: £1,320

Weather: cloudy and dry at first, heavy rain during second half

Progressive score:

Hull	score (min)	Hull Kingston Rovers
	0–2 (4)	Gibson penalty
Stone try	3–2 (10)	
Taylor try	6–2 (30)	
	6–4 (-)	Gibson goal from mark
Devereux try	9–4 (-)	
Taylor try, Kennedy goal	14–4 (55)	
	14–9 (63)	Mulvey try, Gibson goal
	14–11 (-)	Gibson penalty
Kennedy penalty	16–11 (74)	
	16–14 (75)	Cook try

League leaders	P	W	D	L	For	Agst	Pts	Percent
1 Hull Kingston Rovers	32	24	1	7	432	233	49	76.56
2 Hull	36	27	0	9	722	267	54	75.00
3 Halifax	38	27	0	11	492	184	54	71.05
4 Wigan	34	23	1	10	435	238	47	69.12

Semi-finals:

Hull Kingston Rovers 24 Wigan 4
Hull 27 Halifax 10

Head-to-head form guide:

Hull Kingston Rovers 6 Hull 15 (League)
Hull Kingston Rovers 2 Hull 0
(Yorkshire Cup at Headingley, Leeds)
Hull 4 Hull Kingston Rovers 8 (League)

three conversions, although each try was in the corner, his second effort hitting the far post.

Ahead 9–4, Hull began the second half with 12 men, forward Danny Wyburn having retired prior to Devereux's try following a kick to his head. He soon resumed to 'loud cheers' with his head bandaged, a doctor having been located in the spectators' stand. It was Wyburn, later dubbed 'the hero of the day' after a courageous second half performance that set up Hull's next try. As the Rovers pack attempted to dribble the ball through the Hull ranks Wyburn retrieved it, his powerful charge downfield taking him to the opposition's 25-yard line. Faced by Osbourne, he off-loaded to the supporting Taylor who raced round the back of the posts, Kennedy adding his elusive goal. Rain began falling heavily as Rovers bravely mounted a late comeback. Winger H. Mulvey crossed in the corner off Tommy McGiever's pass, despite an attempted intercept by Milner, racing round behind the posts. Gibson appended and tagged on a penalty following a scrum offence, putting his side within three points. The pace became frantic in the closing stages as Rovers sensed possible victory, Kennedy providing relief for Hull with a penalty. But a late Rovers try by Jimmy Cook, who burst through a gap after Lou Harris caught the ball on the restart, set up a heart-stopping moment but Gibson missed the all-important kick that would have forced the replay. ,Minutes later the supporters in black and white 'favours' began celebrating their club's feat of retaining the Championship.

Billy Stone claimed the opening try

The *Hull Daily Mail*, who claimed it was 'a big mistake' taking the game to Leeds, provided a postscript, revealing the Northern Union authorities had reached agreement with soccer club, Hull City to stage the final. Hull agreed, but at the NU Council meeting in Leeds the preceding Monday, Rovers' president, Mr E.W. Brown, reportedly said it was the first he knew of it and needed to consult his club's directors. As NU officials required a decision, he apparently said his club 'was prepared to abide by the rules of the NU and play the League Final on a neutral ground in a neutral city as previously arranged.'

Hull's successful 1920/21 squad. Back: Batten (inset), Beasty, Wyburn, Grice, Ellis. Third row: Newsome, Taylor, Charles, Shield, Herridge, Francis, Holdsworth. Seated: C.N. Lofthouse (secretary), Garrett, Rogers, Kennedy, Devereux, Stone, Humphries, G.W. Miller (chairman). On ground: Milner, Caswell

1922 Northern Rugby League Championship Final
WIGAN V OLDHAM

Pure magic from Wigan's Welsh centre Jerry Shea settled the destination of the 1922 Championship title. Trailing 6–2, disaster struck for Oldham in the 63rd minute when their stand-off Alf Bates threw out a pass near his own 25-yard area. Shea intercepted and sprinted towards the corner, sidestepping full-back Ernie Knapman before turning inside to go round Billy Hall, evading Reg Farrar's would-be tackle to finish behind the posts for the only try of the match. Jim Sullivan added the extras and at 11–2 Wigan was set for victory.

Northern Union League Final Filmed.

WIGAN v. OLDHAM

ALL THIS WEEK.

AT THE

County Playhouse,

THREE DAYS COMMENCING MONDAY MAY 8,

AT THE

QUEEN'S THEATRE,

PEMBERTON,

CARLTON THEATRE,

PEMBERTON, and also

THURSDAY, FRIDAY, SATURDAY, MAY 11, 12, 13

AT THE

PALACE, Platt Bridge.

The climax to the 1921/22 season brought Wigan and Oldham into Championship Final opposition for the fourth time, having met in the deciders of 1909, 1910 and 1911. It was claimed in Wigan's local press that more motor coaches left the borough for the final than any previous match. The Central Park side decided not to risk half-back Danny Hurcombe, injured a month earlier, his place going to Ted Smith who three days previous helped the reserves win the Lancashire Senior Competition Final. Staged at The Cliff – which earned plaudits for marker flags 'composed of Union Jacks and other patriotic emblems,' but was advised, 'the turnstile accommodation needs improving' as many spectators did not enter until after the kick-off – the match attracted 26,000 who paid £1,825. Both figures created new Championship Final records.

The ever-accurate boot of Wigan's Sullivan opened the scoring with an early penalty after scrum half Sid Jerram was obstructed. Centre Tommy Howley doubled the lead three minutes later with a drop-goal after Knapman spilled the ball. The earliest try scoring chances, though, fell to Oldham. Firstly Hall – put in possession from a quick bout of passing after Jerram lost possession – looked to have the line at his mercy but chose to feed wing partner Jim Finnerty, who failed to hold on. Minutes later the Roughyeds had an opportunity on the other flank through the normally dependable Farrar, but the ball again hit the deck. In a nail-biting encounter, each side continued to apply pressure with several near misses at each end as the protagonists defended strongly. Sullivan got the final points of the opening half with a superb goal from near halfway, Shea having called for a mark after catching an Oldham drop out on the full.

Both teams created good chances in an equally tense second half, Sullivan almost scoring a try after kicking the ball round

CHAMPION CAPTAIN

Percy Coldrick (Wigan 1922)

Percy Coldrick had six rugby union appearances with Wales under his belt before signing with Wigan in 1912. Born in Caerleon, South Wales, the speedy, mobile forward had previously played for Crumlin, Weston-super-Mare and Newport. His club honours whilst at Central Park included the Championship (1921/22), Lancashire Cup (1912, 1922), and Lancashire League (1912/13, 1913/14, 1914/15, 1920/21, 1922/23, 1923/24). He made four Test appearances – all during the 1914 tour to Australia and New Zealand – and represented Wales (twice) and Other Nationalities (once). His last match for Wigan was in 1924, transferring to St Helens a year later, with whom he played in several matches during the 1925/26 campaign before retiring.

A postcard celebrating Wigan's 1921/22 Championship success with team captain Percy Coldrick standing proudly behind the trophy

Knapman, Hall just beating him to the touch. The next points on the board – the only ones from Oldham – also resulted from a mark when Wigan forward Tom Woods' drop-out was fielded by Maurice Tighe, Farrar kicking an easy goal. At 6–2, Oldham started to move the ball earnestly, determined to get the try that would put them in front but it all went pear-shaped when Shea grabbed his moment of glory. With two minutes left, Oldham forward Rod Marlor was dismissed after Jerram had been brought down a yard short of the try-line. Marlor, who a few minutes earlier had been involved in a spat with Sullivan, allegedly kicked out at Jerram and was promptly sent off, Sullivan's successful penalty completing the scoring as Wigan claimed their second Championship.

The *Manchester Guardian* claimed 'It was a keen though rather disappointing final', the *Daily Dispatch* explaining, 'The backs (of both teams) were handicapped by the strong wind and new ball on a lively ground' exonerating full-backs Knapman and Sullivan, who 'both fielded with accuracy and kicked with splendid length and judgement.' The occurrence of two goals from a 'mark' clearly lacked appeal for the game's administrators. At the Northern Union's annual general meeting the following June, when the decision was also taken to rename itself The Rugby Football League, officials voted to no longer allow the option of kicking a goal from a mark although 'free kicks' downfield would still be permitted.

STATS

Wigan 13 Oldham 2

Saturday 6 May at The Cliff, Broughton (3.30 pm)

Wigan: (blue): Sullivan, Coles, Howley, Shea, Smith, Jerram, Hesketh, Banks, Coldrick (captain), Hodder, Roffey, Shaw, Woods. Trainer: T. McCarty

Oldham: (red and white hoops): Knapman, Finnerty, Hall, Davies, Farrar, Bates, Tighe, Brown, Collins, Hilton (captain), Marlor, Sloman, Tomkins. Trainer: C. Marsden

Half-time: 6–0　**Referee:** R. Robinson
Attendance: 26,000　**Receipts**: £1,825

Weather: bright sunshine, strong wind

Progressive score:

Wigan	score (min)	Oldham
Sullivan penalty	2–0 (4)	
Howley drop-goal	4–0 (7)	
Sullivan goal from mark	6–0 (33)	
	6–2 (45)	Farrar goal from mark
Shea try, Sullivan goal	11–2 (63)	
Sullivan penalty	13–2 (78)	

League leaders	P	W	D	L	For	Agst	Pts	Percent
1 Oldham	36	29	1	6	521	201	59	81.94
2 Wigan	32	22	1	9	446	159	45	70.31
3 Hull	38	25	0	13	538	326	50	65.79
4 Huddersfield	36	23	1	12	608	271	47	65.28

Semi-finals:
Oldham 13 Huddersfield 5
Wigan 27 Hull 8

Head-to-head form guide:
Wigan 14 Oldham 5 (League)
Oldham 4 Wigan 2 (League)

1923 Northern Rugby League Championship Final
HULL KINGSTON ROVERS V HUDDERSFIELD

Hull Kingston Rovers sneaked through almost unnoticed during the latter half of the 1922/23 campaign to capture their first Championship, edging Wigan out of fourth play-off spot through winning 18–5 at Barrow in their last League game of the season. It climaxed a 16-match run that saw them ascend the League ladder with 14 wins and a draw. Sweeter still was their 16–2 victory over League leaders and neighbours Hull at the Boulevard in the play-off.

Jimmy Cook scored a vital Rovers' try 15 minutes from the end

In an unspectacular final they were comfortable winners over Huddersfield, building their victory platform with resolute tackling and an efficient kicking game. Huddersfield was virtually a new-look line-up from the great 'Team of All the Talents' of the previous decade with just a few veterans remaining, one of them, club captain Harold Wagstaff, being indisposed due to a stomach ulcer that required an operation. The Claret and Golds incurred further disruption during the final; Johnny Rogers was injured in the opening minutes, being barely able to run afterwards, and Arthur Swinden suffered a badly gashed head after coming into contact with a boot towards the end of the first half, returning just before the interval with his head protected.

The early scoring chances came from penalty awards, Huddersfield's Ben Gronow missing two shots either side of an attempt from Rovers' Laurie Osbourne, who miscued from in

Hull Kingston Rovers 1922/23 – Champions for the first time! Standing: J.H. Wilkinson, Westerdale, Boagey, J.R. Wilkinson, Bielby, Clark. Seated: T. Williams (secretary), Austin, Rees, Moore, Harris, Osbourne, E.W. Brown (chairman). On ground: Jacques (trainer), Hoult, McIntyre

front of goal, both marksmen seeking their 100th two-pointer of the season. Osbourne was the first to succeed with a well-judged drop-goal after catching a hasty clearance kick from Huddersfield's Gwyn Thomas following a Rovers forward rush. Gronow, meanwhile, was off target again, failing with a third penalty attempt. A try-scoring opportunity presented itself to the Robins when Lou Harris broke away but, with four colleagues in support, he failed to deliver a pass, being tackled by Thomas in the last significant move of the half.

Harris was again to the fore at the start of the second period with a 50-yard sprint. It did not conclude with a try but, with confidence building in their side, Dick Rees raced through shortly afterwards to score near the posts. Osbourne's goal extended the lead to 7–0. Huddersfield responded quickly when Osbourne misjudged a George Davidge kick, Duggie Clark following up to boot the ball towards the Rovers' line, Stanley Williams joining the chase to touch down near the posts. Gronow appended the goal, completing his elusive century. Just two points in arrears, Huddersfield looked for the go-ahead score, a chance coming when Williams again got away but his pass to Clark was disappointing. Moments later Clark appeared to have forced his way over the whitewash for a try only for referee Frank Fairhurst to dismiss the claim.

The immobility of Rogers forced Huddersfield to reshuffle their side: Farragher Stamper moving to full-back, Thomas to centre and Jack Howarth to stand-off. Disaster struck, though, when Stamper lost possession on his line and, as he tried to rescue the situation, Jimmy Cook raced up to claim the score, Osbourne being unable to add the extra points. The Rovers then embarked on a flurry of drop-goal attempts, Osbourne missing three – the first of which bounced back off the post – and captain Arthur Moore, one. Another error from Stamper – clearly struggling as emergency full-back – resulted in the Rovers' third and final try when he was slow to recover a loose ball, Jack Hoult gathering it up before placing it over the line. Osbourne's goal made it 15–5.

It was a great moment for the club when Moore received the trophy from Sir Edwin Airey, the *Hull Daily Mail* correspondent 'Robin Adair' – who had referred to the team as 'the Gallant Reds of Craven Park' – noting 'their team included no fewer than eleven local players all brought up in Hull and District, and this, indeed, was a triumph for local junior football in Hull.'

CHAMPION CAPTAIN

Arthur Moore (Hull Kingston Rovers 1923)

Back-row forward Arthur Moore signed for Hull Kingston Rovers under the name of Arthur Mawr from the local Hull St Patrick's club in 1907 making his senior debut in 1909, the first of 341 appearances for the club. Having won the Championship (1922/23) and Yorkshire Cup (1920), he left midway through the 1924/25 campaign, age 39, joining Dewsbury for a reported £250. With them he won the Yorkshire Cup again (1925), his final match being in 1926. He represented England once (versus Wales in 1913) and Yorkshire (6 times).

STATS

Hull Kingston Rovers 15 Huddersfield 5

Saturday 5 May at Headingley, Leeds (3.30 pm)

Hull Kingston Rovers: (white with red band): Osbourne, Harris, Cook, Rees, Austin, McIntyre, Hoult, Bob Wilkinson, F. Boagey, Jack Wilkinson, Westerdale, Bielby, Moore (captain). Trainer: W. Jacques

Huddersfield: (claret with narrow gold hoops): Thomas, Davidge, Reid, Howarth, Watts, Rogers, Williams, Swinden, Gronow (captain), Fenwick, Clark, Sherwood, Stamper. Trainer: unknown

Half-time: 2–0 **Referee:** F. Fairhurst
Attendance: 14,000 **Receipts**: £1,370

Weather: sunny and warm

Progressive score:

Hull Kingston Rovers	score (min)	Huddersfield
Osbourne drop-goal	2–0 (32)	
Rees try, Osbourne goal	7–0 (45)	
	7–5 (50)	Williams try, Gronow goal
Cook try	10–5 (65)	
Hoult try, Osbourne goal	15–5 (80)	

League leaders	P	W	D	L	For	Agst	Pts	Percent
1 Hull	36	30	0	6	587	304	60	83.33
2 Huddersfield	34	26	0	8	644	279	52	76.47
3 Swinton	36	27	0	9	467	240	54	75.00
4 Hull Kingston Rovers	36	26	1	9	597	231	53	73.61

Semi-finals:
Hull 2 Hull Kingston Rovers 16
Huddersfield 16 Swinton 5

Head-to-head form guide:
Huddersfield 18 Hull Kingston Rovers 11 (League)
Hull Kingston Rovers 32 Huddersfield 5 (League)

1924 Northern Rugby League Championship Final
BATLEY V WIGAN

Batley enjoyed one of their finest moments by conquering favourites Wigan 13–7 in the 1924 Championship Final. The Yorkshire League Champions achieved their success minus outstanding forward and captain Frank Gallagher, who had set sail for Australia with the touring team, although Wigan had five players on board in Tommy Howley, Danny Hurcombe, Jack Price, Johnny Ring and Jim Sullivan. The bottom line, though, is the tour deprived the teams of one forward each and it was in the battle up front that the match was won and lost. Whereas the workmanlike, solid Batley six hardly noticed the absence of Gallagher, Wigan missed the pace and creativity of loose forward and skipper, Price.

Batley eagerly set about their task from kick-off, taking three minutes to score a try following a scrum in Wigan's half. Acting captain Ike Fowler picked up, transferring to George Davidge who cut inside, setting off on a long run. His pass to Harry Rees was fumbled but somehow the centre held on and, when confronted by Jerry Shea, passed to Bert Murray, who showed great pace to score in the corner despite the attention of Attie van Heerden who raced across from the opposite flank. Rees missed with the kick.

A period of Wigan pressure, despite the four-minute loss of injured George Owens, came to nought, Batley regaining the ascendancy. Excellent passing by Davidge and Rees almost got Fred Carter away for a second try but

CHAMPION CAPTAIN

Ike Fowler (Batley 1924)

Welsh scrum half Ike Fowler signed with Batley for a reported £250 from Llanelli Rugby Union Club in 1919, commencing a professional career that continued until 1931. Born in Pantyffynnon, near Ammanford, he had made one international appearance for Wales, against the New Zealand Army in 1919. His Championship success in 1923/24 gives him the distinction of being the only player, to date, to lead Batley to the title, the Yorkshire League also being secured that season. Second on Batley's all-time appearance list with 386, he also made two international rugby league appearances, both against England in 1926; for Wales (at Pontypridd) and Other Nationalities (at Whitehaven).

Batley with the Yorkshire League (left) and Northern League Championship trophies after, arguably, the clubs best ever season. Standing: A. Armitage (trainer), Brooke, Gledhill, F. Carter, Smith, C. Armitage, Douglas, Ramsbottom, G Thwaites (asst. trainer). Seated: W. Rees, Davidge, Scott, Fowler, Robinson, H. Rees, Murray. On ground: Williams, A. Carter

Tommy Parker gave chase to pull off a great tackle. Eventually Wigan did get on the scoreboard midway through the half, Sol Oakley landing a penalty awarded for a scrum offence. The Cherry and Whites started showing better form, but almost went further behind when penalised for obstruction, Rees being just short with his kick. Then van Heerden, in one of his rare attacks on the day, got away from Batley's cover but was eventually put into touch by Davidge.

Holding a one-point lead, Batley had the advantage of a light wind in the second half. Rees missed an early opportunity to stretch the margin with a penalty after Owens obstructed Joe Robinson. However, a more crucial score quickly followed when Robinson fielded a kick and transferred to Murray. The winger raced away before cross-kicking towards Wigan's line. Robinson, following up, missed the ball but his presence distracted Oakley, allowing Jack Leeming to pick up and dive over. Rees added the goal for an 8–2 lead.

Ike Fowler ably led Batley in Frank Gallagher's absence

Rees failed with another penalty chance before a smart Batley break almost resulted in another Leeming try, the forward being held a yard short after losing his footing. Batley continued applying pressure through their domineering pack and, from a scrum, Fowler put in a short kick, collected by Rees. After drawing his man, Rees gave an inside pass to Murray, sending him over near the posts for his second touchdown. Rees kicked the goal for what looked a winning 13–2 lead. Seven minutes later, though, Oakley reduced the arrears to nine points, Batley being penalised at a scrum, but was wide with a further attempt, given for obstruction shortly after. In a frenzied close, Wigan finally managed to get the ball down over the Batley line. Ten minutes from time, Dick Armstrong squeezed into the corner off a Shea pass, Oakley missing the vital goal that would have put them within one score. Wigan soon ran out of time, though, Batley thoroughly deserving their moment of glory after a match in which their full-back Robinson had played a key role by repelling whatever Wigan had thrown at him.

After Batley left the reception at their Town Hall they journeyed to Clark Green where a visit was made to the house of absent team captain Frank Gallagher. On reaching the Commercial Hotel, of which he was licensee, a band duly played 'Auld Lang Syne.'

STATS

Batley 13 Wigan 7

Saturday 3 May at The Cliff, Broughton (3.30 pm)

Batley (cerise): Robinson, Williams, Davidge, H. Rees, Murray, Scott, Fowler (captain), Ramsbottom, Brooke, Leeming, Smith, Douglas, F. Carter. Trainer: A. Armitage

Wigan: (cherry and white hoops): Oakley, Armstrong, Shea (captain), Parker, van Heerden, Jerram, Owens, Webster, Banks, Brown, van Rooyen, Roffey, Coldrick. Trainer: T. McCarty

Half-time: 3–2 **Referee:** F. Mills
Attendance: 13,729 **Receipts**: £968

Weather: cloudy, dry and windy

Progressive score:

Batley	score (min)	Wigan
Murray try	3–0 (3)	
	3–2 (21)	Oakley penalty
Leeming try, Rees goal	8–2 (45)	
Murray try, Rees goal	13–2 (55)	
	13–4 (62)	Oakley penalty
	13–7 (70)	Armstrong try

League leaders	P	W	D	L	For	Agst	Pts	Percent
1 Wigan	38	31	0	7	824	228	62	81.57
2 Batley	36	24	3	9	432	287	51	70.83
3 Oldham	36	23	2	11	579	296	48	66.66
4 Leigh	34	20	3	11	407	250	43	63.23

Semi-finals:
Wigan 27 Leigh 0
Batley 38 Oldham 0

Head-to-head form guide:
Batley 13 Wigan 9 (League)
Wigan 34 Batley 8 (League)

1925 Northern Rugby League Championship Final
HULL KINGSTON ROVERS V SWINTON

Hull Kingston Rovers won their second Championship in three seasons after a tightly fought battle with Swinton at Rochdale's Athletic Grounds, described by 'Leonard' in the *Salford Reporter* as 'one of the most exciting matches I have witnessed for many a long day.' They earned their success with some 'deadly tackling', often withdrawing a man from the scrum to nullify the threat of a quick breakaway posed by Swinton's talented backs. Having lost to Oldham in the previous week's Challenge Cup Final, the Rovers rang the changes to (in the words of the *Hull Daily Mail*) give 'greater attacking power to the three-quarters' and 'increased speed in the forwards.' Consequently Lou Harris lost his right wing place to Jack Hoult whose usual centre slot went to incoming Ralph Rhoades, whilst forwards Bob Wilkinson and Billy Westerdale gave way to Ben Britton and Harold Binks. Swinton was without influential centre and captain Hector Halsall (knee injury) and suspended forward Bert Morris (dismissed during the semi-final win over St Helens Recreation).

Swinton's forwards took control in the early stages, winger Chris Brockbank, generally considered the Lions' best performer on the day, almost claiming a try in the opening minutes but for good defence from Jimmy Cook. Bryn Evans twice came close to breaching Rovers' line, being pushed back each time, and Brockbank actually placed the ball over the whitewash, a forward pass being ruled. After Rovers missed a couple of penalty attempts by Rhoades (from inside his own half) and skipper Laurie Osbourne (his high kick sailing wide), Hoult

CHAMPION CAPTAIN

Laurie Osbourne (Hull Kingston Rovers 1925)

Hull-born Laurie Osbourne plied his trade at full-back in the colours of Hull Kingston Rovers from 1920 until 1932, appearing 432 times. During what was one of the Robins' most rewarding periods, he won the Championship (1922/23, 1924/25), Yorkshire Cup (1920, 1929) and Yorkshire League (1924/25, 1925/26). Reliable and steady in defence he was, reportedly, capable of clearing his line with either foot. A reputable goal kicker, his marksmanship was a crucial factor in both Rovers' championship successes during the 1920s. He was selected for England (twice) and Yorkshire (9 times).

STATS

Hull Kingston Rovers 9 Swinton 5

Saturday 2 May at The Athletic Grounds, Rochdale (3.30 pm)

Hull Kingston Rovers: (white with red band): Osbourne (captain), Hoult, Cook, Rhoades, Austin, McIntyre, Raynor, Britton, F. Boagey, Jack Wilkinson, Binks, Bielby, Camichael. Trainer: W. Jacques

Swinton: (navy blue): Williams, F. Evans, Sulway, J. Evans (captain), Brockbank, Rees, B. Evans, H. Entwistle, Blewer, Strong, J. Entwistle, Halliwell, Beswick. Trainer: W. Kearns

Half-time: 0–5 **Referee:** A. Brown
Attendance: 21,580 **Receipts**: £1,504

Weather: fine and dry at first with slight crosswind, drizzle at start of second half

Progressive score:

Hull Kingston Rovers	score (min)	Swinton
	0–2 (31)	Brockbank penalty
	0–5 (38)	Brockbank try
Rhoades try, Osbourne goal	5–5 (45)	
Osbourne penalty	7–5 (68)	
Osbourne penalty	9–5 (73)	

League leaders	P	W	D	L	For	Agst	Pts	Percent
1 Swinton	36	30	0	6	499	244	60	83.33
2 Hull Kingston Rovers	34	25	3	6	492	171	53	77.94
3 Wigan	36	27	1	8	784	258	55	76.38
4 St Helens Recreation	38	26	3	9	564	267	55	72.36

Semi-finals:

Swinton 20 St Helens Recreation 2

Hull Kingston Rovers 13 Wigan 4

Head-to-head form guide:

Swinton 5 Hull Kingston Rovers 8 (League)

Hull Kingston Rovers 0 Swinton 6 (League)

Hull Kingston Rover with the Northern League and Yorkshire League Championship trophies. Standing: Binks, Westerdale, T. Williams (secretary), J.R. Wilkinson, F. Boagey, J.H. Wilkinson, Britton, Jacques (trainer), McIntyre, Bielby. Seated: Cook, Rhoades, Clark, E.W. Brown (chairman), Osbourne, Hoult, Austin. On ground: Webb, Lyons, Raynor. Carmichael

made a spectacular break, Brockbank producing a try-saving tackle. Brockbank then ended the stalemate with a 31st minute penalty, given for a Frank Bielby obstruction. Seven minutes later, he followed it with a 'picture-book' try. Jack Evans shot between the opposing centres following a scrum, delivering an inside pass to his brother, Bryn, who directed a beautifully weighted ball to the flank. Brockbank took it at speed off a perfect bounce to go over in the corner, although missing the conversion.

Laurie Osbourne's three second half goals for Rovers made the difference

Thoughts of Swinton increasing their 5–0 lead after the interval was dispelled within five minutes of the restart. A wide pass from Rovers' half-back John McIntyre went to ground, the situation looking harmless until Rhoades reached the ball first, twice getting his boot to it. Catching Brockbank and Bob Williams in two minds he picked up and went over for the touchdown, Osbourne adding the goal. There was an element of fortune in that Swinton's Miller Strong was being treated for an eye injury at the time, but there was no denying the Yorkshiremen after that. Fuelled with vigour, they concentrated on an intimidating 'kick and rush' approach and began to dominate proceedings. Swinton, who had an opportunity when Jack Evans was tackled on the line after intercepting, was forced on the defensive for long periods. But their line remained intact, the Robins sealing it through two Osbourne penalties in the last 12 minutes. The latter was for a Jack Evans obstruction, whilst the former, which put Rovers ahead for the first time, was tinged with controversy. Awarded through the intervention of a touch-judge, Fred Beswick allegedly 'striking' an opponent, referee Arthur Brown being unmoved by claims of mistaken identity and the insistence that it was a retaliatory blow.

Hull Kingston Rovers' triumph was a great fillip for the club after their Challenge Cup Final setback. The Lions, on the verge of a great period in their history, had seemed inhibited, their local paper *The Journal* commenting: 'There was far too much individualism on the part of the Swinton players, and their display was in great contrast to that of Hull (Kingston Rovers), who had the right team spirit and worked collectively.'

1926 Northern Rugby League Championship Final
WIGAN V WARRINGTON

Wigan took their third Championship title during the period of Britain's first general strike, invoked by the Trades Union Congress to support the striking miners. The all-out stoppage – eventually lasting 10 days – had reached its sixth day, one of its effects being the disruption of public transport. Undeterred, many of the Wigan fans did manage to secure some form of conveyance to Knowsley Road for the final whilst others walked the 10 miles or so to the ground! Their reward was to see their team defeat Warrington for the fourth time that season, registering six tries to two in winning 22–10. Both teams were virtually at full strength, the notable exception being two players nearing the end of their illustrious playing careers; Wigan half-back Sid Jerram, whose recent poor form had cost him his place, and Warrington full-back Ben Jolley, injured at Hull almost two months earlier.

Although Wigan 'played with the wind and the slope' in the opening half, Warrington struck first when centre Ned Catterall landed a penalty goal after the Cherry and White's South African half-back David Booysen passed the ball after being grounded in a tackle. Johnny Ring had the opportunity to put Wigan in front a few minutes later, but dropped the ball with the line open. He quickly made up for that when, in the 10th minute, he sprinted to the opposing wing before transferring to Attie van Heerden, who then passed to the supporting Tommy Howley for the first try. Jim Sullivan missed the kick and, at the other end, Catterall did likewise, spurning a penalty chance that would have put the Wires back in the lead. Warrington was now under pressure and, with a quarter of the match gone, Howley set up Wigan's second touchdown, cleverly sidestepping past several defenders before sending Ring racing over at the corner flag. Wigan were now on a roll and, five minutes later, Booysen cut through the middle before feeding the supporting Tommy Parker who sent van Heerden on an unchallenged run over the line. Sullivan's conversion made it 11–2. That was to be the last score of the opening period, although van Heerden nearly registered his

STATS

Wigan 22 Warrington 10

Saturday 8 May at Knowsley Road, St Helens (3.30 pm)

Wigan: (cherry and white hoops): Sullivan (captain), Ring, Howley, Parker, van Heerden, Owens, Booysen, Hodder, Bennett, Beetham, van Rooyen, Stephens, Price.
Trainer: T. McCarty

Warrington: (primrose and blue hoops): Frowen, Blackburn, Walker, Catterall, Roberts, Flynn, Ryder (captain), W. Cunliffe, Peacock, Harrop, T. Cunliffe, Tranter, Williams.
Trainer: J. Fish

Half-time: 11–2 **Referee:** R. Robinson
Attendance: 20,000 **Receipts**: £1,100

Weather: cloudy, dry and windy

Progressive score:

Wigan	score (min)	Warrington
	0–2 (6)	Catterall penalty
Howley try	3–2 (10)	
Ring try	6–2 (20)	
van Heerden try, Sullivan goal	11–2 (25)	
Howley try	14–2 (52)	
	14–7 (54)	Peacock try, Catterall goal
Ring try, Sullivan goal	19–7 (66)	
Ring try	22–7 (72)	
	22–10 (79)	Ryder try

League leaders	P	W	D	L	For	Agst	Pts	Percent
1 Wigan	38	29	3	6	641	310	61	80.26
2 Warrington	36	27	1	8	472	279	55	76.38
3 Swinton	36	26	2	8	442	223	54	75.00
4 Hull	38	24	3	11	547	329	51	67.10

Semi-finals:
Wigan 34 Hull 0
Warrington 11 Swinton 8

Head-to-head form guide:
Wigan 14 Warrington 10 (Lancashire Cup)
Wigan 20 Warrington 5 (League)
Warrington 4 Wigan 38 (League)

Wigan (including four players in 'civvies') photographed earlier in the season. Back: Price, Hodder, Ilsley, Stephens, van Rooyen, Sherrington, Beetham, Roffey, Jerram. Front: Sullivan Owens, Booysen, Hurcombe, Oakley, Ring, Howley, van Heerden

second try when his attempt to ground the ball after kicking to the Wires' in-goal area was denied.

Warrington began the second half determined to pull back the deficit and George Walker, Tommy Flynn, Fred Ryder and Jimmy Tranter all caught the eye during an unrelenting period of attack. Their efforts came to nought and it looked all but over when Wigan scored their fourth try. It came as the result of skilful play from Howley, the centre intercepted a pass before sending a neat grubber kick beyond Wires' full-back Arthur Frowen, regaining possession to score. Warrington still had some fight left and a forward rush was utilised by Ryder, who put Alf Peacock in for their first try. Catterall augmented and, at 14–7 with some 25 minutes left on the clock, Wigan still had a job to do. Warrington was now pumped up and Tommy Roberts and Walker were both held inches short of the try-line. But, once again, they became their own worst enemy with another intercepted pass, Parker plucking the ball out of the air, quickly passing to Howley, who sent the irrepressible Ring flying over. Sullivan's goal made it 19–7 and Wigan was back in control. Eight minutes from time, Ring completed his hat-trick with a try in the corner, Ryder concluding the scoring with a consolation try for Warrington after a Sullivan clearance was charged down.

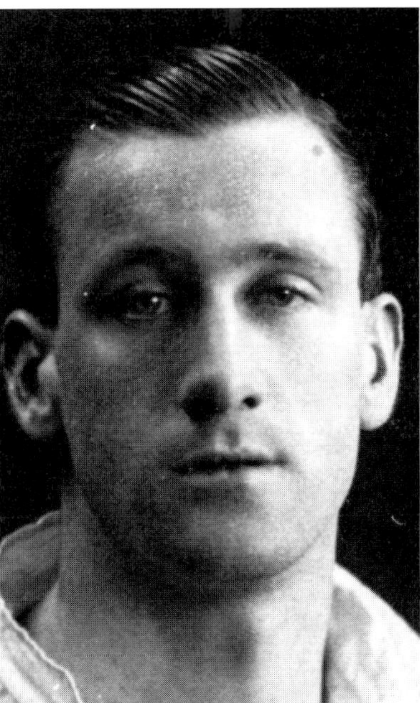

Johnny Ring grabbed a 'hat-trick' of tries on the way to a club record 62 for the season

Jubilant Wigan skipper Sullivan said, as he accepted the cup from the Mayor of St Helens, Alderman Hamblett, that he was 'very proud.' He also added that 'as Wigan had been on top all of the season they deserved to win,' a reference to the amazing fact that it was the first time since 1915 that the League leaders had gone on to secure the title.

1927 Northern Rugby League Championship Final
SWINTON V ST HELENS RECREATION

In winning their first Championship in 1927, Swinton's gifted side did so against surprise package, St Helens Recreation. The works team, funded by Pilkington Brothers Glassworks, had only competed in the senior echelons since 1919, reaching the final through defeating established cross-town rivals, St Helens, 33–0 in the play-off. Swinton overcame the 'Recs' 13–8 in a match hailed as great entertainment for the bumper 24,432 crowd, beating the previous Wilderspool ground record by almost 1,000. The *St Helens Reporter* echoed the thoughts of many: 'It was a great game, a fine, clean and sparkling exhibition, which, a credit to both sides, was heralded as the most magnificent final tie seen for years.' Both teams fielded strong sides, although Swinton caused a surprise in selecting Harry Entwistle ahead of Dick Cracknell in the second row.

A dominant feature was Swinton's overwhelming scrum possession, taking the first half heels 27–18 and the second 26–6. Despite that, they trailed at half-time to a Recs side determined to stifle the potential threat posed by the Lions talented backs, particular 'the master of the reverse pass' Billo Rees. Their 'spotting' tactics worked well during the first period, Swinton, playing against the wind, being penned in their own territory for long periods. As one writer succinctly put it: 'In the first forty minutes Swinton had the ball but no field to play in, whilst the Recs had a field but no ball to play with.'

Johnny Greenall – captain of St Helens Recreation

Bert Morris put Swinton 2–0 up after five minutes with a penalty, Bob Innes having played the ball incorrectly. Joe McComas missed with a drop-goal for Recs before Swinton almost scored a try after excellent inter-passing between Rees and Frank Evans, breaking down when the latter delivered a forward pass. Tommy Dingsdale then tried to open Recreation's account, but his 45-yard drop-goal attempt proved too ambitious. When Swinton skipper Hector Halsall attempted a clearance kick, the Recs' Billy Mulvanney grabbed his chance, charging it down and dribbling across the try-line. Frank Bowen, racing up in support got the touch near to the posts ahead of Swinton's Elwyn Leigh. Dingsdale surprisingly missed the goal, later failing with a more difficult touchline penalty. Encouraged by their

CHAMPION CAPTAIN

Hector Halsall (Swinton 1927, 1928)

Plucked from the obscurity of Wigan's reserves in 1920, centre Hector Halsall became one of the stars in Swinton's magnificent side of the 1920s. A quick-witted, inspirational player, he quickly established himself, becoming club captain in 1922/23, a role he retained until his final appearance in 1930. With the Lions, he won the Championship (1926/27, 1927/28), Rugby League Challenge Cup (1928 – he missed out in 1926 although contributing in the previous rounds), Lancashire Cup (1925, 1927) and Lancashire League (1924/25, 1927/28, 1928/29). Halsall played in just one Test – against Australia at Swinton in 1929 – and for Lancashire twice. He also opposed the 1929 Australian side at St James' Park, Newcastle, when he represented a Northern Rugby League XIII. Following his retirement he became coach at Leigh, taking a similar appointment at Barrow in 1932 that he held until 1950.

Swinton honour their first Championship title in 1926/27. Third row (players only): Cracknell, H. Entwistle, Morris, Blewer, Strong, Halliwell, Beswick, Leigh. Seated: F. Evans, Sulway, J. Evans, Halsall, Brockbank, B. Evans. On ground: Atkinson, Rees

STATS

Swinton 13 St Helens Recreation 8

Saturday 30 April at Wilderspool, Warrington (3.30 pm)

Swinton: (navy blue): Leigh, F. Evans, Halsall (captain), J. Evans, Brockbank, Rees, B. Evans, Blewer, Morris, Strong, H. Entwistle, Halliwell, Beswick. Trainer: W. Kearns

St Helens Recreation: (red, amber and black hoops): Dingsdale, Wilson, McComas, Innes, Wallace, Honey, Greenall (captain), Highcock, King, Bowen, Smith, Fildes, Mulvanney. Trainer: E. Forber

Half-time: 2–5 **Referee:** H. Horsfall
Attendance: 24,432 **Receipts**: £1,803

Weather: cloudy, dry and windy

Progressive score:

Swinton	score (min)	St Helens Recs
Morris penalty	2–0 (5)	
	2–3 (25)	Bowen try
	2–5 (35)	Dingsdale penalty
B Evans try	5–5 (45)	
Beswick try	8–5 (55)	
B Evans try, Morris goal	13–5 (64)	
	13–8 (77)	Innes try

League leaders	P	W	D	L	For	Agst	Pts	Percent
1 St Helens Recreation	38	29	3	6	544	235	61	80.26
2 Swinton	38	29	2	7	471	275	60	78.98
3 Wigan	40	29	0	11	691	366	58	72.50
4 St Helens	34	23	1	10	538	283	47	69.11

Semi-finals:

St Helens Recreation 33 St Helens 0
Swinton 23 Wigan 3

Head-to-head form guide:

Swinton 19 St Helens Recreation 2 (League)
St Helens Recreation 18 Swinton 2 (League)

lead, the St Helens outfit stormed the Lions territory, coming close to increasing their score several times. When their centre Joe McComas broke through and kicked ahead he was obstructed, Dingsdale kicking the resultant penalty for a 5–2 interval lead.

Jimmy Honey retired before the break after a 'collision' with Swinton forward Miller Strong, returning for the second half, although it was the Lions that came out more resolute. A scrum 25 yards from the Recs line resulted in Bryn Evans receiving the ball from Rees and offering two dummy passes as he raced through the defence for an excellent try near the posts. Morris missed an easy goal, but the scores were level. Rees was now finding space to utilise his deadly kicking game as Swinton continually pushed the Recs back, their wingman Chris Brockbank being wide with a drop-goal. Then Dingsdale spilled the ball when tackled by Morris near his line, Fred Beswick picking up to score near the corner flag. Morris failed with the difficult kick. Further goal chances were missed at each end, Dingsdale (penalty) and Leigh (drop-goal) both being off target. The Lions went two scores ahead when Bryn Evans, taking the ball from a scrum, kicked ahead, brother Jack retrieving and turning the ball inside for Bryn to go behind the posts. Morris' goal made it 13–5. With minutes to spare Innes scored a late consolation in the corner after a good passing move, Dingsdale missing the goal.

1928 Northern Rugby League Championship Final
SWINTON V FEATHERSTONE ROVERS

Swinton earned the distinction of being the only Lancashire side to complete the 'All Four Cups' feat by retaining the Championship in 1928, having already garnered the Rugby League Challenge Cup, Lancashire League and Lancashire Cup. As in 1927, Swinton took the Championship title by defeating a relative 'new kid on the block' in the final in Featherstone Rovers, a former junior club that achieved professional status in 1921. Labelled the shock team of the season, the Rovers reached the final by virtue of a surprise 15–12 win over second-placed Leeds at Headingley. Their elevation to the play-offs was, according to one report, due to them replacing their former 'kick and rush' tactic to 'indulge in crisp and unorthodox passing.' Their performance in the final, though, was considered to be well below their showing at Leeds. It disappointed their estimated 1,000 fans that made the trip to Oldham from their mining village. Swinton, whose following greatly outnumbered that of the Yorkshire side, showed far more enterprise, particularly amongst the backs, against a team that the *Pontefract & Castleford Express* accused of missing their opportunities through 'stage fright.'

Jim Denton - Featherstone Rovers captain

Both teams had players on the latest tour Down Under with Bryn Evans, Jack Evans, Billo Rees (all Swinton) and Tommy Askin (Featherstone) having all departed. The Lancashire outfit was also without first choice full-back Jack Pearson, who had been injured during the Easter fixtures and centre Elwyn Leigh. Although not a regular, Leigh – brought into the side to cover for Jack Evans' absence – had been hurt five days before the Championship Final when Swinton officials – amazingly by today's standards – paraded a full strength team for a charity game, Wilf Sulway coming in as an 11th hour replacement.

Swinton dominated an opening 15 minutes that was almost exclusively fought out in the Rovers' half, during which time skipper Hector Halsall scored the first try in the corner. It followed good approach play by Miller Strong who collected a loose ball following a scrum on the Featherstone 25-yard line before transferring to Sulway who, in turn, provided the scoring pass. Bert Morris failed with the tricky kick. The 'dust-dry' pitch suited Swinton's brand of attacking play perfectly, although the *Pontefract & Castleford Express* accused Rovers' half-backs, Jim Rudd and Jimmy Williams, of not helping their cause because they 'persisted in giving Swinton possession by making short ground kicks.' Billy Young tried unsuccessfully to increase the Lions lead, missing with a drop-goal. In the latter stages of the first half, Featherstone, at last, began to impress, their pack producing a 'terrific onslaught' but Swinton's line held. Minutes before half-time the Rovers' Jim Denton frustrated the Yorkshire fans by missing an easy penalty in front of goal.

Wingman Chris Brockbank was appearing in his third final for Swinton

Featherstone began the second half well, but Swinton continued to put up a 'rock like' defence, the closest Rovers came being when

STATS

Swinton 11 Featherstone Rovers 0

Saturday 5 May at Watersheddings, Oldham (3.30 pm)

Swinton: (navy blue): Young, F. Evans, Halsall (captain), Sulway, Brockbank, H. Evans, Atkinson, Strong, Blewer, Morris, Hodgson, Cracknell, Beswick. Trainer: W. Kearns

Featherstone Rovers: (chocolate and white broad hoops): S. Denton, J. Denton (captain), Hirst, Whittaker, Taylor, Rudd, Williams, Barraclough, Hall, Smith, Blakeley, Haigh, Morgan. Trainer: unknown

Half-time: 3–0 **Referee:** Revd F.H. Chambers
Attendance: 15,451 **Receipts**: £1,136

Weather: fine and warm; ground hard

Progressive score:

Swinton	score (min)	Featherstone Rovers
Halsall try	3–0 (11)	
F. Evans try	6–0 (57)	
Cracknell try, Young goal	11–0 (68)	

League leaders	P	W	D	L	For	Agst	Pts	Percent
1 Swinton	36	27	3	6	439	189	57	79.16
2 Leeds	42	32	0	10	619	307	64	76.19
3 Featherstone Rovers	36	25	1	10	387	234	51	70.83
4 Hunslet	40	28	0	12	546	308	56	70.00

Semi-finals:
Swinton 12 Hunslet 2
Leeds 12 Featherstone Rovers 15

Head-to-head form guide:
No previous meetings during season

Williams broke only for Arthur Haigh to drop his pass when a try looked possible. Swinton doubled their lead to 6–0 with an unconverted try after brilliant attacking play from winger Frank Evans who, having received the ball from half-back Albert Atkinson, sped down the touchline, fending off Sid Denton in the process. Jim Denton missed a second penalty chance, before Swinton's Dick Cracknell scored what many rated as the try of the match. The forward, having received the ball near halfway following a terrific break from Harold Evans, sprinted like a three-quarter towards the Featherstone posts before planting the ball down. Young's goal completed the scoring at 11–0.

Realising the enormity of their side's achievement, particularly without their tourists, the Swinton supporters, according to *The Journal* correspondent 'danced for joy when referee (Reverend Frank) Chambers sounded the final solo at the close', adding 'there were remarkable scenes of enthusiasm as the spectators swarmed across the playing pitch to congratulate the players.'

The Swinton squad of 1927/28 proudly show off their collection of trophies; the famed 'All Four Cups' plus the Salford Royal Hospital Cup (extreme left). Fourth row (players only): Pardon, Buckingham, Fairhurst, Strong, Pearson, Leigh, Sulway. Third row: Beswick, Entwistle, Halliwell, Butters, Hodgson, Cracknell, Grimshaw, Morris, Young. Seated: H. Evans, Brockbank, J. Evans, Halsall, B. Evans, F. Evans. On ground: Atkinson, Rees

1929 Northern Rugby League Championship Final
HUDDERSFIELD V LEEDS

Incredibly, the 1929 Championship Final between Huddersfield and Leeds was remembered as 'very fast and keenly contested', the *Huddersfield Daily Examiner* headline describing it a 'Stirring Rugby League Final.' Yet anybody hearing the final score was 2–0, the lowest in Championship Final history with just one penalty goal to show for 80 minutes endeavour, may have thought otherwise. It was a score-line all the more unexpected when it is realised that the conditions – described by one journalist as 'cricket weather' – were ideal for a high scoring match. But, on the day, both defences were equally robust in a game that kept the crowd enthralled until the final whistle.

Before the match it was expected that the attendance record for Halifax's Thrum Hall enclosure that stood at 29,122 would be surpassed. Although not reaching that figure, the official paying admittance of 25,604 was the second highest for a Championship Final so far, receipts topping £2,000 for the first time. The *Huddersfield Daily Examiner* writer observed that the crowd, as they waited for the kick-off to arrive, amused themselves with 'parodies on popular songs made applicable to football and war chants on the lines of Australian and New Zealand cries.' After the team emerged on to the field the band went through the then traditional patriotic pre-final routine of playing 'God Save the King.' The two teams, excepting Huddersfield full-back John Stocks, who had injured a finger several weeks earlier, lined up at full strength.

The contest produced early chances for tries at both ends of the field, during which Joe Thompson missed a 'not too difficult' penalty opportunity for Leeds. It was Huddersfield full-back, Joe Brook, though, that claimed what turned out to be the crucial goal with a well struck 10th minute penalty from the touchline, awarded on the intervention of a touch-judge.

Huddersfield 1928/29 (players only). Third row: Baxter, Morton, Young, Halliday, Carter, Rudd, Tiffany. Kneeling (left): Stocks. Seated: Brook, Mills, Bowkett, Parker, Smart, Gee. On ground: Williams, Spencer

CHAMPION CAPTAIN

Len Bowkett (Huddersfield 1929, 1930)

Full-back or centre Len Bowkett arrived at Huddersfield in late 1926 from his hometown Coventry Rugby Union Club. Noted for his powerful defence-splitting breaks, he was also a reliable goal-kicker, notching a match-winning six against Warrington at Wembley in the 1933 Challenge Cup Final. He was destined to lead the Fartowners to six major trophy successes; Championship (1928/29, 1929/30), Rugby League Challenge Cup (1933), Yorkshire Cup (1931) and Yorkshire League (1928/29, 1929/30). A former Warwickshire county cap at the 15-man game, he represented England against Wales at Salford in 1932. His final senior appearance for Huddersfield was in 1935, subsequently playing two matches on loan to Batley during 1936 before joining Keighley as player-coach.

Shortly afterwards, the Fartowners almost added the first try, half-back Eddie Williams being stopped just a few yards short of the Leeds try line, following a dribbling move by his forwards. As the tension mounted, two of the protagonists were 'hauled up' by a touch-judge following an altercation. In a non-stop opening half, Leeds began to press with some fine attacking play but was repelled by determined Huddersfield resistance. Just before the interval Brook attempted a long-range penalty goal but was just short. The half-time score of 2–0 to Huddersfield reflected that there was little to choose between the two teams during a first half in which both sets of forwards had worked extremely hard, with some good passing movements amongst the backs to entertain the crowd, particularly by Leeds.

Freddie Smart came close to scoring a Huddersfield try during the second period

Huddersfield opened the second half with a dangerous looking run from wingman Ernie Mills but, having kicked ahead, he overran the ball close to the try-line. Another try beckoned for the Claret and Golds after Leeds' full-back Jim Brough had booted the ball away from his line only for Brook to run it back before passing to the supporting centre Gwyn Parker. A try looked certain but Parker went too close to the touchline before parting to Freddie Smart, his winger running out of space as a consequence. Leeds also missed out on scoring chances; George Andrews dropping the ball after being put through by Bill Davis and Mel Rosser, likewise Davis after being given an opportunity by Jeff Moores. As the afternoon temperature rose, so did the temper of the forwards, requiring the referee Frank Fairhust to lecture P. Carter (Huddersfield) and Frank Gallagher (Leeds). With players wilting in the sapping heat, both teams looked for goals as a means of salvation. Dan Pascoe and Thompson both tried and failed to bring Leeds level with penalty attempts, and Brook missed with another lengthy penalty effort at the other end. Huddersfield forward Clifford Morton's late drop-goal attempt reflected the exhaustion of the participants, the ball hardly rising above ground level.

STATS

Huddersfield 2 Leeds 0

Saturday 11 May at Thrum Hall, Halifax (3.30 pm)

Huddersfield: (claret with narrow gold hoops): Brook, Mills, Bowkett (captain), Parker, Smart, Spencer, Williams, Gee, Halliday, Rudd, Morton, Carter, Young. Trainer: J.T. Withers

Leeds (amber with blue bands): Brough, Andrews, Rosser, O'Rourke, Lloyd, Moores (captain), Swift, Thompson, Demaine, Pascoe, Davis, Thomas, Gallagher. Trainer: B. Heyhirst

Half-time: 2–0 **Referee:** F. Fairhurst
Attendance: 25,604 **Receipts**: £2,028

Weather: sunny and hot

Progressive score:

Huddersfield	score (min)	Leeds
Brook penalty	2–0 (10)	

League leaders	P	W	D	L	For	Agst	Pts	Percent
1 Huddersfield	38	26	4	8	476	291	56	73.68
2 Hull Kingston Rovers	40	27	3	10	436	239	57	71.25
3 Leeds	38	26	2	10	695	270	54	71.05
4 Salford	34	23	2	9	395	222	48	70.58

Semi-finals:

Huddersfield 13 Salford 2

Hull Kingston Rovers 4 Leeds 7

Head-to-head form guide:

Huddersfield 0 Leeds 11 (League)

Leeds 5 Huddersfield 7 (League)

1930 Northern Rugby League Championship Final
HUDDERSFIELD V LEEDS

Huddersfield in 1929/30 with the Yorkshire Championship Cup, Huddersfield Royal Infirmary Cup and Northern League Championship Cup. Standing: Gee, Banks, Rudd, Halliday, Young, Tiffany, Morton. Seated: Overton (asst. trainer), Brook, Brogden, Stocks, Bowkett, Mills, Parker, Smart, Withers (trainer). On ground: Williams, Thompson, Spencer, Royston

Huddersfield retained their title, winning the first replayed final for 22 years by 10–0 against Leeds at Halifax. The teams drew 2–2 at Belle Vue, Wakefield, two days earlier in a match that was almost a repeat of last year in that it defied its low score to provide wonderful entertainment. It was watched by 32,095 who paid £2,111, both records for the Wakefield ground and the Championship Final, some later arrivals being perched precariously on the popular side stand roof, others settling on the end of a big advertisement board to obtain a view. Several key players were unfit for selection including three-quarters Stanley Brogden and Joe Brook for Huddersfield, and full-back Jim Brough (a long term absentee), three-quarter George Andrews and half-back Walter Swift for Leeds.

Although described by the *Huddersfield Daily Examiner* as containing 'end to end' rugby played at a 'cracking' pace, the four wingmen had only one real try-scoring chance between them, falling to Huddersfield's Ernie Mills in the opening minutes. His centre, and team captain, Len Bowkett, though, delayed his pass too long, allowing Leeds to recover when Mills appeared to have had a clear run. It was left to the marksmen on view to settle the issue and, after Joe Thompson (Leeds) missed with a penalty and John Stocks (Huddersfield) had failed with a 30-yard drop-kick, the scoreboard finally saw some activity. It came with the blink of an eye; Stocks converting a 36th minute penalty in front of the posts just outside the Leeds 25 area, Thompson replying in kind two minutes later with a great touchline kick that rebounded off the far post. Huddersfield, though, would face the second half a man short, Tom Banks being dismissed shortly before the two penalties were struck, for allegedly putting his knee into an opponent during a tackle.

Leeds – beaten again by Huddersfield at the last hurdle! Standing: Askin, Douglas, Williams, Moores, Rosser, Pascoe, O'Rourke. Kneeling: Swift, Demaine, Thomas, Andrews, Jenkins, Evans

The intensity of the first half was not sustained after the break, few chances being presented. Stocks had two more penalty attempts and Bowkett also tried, although none succeeded. Herbert Campbell, in the *Leeds Mercury*, said, 'Victory fluttered like a feather in the breeze.' The crowd shouted for 'more' as an announcement was made that the hurriedly arranged replay would be at Halifax the following Monday with an early evening kick-off.

An unchanged Huddersfield line-up began the rematch the more determined side and kept up the pressure throughout. Leeds – who made several changes with the loss of skipper Jeff Moores and James Gill through injury being particular blows – failed to settle and always looked second best. Stocks missed two early penalties, sandwiching a near miss when Bowkett made a break, Mills coming in too close to receive the pass instead of utilising space further out. The Fartowner's claimed the first try of the final when Stanley Spencer broke away from a scrum on the halfway line, his lengthy kick going over full-back George Goldie's head, Ernie Thompson following at 'astonishing' speed to gain the touchdown. Stocks converted, adding an easy penalty after being obstructed in front of Leeds' posts supporting a Mills break. Huddersfield made it 10–0 before the interval through a Gwyn Parker try, finding himself on the end of an excellent move by Harold Young, Spencer and Bowkett. Stocks missed the goal.

After the break Stocks failed to increase the lead when his penalty was just short. Leeds' luck, though, was disappearing fast, losing Evan Williams who was rushed to Leeds Infirmary with a head injury after colliding with colleague David Jenkins. Consequently, Tommy Askin took his place at stand-off, Jenkins moving to centre. As the match drew to its inevitable conclusion, Spencer, the acclaimed Huddersfield stand-out performer having 'proved himself a great man for a great occasion', broke away, his cross-field kick to Frank Royston being cleanly taken, but he was just tackled a few yards short from behind.

The *Daily Dispatch* said 'Huddersfield were a team in every sense of the word; Leeds a set of units playing a lot of clever football but mostly without method or purpose.' For Leeds, it was their third defeat in three Championship Final appearances, all to Huddersfield!

STATS

Huddersfield 2 Leeds 2

Saturday 10 May at Belle Vue, Wakefield (3.30 pm)

Huddersfield: (claret with narrow gold hoops): Stocks, Mills, Bowkett (captain), Parker, Royston, E. Thompson, Spencer, Rudd, Halliday, Gee, Tiffany, Banks, Young. Trainer: J.T. Withers

Leeds: (amber with blue bands): Rosser, Jones, Askin, Moores (captain), Smith, Williams, Adams, Davis, Demaine, Pascoe, J.F. Thompson, Douglas, Gill. Trainer: B. Heyhirst

Half-time: 2–2 **Referee:** A.E. Harding
Attendance: 32,095 **Receipts**: £2,111

Weather: cloudy, dry and slight breeze

Progressive score:

Huddersfield	score (min)	Leeds
Stocks penalty	2–0 (36)	
	2–2 (38)	Thompson penalty

Replay: Huddersfield 10 Leeds 0

Monday 12 May 1930 at Thrum Hall, Halifax (5.30 pm)

Huddersfield: (claret with narrow gold hoops) unchanged

Leeds: (amber with blue bands) Goldie, Smith, Askin, Rosser, O'Rourke, Williams, Adams, Demaine, Pascoe, J.F. Thompson, Thomas, Jenkins, Evans.

Half-time: 10–0 **Referee:** A.E. Harding
Attendance: 18,563 **Receipts**: £1,319

Weather: cloudy and dry; ground soft from earlier rain

Progressive score:

Huddersfield	score (min)	Leeds
E. Thompson try, Stocks goal	5–0 (10)	
Stocks penalty	7–0 (-)	
Parker try	10–0 (-)	

League leaders	P	W	D	L	For	Agst	Pts	Percent
1 St Helens	40	27	1	12	549	295	55	68.75
2 Huddersfield	38	25	2	11	510	317	52	68.42
3 Salford	36	23	3	10	397	214	49	68.05
4 Leeds	40	25	2	13	672	302	52	65.00

Semi-finals:
St Helens 6 Leeds 10
Huddersfield 15 Salford 10

Head-to-head form guide:
Huddersfield 16 Leeds 0 (League)
Leeds 36 Huddersfield 0 (League)

1931 Northern Rugby League Championship Final
SWINTON V LEEDS

Swinton made it three title wins in five seasons, consigning Leeds to a third consecutive Championship Final loss with a 14–7 score-line. Staged at Wigan's Central Park for the first time, the result went against general pre-match opinion that, despite the Lions being League leaders, Leeds was 'a more polished 13' particularly amongst the backs. The delighted Swinton chairman Ted Worsley said of his side afterwards: 'Considering that they had lost their international three-quarter line, the team had done exceptionally well' a reference to the absence of Chris Brockbank, Hector Halsall and unrelated Jack and Frank Evans over the past few seasons, for varying reasons, including retirement in two instances. Swinton, though, still boasted a formidable set of forwards and two fine half-backs in Billo Rees and Bryn Evans.

Leeds went into the match without prolific try-scoring winger Eric Harris and scrum half Lesley 'Juicy' Adams, who both failed fitness tests, although their replacements, Les Grainge and Jimmy Fawcett (making his senior debut!) performed well on the day. But, whilst Swinton delighted their supporters with a fine display of teamwork, Leeds, except for the opening 20 minutes of the second half, was a disappointment.

The Headingley side was under the cosh from the start, Swinton's pack dominating early scrum possession allowing their halves, who were in sparkling form, to dictate affairs. After Martin Hodgson started the scoreboard ticking in their favour with two penalties, George Whittaker, Rees and Fred Butters all went close to crossing the whitewash. It was the latter who claimed the first three-pointer when he scored in the corner after 24 minutes, after a pass from Fred Beswick who picked up a loose ball following some 'strong' forward play near the Leeds line. Hodgson added a great touchline goal for a 9–0 lead. Leeds responded with a Joe Thompson penalty for obstruction, Swinton

Another trophy-laden season for Swinton! Players only, are, fourth row: Salmon, Pearson, Cheetham, Troughton, Hodgson. Third row: Brockbank, Turner, Jones, Sulway, Hurst, Leigh, Kennedy, Shaw. Second row: Grimshaw, Buckingham, Mansfield, Wright, Strong, Morris, Butters, Halsall, Woodall. Seated: Atkinson, Beswick, Whittaker, B. Evans, Rees, H. Evans, Kenny, Scott

replying in kind through Hodgson's fourth goal of the half. Bob Scott almost added a second try for the Lions when he sprinted through off an inside pass but was thwarted from going under the posts by the bounce of the ball after kicking past Jim Brough.

Down 11–2, Leeds rallied at the start of the second period as their forwards started to heel more scrum possession, Swinton having to do some desperate defending at times. After Hodgson and Thompson had exchanged, and missed, penalty kicks, Grainge threw himself over the line for a try in the corner after receiving the ball from Thompson following a magnificent break down the middle by Frank O'Rourke. Thompson hit the upright with his goal attempt, again striking a post with a subsequent penalty before landing one following an indiscretion by Bryn Evans at a scrum, narrowing the score to 11–7. Instead of panicking, Swinton got a 'second wind' and was on top again in the closing stages, although Thompson again missed with a penalty for Leeds. Swinton winger Frank Buckingham actually crossed the Leeds line but was denied because of a forward pass, Whittaker finally placing daylight between the teams with a Championship-clinching try seven minutes from the end after collecting Harold Evans' high kick on the bounce to fly over. Hodgson missed the goal but at 14–7 it was a winning lead, although Jack Kenny could have increased it had he not knocked-on in the closing stages when another score looked certain.

Following the presentation of the trophy to skipper Bryn Evans by Lord Daresbury, the excited and delighted Swinton supporters 'chaired' their hero to the changing rooms!

CHAMPION CAPTAIN

Bryn Evans (Swinton 1931, 1935)

Scrum half Bryn Evans was the genius behind Swinton's talented side of the 1920s and 1930s. His eye for an opening that created so many exciting breaks earned him a tour spot to Australasia in both 1928 and 1932. Born locally and acquired from Swinton Park Rangers in 1920, he was one of three brothers who joined Swinton, their father – a former Wales rugby union international – having previously signed for the club in 1897. He played 416 times for Swinton, the last being in 1936, having won the Championship (1926/27, 1927/28 – missing the final due to the tour, 1930/31, 1934/35), Rugby League Challenge Cup (1926, missing the 1928 final win due to touring), Lancashire Cup (1925, 1927) and Lancashire League (1924/25, 1927/28, 1928/29, 1930/31). He appeared in 10 Tests and also represented England (4 times) and Lancashire (21). After retiring he coached Swinton for the 1936/37 season.

STATS

Swinton 14 Leeds 7

Saturday 9 May at Central Park, Wigan (3.30 pm)

Swinton: (navy blue): Scott, Buckingham, Whittaker, H. Evans, Kenny, Rees, B. Evans (captain), Wright, Blewer, Morris, Hodgson, Beswick, Butters. Trainer: W. Kearns

Leeds: (white): Brough, Grainge, Moores (captain), O'Rourke, S. Smith, Williams, Fawcett, Demaine, J.F. Thompson, Thomas, R. Smith, Douglas, Gill. Trainer: B. Heyhirst

Half-time: 11–2 **Referee:** F. Peel
Attendance: 31,000 **Receipts**: £2,100

Weather: very hot and sunny

Progressive score:

Swinton	score (min)	Leeds
Hodgson penalty	2–0 (17)	
Hodgson penalty	4–0 (19)	
Butters try, Hodgson goal	9–0 (24)	
	9–2 (30)	J.F. Thompson penalty
Hodgson penalty	11–2 (38)	
	11–5 (57)	Grainge try
	11–7 (60)	J.F. Thompson penalty
Whittaker try	14–7 (73)	

League leaders	P	W	D	L	For	Agst	Pts
1 Swinton	38	31	2	5	504	156	64
2 Leeds	38	29	1	8	695	258	59
3 Wigan	38	28	2	8	657	199	58
4 Oldham	38	27	4	7	464	178	58

Semi-finals:
Swinton 16 Oldham 3
Leeds 13 Wigan 0

Head-to-head form guide:
No previous meetings during season

Swinton's brilliant Welsh stand-off Billo Rees formed a lethal half-back partnership with his skipper Bryn Evans

1932 Northern Rugby League Championship Final
ST HELENS V HUDDERSFIELD

St Helens' hard fought 9–5 win over Huddersfield in the 1932 Championship Final got the club off the ground as the winner of a major rugby league prize. The team had gone down in three Challenge Cup Final appearances to date, including a 37–3 drubbing by Huddersfield in 1915 and an unexpected defeat to local rivals Widnes two years earlier at Wembley. It was a finale again hit by tour commitments; Alf Ellaby, Albert Fildes (both St Helens) and Stanley Brogden (Huddersfield) all having left British shores. Saints pair George Lewis and Tom Winnard was doubtful during the preceding week with injuries but both played, scoring all their side's points between them! Team captain Lewis, in particular, landed two tremendous touchline goals on a day when 'two-pointers' proved vital.

Most of the early pressure came from St Helens; Winnard missing two penalty chances, Roy Hardgrave (stepping in touch as he went over the try-line) and Jack Arkwright (pulled up a yard short by Len Bowkett) both going close to a touchdown. Another opportunity came after a Huddersfield cross-kick was miscued. It headed towards an unmarked Winnard who, with an open line, could only get fingertips to it, to the chagrin of Saints fans who 'groaned' with dismay! But the pressure eventually paid off. Huddersfield's Gwyn Parker lost the ball near halfway, Billy Mercer recovering it for St Helens, transferring to Jack Garvey who sprinted towards the right corner with three defenders giving chase. As Henry Tiffany hauled him down, he transferred to Winnard, who had a 'roving commission looking for these sorts of chances', the centre going past Robert Walker for a try in the corner. Lewis' well-struck conversion made it 5–0. Huddersfield tried to retaliate, H. Walshaw missing a drop-kick, and Bowkett failing with a difficult penalty attempt. Then Harry Frodsham almost scored another for Saints, but knocked on after intercepting. Lewis' touchline penalty, after Ernie Thompson illegally fed the scrum, closed the first half scoring, Saints leading 7–0.

Huddersfield, with the wind behind them, began the second half well, Harold Young putting skipper Ernie Mills away, Hardgrave saving a desperate looking moment with an ankle tap on the winger. More danger threatened for St Helens when Tiffany was brought down three yards short. The Knowsley

STATS

St Helens 9 Huddersfield 5

Saturday 7 May at Belle Vue, Wakefield (3.30 pm)

St Helens: (white with red band): Lewis (captain), Hardgrave, Mercer, Winnard, Jones, Garvey, Frodsham, Atkin, Cotton, Hill, Arkwright, Halfpenny, Groves. Trainer: E. Smith

Huddersfield: (claret with narrow gold hoops): Bowkett, Mills (captain), Parker, Walshaw, Walker, Richards, Thompson, Rudd, Halliday, Sherwood, Tiffany, Banks, Young. Trainer: J.T. Withers

Half-time: 7–0 **Referee:** F. Fairhurst
Attendance: 19,386 **Receipts**: £943

Weather: fine and dry, some sunshine; overhead storm clouds passed by

Progressive score:

St Helens	score (min)	Huddersfield
Winnard try, Lewis goal	5–0 (17)	
Lewis penalty	7–0 (37)	
	7–2 (43)	Bowkett drop-goal
Lewis penalty	9–2 (49)	
	9–5 (65)	Walker try

League leaders	P	W	D	L	For	Agst	Pts
1 Huddersfield	38	30	1	7	636	368	61
2 St Helens	38	29	2	7	699	279	60
3 Leeds	38	27	1	10	603	307	55
4 Hunslet	38	27	1	10	672	359	55

Semi-finals:
Huddersfield 12 Hunslet 9
St Helens 9 Leeds 0

Head-to-head form guide:
Huddersfield 5 St Helens 2 (League)
St Helens 21 Huddersfield 8 (League)

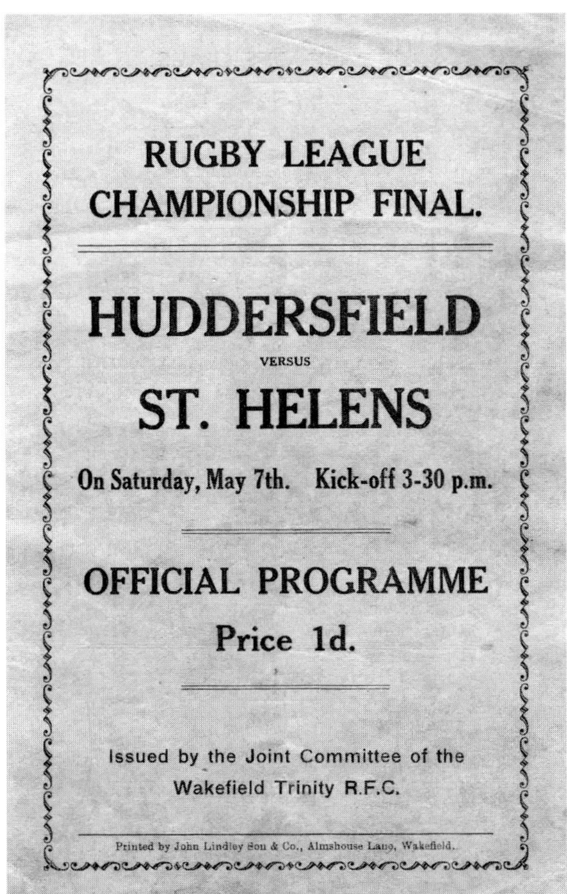

RUGBY LEAGUE
CHAMPIONSHIP FINAL.

HUDDERSFIELD

VERSUS

ST. HELENS

On Saturday, May 7th. Kick-off 3-30 p.m.

OFFICIAL PROGRAMME

Price 1d.

Issued by the Joint Committee of the
Wakefield Trinity R.F.C.

Printed by John Lindley Son & Co., Almshouse Lane, Wakefield.

Whilst St Helens were taking part in their first Championship Final, Huddersfield were notching up their ninth appearance

CHAMPION CAPTAIN

George Lewis (St Helens 1932)

Welsh centre George Lewis signed for St Helens, along with his brother Stan, from hometown Pontypool Rugby Union Club in 1922. A tricky, elusive performer, he initially played at scrum half before being transformed into a centre-cum-full-back. With the Saints he won the Championship (1931/32), Lancashire Cup (1926) and Lancashire League (1929/30, 1931/32). In 1930 he had the disappointment of losing at Wembley in his only Challenge Cup Final, when he was also captain. Under rugby league rules, he represented Wales and the combined Glamorgan & Monmouthshire side three times each and also played for Monmouthshire in a one-off game against Glamorgan at Pontypridd in 1927. He played his final match for St Helens in 1936 after 428 appearances during which he kicked 850 goals, subsequently coaching the club for one season.

Road side managed to clear their line, but only as far as Bowkett, who dropped a neat goal for his side's first points of the day. St Helens responded, Garvey being illegally tackled by Gwyn Richards after kicking the ball through, Lewis adding the resultant penalty against the strong wind. Bowkett, having gone wide with a penalty attempt, left for treatment after colliding with Ben Halfpenny. He returned but worse followed for Huddersfield when Walshaw dislocated his shoulder, resuming after having it put back. Bowkett missed another penalty but then an unexpected mix up gifted Huddersfield a try. Lewis fielded a kick, beat a man and ran towards colleague Bob Jones on the right touchline, but there appeared to be uncertainty between the pair, Lewis losing the ball as a tackle came in. Walker gratefully scooped it up to go over for the touchdown. Winnard, to his credit, raced up to force the scorer into the corner rather than under the posts. Consequently, Bowkett failed to convert from the more acute ankle, the score standing at 9–5. Some powerful play ensued from Huddersfield in the final 15 minutes, led by forwards Tom Banks, Ttiffany and Young but they could not find the winning score.

The *Daily Express* said of the St Helens team: 'Undoubtedly they were better than Huddersfield. Without touching their best form, they gave ample proof of their superiority in a match that did not reach the high level of some of the other finals.'

St Helens captain George Lewis is surrounded by 'well wishers' as he clings to the Championship cup

1933 Northern Rugby League Championship Final
SALFORD V SWINTON

Salford defeated derby rivals Swinton 15–5 in the 1933 Championship Final, their first title for 19 years. It was a match that, after the opening 20 minutes, developed into a heated encounter, described by one journalist as 'a local Battle Royal.' Club officials also got hot under the collar after the Management Committee decided Wigan's Central Park should stage the match, ignoring claims for the more convenient Broughton Rangers' ground. The verdict 'aroused on all sides in Salford and district a storm of criticism of unprecedented dimensions.' The detractors were proved right, the 18,000 attendance being less than watched both League matches between the clubs. Swinton had several players unavailable, the most crucial being mighty forward Martin Hodgson, sidelined for the latter months of the season through a knee cartilage injury.

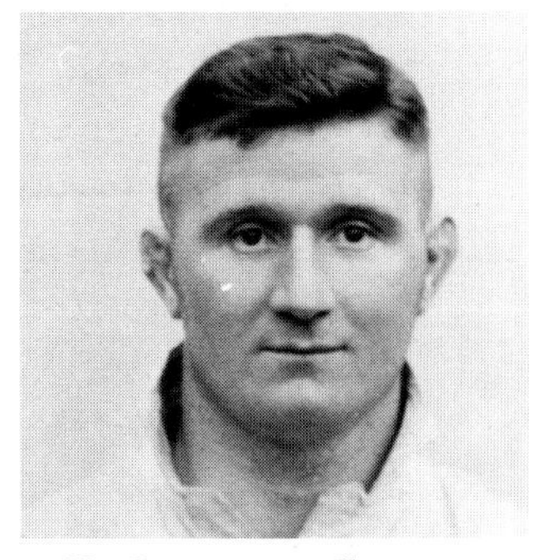

Salford captain Billy Williams

Salford took a 7th minute lead, Emlyn Jenkins putting Gus Risman through a gap, the centre drawing Bob Scott before sending Bob Brown racing over in the corner. Risman missed the goal, having more success six minutes later after Jenkins added a second try through following up a kick towards the Lions' try-line that was mishandled by Scott. It stood up perfectly, however, for the Welsh stand-off who outmanoeuvred two more defenders to score. Risman had chances to increase their 8–0 lead, knocking on when in the clear and also missing an angled penalty attempt. After back-peddling, Swinton started asserting themselves, Bryn Evans making an impressive break, his perfectly judged grubber kick deceiving Harold Osbaldestin, the chance being lost when George Whittaker spilled the ball. Scott then missed with two penalty attempts, the first being an ambitious shot from near halfway.

As the combative nature of the game increased, Jenkins and Swinton's Fred Beswick were injured during a tackle, the pair departing for attention. The Lions forward returned five minutes later, but a heavily concussed Jenkins missed 30 minutes play, Sammy Miller going to stand-off, Brown to centre, Jack Feetham

STATS

Salford 15 Swinton 5

Saturday 29 April at Central Park, Wigan (3.30 pm)

Salford: (red): Osbaldestin, Hudson, Miller, Risman, Brown, Jenkins, Watkins, Williams (captain), Day, Bradbury, Casewell, Middleton, Feetham. Team manager: L.B. Todd

Swinton: (navy blue): Scott, Jones, Whittaker, H. Evans, Kenny, Rees, B. Evans (captain), Strong, Armitt, Wright, Shaw, Beswick, Butters. Trainer: W. Kearns

Half-time: 8–5 **Referee:** H. Swift
Attendance: 18,000 **Receipts**: £1,053

Weather: fine and dry, slight wind

Progressive score:

Salford	score (min)	Swinton
Brown try	3–0 (7)	
Jenkins try, Risman goal	8–0 (13)	
	8–5 (38)	Shaw try, Scott goal
Risman penalty	10–5 (60)	
Feetham try, Risman goal	15–5 (79)	

League leaders	P	W	D	L	For	Agst	Pts
1 Salford	38	31	2	5	751	165	64
2 Swinton	38	26	2	10	412	247	54
3 York	38	24	4	10	571	273	52
4 Wigan	38	25	2	11	717	411	52

Semi-finals:
Salford 14 Wigan 2
Swinton 11 York 4

Head-to-head form guide:
Salford 25 Swinton 11 (Lancashire Cup)
Swinton 3 Salford 11 (League)
Salford 17 Swinton 2 (League)

covering the wing. Scott missed two further penalties but augmented Billy Shaw's touchdown just before the interval. It came after Harold Evans collected the ball in midfield, Shaw accepting his pass before launching a towering kick towards the Salford line which he followed up quickly, taking advantage of Osbaldestin's fumble.

Salford had a scare after the break when a 'fierce' Swinton siege saw Fred Butters cross in the corner after an excellent move, only to be recalled for stepping into touch. Risman, who missed a penalty prior to Butters' effort, failed twice more before finally landing one; given for obstruction after an hour's play. It stretched the Reds' lead to 10–5. Butters left the field with a damaged eye, returning soon after, being followed 'amid great applause' by Jenkins, who went on the wing. Swinton looked certain to score after Bryn Evans got the ball away quickly from a scrum for Billo Rees to send Whittaker scything through. But, with only Osbadestin barring the way, he ignored unmarked Johnny Jones and Harold Evans to his right, and succumbed to the tackle. With time almost over, Feetham followed up a kick and, with Scott losing the ball, dived on it for a try near the posts. Risman's goal was his 100th of the campaign for the club, the first Salford player to do so. He was congratulated by virtually every player, Jack Kenny sportingly handing the ball to him after the final whistle.

Salford captain Billy Williams later told the *Salford City Reporter* 'we should have been heartbroken had we not won the Championship after all we have done this season, and although it was a hard match, perhaps a little too hard, in fact, we did the trick, thanks to a fine start and a fine finish.' The trophy presented afterwards was the Lancashire League Cup already awarded to them the previous week, the League Championship Trophy being at the National Sporting Trophies Exhibition in London!

CHAMPION CAPTAIN

Billy Williams (Salford 1933)

Welsh prop forward Billy Williams signed for Salford from hometown Crumlin Rugby Union Club in 1927. A formidable opponent, he was an intelligent packman, taking over as team captain in 1931. A tourist twice (1928, 1932), he played in two Tests for Great Britain, and made appearances for Wales (3 times – adding to his four Welsh rugby union caps), Other Nationalities (1) and Glamorgan & Monmouthshire (5). With Salford, he won the Championship (1932/33, 1936/37), Rugby League Challenge Cup (1938), Lancashire Cup (1931, 1934, 1935, 1936), and Lancashire League (1932/33, 1933/34, 1934/35, 1936/37). He handed the Salford captaincy to Gus Risman in 1935, playing his final match for the club in 1938.

The Salford line-up. Standing: Dawson (trainer), Feetham, Hudson, Bradbury, Middleton, Casewell, Risman, Osbaldestin. Seated: Day, Brown, Williams, Miller. On ground: Jenkins, Watkins

1934 Northern Rugby League Championship Final WIGAN V SALFORD

Wigan claimed their fourth Championship in 1933/34, beating pre-match favourites Salford, who led the table 11 points clear of the Central Park outfit, by 15–3. It climaxed an incredible turn in fortunes for the Cherry and Whites that, in January, looked out of contention even for a play-off spot. They then embarked on a 'Grandstand' finish, claiming 11 victories from their remaining 12 fixtures, completing a 'double' over Salford with an emphatic 21–10 win at The Willows. Despite the morning press leaning to the Reds, Wigan's players and supporters travelled to Warrington with plenty of confidence.

The final created huge interest, the enthusiastic 31,564 attendance producing record £2,114 receipts for the Championship Final and Wilderspool. The crowd overflowed onto the playing area during the first half, having taken up positions behind the posts and along the touchlines. Salford missed winger Barney Hudson through a leg injury, Wigan continuing the experiment of including robust New Zealand forward Len Mason in the centre, primarily to mark the brilliant Gus Risman.

After Risman missed two Salford penalty efforts, Wigan centre Gwynne Davies scored the first points, intercepting a 10th minute pass after Salford won a scrum in Wigan territory. Sprinting through, he drew Harold Osbaldestin before passing inside to Ossie Griffiths who made a long run downfield, the ball eventually returning, via George Bennett, to Davies, who scored near the posts. Sullivan added the extra points. Risman failed with two more penalty attempts, the latter after a touch-judge had raised his flag behind the posts to signal a 'goal', referee Albert Dobson overruling. Wigan struck a second time just before the break, again from a Salford error, Jack Morley retrieving a lost ball on the halfway line. Evading opposing winger Bob Brown, he won the race for the touchdown after his perfectly weighted kick put the ball just over the try-line. Sullivan again converted giving Wigan a 10–0 interval lead.

Salford showed greater determination in the second period, looking much more dangerous than in the opening half. It paid off when scrum

CHAMPION CAPTAIN

Jim Sullivan (Wigan 1926, 1934)

Jim Sullivan is generally considered the most legendary figure in the Wigan club's history, a strong claim considering the many great players that have worn the famous cherry and white jersey. He was 17 years old when enticed from hometown Cardiff Rugby Union Club in 1921, becoming the dominant full-back in British rugby league throughout the 1920s and 1930s. His capability as tactician, leader and defender was second to none and his incredible appetite for scoring goals set records that are still intact today. At Wigan, he retains club career records for goals (2,317), points (4,883) and appearances (774), whilst, in all matches, he holds the rugby league record for goals (2,867) and appearances (928). His 22 goals in a match against amateurs Flimby & Fothergill United in the 1925 Challenge Cup also remains a record. His honours with Wigan, where he became captain in 1925, include the Championship (1921/22, 1925/26, 1933/34), Rugby League Challenge Cup (1924, 1929), Lancashire Cup (1922, 1928, 1938), and Lancashire League (1922/23, 1923/24, 1925/26). He toured on three occasions (1924, 1928, 1932), the latter as captain, rejecting a record fourth (1936) through personal reasons. He represented Great Britain (25 Tests – 15 as captain) Wales (26 times – a record, 18 as captain), England (3), Other Nationalities (6), Glamorgan & Monmouthshire (12) and Glamorgan (1). In 1932 he became Wigan player-coach, his final appearance being in 1946. He continued as coach until 1952, later taking over at St Helens (1952–59) and Rochdale Hornets (1959–61). He returned to Wigan as coach in 1961 but ill health prevented him commencing his duties, and he retired. During the Second World War he made guest appearances for Dewsbury, Keighley and Bradford Northern. He was an inductee to the Rugby League Hall of Fame in 1988.

half Billy Watkins, securing the ball from a scrum near Wigan's line, shot away to put stand-off Emlyn Jenkins through with a neat reverse pass. Risman, having no luck with his kicking, again missed the target. Wigan, though, recovered to take control once more, Bennett coming close to a further try for Wigan. Sullivan, after two abortive attempts by colleagues, succeeded with a drop-goal to push his side 12–3 ahead. Wigan prop Bill Targett grabbed the final points of the afternoon, his late try capitalising on good work by Davies and Bennett, again after Salford had lost possession. With the final whistle about to sound, Sullivan was excused for missing the conversion, Wigan being clear winners.

The *Daily Express* writer had no doubts about Wigan's success, saying: 'Their superiority was clearly defined. Never was a final more decisively won.'

Jim Sullivan holds the Championship trophy after his Wigan team had upset the odds in beating Salford

STATS

Wigan 15 Salford 3

Saturday 28 April at Wilderspool, Warrington (3.30 pm)

Wigan: (cherry and white hoops): Sullivan (captain), Morley, Mason, Davies, Twose, Bennett, Gee, Targett, Golby, Edwards, Hathway, Davis, Griffiths. Player-coach: J. Sullivan

Salford: (red): Osbaldestin, Pearson, Miller, Risman, Brown, Jenkins, Watkins, Williams (captain), Day, Bradbury, Casewell, Middleton, Feetham. Team manager: L.B. Todd

Half-time: 10–0 **Referee:** A.S. Dobson
Attendance: 31,564 **Receipts**: £2,114

Weather: fine and dry with strong crosswind; ground soft from earlier rain

Progressive score:

Wigan	score (min)	Salford
Davies try, Sullivan goal	5–0 (10)	
Morley try, Sullivan goal	10–0 (38)	
	10–3 (47)	Jenkins try
Sullivan drop-goal	12–3 (72)	
Targett try	15–3 (80)	

League leaders	P	W	D	L	For	Agst	Pts
1 Salford	38	31	1	6	715	281	63
2 Wigan	38	26	0	12	739	334	52
3 Leeds	38	26	0	12	597	376	52
4 Halifax	38	26	0	12	457	340	52

Semi-finals:
Salford 28 Halifax 3
Wigan 14 Leeds 10

Head-to-head form guide:
Wigan 15 Salford 9 (League)
Salford 10 Wigan 21 (League)

Wigan with their Championship prize. Back: Seeling, Edwards, Davis, Targett, Golby, Hathway, Griffiths. Seated: Morley, Mason, Sullivan, Twose, Wilson, Davies. On ground: Bennett, Gee

1935 Northern Rugby League Championship Final
SWINTON V WARRINGTON

Swinton was acclaimed as the 'Jubilee Champions' by the headline in the *Salford City Reporter* after disposing of Warrington by a comfortable 14–3 score-line in the 1935 Championship Final, a reference to the fact that they did it during the King's 'Royal Silver Jubilee Week' celebrating 25 years since King George V had succeeded to the throne. The Lions were worthy winners against a Warrington side whose pack, apart from the opening quarter of the match, struggled to contain the Swinton sextet, Martin Hodgson, in particular, playing a dominant part.

There was no hint of the final outcome to the match in the opening 20 minutes with Warrington starting well on top, Nat Bentham out-hooking Tommy Armitt in the battle for scrum possession. Swinton, though, did manage to take the lead during this period with a 12th minute Hodgson penalty from near halfway after a scrum infringement. Warrington centre Billy Dingsdale almost got over for the first try, his brilliant run being halted by Bob Scott near the try-line. Eventually, aided by an improved share of possession, Swinton got a foothold in the match and their backs, brilliantly led by captain Bryn Evans, started to give the ball plenty of air. Hodgson missed two further penalties and Warrington's Billy Holding hit the post with a long-range attempt, before the Lions obtained the first try four minutes before the break. The scorer was Dick Green who got over near the posts after some good approach work by Arthur Hickman and Harold Evans, Hodgson's goal just sneaking over off the crossbar for a 7–0 lead.

Caricature featuring Warrington try-scorer Billy Dingsdale

Warrington – no doubt motivated by their half-time talk – restarted the match in a very determined manner, being rewarded after just six minutes with a try. Swinton's Jim McGregor was deceived by the bounce of the ball, the Wires' Jack Garrett seizing hold to race down

STATS

Swinton 14 Warrington 3

Saturday 11 May at Central Park, Wigan (3.30 pm)

Swinton: (navy blue): Scott, Buckingham. Hickman, H. Evans, McGregor, Green, B. Evans (captain), Wright, Armitt, Hughes, Hodgson, Beswick, Sullivan. Trainer: W. Kearns

Warrington: (primrose): Holding, Garrett, Hawker, Dingsdale, Jenkins, Shankland (captain), Goodall, Hardman, Bentham, Miller, King, Arkwright, Chadwick. Trainer: W. Bennett

Half-time: 7–0 **Referee:** F. Peel
Attendance: 27,700 **Receipts**: £1,710

Weather: very hot and sunny

Progressive score:

Swinton	score (min)	Warrington
Hodgson penalty	2–0 (12)	
Green try, Hodgson goal	7–0 (36)	
	7–3 (46)	Dingsdale try
Hodgson penalty	9–3 (61)	
Sullivan try, Hodgson goal	14–3 (76)	

League leaders	P	W	D	L	For	Agst	Pts
1 Swinton	38	30	1	7	468	175	61
2 Warrington	38	28	3	7	445	253	59
3 Wigan	38	26	4	8	790	290	56
4 Salford	38	27	1	10	478	272	55

Semi-finals:
Swinton 21 Salford 2
Warrington 9 Wigan 0

Head-to-head form guide:
Swinton 15 Warrington 2 (League)
Warrington 7 Swinton 5 (League)

the wing before sending Dingsdale over in the corner. Holding just missed with his goal attempt. The score inspired Warrington but they could not penetrate the Lions defence again, Swinton regaining the initiative when Hodgson put his team two scores ahead with a second penalty just after the one hour mark. It got worse for Warrington when Holding was carried off injured, Rex King being withdrawn from the forwards to cover his departure. Swinton was now well on top and confirmed their win with a late try from loose forward Joe Sullivan, who picked up the ball as it emerged from a scrum before dummying his way over. Hodgson added the goal to complete the scoring. Warrington's day of woe was completed with the dismissal of Bentham just before the final whistle.

Delighted Lions skipper Bryn Evans was in patriotic mode after the match stating: 'Our victory was achieved by the greatness of team work and the wonderful backing up of every one of the thirteen who marked the occasion of the King's Silver Jubilee by proving that we were real League Champions.' The team captain received due credit for his performance from 'Onlooker' in *The Journal*, who said: 'Bryn Evans excelled as a leader, his skill and enterprise being a dominant factor in the success and far more than the Warrington men could cope with.' For 'Leonard' of the *Salford City Reporter*, though, one player stood out above all others: 'I must single out Hodgson as the hero of the match. Whether in defence, attack, fielding or kicking, he was ubiquitous. The new ball, the hard ground, the wind or the blazing sun had no terrors for this great forward.'

Caricature featuring Swinton skipper Bryn Evans

The 1934/35 Swinton squad. Back: Lee, Stoddart, Wright, Hughes, Spruce, Armitt. Second row: Mee (trainer), McGregor, McGurk, Hodgson, Sullivan, Butters, Green, Cheetham, Shaw, H. Evans, Millar, Kerns (trainer). Seated: Buckingham, Hickman, T. Crossley (chairman), B. Evans, S. Jones (secretary), Woodall, Kenny. On ground: Scott, Marsden, F. Evans, Holland

1936 Northern Rugby League Championship Final
HULL V WIDNES

Hull won their third Championship in 1936, defeating Final debutants Widnes 21–2, in a match finely balanced at 2–2 until fate took a hand in the 47th minute. It began when a Hull play-the-ball was being enacted in midfield, referee Paul Cowell blowing his whistle to signal an infringement. Widnes took hold of the ball thinking they had been awarded a free-kick. The official, however, indicated the verdict was in Hull's favour, the ball being handed back. Hull captain Joe Oliver then produced a wonderful kick to touch near the Widnes line, subsequently scoring the opening try himself from the resultant scrum. It occurred after Hull scrum half Jim Courtney took possession as the ball emerged, transferring to stand-off Ernie Herbert who, seeing his route to the posts blocked, lobbed the ball wide for Oliver to touchdown. Oliver then appended the goal for a 7–2 lead.

Up to that point Widnes had probably exceeded theirs and their supporters' expectations in holding the powerful Hull side for the majority of the game, the *Widnes Weekly News* preview conceding 'Widnes may not be the fancied team.' They certainly contested every blade of grass during the first half and could even have been ahead at the interval. Hull, though, had the first chance when full-back Freddie Miller was wide with a drop-goal attempt. They did take the lead, however, in the 22nd minute when Oliver sent the ball through the uprights after Widnes was penalised at a play-the-ball. Percy Jacks for Widnes and Oliver, with a 'poor' shot, both missed further penalties, the former levelling the scores with his second attempt, from long distance, in

CHAMPION CAPTAIN

Joe Oliver (Hull 1936)

Maryport-born Joe Oliver made a tremendous impact with Hull during 12 seasons at the Boulevard. The powerfully built Cumbrian – who played at full-back and centre and renowned for his surging breaks – still retains the career record at Hull for goals (687) and points (1,842). He joined Hull in 1928 from Batley in a reported £800 deal, having just completed his only tour during which he appeared in four Tests; three in Australia, one in New Zealand. Originally with Glasson Rangers, he signed for Huddersfield in 1923, subsequently winning the Yorkshire Cup with the Fartowners (1926), transferring to Batley in 1927 for £300. Following his time at Hull, during which he was a Championship winner (1935/36), he moved east of the city in 1938 to join Hull Kingston Rovers, retiring a year later. He returned to the Boulevard, however, during the latter years of the Second World War, appearing from 1943 to 1945. He represented England (4 times) and Cumberland (35 – a record for the county). His 22 years as a player yielded an aggregate of 2,333 points from 217 tries and 841 goals in 679 matches. In the early post-war years he coached at both Hull Kingston Rovers and Hull.

Hull with the Northern Rugby League (right) and Yorkshire League Championship trophies. Standing: Caswell (trainer), Booth, Thacker, G. Barlow, Wilson, Stead, Corner, Bateman, L. Barlow. Seated: Overton, Fifield, G. W. Miller (chairman), Oliver, J. H. Dannatt (vice-chairman), Miller, Carmichael. On ground: Herbert, Courtney

the 32nd minute. It was a score that gave the Chemics confidence and they attacked more vigorously, but Hull defended just as keenly. Jacks then had a golden opportunity to put his team in front before the break, but his penalty was 'inches' wide.

At the start of the second half, Hull forward Laurie Barlow was injured and had to go off for attention, returning in time to witness the aforementioned opening try by Oliver. Motivated by their five point lead, Hull's pack exerted more pressure and, in one marauding run, Widnes full-back Walter Bradley was forced to hastily kick the ball clear only to see it land into the arms of Miller, who took careful aim before dropping a goal. Hull at this stage was moving the ball around well and, having popped over another penalty (given for obstruction) Oliver made a wonderful break through the Widnes ranks nine minutes from the end. Racing in from 25 yards out, he bamboozled the Widnes defence before crossing for what was rated the best try of the match. His goal made the score 16–2. They finished the job off with a try from Laurie Barlow, Dickie Fifield creating the opening after Bradley had failed to gather a kick propelled from Hull's half of the field. Oliver added the goal.

Having led his team to victory by scoring 16 of their 21 points, Oliver received most of the post-match accolades after an outstanding performance, 'Kingstonian' of the *Hull Daily Mail* even suggested it should be remembered as 'Oliver's Final.' Both teams had taken part without key personnel due to the latest tour; Hull losing loose forward Harold Ellerington, Widnes minus scrum half Tommy McCue and team captain and prop forward Nat Silcock. In addition, Hull winger Bob Corner withdrew with a damaged toe and Widnes had three-quarter Ken Barber indisposed.

STATS

Hull 21 Widnes 2

Saturday 9 May at Fartown, Huddersfield (3.30 pm)

Hull: (white with black 'three crowns' emblem of Hull on left breast): Miller, Wilson, Oliver (captain), Fifield, Overton, Herbert, Courtney, Stead, G. Barlow, Thacker, L. Barlow, Booth, Dawson. Trainer: E. Caswell

Widnes: (black and white hoops): Bradley, A.H. Evans, Topping, Jacks, Gallimore, Shannon (captain), A. Evans, Higgins, Jones, Roberts, McDowell, Sherratt, Millington. Trainer: P. Lyons

Half-time: 2–2 **Referee:** P. Cowell
Attendance: 17,276 **Receipts**: £1,208

Weather: overcast and dry

Progressive score:

Hull	score (min)	Widnes
Oliver penalty	2–0 (22)	
	2–2 (32)	Jacks penalty
Oliver try, Oliver goal	7–2 (47)	
Miller drop-goal	9–2 (49)	
Oliver penalty	11–2 (60)	
Oliver try, Oliver goal	16–2 (71)	
L. Barlow try, Oliver goal	21–2 (79)	

League leaders	P	W	D	L	For	Agst	Pts
1 Hull	38	30	1	7	607	306	61
2 Liverpool Stanley	38	27	2	9	426	248	56
3 Widnes	38	25	4	9	543	328	54
4 Wigan	38	25	1	12	481	261	51

Semi-finals:
Hull 13 Wigan 2
Liverpool Stanley 9 Widnes 10

Head-to-head form guide:
No previous meetings during season

Widnes 1935/36. Back: Millington, Gallimore, Higgins, Tennison, McDowell, Jones, Silcock, Sherratt. Front: Jacks, Shannon, Evans, Bradley, Topping.

1937 Northern Rugby League Championship Final
SALFORD V WARRINGTON

Salford stole the 1936/37 Championship from under Warrington's nose with a dramatic late converted try. It provided a sensational finish to a final described as 'one of the dullest in the history of the competition.' Trailing 11–8 with five minutes remaining, Salford finally began to play like champions. Inspired by their legendary Welsh skipper, Gus Risman, they found the extra gear that had eluded them for much of the contest. From a scrum inside Warrington territory, they instigated a planned move as scrum half Billy Watkins retrieved the ball and raced infield. Instead of the anticipated off-load to Emlyn Jenkins, he passed over his half-back partner's head to Risman, who had sprinted forward to create the extra man. Pausing slightly to draw the cover, he handed on, via Albert Gear and Harold Osbaldestin, to powerful winger Barney Hudson who squeezed through the tightest opening to score in the corner. With the scores level and an awkward wind adding to the pressure, Risman landed a great touchline conversion to put Salford ahead for the first time and secure victory, 13-11.

The outcome had looked so different for the Wires 11 minutes from time when their hooker Dave Cotton pushed his way through off a Jack Miller pass for the first try of the game, having won a scrum near Salford's line. With a three-point lead in what had been a tightly contested match it had given the Warrington faithful real hope of a first ever Championship.

Although Salford had finished two points ahead of Warrington in the League, it was the Wilderspool outfit that went into the match as slight favourites, having knocked Salford out of the Challenge Cup in front of a ground record 26,470 crowd at The Willows the previous February. Excepting Salford three-quarter Bob Brown, out with a rib injury, the two teams began at full strength.

Salford mounted the first real attack with a powerful run from Gear that took him into Warrington's 25 area, the centre being obstructed after kicking ahead. Risman missed the resultant penalty but the incident seemed to set the tone for a final in which, according to one report, 'from beginning to end there was not a really good constructive movement.'

In a match dominated by the two packs, Warrington was accused of stifling the play but, with a depleted side for much of the game, it was an understandable tactic against a Salford side that possessed a lethal back division. Wires' centre Dave Brown had to leave the field midway through the opening half, returning as a passenger on the wing. No sooner had he resumed than their full-back Billy Holding began limping, eventually collapsing in the in-goal area. Unable to continue as the last line of defence, he moved to the wing, surprisingly to play outside of Brown, the two forming a right wing pairing that

The Salford squad. Back: Hudson, Cambridge, Day. Third row: Harris, Bradbury, Dalton, Feetham, Osbaldestin. Seated: Edwards, C. B. Riley (chairman), Gear, Risman, Williams, Todd (manager), Jenkins. On ground: Watkins, Miller

Salford captain Gus Risman looks for an opening

STATS

Salford 13 Warrington 11

Saturday 1 May at Central Park, Wigan (3.30 pm)

Salford: (red): Osbaldestin, Hudson, Gear, Risman (captain), Edwards, E. Jenkins, Watkins, Williams, Day, Bradbury, Dalton, Cambridge, Feetham. Team manager: L.B. Todd

Warrington: (primrose with blue collar): Holding, Shankland, Brown, Dingsdale, G. Jenkins, de Lloyd, Goodall, Rankin, Cotton, Miller, Arkwright (captain), Welsby, Chapman. Team manager: C. Brockbank

Half-time: 4–6 **Referee:** F. Peel
Attendance: 31,500 **Receipts**: £2,000

Weather: hot and sunny with slight breeze

Progressive score:

Salford	score (min)	Warrington
	0–2 (9)	Holding penalty
	0–4 (15)	Holding penalty
Risman penalty	2–4 (22)	
Risman penalty	4–4 (25)	
	4–6 (37)	Shankland penalty
	4–8 (43)	Welsby drop-goal
Risman penalty	6–8 (47)	
Risman penalty	8–8 (52)	
	8–11 (69)	Cotton try
Hudson try, Risman goal	13–11 (75)	

League leaders	P	W	D	L	For	Agst	Pts
1 Salford	38	29	3	6	529	196	61
2 Warrington	38	28	3	7	468	189	59
3 Leeds	38	28	1	9	627	262	57
4 Liverpool Stanley	38	26	3	9	425	226	55

Semi-finals:
Salford 15 Liverpool Stanley 7
Warrington 12 Leeds 2

Head-to-head form guide:
Salford 11 Warrington 5 (League)
Warrington 11 Salford 0 (League)
Salford 4 Warrington 10 (Challenge Cup)

looked vulnerable against the threat of wingman Alan Edwards, although Salford failed to fully capitalise. Loose forward Bill Chapman was withdrawn from the scrum to help cover the potential danger, Shankland taking over at full-back.

The match provided few try-scoring opportunities prior to those two late touchdowns, the closest being Brown in the opening minutes, failing to hold a Billy Dingsdale pass with Bill Shankland unmarked outside him, and Edwards in the second half when Emlyn Jenkins' cross-kick bounced perfectly for him to take it at top speed, Shankland making a crucial tackle in the corner.

At one stage it looked odds-on the title being settled by penalty kicks, Risman having eight attempts and Warrington, collectively, having the same. Holding – before his injury – landed the first two, both for obstruction, Risman succeeded with his third and fourth efforts to level the scores, Shankland restoring Warrington's lead three minutes before half-time with a shot from just outside the 25-yard line. Three minutes after the resumption, Wires second-row man E. Welsby snapped up a loose ball in Salford territory, dropping a goal on the turn from an almost impossible angle to widen the gap to four points. Risman then tied the score at 8–8 with two more penalties, setting the stage for a frantic finish.

1938 Northern Rugby League Championship Final
HUNSLET V LEEDS

The 1938 Championship Final has entered rugby league folklore as 'The All-Leeds Final', a unique slice of history where the city of Leeds' two premier rugby clubs fought it out on neutral territory at Leeds United Football Club's Elland Road headquarters. It was a match that galvanised the community, 54,112 spectators turning up to produce a record crowd for the game in Britain, surpassing the 51,250 that attended the 1936 Challenge Cup Final at Wembley and over 22,000 more than the previous Championship Final record set in 1930. It was reported that thousands more were unable to gain entrance with many giving up and returning home some 20 minutes before kick-off time. Needless to say the attendance generated new record receipts for the Championship Final of £3,572.

It was, though, an event that would not have happened had it not been for the foresight and determination of the two clubs' officials – particularly Leeds' chairman Sir Edwin Airey – who agitated for the match to be transferred from Wakefield Trinity's ground, the original choice of the Rugby League hierarchy. The first Championship Final to take place on an Association Football ground, it was the fourth meeting of the two clubs that season, Hunslet having completed a League 'double' over their neighbours, but losing the annual pre-season Lazenby Cup charity fixture at Headingley 26–3. The pitch was transformed into a rugby league arena the day before the match, Hunslet's posts

STATS

Hunslet 8 Leeds 2

Saturday 30 April at Elland Road, Leeds (3.30 pm)

Hunslet: (myrtle with flame and white bands) Walkington (captain), Batten, Morrell, Winter, O'Sullivan, Morris, Thornton, Tolson, White, Bennett, Newbound, Stansfield, Plenderleith. Trainer: W. Hannah

Leeds (blue with amber bands) Eaton, Harris, Williams, Brogden, Smith, Hey (captain), Jenkins, Murphy, Satterthwaite, Prosser, Tattersfield, Dyer, Duffy. Trainer: W. Smith

Half-time: 6–2 **Referee:** F. Fairhurst
Attendance: 54,112 **Receipts**: £3,572

Weather: fine, dry and windy

Progressive score:

Hunslet	score (min)	Leeds
	0–2 (9)	Tattersfield penalty
Winter try	3–2 (24)	
O'Sullivan try	6–2 (34)	
Walkington drop-goal from penalty	8–2 (75)	

League leaders	P	W	D	L	For	Agst	Pts
1 Hunslet	36	25	3	8	459	301	53
2 Leeds	36	25	2	9	530	227	52
3 Swinton	36	24	2	10	392	198	50
4 Barrow	36	25	0	11	447	260	50

Semi-finals:
Hunslet 13 Barrow 7
Leeds 5 Swinton 2

Head-to-head form guide:
Hunslet 16 Leeds 10 (League)
Leeds 5 Hunslet 8 (League)

Hunslet winger Eric Batten (with ball) is forced into touch by a posse of Leeds defenders

CHAMPION CAPTAIN

Jack Walkington (Hunslet 1938)

Leeds-born Jack Walkington was a product of local Burley Rugby Union Club, signing with Hunslet for £300 in 1927. Beginning as a centre, he soon established himself as a cool, resolute full-back, capable of fielding the most difficult of kicks and clearing his line with consummate ease. He won medals for the Championship (1937/38) and Rugby League Challenge Cup (1934) – both times as captain – and Yorkshire League (1931/32), his lengthy Parkside career ending in 1948, following a club record 572 matches. He also appeared as a guest player during the Second World War for Batley, Bramley, Dewsbury and Leeds. He represented England (3 times – including one wartime international) and Yorkshire (15) and was appointed Hunslet team manager in 1950.

being used because their Parkside ground was closest, plus transporting the Headingley posts would have been a challenge as they were 'the tallest and heaviest in rugby league.' Both teams were without leading forwards; Hunslet's Henry Tiffany having been taken badly ill with bronchitis a couple of weeks earlier, and Leeds' Ken Jubb being suspended.

Leeds went ahead in the 9th minute through a successful penalty attempt from back-row forward Ted Tattersfield. An ankle injury to prop Mark Tolson caused Hunslet some scrum disruption as he moved from open-side to the less demanding blind side before reluctantly leaving the field for 10 minutes to receive attention. Leeds, though, failed to cash in on their temporary numerical advantage and missed several chances to cross the whitewash. First, a pass from Welsh centre Evan Williams aimed at his Australian wing partner Eric Harris was too high, then full-back Charlie Eaton failed to hold on to a scoring pass and, when their skipper and stand-off Vic Hey burst through, he lacked support and was apprehended by Jack Walkington.

Hunslet made the Loiners pay with two quick, unconverted, tries of their own. Centre Ernest Winter got the first with a breath-taking run which left two defenders trailing in his wake, before dummying through a couple more and outpacing Dai Jenkins in a race for the line. Ten minutes later Winter was again the hero when he penetrated the Leeds defence before drawing Harris and sending Irish winger Jimmy O'Sullivan over in the corner. Cyril Morrell almost scored a third but his long dazzling run was finally closed down.

Hunslet captain Walkington, whose first half kicking for territory against the wind had kept Leeds in check, bombarded winger Stanley Smith – struggling with a sprained ankle incurred early in the match – with more of the same after the interval. Leeds suffered further handicap when the influential Hey pulled both thigh muscles and moved to centre and, in the closing stages, to the wing, Stanley Brogden assuming his stand-off role. Despite being depleted, the Headingley side held on gamely, restricting their opponents to a late drop-goal from Walkington after a penalty had been awarded. Hunslet, though, had essentially won the match in the opening half.

The Hunslet side that bridged a 30-year Championship gap in 1937/38. Inset: Winter, Tiffany, Yates. Standing: Hannah (trainer), Bennett, Newbound, Tolson, White, Stansfield, Thompson, J. Laithwaite (chairman). Seated: Batten, Morrell, Walkington, Plenderleith, O'Sullivan. On ground: Thornton, Morris

1939 Northern Rugby League Championship Final
SALFORD V CASTLEFORD

Salford repeated their 'Great Escape' act of two years earlier in defeating a gallant Castleford side 8–6 in the 1939 Championship Final. As before, Salford's late winner, seven minutes from the end, put them ahead for the first time. Their centre Albert Gear had taken possession and, realising Jimmy Robinson and Bernard Cunniffe had moved across to cover colleagues Gus Risman and Alan Edwards, he sprinted forward, sending a short kick to the left touchline. Edwards, showing tremendous pace, raced after it, taking the perfect bounce at speed on the halfway line before sidestepping George Lewis to go over the try-line, Jim Croston desperately hanging on.

The last peacetime Championship decider prior to the Second World War proved to be a record-breaker. Following last year's initiative of taking the event to a soccer stadium, the 1939 finale was held at Manchester City Football Club's Maine Road enclosure. The Rugby League authorities were rewarded for their enterprise with a British record attendance of 69,504, beating the 64,453 that watched the Leeds-Halifax Challenge Cup semi-final at Odsal the previous month. The receipts of £4,301 were also the highest outside Wembley. The posts were those of Broughton Rangers, based at the nearby Belle Vue speedway stadium.

The teams came out side-by-side onto a ground described by the *Pontefract & Castleford Express* as 'level as a billiard table, but with most of the turf worn away with the season's play.' Salford was minus full-back Harold Osbaldestin who suffered what was to be a career ending Achilles tendon injury at Wembley in the previous week's Challenge Cup Final, Sammy Miller deputising. Castleford, appearing in their first Championship Final, was without centre and captain, Arthur Atkinson, a cartilage injury sidelining him since mid-January.

Castleford set off at a ferocious pace and, in the sixth minute, drew first blood. Scrum half 'Juicy' Adams, having already worked the same move twice, dummied through the defence before giving Fred Brindle a perfect reverse pass, the loose forward racing over the try line virtually unopposed. Lewis missed the

This photograph, taken from the Leeds Mercury, shows Castleford loose forward Fred Brindle (left) vainly attempting to block the path of Tom Kenny (with ball) as he races in for Salford's first try

Salford's team captain Gus Risman (right) and 21-year-old prop Dai Davies display the spoils of victory

conversion. The lead lasted six minutes, Salford striking back after Edwards pressured Lewis, causing him to fumble a high kick. From the resulting scrum Billy Watkins demonstrated his own dummying skills to send stand-off Tom Kenny over in the corner despite Brindle's tackle. Risman, wide with a penalty moments earlier, just failed with the conversion.

Quick Salford passing saw Gear send Barney Hudson charging down the right wing but his return pass went astray with the defence broken. Risman missed another penalty before Adams, who had an outstanding game, split Salford wide open to cut through brilliantly, sending a high pass to Croston who put Robinson over at the corner. Agonisingly, Lewis hit the crossbar with his goal effort, Castleford leading 6–3. Risman reduced the deficit with a penalty for offside and, as half-time approached, Adams made another fabulous break, being brought down 'inches short.'

Castleford began to show signs of tiredness after the break, the opening 30 minutes of the second half developing into a stalemate. The Yorkshire side had their chances, Lewis (drop) and Croston (penalty) both failing to land goals. In the latter stages, though, Castleford was visibly wilting having 'run to a standstill'. Salford seized their moment to score the winner. Risman missed the conversion but, Castleford were shaken. Watkins' neat kick towards the try-line, minutes later, was collected by Kenny, but he failed to ground properly and, just before the final whistle, Watkins missed with a drop-goal.

Salford manager Lance Todd, interviewed by Jim Sullivan for the *News of the World*, referring to the influenza outbreak that hit his team for the previous week's Wembley Challenge Cup Final, said afterwards, 'We knew the boys could not be expected to reveal the same stamina as Castleford after their epidemic and I told them to reserve their energy. They did so and when I told Jack Feetham 12 minutes from the end "It's now or never", he knew what I meant. They crowded on full sail and I had no doubts about the result once Edwards had scored that picture try.' Although Salford and Castleford were known for playing an attractive brand of rugby league, it was noted that 'none excelled' in the final, although they still served up an entertaining, nerve-jangling match for the vast crowd on a pitch with 'dust flying as thick as a Sahara sandstorm.'

STATS

Salford 8 Castleford 6

Saturday 13 May at Maine Road, Manchester (3.30 pm)

Salford: (red) Miller, Hudson, Gear, Risman (captain), Edwards, Kenny, Watkins, Davies, Day, Bradbury, Dalton, Thomas, Feetham. Team manager: L.B. Todd

Castleford: (white with amber and black chevron) Lewis, Cunniffe, Robinson, Croston, Lloyd, Hardy, Adams (captain), Stead, Haley, Taylor, Horan, Sadler, Brindle.
Trainer: W. Rhodes

Half-time: 5–6 | **Referee:** S. Adams
Attendance: 69,504 | **Receipts**: £4,301

Weather: fine and dry

Progressive score:

Salford	score (min)	Castleford
	0–3 (6)	Brindle try
Kenny try	3–3 (12)	
	3–6 (30)	Robinson try
Risman penalty	5–6 (34)	
Edwards try	8–6 (73)	

League leaders	P	W	D	L	For	Agst	Pts
1 Salford	40	30	3	7	551	191	63
2 Castleford	40	29	3	8	502	287	61
3 Halifax	40	28	3	9	544	349	59
4 Huddersfield	40	28	2	10	647	345	58

Semi-finals:
Salford 15 Huddersfield 0
Castleford 21 Halifax 4

Head-to-head form guide:
Salford 17 Castleford 0 (League)
Castleford 12 Salford 5 (League)

WAR EMERGENCY LEAGUE CHAMPIONSHIP FINAL

Great Britain and France declared war against Germany on 3 September 1939, following Germany's invasion of Poland, the new season being just a few weeks old, the New Zealanders having commenced their tour the previous day. Whilst plans were quickly made for the tourists to return home at the earliest opportunity, it was not until 11 September that the Rugby League Council confirmed that the League programme and early season county cup competitions were to be shelved. In their place, and to reduce travel, were to be two separate Lancashire and Yorkshire Emergency Leagues, an Emergency Committee being appointed to oversee the sports affairs for the duration of the war. Three days later, it was agreed that players who had problems travelling to matches could, provided their own club agreed, play for another, more accessible club. With the fear of enemy bombing, government restrictions limited crowds to 8,000, whilst grounds holding over 60,000 (which affected Bradford Northern) were allowed to house 15,000. These upper levels were later raised as the war progressed.

At that stage, there was no thought of a Championship Final taking place, quite the reverse in fact, considering large gatherings were discouraged. But, when the Emergency Committee met on 17 January 1940 at the Grosvenor Hotel, Manchester, it was, according to the minutes, 'decided to play a Grand Championship Final between the winners of the Lancashire and Yorkshire Leagues, this to be played on each home ground on Saturday May 4 and 11.' The dates were subsequently pushed back slightly but the wheels were in motion. Quite by accident, the term 'Grand Final' had slipped into rugby league's vocabulary some 58 years ahead of its summer revolution. The front cover of the programme for the second leg, when Bradford was at home to Swinton, said the match was 'to decide Rugby League's War-time Championship. Neither medals or a cup will be presented but the "grand final" as it has been called in official circles is for the game's championship.'

Having been arranged at comparatively short notice, and with no silverware on offer, not to mention the fact that there were more serious matters to worry about, the first wartime 'championship' contest was not taken too seriously. Although, for Bradford Northern it would be their first cup final win since being resurrected in 1907, the *Yorkshire Post* simply referred to them winning 'the war-time substitute for the Rugby League Championship.' After the war, when Bradford was set to meet Wigan in the 1952 Championship Final, its wartime success still went unrecognised by the *Bradford Telegraph & Argus* who referred to the club 'trying to win the Championship for the first time.'

References to a 'grand final' appeared again in 1941 when the Lancashire (Wigan) and Yorkshire (Bradford) winners' met. As hostilities continued many clubs ceased playing, either for financial reasons or because their ground had been requisitioned for the war effort. This was particularly true of the Lancashire clubs and, with only three remaining, one league operated

FIRST WORLD WAR

The situation had been very different during the First World War. Unlike the Second World War when sporting activities were encouraged, competitive sport was generally frowned upon, with so many young men (including many Northern Union players it must be said) sacrificing their lives in Europe. From the 1915/16 season only friendly games took place, although the press used to compile unofficial tables. Curiously, though, an arrangement was made in 1917/18 for the top two Lancashire and top two Yorkshire placed clubs to play-off for the 'championship.' Dewsbury, who beat Leeds, and Barrow, who overcame Broughton Rangers, qualifying for the 'final' which the Northern Union agreed could go ahead in May, receipts going to charities. The final though did not take place as Dewsbury (who wanted to play the final at Headingley) and Barrow (who suggested two legs or a one-off game at Warrington) could not reach an agreement.

from 1941/42 with a top-four play-off deciding the winners. Conversely, most Yorkshire sides were to continue throughout the war with several, such as Bradford, Dewsbury, Halifax and Leeds, able to 'strengthen' their teams with 'guest' players due to military camps being located nearby.

The decision not to present a trophy was repeated several times up to the 1944 final, the players being rewarded with War Saving Certificates instead of medals. It seems that the absence of silverware was not well publicised, leading to frustration for supporters. When Dewsbury won in 1942, the *Dewsbury Reporter* said: 'It was perhaps a little disappointing that when the final whistle had sounded there was no cup presentation but as this was the emergency league, there is no trophy for competition and thus none of the usual rejoicing and celebration of the success.' In 1944 when Wigan secured victory, the *Wigan Examiner* said: 'After the finish Wigan's enthusiastic supporters gathered in front of the stand evidently hoping that the cup would be presented (but) the crowd was disappointed there was no cup presentation ceremony.'

Interestingly, an exception was made for the Dewsbury-Halifax final in 1943, the *Dewsbury & District News & Chronicle* saying ahead of the match: 'Of course the prestige and honour of winning the cup cannot be measured in (pounds, shillings and pence) and Dewsbury will be more than satisfied if they win the trophy for the first time in the club's history. This is the first time during the war period that the Championship cup has been played for.' Dewsbury did win. The name of skipper Barney Hudson was inscribed on the cup's plinth, joining the list of previous captains (no names appear for 1940, 1941, 1942 and 1944) but, subsequently, as explained in the pages covering the 1943 final, the club was stripped of the title after a protest by Bradford. Suffice to say here that there was an irony involved in that incident because, after Dewsbury had lost 8–3 to Bradford in the semi-final, they claimed J.E. 'Sandy' Orford (a guest player from Wakefield Trinity) had not played the minimum four League fixtures for Northern prior to the play-offs. The Emergency Committee upheld their protest and Dewsbury replaced Bradford in the final.

The troubled 1943 play-offs had already been beset with problems. The Emergency Committee had decided that the top four after the Easter Monday (26 April) games would play-off for the Championship. Leeds subsequently arranged a match with Batley for Easter Monday morning (4½ hours before the second leg of their Challenge Cup Final against Dewsbury), presumably to try to get into the top four. Halifax (who finished fourth) objected. The Emergency Committee met on Good Friday, 23 April, and came up with a compromise solution, in that the clubs finishing third to sixth would meet to decide two of the semi-final places. But then Leeds cancelled their match with Batley and withdrew from the play-offs leaving Bradford (third) to play Huddersfield (sixth), Halifax receiving a 'bye'.

The last wartime Championship Final in May 1945 (the war in Europe having ended earlier that month) concluded with the trophy reappearing and being presented to winning Bradford captain Ernest Ward by R. 'Dicky' Lockwood, the Chairman of the Rugby Football League and father of the opposing Halifax captain who, himself, was destined to hold similar office.

The Rugby Football League's Report and Balance Sheet for 1944/45 contained the following comment regarding the Wartime Emergency League: 'The competition has served the Rugby League game well during the war, but we part with it without regret. The Northern League will resume Championship Football next season.'

1940 War Emergency League Championship Final
BRADFORD NORTHERN V SWINTON

The first wartime Championship Final gave Bradford Northern their first major success since being reformed under that title in 1907. Played over two legs, their 37–22 aggregate victory over Swinton owed a lot to the industry of their younger, energetic forwards, who demonstrated in both ties that they possessed more staying power than the Lions veteran pack. It was a match billed as a 'Grand Final', pitting together the winners of the Lancashire and Yorkshire sections of the War Emergency League.

Both teams were handicapped by Forces commitments; Bradford being without winger Des Case for both legs, stand-off Willie Davies (RAF) missing the second, whilst Swinton lost full-back Harold Palin and forward Gomer Hughes, both having 'joined up' on the Thursday preceding the opening leg. Bradford also had to manage in both ties without injured centre Ernest Ward. Swinton hosted the first leg, attracting a below-par attendance of 4,856, blamed by 'Onlooker', in *The Journal*, on the 'counter-attraction' of the Manchester Races at Castle Irwell racecourse.

The home side got off to a whirlwind start, Randall Lewis breaking through the Bradford ranks only for Bill Hopkin to be held at the critical moment. Then, after their captain, Martin Hodgson, had missed with an 'easy' penalty, Tommy Holland crossed the Bradford line in the corner but a knock-on was ruled. The Lions got their reward in the 12th minute when, from a scrum, Frank Bowyer flung the ball out to Lewis who sent Hopkin haring past several defenders for a spectacular touchdown in the corner. Hodgson missed the difficult kick. Bradford responded three minutes later when a passing move, led by their centres Stanley Brogden and Tom Winnard, resulted in a try for George Harrison near the posts, George Carmichael's goal placing them ahead 5–3.

Midway through the half, Swinton scored what many considered the try of the match,

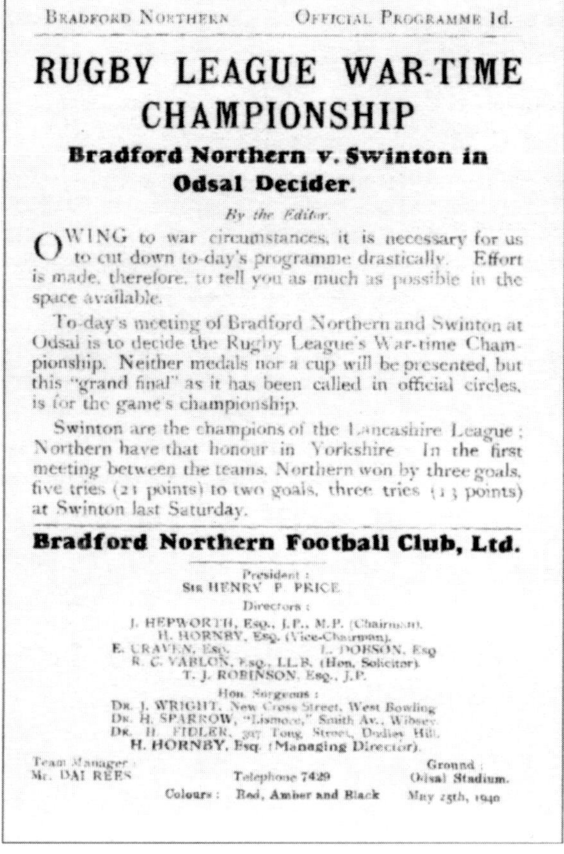

BRADFORD NORTHERN — OFFICIAL PROGRAMME 1d.

RUGBY LEAGUE WAR-TIME CHAMPIONSHIP

Bradford Northern v. Swinton in Odsal Decider.

By the Editor.

OWING to war circumstances, it is necessary for us to cut down to-day's programme drastically. Effort is made, therefore, to tell you as much as possible in the space available.

To-day's meeting of Bradford Northern and Swinton at Odsal is to decide the Rugby League's War-time Championship. Neither medals nor a cup will be presented, but this "grand final" as it has been called in official circles, is for the game's championship.

Swinton are the champions of the Lancashire League; Northern have that honour in Yorkshire. In the first meeting between the teams, Northern won by three goals, five tries (21 points) to two goals, three tries (13 points) at Swinton last Saturday.

Bradford Northern Football Club, Ltd.

President:
SIR HENRY F. PRICE.

Directors:
J. HEPWORTH, Esq., J.P., M.P. (Chairman).
H. HORNBY, Esq. (Vice-Chairman).
E. CRAVEN, Esq. L. DOBSON, Esq
R. C. VABLON, Esq., LL.B. (Hon. Solicitor).
T. J. ROBINSON, Esq., J.P.

Hon. Surgeons:
DR. J. WRIGHT, New Cross Street, West Bowling.
DR. H. SPARROW, "Lismore," Smith Av., Wibsey.
DR. H. FIDLER, 307 Tong Street, Dudley Hill.
H. HORNBY, Esq. (Managing Director).

Team Manager: Mr. DAI REES — Telephone 7429 — Ground: Odsal Stadium.
Colours: Red, Amber and Black — May 25th, 1940

The programme for the second leg referred to the Bradford-Swinton clash as a 'Grand Final'

CHAMPION CAPTAIN

Stanley Brogden (Bradford Northern 1940 – 1st leg)

Locally-born Stanley Brogden made his Bradford Northern debut aged 17 in 1927. The quick, elusive centre joined Huddersfield for a Rugby League record-equalling £1,000 transfer (1929), setting a new £1,200 high when joining Leeds (1934), a figure matched when he went to Hull (1938). Still living in Bradford, he played for Northern and Hull during the war, subsequently joining Rochdale Hornets (1945), Salford (1947) and Whitehaven (1948), where he spent one final season. His honours include the Championship (with Huddersfield 1929/30 - missing the final through injury, Dewsbury 1939/40), Challenge Cup (Huddersfield 1933, Leeds 1936), Yorkshire Cup (Leeds 1934, 1935, 1937) and Yorkshire League (Huddersfield 1929/30, Leeds 1934/35, 1936/37, 1937/38). He represented Great Britain (16 times), England (15), Yorkshire (19) and was a tourist in 1932 and 1936.

STATS

Swinton 13 Bradford Northern 21 (1st leg)

Saturday 18 May at Station Road, Swinton (3.30 pm)

Swinton: (navy blue) Bartram, Hopkin, Lewis, Shaw, McGurk, Bowyer, Holland, Wright, Armitt, Stoddart, Williams, Hodgson (captain), Garner. Trainer: W. Kearns

Bradford Northern: (white with red, amber and black band) Carmichael, Jenkins (Keighley), Winnard, Brogden (captain, Hull), Walters, Davies, D. Ward, Whitcombe, Dilorenzo, Smith, Harrison, Foster, Moore. Team manager: D. Rees

Half-time: 8–10 **Referee:** J.E. Taylor
Attendance: 4,856 **Receipts**: £237

Weather: hot and sunny

Progressive score:

Swinton	score (min)	Bradford Northern
Hopkin try	3–0 (12)	
	3–5 (15)	Harrison try, Carmichael goal
McGurk try, Hodgson goal	8–5 (20)	
	8–10 (40)	Smith try, Carmichael goal
	8–15 (45)	Whitcombe try, Carmichael goal
Shaw try, Hodgson goal	13–15 (-)	
	13–18 (-)	Davies try
	13–21 (-)	Brogden try

War Emergency League leaders

Lancashire section	P	W	D	L	For	Agst	Pts
1 Swinton	22	17	0	5	378	158	34
2 Salford	22	16	2	4	328	171	34
3 Wigan	22	16	1	5	301	157	33

Bradford Northern 16 Swinton 9 (2nd leg)

Saturday 25 May at Odsal Stadium, Bradford (3.30 pm)

Bradford Northern: (white with red, amber and black band) Carmichael (captain), Foster, Winnard, Jenkins (Keighley), Lambert, D. Ward, Hayes, Whitcombe, Dilorenzo, Higson, Smith, Harrison, Moore

Swinton: (navy blue) unchanged

Half-time: 8–2 **Referee:** P. Cowell
Attendance: 11,271 **Receipts**: £570

Weather: unknown

Progressive score:

Bradford Northern	score (min)	Swinton
D. Ward try	3–0 (-)	
	3–2 (-)	Hodgson drop-goal
Winnard try, Carmichael goal	8–2 (28)	
Whitcombe try	11–2 (51)	
	11–5 (-)	Williams try
Winnard try, Winnard goal	16–5 (-)	
	16–7 (76)	Hodgson penalty
	16–9 (79)	Hodgson penalty

War Emergency League leaders

Yorkshire section	P	W	D	L	For	Agst	Pts
1 Bradford Northern	28	21	0	7	574	302	42
2 Huddersfield	28	19	1	8	545	340	39
3 Hull	26	18	0	8	376	265	36

Head-to-head form guide:

No previous meetings during season

Holland beating a succession of would-be tacklers on a blind side break, drawing Carmichael before sending Jack McGurk over in the corner. Hodgson added a great goal to put his team three points up. Swinton had further chances; Hopkin and Billy Shaw both went close, Hodgson missing a couple of penalties. An enthralling first half ended with Bradford regaining the lead just before the break, Emlyn Jenkins racing down the touchline, sidestepping two opponents before his cross-kick found Bert Smith who caught the ball on the bounce to score under the posts. Carmichael appended the goal and Northern went in at half-time 10–8 to the good.

The *Yorkshire Post's* correspondent said that, despite trailing by two points at the interval, 'all the best football had been played by Swinton.' The second half told a different tale, the same writer saying that after the break 'Northern's forwards became more and more aggressive in the loose' whilst for Swinton's pack 'the strain of

CHAMPION CAPTAIN

George Carmichael (Bradford Northern 1940 – 2nd leg)

Steady, dependable full-back George Carmichael made his debut for Hull Kingston Rovers (the club his father Alf 'Bunker' Carmichael, also a full-back, played for before the First World War) in 1929. He moved to Bradford Northern in 1934, retiring in 1950 after 481 appearances. With Northern, he won the Championship (1939/40, 1040/41), Challenge Cup (1944, 1947), and Yorkshire Cup (1941 – April, 1941 – December, 1943, 1945). He represented Yorkshire four times.

summer football sapped the energy of some of the side's mighty veterans.' Bradford got an early score after the restart when heavyweight prop Frank Whitcombe pushed his way over the line for a try beneath the posts, Carmichael adding the goal. Shaw gave the Lions fans hope when he hit back, diving over for a try that was converted by Hodgson. But it was their last contribution to the score, Bradford adding two unconverted tries through Davies, scoring in the corner after following up a failed penalty by Winnard that came back off the post, and Brogden.

Despite returning to Odsal with an eight-point lead, there were concerns in the Bradford camp as to whether they could protect it. Whilst Swinton fielded an unchanged team, the Odsalites' back division, already unable to call on Case, Davies and Ernest Ward, lost three-quarters Brogden and Emlyn Walters due to first leg injuries. In the end, though, it was Bradford's pack that determined the outcome of a contest that was described as 'a patchy display by both teams.'

After Swinton forward Cledwyn Williams was stopped 'inches' from the try-line it was Bradford – looking the more confident outfit at the start – that got the first try through Donald Ward, taking a pass off Jenkins. Carmichael missed the goal. Hodgson was unsuccessful with a penalty but made amends with a drop–goal. Twelve minutes before half-time, Winnard grabbed Bradford's second try, scoring in the corner after intercepting a pass, despite attention from Tommy Bartram. Carmichael added the extra points and Northern led 8–2 at the break, their overall 14 points' lead looking safe.

The second half scoring proved tighter than anticipated. Bradford increased their lead when Carmichael put Whitcombe over but, following a poor penalty attempt by Jenkins, Swinton replied through a Williams try after Holland and McGurk had created the opening. The Lions suffered a blow when Hopkin had to quit with an ankle injury, following which a try from Winnard, that he converted himself, gave Bradford an unassailable 19-point aggregate lead. Swinton, or rather Hodgson, saved the best until last with two magnificent penalty goals. The *Yorkshire Observer* described them as 'the highlights of this poor game,' adding, 'despite the boos ringing the ground, Hodgson kicked perfect goals, with one of the shots within a yard of halfway.' The match ended on an unfortunate note with Bowyer and Jenkins being sent off for fighting two minutes for time, Swinton, therefore finishing with 11 men, Bradford 12.

During the week of the final, Swinton officials announced that they would be withdrawing from future League competition as their ground was being requisitioned for the war effort. Although they emerged, briefly, the following season, playing some home games at the ground of neighbours Salford, it effectively ended their challenge for 'honours' until peace resumed. Sadly the Lions scrum half Holland did not survive the conflict.

Bradford pose for the camera before the second leg at Odsal. Back: Foster, Smith, Jenkins, Harrison, Higson, Winnard, Lambert, Whitcombe. Front: D. Ward, Dilorenzo, Moore, Carmichael, Hayes

1941 War Emergency League Championship Final
BRADFORD NORTHERN V WIGAN

The 1941 Championship Final between Bradford Northern and Wigan was settled over the Easter holiday weekend, the second leg at Odsal Stadium being watched by 20,205 who paid £1,148, both new records for the Second World War period. This was despite the fact Bradford had taken the opening leg 17–6 at Central Park – the first meeting between the two since 1934 – eventually retaining their title with a 45–15 aggregate. As with their previous year's success, the forwards played a key role, the *Wigan Examiner* conceding 'Bradford were bigger, faster and better than Wigan. They fully deserved to win the Rugby League Championship.' Bradford had to do it without the help of regular scrum half, Donald Ward, who had not sufficiently recovered from wrenching his leg muscles in the previous weekend's Yorkshire Cup Final.

The first encounter began with Wigan claiming most of the early possession, the final scrum count being 49–31 in their favour. After 26 scoreless minutes, though, it was Bradford that cut loose with three first half tries; Len Higson (a simple touchdown off Cliff Carter's off-load after the hooker's outrageous dummy took him through a gap), Gus Risman (taking a pass from the scrum and escaping a defender although he looked held), and Emlyn Walters (flying down the wing to go over in the corner after some quick passing). Ernest Ward converted the latter from the touchline following failures by Risman and George Carmichael to append the first two. Risman also missed with a drop-goal attempt whilst, in the early stages, Johnny Lawrenson was off-target with a penalty for Wigan.

After the half-time break, Bradford set about building on their 11–0 lead. Northern's next score was another try from Walters, hailed as the most spectacular of the match, the winger racing half the length of the field before re-gathering his own kick in the in-goal area. The move had started in front of the Northern posts, Walters,

Two of Bradford Northern's all-time greats, Ernest Ward (left) and Trevor Foster, played their part in helping the Odsal-based club retain their wartime title

from his left wing position, moving across field tracking colleague after colleague as the ball was transferred to the right. Eventually he collected the ball off an inside pass from Walter Best who had already beaten two defenders himself. Carmichael missed the goal. Best himself claimed the next, placing the ball in the corner after another exciting move. This time it was Ward that was off-track with the goal-kick, but Bradford looked secure with a 17–0 lead.

Wigan finally earned some points through quick thinking from Joe Jones who, when Bradford was penalised, put in short kick, regathering the ball for the touchdown. Lawrenson, whose conversion attempt was poor, concluded the scoring, running diagonally across

STATS

Wigan 6 Bradford Northern 17 (1st leg)

Saturday 12 April at Central Park, Wigan (3.30 pm)

Wigan: (cherry and white hoops) Jones, Aspinall (Liverpool Stanley), Lawrenson, Maloney (Liverpool Stanley), Johnson, Cunliffe, Bradshaw, Curran (Salford), Egan, Gee, Jack Bowen, Cayzer (Hull KR), Simpson. Trainer: E. Parkes

Bradford Northern: (white with red, amber and black band) Carmichael, Best, Winnard, E. Ward, Walters, Risman (captain, Salford), Hayes, Whitcombe, Carter (Leeds), Higson, Foster, Smith, Moore. Team manager: D. Rees

Half-time: 0–11 **Referee:** A.S. Dobson
Attendance: 11,245 **Receipts**: £642

Weather: fine, dry and windy

Progressive score:

Wigan	score (min)	Bradford Northern
	0–3 (27)	Higson try
	0–6 (29)	Risman try
	0–11 (34)	Walters try, E. Ward goal
	0–14 (-)	Walters try
	0–17 (-)	Best try
Jones try	3–17 (-)	
Lawrenson try	6–17 (-)	

War Emergency League leaders

Lancashire section	P	W	D	L	For	Agst	Pts
1 Wigan	16	15	1	0	297	71	31
2 Warrington	16	13	0	3	236	42	26
3 St Helens	14	10	1	3	280	83	21

Bradford Northern 28 Wigan 9 (2nd leg)

Monday 14 April at Odsal Stadium, Bradford (3.30 pm)

Bradford Northern: (white with red, amber and black band) unchanged

Wigan: (cherry and white hoops) unchanged except Sharratt for Curran, Curran for Cayzer

Half-time: 8–6 **Referee:** P. Cowell
Attendance: 20,205 **Receipts**: £1,148

Weather: unknown

Progressive score:

Bradford Northern	score (min)	Wigan
	0–3 (-)	Aspinall try
Winnard try	3–3 (-)	
Risman try, E. Ward goal	8–3 (35)	
	8–6 (38)	Johnson try
Risman try, E. Ward goal	13–6 (-)	
Winnard try	16–6 (-)	
Walters try, E. Ward goal	21–6 (-)	
Moore try, E. Ward goal	26–6 (-)	
E. Ward penalty	28–6 (-)	
	28–9 (75)	Bowen try

War Emergency League leaders

Yorkshire section	P	W	D	L	For	Agst	Pts
1 Bradford Northern	25	23	1	1	469	126	47
2 Hull	26	20	0	6	341	227	40
3 Huddersfield	25	14	2	9	422	297	30

Head-to-head form guide:
No previous meetings during season

the pitch after receiving from Tommy Bradshaw. Kicking towards the corner he followed up with a spectacular dive to score. Cunliffe missed the goal.

As they journeyed to Odsal for the concluding match on Easter Monday, Bradford's fans must have thought the title was as good as theirs. But, as the *Yorkshire Observer* subsequently noted, 'in the early stages the Wigan enthusiasm was such that the visitors looked like wiping out their 17–6 deficit.' Wigan struck early, Bradshaw's cross-kick putting George Aspinall over in the corner, Lawrenson's goal attempt grazing the wrong side of the far post. Northern, though, soon reasserted themselves by scoring the next two tries. The first by Tom Winnard came after Walters slipped the ball to him despite being held up in the corner by Jones, the position having been set up with a wide pass from Trevor Foster after bursting down the middle. Risman got their second in the corner five minutes before the break, Ward adding a great touchline goal after missing with the earlier effort. Almost on the stroke of half-time an adventurous Wigan attack involving six players ended with Vic Johnson scoring. Lawrenson, having already seen his earlier penalty shot rebound off a post, failed to add the extra points. Bradford led 8–6 at the interval and by 13 points overall.

Early in the second half, hookers Joe Egan and Carter were dismissed by referee Albert Dobson following several warnings related to scrum offences. Bradford, though, continued to impress with their speed and skill, adding four more tries to seal the team's victory; Risman (his

Bradford right-centre Tom Winnard (left) crossed the whitewash for two important tries during the second leg. Playing directly opposite him in the Wigan three-quarter line was Jack Maloney (right), on loan from Liverpool Stanley

scoring dash ending behind the posts after Winnard had broken the defence before delivering the pass), Winnard (cutting inside after receiving from Risman), Walters (on the way to a club record 35 for the season after Higson made the opening), and Jack Moore. Ward tagged the goals to all but Winnard's effort, adding a penalty for good measure. Persistence and determination by Jack Bowen produced a consolation try in the corner for Wigan, Lawrenson missing the goal.

The *Yorkshire Observer* said: 'Once Northern had found their feet, their achievement (at Wigan) was repeated, though, perhaps, not in the same spectacular way. Their power in the loose among the forwards and skill in the backs, if for some time latent, eventually asserted itself,' adding, 'Wigan played better than the final score of 28–9 suggests, but they hadn't the forward strength nor the back skill of opponents who have blended into an efficient team.'

A sad postscript, and a sign of the times, was that Bradford's loose forward Moore, who was in the Navy, drowned when his ship HMS Electra sank on 27 February 1942 during a naval battle off Java.

RUGBY LEAGUE CHAMPIONSHIP.

WIGAN WELL BEATEN.

Bradford Northern's Superiority.

BIG CROWD AT ODSALL.

BRADFORD NORTHERN secured their third trophy of the season on Easter Monday, when in the second match of the Rugby League championship final against Wigan they made the aggregate in their favour 45 pts. to 15. The Northern were worthy winners. At Wigan, on Saturday, they gained a winning lead of 11 pts. Despite this the crowd at Odsall on Monday numbered 21,000. The receipts were £1,143, a record for Rugby League war-time football. The clubs had finished on top of their respective county leagues and the championship of the Rugby League was decided on the home and away principle. Bradford have also won the Yorkshire Challenge Cup.

Champions again! The headline as it appeared in the Wigan Examiner

1942 War Emergency League Championship Final
DEWSBURY V BRADFORD NORTHERN

Dewsbury's Welsh centre Alan Edwards provided the defining moment of the 1942 Championship Final with an incredible and unexpected 40-yard drop-goal 15 minutes from the end, his side going on to deny Bradford Northern a third consecutive Championship with a 13–0 win at Headingley. It had followed 65 scoreless minutes in which an over enthusiastic Dewsbury – including Edwards himself – had spurned chances in their eagerness to clinch a first ever title for the Crown Flatt club. According to the *Dewsbury News*, Edwards, having obtained possession inside the Bradford half, 'swung round like lightening and sent the ball soaring high over the Bradford crossbar.'

From that moment they were in control as nerves settled and their rugby became more fluid, their inspired pack taking command to push the much-vaunted Northern pack off the ball. Dewsbury skipper Gus Risman attempted to emulate his colleague in the next attack but was not as successful. Their first try inevitably followed as Harry Royal got Tom Kenny away on a run. He swept Willie Davies out of the way before off-loading to Edwards who made further yardage before transferring to right wingman Barney Hudson who then charged towards the corner 'like a steam engine' for the score. Risman missed the goal. Another assault soon followed, Hudson running into a gap inside his centre, Edwards, to take the ball up before handing on to Risman who, in turn, fed Roy Francis, the left winger flying into the corner before the defence could get across. Risman added the touchline kick opening up a 10–0 lead. Bradford tried to rally, Hudson saving his line with a telling tackle whilst, at the other end of the field, Francis was bundled into touch just short of the line. In the dying minutes, Kenny shrugged off the opposition as he went over for a third touchdown, having taken the ball at speed off a pass from Royal. Risman missed the kick.

The final, which the *Dewsbury News* predicted 'will be a battle between Dewsbury's backs and Bradford Northern's fiery forwards', began 15 minutes late due to the thousands still outside at the scheduled start time of 3.30 pm. This, despite the fact that the 18,000 attendance was described as 'disappointing', a factor blamed on 'transport difficulties' due to wartime limitations. Despite the war situation both teams were able to feature strong sides although Bradford scrum half Donald Ward was unavailable, Keighley's Ken Davies deputising.

Until Edwards' dramatic game-breaker, the two defences had dominated the match,

Alan Edwards - his spectacular second half drop-goal put Dewsbury on the road to victory

STATS

Dewsbury 13 Bradford Northern 0

Saturday 18 April at Headingley, Leeds (3.30 pm)

Dewsbury: Miller (Salford), Hudson (Salford), Edwards (Salford), Risman (captain, Salford), Francis (Barrow), Kenny (Salford), Royal, Hammond, Nicholson, Gardner (Salford), Kershaw, Curran (Salford), Bunter (Broughton Rangers).
Team manager: E. Waring

Bradford Northern: Carmichael, Best, Billington, E. Ward, Walters, W. Davies, K. Davies (Keighley), Whitcombe, Carter (Leeds), Higson, Foster, Smith, Hutchinson.
Team manager: D. Rees

Half-time: 0–0 **Referee:** G.S. Phillips
Attendance: 18,000 **Receipts**: £1,121

Weather: sunny and windy

Progressive score:

Dewsbury	score (min)	Bradford Northern
Edwards drop-goal	2–0 (65)	
Hudson try	5–0 (-)	
Francis try, Risman goal	10–0 (-)	
Kenny try	13–0 (78)	

War Emergency League leaders

	P	W	D	L	For	Agst	Percent
1 Dewsbury	24	19	1	4	431	172	81.25
2 Bradford Northern	17	13	1	3	318	130	79.41
3 Halifax	17	13	0	4	262	139	76.47
4 Hull	18	12	0	6	265	146	66.66

Semi-finals:
Dewsbury 32 Hull 18
Bradford Northern 15 Halifax 8

Head-to-head form guide:
Bradford Northern 17 Dewsbury 8 (League)
Dewsbury 5 Bradford Northern 5 (League)

Bradford suffering first half casualties with Trevor Foster sustaining an injured jaw in the opening minutes and Cliff Carter having damaged ribs, although both continued. Ernest Ward missed two penalty attempts for Northern before their first try-scoring opportunity presented itself; Foster breaking away before being stopped in his tracks by Hudson. Walter Best provided their next threat before being dealt with by a brilliant Risman tackle. George Carmichael then tried his hand at taking a Bradford penalty but was also off-target, the opening half ending with Dewsbury testing Northern's defence, Francis being held three yards out as he attempted to 'wriggle' over.

Bradford attacked strongly after the resumption before Dewsbury rallied. Scoring chances, though, went begging for Dewsbury through continual handling errors, Royal losing the ball as he went over for a 'try.' Further near misses came their way, Joe Gardner being held up in the in-goal area and Royal getting over again but unable to place the ball. Then, when it looked like a score was never going to come, Edwards performed his miracle.

Dewsbury's success owed much to the entrepreneurial skills of their young team manager, and future television commentator and personality, Eddie Waring, who utilised nearby Caulms Wood army camp to boost his squad, a total of 45 different 'guest' players being used during the season, with seven Salford men in their line up against Bradford!

The 1941/42 Championship was the first to be won by Dewsbury. Standing: Sullivan, Waring (manager), Kershaw, Hammond, Curran, Gardner, Hudson, McManus, Kenny, Nicholson, H. Smithson (trainer), G. Davies (kitman). Seated: Walsh, Royal, Risman, Miller, Francis. Inset: Edwards, Bunter

1943 War Emergency League Championship Final
DEWSBURY V HALIFAX

The Dewsbury-Halifax meetings to determine the 1943 Championship could well be labelled 'The final that never was!' Dewsbury won the encounter with a convincing 33–16 aggregate but celebrations began turning sour a month later. On 23 June Bradford Northern protested to the Emergency League Committee that Dewsbury included Castleford forward Frank Smith when they met in the play-off, although not appearing in the minimum four League games. The rule, which applied to 'guest' players, was introduced to stop clubs strengthening for the Championship play-offs. Dewsbury overlooked the fact that, although Smith had played for them 15 times during the season, 12 games had been in cup competitions. The committee had little option but to declare on 7 July that the Championship was 'null and void', fining Dewsbury £100. It was all so different during May, when Dewsbury supporters thought the club had retained their 1942 crown and completed a treble, having won the Rugby League Challenge Cup and Yorkshire Cup.

The first leg was at Crown Flatt, the 7,000 attendance being considered a good one 'despite the lack of travel facilities' due to a bus strike. The only real absentee was Halifax winger Arthur Bassett, committed to appearing in a rugby union game in Wales, Glyn Elias taking his place. Dewsbury could not, initially, confirm their full-back, despite having used 11 already that season, the pseudonym 'A.N. Other' being published in the selected side. Wigan's Joe Jones eventually filled the role.

Dewsbury's veteran skipper Barney Hudson proved he was still a threat down the right wing

CHAMPION CAPTAIN

Barney Hudson (Dewsbury 1943)

Bernard 'Barney' Hudson was already a seasoned performer before 'guesting' with Dewsbury during the Second World War. A no-nonsense right winger with a direct running style, he was a native of Horden, County Durham, joining Salford in 1928 from Hartlepool Rovers Rugby Union Club. At Salford, he won the Championship (1932/33, 1936/37, 1938/39), Rugby League Challenge Cup (1938), Lancashire Cup (1931, 1934, 1935, 1936, missing the latter final through injury), and Lancashire League (1932/33, 1933/34, 1934/35, 1936/37, 1938/39). He represented Great Britain (8 times) and England (6), being a tourist twice (1932, 1936). Well into his mid-30s when appearing in Dewsbury colours, he helped them win the Championship (1941/42), Yorkshire Cup (1942) and Challenge Cup (1943). He was captain for the latter and skipper in the nullified Championship bid of 1942/43. His final match was for Salford in 1946, where he set a club career record of 282 tries that stood until 1983.

The match was one of contrasts, Halifax being on top in the first 40 minutes, Dewsbury controlling the second period. The Thrum Hallers had a number of chances to gain a commanding lead before the interval but generally spurned them. In the opening minutes, Hubert Lockwood's penalty fell short, and later, loose forward Harry Millington had a 'try' ruled out for an infringement. Eventually, the pressure told, Tommy Shannon touching down, too far out for Lockwood to convert. Millington almost went under the posts for another just before half-time but Roy Francis

STATS

Dewsbury 11 Halifax 3 (1st leg)

Saturday 15 May at Crown Flatt, Dewsbury (3.30 pm)

Dewsbury: Jones (Wigan), Hudson (captain, Salford), Morrell (Hunslet), Robinson (Castleford), Francis (Barrow), Kenny (Salford), Royal, Hammond, Curran (Salford), Gardner (Salford), Kershaw, Bunter (Broughton Rangers), Seeling. Team manager: E. Waring

Halifax: (blue and white hoops) Lockwood (captain), Bevan, Smith, Todd, Elias, Shannon (Widnes), McCue (Widnes), McDowell (Widnes), Jones (Broughton R.), Irving, Meek, Brereton, Millington (Widnes). Trainer: W. Bennett

Half-time: 0–3 **Referee:** A.S. Dobson
Attendance: 7,000 **Receipts**: £400

Weather: unknown

Progressive score:

Dewsbury	score (min)	Halifax
	0–3 (23)	Shannon try
Royal try	3–3 (52)	
Francis try	6–3 (65)	
Francis try, Seeling goal	11–3 (-)	

War Emergency League leaders

	P	W	D	L	For	Agst	Percent
1 Wigan	16	13	0	3	301	141	81.25
2 Dewsbury	16	12	1	3	270	117	78.12
3 Bradford Northern	19	13	1	5	312	183	71.05
4 Halifax	19	13	0	6	297	149	68.42
5 Leeds	17	11	1	5	337	145	67.64
6 Huddersfield	18	12	0	6	215	189	66.66

Halifax 13 Dewsbury 22 (2nd leg)

Saturday 22 May at Thrum Hall, Halifax (3.30 pm)

Halifax: (blue and white hoops) unchanged except Bassett foe Elias

Dewsbury: unchanged except Walsh (Castleford) for Francis

Half-time: 8–6 **Referee:** A.S. Dobson
Attendance: 9,700 **Receipts**: £683

Weather: fine and dry with slight wind

Progressive score:

Halifax	score (min)	Dewsbury
McCue try	3–0 (-)	
Lockwood penalty	5–0 (20)	
	5–3 (-)	Hudson try
	5–6 (-)	Royal try
Bevan try	8–6 (-)	
	8–9 (-)	Hudson try
McCue try, Lockwood goal	13–9 (-)	
	13–14 (-)	Morrell try, Walsh goal
	13–17 (-)	Kenny try
	13–22 (-)	Curran try, Walsh goal

Play-off qualifier:
Bradford Northern 16 Huddersfield 13

Semi-finals:
Wigan 4 Halifax 13
Dewsbury 3 Bradford Northern 8
(Bradford had ineligible player; match awarded to Dewsbury)

Head-to-head form guide:
Halifax 10 Dewsbury 8 (League)

appeared from 'nowhere' to take 'man and ball to earth' in a tackle that probably changed the outcome of the match.

After the interval Dewsbury utilised their famous slope to gain valuable yardage through well-aimed kicks into the corner. It was Harry Royal, running the ball in from 40 yards off a Charlie Seeling pass, that levelled the scores 12 minutes after the restart. Seeling failed to add the extras and then hit the post with a penalty attempt. Fifteen minutes from the end, Jones spotted a gap to race downfield and, with Halifax's defence in disarray, he got the ball across to Seeling who fed Francis for Dewsbury's second try. Seeling missed the goal. Dewsbury got a third when, with Seeling again providing the pass, the home fans were treated to a 'Francis special' as the winger cut inside to fly past two defenders and finish behind the posts. Seeling added the goal to win 11–3. Late inclusion Jones, after a quiet first half, was the stand-out player, the *Dewsbury Reporter* claiming he gave the 'best full back exhibition seen for long time.'

Dewsbury visited Thrum Hall for the second game without two-try hero Francis, who was representing the West Riding Army team in the Northern Command rugby union sevens at Headingley the same afternoon. Lockwood was also involved in the tournament but Halifax, who also welcomed Bassett back, arranged for him to be transported to Thrum Hall afterwards.

Hooker George Curran, who appeared in four consecutive wartime Championship Finals (1941 to 1944), scored the last try to seal Dewsbury's win

From the *Halifax Courier* viewpoint the 'Championship' was 'won and lost' in the opening 20 minutes. During this period Halifax had try claims by Hudson Irving and Mel Meek disallowed as they desperately tried to close the eight-point deficit. Nonetheless, they did go ahead on the day after Tommy McCue burst through for a brilliant solo try after charging down a Barney Hudson kick. Lockwood missed the goal but then landed a penalty. With the arrears down to three points, Halifax looked capable of pushing on for victory but, conversely, began to slow down. It was Dewsbury that got the next two tries; Hudson (racing under the posts from halfway after a scissors move with Cyril Morrell), and Royal (following a neat sidestep and pass from Tom Walsh) being the scorers. Seeling missed the goals, the first being in front of the posts. Jim Bevan scored another try for Halifax, Lockwood failing to augment, the half-time score favouring the home team, 8–6.

Hudson roared over for his second after the interval, picking up a loose ball from 35–yards out 'with all his old speed and strength' at the age of 37. This meant Dewsbury led 9–8. McCue, Halifax's best player on the day, replied with his second try, Lockwood's goal pushing them 13–9 in front. Only four points behind overall, the expected Halifax surge did not materialise and, instead, Dewsbury dominated the remainder of the match. They added three more tries on the way to a 22–13 triumph through Morrell, Tom Kenny and George Curran, Walsh converting two.

Victorious captain, Hudson, said at a celebration dinner afterwards that: 'The team spirit has been fine and the man who has made that spirit is (team manager) Eddie Waring. All the players have felt they could not let him down. At Salford we tried to sweep the board and I congratulate Dewsbury, Mr Waring and the players for doing it here this season.'

Dewsbury 1942/43. Standing: Robinson, Seeling, Smith, Curran, Hammond, Gardner, Kershaw. Seated: Walsh (in uniform), Bunter, Edwards, Hudson, Waring (manager), Francis, Royal, Kenny, Morrell (in suit)

1944 War Emergency League Championship Final WIGAN V DEWSBURY

Wigan defeated Dewsbury 25–14 over two legs in the 1944 decider, Jim Sullivan being drafted into the side for the second tie, the last cup final of a glittering career at the age of 40. Although not in training he was, reluctantly, 'pressed into service' at the request of club directors when full-back Joe Jones reported unfit. He gave a remarkable performance, the *Dewsbury Reporter* noting: 'The coolness and general-ship of Jim Sullivan had much to do with their (Wigan's) success. He was rarely out of position and with the wind put the ball where he wanted.'

Wigan, who had the choice, staged the first leg hoping to build a winning score, probably expecting more than the four-point advantage they achieved, although the Wigan public saw an exciting game. Described by the *Wigan Observer* as 'a thriller in every sense of the word' the lead changed hands four times during the opening half. Wigan's Jim Featherstone scored the first try after Jack Blan worked the opening, but went from hero to villain five minutes later. Tom Walsh intercepted his pass and scored under the posts, adding the goal himself for a

STATS

Wigan 13 Dewsbury 9 (1st leg)

Saturday 13 May at Central Park, Wigan (3.30 pm)

Wigan: Jones, Fleming, Belshaw (Warrington), Lawrenson, Ashcroft, Ryan, H. Gee, K. Gee, Egan (captain), J. Blan, Featherstone, Cayzer (Hull KR), Bowen. Trainer: E. Parkes

Dewsbury: Lowe (Wigan), Hudson (captain, Salford), Robinson (Castleford), Francis (Barrow), Edwards (Salford), Hey, Walsh (Castleford), Hammond, Curran (Salford), Gardner (Salford), Kershaw, Bunter (Broughton Rangers), Bradbury (St Helens). Team manager: E. Waring

Half-time: 8–7 **Referee:** A.S. Dobson
Attendance: 14,000 **Receipts**: £915

Weather: unknown

Progressive score:

Wigan	score (min)	Dewsbury
Featherstone try	3–0 (10)	
	3–5 (15)	Walsh try, Walsh goal
K. Gee try	6–5 (-)	
	6–7 (-)	Walsh penalty
Lawrenson drop-goal	8–7 (38)	
Egan drop-goal	10–7 (-)	
Lawrenson try	13–7 (-)	
	13–9 (-)	Walsh penalty

Semi-finals:
Wakefield Trinity 5 Dewsbury 11
Wigan 27 Hull 10

Head-to-head form guide:
Wigan 14 Dewsbury 3 (Challenge Cup)
Dewsbury 2 Wigan 11(Challenge Cup)

Dewsbury 5 Wigan 12 (2nd leg)

Saturday 20 May at Crown Flatt, Dewsbury (3.30 pm)

Dewsbury: unchanged except Royal for Walsh, Seeling for Bradbury

Wigan: unchanged except Sullivan for Jones, Bradshaw for H. Gee, Watkins for Cayzer

Half-time: 5–3 **Referee:** A. Holbrook
Attendance: 9,000 **Receipts**: £680

Weather: unknown

Progressive score:

Dewsbury	score (min)	Wigan
Seeling penalty	2–0 (15)	
	2–3 (26)	Fleming try
Francis try	5–3 (39)	
	5–5 (48)	Sullivan penalty
	5–7 (69)	Sullivan penalty
	5–12 (80)	Egan try, Sullivan goal

War Emergency League leaders

	P	W	D	L	For	Agst	Percent
1 Wakefield Trinity	22	19	0	3	359	97	86.36
2 Wigan	21	17	0	4	302	143	80.95
3 Hull	21	15	0	6	236	189	71.42
4 Dewsbury	22	15	1	6	304	169	70.45

5–3 Dewsbury lead. Wigan tried to regain their advantage, Blan just failing to connect when diving on a loose ball in Dewsbury's in-goal area, Featherstone eventually sending Ken Gee over to put Wigan 6–5 ahead. Within five minutes, Hector Gee was penalised for being offside, Walsh's goal nosing the Yorkshire side back in front. The Cherry and Whites led 8–7 at the interval, following a magnificent Johnny Lawrenson drop-goal.

Wigan increased the tempo after the break and, after Jones failed with a similar effort, Joe Egan dropped a goal. Lawrenson then claimed Wigan's third try, going over the line with Jimmy Lowe (who was actually on Wigan's books) clinging on to no avail for the last few yards. Billy Belshaw missed his third conversion, Dewsbury claiming morale victory after Walsh reduced the final deficit with a penalty.

Apart from Jones crying off for the return leg, Wigan lost Hector Gee, who was outstanding in the first match, due to a pulled leg muscle. Tommy Bradshaw, back from a six-week injury lay-off, replaced him. Dewsbury included Charlie Seeling in place of Jack Bradbury, the *Dewsbury Reporter* commenting that the club 'slipped badly' in choosing Bradbury over the guile of Seeling for the first meeting. The last-minute uncertainty of team selection during the war was demonstrated when Walsh was stood down just before kick-off. With Harry Royal available to reclaim his usual scrum half slot, Walsh was assigned to the wing. Former Test winger Barney Hudson, thought to be indisposed, then arrived and Walsh had to sit it out!

Dewsbury made a 'hurricane' start with Seeling and Roy Francis almost getting Joe Gardner over but for Ernie Ashcroft racing across to cover. Seeling, having failed with two penalties, succeeded with the third, reducing the difference to two points. Sullivan missed a penalty before Wigan scored through Jackie Fleming. Taking a Lawrenson pass, he kicked into the corner, following up to dive on the ball ahead of two hesitant defenders. Sullivan missed the conversion. With Australian half-back Vic Hey in brilliant form, Dewsbury heads did not go down, wingers Alan Edwards and Hudson both going near, whilst Seeling was wide with another penalty in front of the posts. On half-time, Seeling's long pass connected with Francis who, taking the ball at speed raced over. Seeling missed the goal, but Dewsbury led 5–3, just two points behind overall.

The second half began with an ambitious, though unsuccessful, touchline drop-goal attempt by Wigan's Belshaw, Sullivan then landing a 40-yard penalty after Martin Ryan was tripped. Sullivan continued to aim for goal whenever the opportunity arrived, two more efforts failing, the first hitting the post, before he found the target once more after Harry Hammond was given offside. One of the game's best moves ended with Francis being dramatically halted near the line as Dewsbury sought to rescue the day. Wigan finished in style, Sullivan, having missed another penalty, tagging on the points after Joe Egan dummied his way over off a Ken Gee pass.

Wigan captain and hooker Joe Egan in the centre

1945 War Emergency League Championship Final
BRADFORD NORTHERN V HALIFAX

The last Championship decider of the Second World War was also the closest, each team winning their home leg. Played out over the 1945 Whitsuntide holiday break there was a more relaxed, carnival feeling about the event than for previous wartime finals. This was perhaps due to VE Day, marking the end of war in Europe, having been celebrated just 11 days earlier.

Finalists Bradford Northern and Halifax had been the season's top sides, Frank Williams in the *Halifax Daily Courier & Guardian* saying: 'Halifax and Bradford supporters have had to wait eight months for the chance to settle the much debated question as to the merits of their respective teams', a reference to them not meeting in the League during the campaign, although Halifax had beaten Bradford over two legs in a Yorkshire Cup clash. Eventual champions Bradford won it the hard way; finishing top of the League table by virtue of winning their last four fixtures, reaching the final after a narrow 18–15 play-off victory over resolute Wigan, and overcoming a first leg deficit to take the title.

For the opening tie at Thrum Hall, Bradford was without stand-off Willie Davies, due to RAF duties, Halifax missing injured forward Hudson Irving. Both returned for the second leg. Halifax fulfilled most expectations by winning 9–2, the highlight being two tremendous second half penalties from skipper Hubert Lockwood whose judgement against a 'tricky' wind was spot on. Halifax's pack asserted pressure over Northern's from the kick-off, Harry Millington charging through in only the second minute, supplying Tommy McCue with a pass that sent him racing under the posts, Lockwood adding the goal. Ernest Ward got two points back with a penalty, the score being 5–2 at half-time.

A policeman keeps watch as Bradford captain Ernest Ward shows off the Championship trophy to the Northern supporters

Bradford, who struggled to make headway in the opening period, improved after the break but was unable to score. Their best chance was lost when Jack Kitching dropped George Bennett's pass, after the latter broke through the middle. Halifax, too, blew a try-scoring chance when George Todd, having made a terrific break, delivered a forward pass five yards from Northern's line, Lockwood's aforementioned goals producing the only points as play 'deteriorated' in the second half.

Halifax defended their seven point lead on Whit Monday without winger Arthur Bassett and prop forward Bill Morgan, both injured at Thrum Hall. It was suggested Bradford would need 'to sharpen their attack' if they were to have any chance and, initially, it was visitors Halifax, inspired by scrum half McCue, who looked more dangerous, Todd almost scoring an early try. It all fell apart, though, when Northern winger Walter Best pounced on a loose ball just

CHAMPION CAPTAIN

Ernest Ward (Bradford Northern 1945)

Ernest Ward signed for Bradford Northern from Dewsbury Boys' Club in 1936, when he was 16. A skilful centre, master tactician, and reliable goal-kicker, he won the Championship (1940/41, 1944/45), Challenge Cup (1944, 1947, 1949), Yorkshire Cup (1941 – April, 1941 – December, 1943, 1945, 1948, 1949) and Yorkshire League (1939/40, 1940/41, 1947/48) with Northern. He represented Great Britain (21 times), England (20), Yorkshire (11), and was a tourist in 1946 and 1950, being captain for the latter. In 1953 he joined Castleford as player-coach, concluding his playing career with Batley in 1956.

outside his 25 area to race down the flank, beating Lockwood with a brilliant sidestep to score, Ernest Ward adding the goal. It opened the floodgates as they hit a purple patch midway through the half with four touchdowns; Alf Marklew (off Best after a spectacular Eric Batten run beat four defenders including a trademark leap over Mel Meek), Kitching (evading some poor tackling), Alan Edwards (after a passing move involving Bill Hutchinson, Kitching and Batten), and Donald Ward (shooting through a gap in Halifax's demoralised defence). Ernest Ward converted Edwards' effort, the Thrum Haller's managing just two penalties from the boot of Lockwood to trail 19–4 at half-time, eight points adrift overall.

Halifax showed greater spirit after the resumption, giving the ball more air. Another penalty from Lockwood was followed by an unconverted McCue try, bringing the aggregate to only 21–18 in Bradford's favour. The home side was stung into action, Ernest Ward's penalty being followed, nine minutes from time, by a second try from brother Donald, created by Kitching. Halifax staged one last-gasp rally but their only reward was another Lockwood penalty, the final aggregate being 26–20.

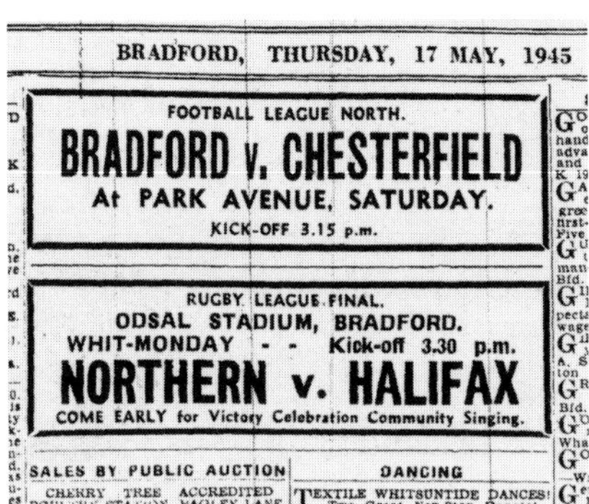
BRADFORD, THURSDAY, 17 MAY, 1945

FOOTBALL LEAGUE NORTH.
BRADFORD v. CHESTERFIELD
At PARK AVENUE, SATURDAY.
KICK-OFF 3.15 p.m.

RUGBY LEAGUE FINAL.
ODSAL STADIUM, BRADFORD.
WHIT-MONDAY - - Kick-off 3.30 p.m.
NORTHERN v. HALIFAX
COME EARLY for Victory Celebration Community Singing.

SALES BY PUBLIC AUCTION
DANCING

The Bradford Telegraph and Argus promoted both codes of football on its front page

STATS

Halifax 9 Bradford Northern 2 (1st leg)

Saturday 19 May at Thrum Hall, Halifax (3.30 pm)

Halifax: (blue and white hoops) Lockwood (captain), Taylor, Todd, Humphrey, Bassett, Rule, McCue (Widnes), Morgan (Broughton R), Jones (Broughton R.), Childs, Meek, Millington (Widnes), Dixon. Trainer: W. Bennett

Bradford Northern: (white with red, amber and black band) E. Ward (captain), Edwards (Salford), Batten, Kitching, Best, Bennett, D. Ward, Whitcombe, Darlison, Higson, Roberts, Marklew, Hutchinson. Team manager: D. Rees

Half-time: 5–2 **Referee:** J.E. Taylor
Attendance: 9,426 **Receipts**: £955

Weather: sunny and warm

Progressive score:

Halifax	score (min)	Bradford Northern
McCue try, Lockwood goal	5–0 (2)	
	5–2 (-)	E. Ward penalty
Lockwood penalty	7–2 (-)	
Lockwood penalty	9–2 (-)	

Semi-finals:
Bradford Northern 18 Wigan 15
Halifax 17 Wakefield Trinity 11

Head-to-head form guide:
Halifax 10 Bradford Northern 0 (Yorkshire Cup)
Bradford Northern 5 Halifax 5 (Yorkshire Cup)

Bradford Northern 24 Halifax 11 (2nd leg)

Monday 21 May at Odsal Stadium, Bradford (3.30 pm)

Bradford Northern: (white with red, amber and black band) unchanged except W. Davies for Bennett

Halifax: (dark blue, light blue and white narrow hoops) unchanged except Elias for Bassett, Irving for Morgan

Half-time: 19–4 **Referee:** A.S. Dobson
Attendance: 16,000 **Receipts**: £1,850

Weather: unknown

Progressive score:

Bradford Northern	score (min)	Halifax
Best try, E. Ward goal	5–0 (10)	
Marklew try	8–0 (-)	
Kitching try	11–0 (-)	
Edwards try, E. Ward goal	16–0 (-)	
	16–2 (-)	Lockwood penalty
	16–4 (-)	Lockwood penalty
D. Ward try	19–4 (-)	
	19–6 (-)	Lockwood penalty
	19–9 (-)	McCue try
E. Ward penalty	21–9 (-)	
D. Ward try	24–9 (61)	
	24–11 (78)	Lockwood penalty

War Emergency League leaders

	P	W	D	L	For	Agst	Percent
1 Bradford Northern	20	17	0	3	337	69	85.00
2 Halifax	16	13	1	2	288	78	84.37
3 Wakefield Trinity	23	17	0	6	380	203	73.91
4 Wigan	24	17	1	6	302	138	72.91

1946 Northern Rugby League Championship Final
WIGAN V HUDDERSFIELD

A touch of half-time inspiration from coach Jim Sullivan set Wigan on the road to winning the first peacetime Championship Final following the cessation of Second World War hostilities. Minus four of their biggest stars – Joe Egan, Ken Gee, Martin Ryan and Ted Ward – who had set off for Australia and New Zealand with the 1946 tourists, Wigan had suffered defeat to Wakefield Trinity 14 days earlier in the Challenge Cup Final at Wembley. Sullivan was anxious to avoid a repetition against Huddersfield, a team that lay 12th in the League at the end of November. The Final, which returned to Maine Road, attracted record receipts for the event of £8,387, over £4,000 up on the 1939 record.

The Championship Final returned to Maine Road in 1946 after 7-years

Although Huddersfield – who themselves had forward Bob Nicholson on tour and back Russ Pepperell out with a pulled muscle – lost the toss and began against a cross-wind, it was Wigan that struggled in the opening exchanges. They came close to conceding the first try when Geoff Bawden, crossed the line but, according to the officials, was prevented by Jack Cunliffe from touching down, Huddersfield protesting otherwise. Bawden did score shortly afterwards, landing a penalty goal after Gordon Ratcliffe strayed offside. Brian Nordgren must have thought his Wembley horror show, where he had missed all seven of his goal efforts, was about to be repeated when, attempting a penalty shot, his boot made contact with the turf and the ball travelled a short distance across the pitch. He was relieved to see his second effort, from a difficult position, level the score. Wigan began opening out and Ernie Ashcroft, backing up a Frank Barton break, scored by the uprights. Nordgren's frustration continued as he missed the easy conversion. Huddersfield still had some ammunition left, Les Baxter and Jock Anderson both coming near to a try and Bob Robson failing with an attempted drop-goal. Wigan went into the break leading 5–2 but, as one report said: 'Huddersfield seemed to have the Wigan defence in a tangle with some swift passing, but just when success looked likely something happened to save the Wigan line – either weak finishing or an unexpected tackle when all seemed lost.'

It was time for Sullivan, calling on his superb tactical brain, to change the Wigan formation for the second half. He moved Reg Lowrey, who was suffering from concussion, to the left wing with Stan Jolley shifting inside to left centre and Ashcroft relocating to stand-off. The changes

CHAMPION CAPTAIN

Eddie Watkins (Wigan 1946)

The war-disrupted playing career of Eddie Watkins at Wigan was brief – in terms of matches – but glorious. Although making just 94 appearances for the club between 1939 and 1946 – he still managed to collect a few medals. His zenith came when temporarily handed the captaincy in place of tourist Joe Egan at the climax to the 1945/46 campaign. He led the team to victory in the Championship Final just two weeks after being skipper in the narrow Challenge Cup Final defeat to Wakefield at Wembley. Born in Caerphilly, he moved to Central Park from Cardiff Rugby Union Club, having represented Wales eight times. A fiercely competitive back-row forward, he added three more appearances for Wales under rugby league rules during the Second World War. Further success with Wigan included the Championship (1943/44) and Lancashire League (1945/46). He later joined Belle Vue Rangers, playing 13 times during the 1946/47 season.

revitalised their attacking play and, although Bawden managed to reduce Huddersfield's deficit to one point with a penalty, they began to dictate the game. A further change, albeit temporary, occurred when Cunliffe moved to stand-off whilst recovering from concussion after a knock. Receiving a quick pass off Tommy Bradshaw from a scrum, he set off down the 'blind side' near the touchline, his swerve taking him past a defender to race over and put the ball down despite an attempted tackle. Nordgren missed the goal attempt, leaving Wigan 8–4 ahead. The final try was claimed by Ashcroft

Alex Fiddes – Huddersfield's Scottish centre and captain

STATS

Wigan 13 Huddersfield 4

Saturday 18 May at Maine Road, Manchester (3.30 pm)

Wigan: (blue) Cunliffe, Nordgren, Ratcliffe, Ashcroft, Jolley, Lowrey, Bradshaw, Banks, J. Blan, Barton, Watkins (captain), Atkinson W. Blan. Coach: J. Sullivan

Huddersfield: (claret and gold) Leake, Anderson, Fiddes (captain), Davies, Bawden, Grahame, Morgan, Mallinson, Whitehead, Bradbury, Aspinall, Baxter, Robson. Coach: unknown

Half-time: 5–2 **Referee:** A.S. Dobson
Attendance: 67,136 **Receipts**: £8,386

Weather: cloudy with some sunshine, windy

Progressive score:

Wigan	score (min)	Huddersfield
	0–2 (10)	Bawden penalty
Nordgren penalty	2–2 (26)	
Ashcroft try	5–2 (36)	
	5–4 (47)	Bawden penalty
Cunliffe try	8–4 (55)	
Ashcroft try, Nordgren goal	13–4 (66)	

League leaders	P	W	D	L	For	Agst	Pts
1 Wigan	36	29	2	5	783	219	60
2 Huddersfield	36	27	1	8	688	286	55
3 Wakefield Trinity	36	26	0	10	707	283	52
4 Bradford Northern	36	24	3	9	544	288	51

Semi-finals:
Wigan 18 Bradford Northern 4
Huddersfield 8 Wakefield Trinity 3

Head-to-head form guide:
No previous meetings during season

who, having received the ball from Bradshaw 25 yards from the Huddersfield line, neatly cut inside before sidestepping full-back Bill Leake. Nordgren added the goal from in front of the posts, extending the final score to 13–4.

Sullivan deflected the praise towards his players, saying 'They won the day because their team was fitter; stamina told in the second half.' For stand-in skipper Eddie Watkins, who broke his thumb during the game, it was a special moment, receiving the trophy in the absence of regular skipper Egan. The result meant that Wigan, with their sixth Championship including one won during the Second World War, had set a new record, previously shared with Huddersfield on five.

1947 Northern Rugby League Championship Final WIGAN V DEWSBURY

Wigan retained their title in 1947, defeating Dewsbury 13–4 at Maine Road in a match pre-empting the birth of summer rugby league 49 years later, the final taking place in late June after a severe winter extended the season. Although the attendance of 40,599 was almost 27,000 down on last year, officials deemed it a good turnout for that time of the year!

Dewsbury, coached by former Leeds and Australia stand-off Vic Hey, surprised many in reaching their first peacetime Championship Final. They fully merited their place, though, after a run of 13 consecutive victories, covering their final 12 League fixtures and the play-off win against Widnes. Despite the Yorkshire side's excellent form, table-toppers Wigan were still favoured to increase their record number of Championship victories to seven.

It was Dewsbury full-back Jimmy Ledgard that caught the eye in the opening minutes, aiming a perfectly judged kick towards the corner flag, forcing Jack Cunliffe to kick dead. Ledgard then fielded the resultant Wigan drop-out producing his own drop-kick which sailed between the posts for a 2–0 lead. Ted Ward failed to convert a couple of Wigan penalty opportunities, a long distance shot just dipping under the bar and another hitting the post from an acute angle. Dewsbury, though, was in the ascendancy, Wigan's defence working overtime to contain their enthusiastic forays. The Cherry and Whites did, however, have their moments; Cec Mountford caught the ball and beat four opponents during a thrilling 40-yard dash before the move broke down, and Johnny Lawrenson

CHAMPION CAPTAIN

Joe Egan (Wigan 1944, 1947)

Hooker Joe Egan had more to his game than winning scrum possession, being wonderfully adroit in setting up attacks for supporting pack colleagues, his long-term front-row partnership with prop Ken Gee being particularly fruitful. He began as a full-back playing for local clubs Wigan St Patrick's and Highfield Old Boys, signing with Wigan in 1937 at 17 years old. He quickly established himself, taking over as skipper in 1942. At Wigan, he received winners' medals for the Championship (1943/44, 1945/46 – missing the final through touring, 1946/47, 1949/50 – again missing the final through touring), Rugby League Challenge Cup (1948), Lancashire Cup (1938, 1946, 1947, 1948, 1949), and Lancashire League (1945/46, 1946/47, 1949/50). A tourist twice (1946, 1950), he appeared in 14 Tests for Great Britain (captain once), representing England (19 times) and Lancashire (10). In 1950 he joined Leigh as captain-coach for a rugby league record £5,000, leading them to Lancashire Cup success in 1952. His last Leigh match was in 1955, continuing as coach before reuniting with Wigan in a similar capacity (1956–61). He later coached Widnes, Warrington and Blackpool Borough and was in charge of Great Britain for the 1954 World Cup. During the Second World War, he made a guest appearance for Oldham in 1943.

Dewsbury captain Harry Royal gets the ball away from the scrum to his stand-off Cyril Gilbertson

Schoolboy admirers join the excited throng that surrounds the Wigan side as skipper Joe Egan is chaired around the Maine Road pitch in triumph

stepped into touch heading towards the corner following another exciting Wigan attack. But it was Dewsbury that finished the first half strongest, almost scoring by the right corner flag as the interval approached, Wigan being relieved to reach the break only two points adrift.

The opening period of the second half saw a completely different Wigan, rediscovering their form to dominate the first 20-odd minutes, Dewsbury being unable to breach their 25 area during that time. Brian Nordgren scored the opening try in the right corner two minutes after the restart, Ward slipping him the ball in a tackle having raced down the right touchline after recovering a neat kick from Ken Gee. Ward added the difficult conversion, the ball rebounding in off the far upright, placing Wigan 5–2 ahead. Lawrenson (just failing to reach the ball before it went in touch) and Ernie Ashcroft (losing possession as he dived over) both came close to adding to the Wigan tally. Dewsbury loose forward Arthur Street was then forced to leave the field for treatment to an injury, Wigan building a winning lead in his absence. Firstly, Tommy Bradshaw and Mountford combined to get Ward away, his pass to Ashcroft being continued on to Lawrenson who scored in the left corner. Ward missed the kick but was then on target minutes later after Bradshaw – having fed Lawrenson from a scrum on the 'blind side' – was on hand for the return pass to go over. Dewsbury tried desperately to rally, coming near several times to earning a consolation try, half-back Cyril Gilbertson – having moved to the right wing – being nearest in the final seconds. Their only reward, though, was a Jack Holt drop-goal four minutes from time.

Although Wigan repeated the previous year's score-line in overcoming Dewsbury, the *Wigan Examiner* told its readers: 'It was by no means a great match and did not produce either the thrills or the sparkling football seen when Wigan defeated Huddersfield (in the 1946 final) on the same ground.'

STATS

Wigan 13 Dewsbury 4

Saturday 21 June at Maine Road, Manchester (3.00 pm)

Wigan: (cherry and white hoops) Cunliffe, Nordgren, Ward, Ashcroft, Lawrenson, Mountford, Bradshaw, Gee, Egan (captain), Banks, Barton, W. Blan, J. Blan. Coach: J. Sullivan

Dewsbury: (red, amber and black hoops) Ledgard, Armitage, Clark, Sacker, Withington. Gilbertson, Royal (captain), Hammond, McKeating, Pearson, Cox, Holt, Street. Coach: V. Hey

Half-time: 0–2 **Referee:** A.S. Dobson
Attendance: 40,599 **Receipts**: £5,894

Weather: cloudy with some sunshine

Progressive score:

Wigan	score (min)	Dewsbury
	0–2 (3)	Ledgard drop-goal
Nordgren try, Ward goal	5–2 (42)	
Lawrenson try	8–2 (59)	
Bradshaw try, Ward goal	13–2 (62)	
	13–4 (76)	Holt drop-goal

League leaders	P	W	D	L	For	Agst	Pts
1 Wigan	36	29	1	6	567	196	59
2 Dewsbury	36	27	1	8	411	158	55
3 Widnes	36	26	2	8	284	149	54
4 Leeds	36	25	2	9	573	305	52

Semi-finals:
Wigan 21 Leeds 11
Dewsbury 5 Widnes 2

Head-to-head form guide:
No previous meetings during season

Graham Morris

1948 Northern Rugby League Championship Final
WARRINGTON V BRADFORD NORTHERN

Warrington won their first Championship in the 1947/48 season, the *Warrington Guardian's* Jack Steel claiming their Maine Road victory over Bradford Northern marked 'the most important day in the Warrington club's long career.' Although Northern blotted their performance with handling errors and Warrington was considered below par through being 'over anxious', the Championship Final was still labelled 'a thrilling affair.' Watched by over 69,000 it created new record receipts (£9,792) for the occasion.

Warrington was without winger Albert Johnson, missing since the end of March through a leg injury, and sensational Australian forward, Harry Bath, who, despite having played 10 League fixtures was ineligible, having signed from Barrow after the 1 March deadline. Northern began the match at full strength although loose forward Ken Traill suffered a thigh injury in the opening minutes, rendering him ineffective for the rest of the match.

Bradford captain Ernest Ward – one of his side's better performers on the day – caused Warrington problems in the opening minutes, with some telling kicks into touch, aided by a strong wind. It was, however, Warrington's Harold Palin that, according to Jack Steel, 'gave the side a tonic equally as good as the Lytham air' when his 9th minute penalty put the Wire in front. Their Aussie wing sensation Brian Bevan, who threatened danger several times during the match, scored his 57th try of the season eight minutes later, Palin missing the goal. Just before half-time one of the crucial moments of the match occurred when Bradford second-row forward Barry Tyler, some 12 yards from the Warrington line, looked a certain scorer but, unexpectedly, turned the ball inside, but only into the waiting arms of Warrington's Jackie Fleming, a great chance to pull level being lost.

After the break, the Wires soon doubled their lead when Stan Powell dived over in the left corner after good combination between props Bill Riley and Bill Derbyshire, Palin adding a great goal. Bradford still had their moments;

Warrington finally took possession of the Championship trophy in 1947/48. Standing: Riley, Davies, Cotton, Bath, Derbyshire, Ryan, Peake. Seated: Pimblett, Knowelden, Powell, Palin, Jones, Johnson, Bevan. On ground: Fleming, Helme

CHAMPION CAPTAIN

Harold Palin (Warrington 1948)

The career of Harold Palin went 'full circle', when he returned to Warrington in 1947 after a 10-year stint at Swinton, where he had won the Lancashire Cup and Lancashire League in 1939/40. Originally a full-back, he made just three appearances for his local side, Warrington, in 1936. Swinton snapped him up in 1937, where he developed into an exciting loose forward whose pace enabled him to provide a perfect link with his backs. He was also reliable with the boot, notching a Warrington club record of 146 in a season (1948/49 – adding 8 tries for a record 316 points) and 14 in a match (v Liverpool City, 1950). He was installed as captain on his return to Warrington leading them to their first ever Championship success in 1948/49, adding the Rugby League Challenge Cup (1950) and Lancashire League (1947/48, 1948/49, 1950/51) to his personal honours list. He transferred to Halifax in 1951, moving to Keighley the following year, for whom he played his last match in 1953. He appeared in two Test matches (both 1953) and represented England (3 times) and Lancashire (5 – the first two whilst at Swinton).

Ernest Ward broke dangerously through the middle but was obstructed after he kicked ahead, and Eric Batten was stopped by 'the tackle of the match' from Les Jones, his team's defence being otherwise in disarray. Bradford was rewarded when, after a sharp passing move, Des Case got over for a try. This led to a bizarre moment with the goal that followed, being described by the *Yorkshire Observer's* George M. Thompson as 'one of the strangest I have seen.' Ernest Ward hit the post, the ball bouncing back into the field of play (a Warrington player catching it on the way down). Referee Albert Dobson who was, apparently, standing behind the posts and gave the goal, explaining afterwards: 'The ball hit the upright, swerved over the bar, then dropped in front of the posts.'

Bradford prop Frank Whitcombe unceremoniously upends a Warrington opponent

With the score at 10–5, it gave Bradford supporters hope, but their team went off the boil just as quickly as they had gone on it and Albert Pimblett, who had an inspirational game, broke down the right to go over for another Wires try. Palin missed the goal but added a long distance penalty, the final score being 15–5.

The *Yorkshire Observer* said Warrington had 'looked far and away the better side' achieving their success against a Bradford team that looked 'leg weary and tired from the start', attributed to a heavy end of the season schedule that included a hard fought win at League leaders Wigan in the play-off and a disappointing loss to the same opposition at Wembley the previous week.

STATS

Warrington 15 Bradford Northern 5

Saturday 8 May at Maine Road, Manchester (3.15 pm)

Warrington: (primrose and blue hoops) Jones, Bevan, Knowelden, Pimblett, Powell, Fleming, Helme, Derbyshire, Cotton, Riley, Featherstone, Ryan, Palin (captain). Team manager: C. Brockbank

Bradford Northern: (white with amber, red and black chevron): Carmichael, Batten, Case, E. Ward (captain), Edwards, Davies, D. Ward, Whitcombe, Darlison, Smith, Foster, Tyler, Traill. Team manager: D. Rees

Half-time: 5–0 **Referee:** A.S. Dobson
Attendance: 69,143 **Receipts**: £9,791

Weather: cloudy with some sunshine, windy

Progressive score:

Warrington	score (min)	Bradford Northern
Palin penalty	2–0 (9)	
Bevan try	5–0 (17)	
Powell try, Palin goal	10–0 (47)	
	10–5 (60)	Case try, E. Ward goal
Pimblett try	13–5 (-)	
Palin penalty	15–5 (-)	

League leaders	P	W	D	L	For	Agst	Pts
1 Wigan	36	31	1	4	776	258	63
2 Warrington	36	30	1	5	688	232	61
3 Huddersfield	36	26	2	8	669	240	54
4 Bradford Northern	36	26	0	10	549	310	52

Semi-finals:
Wigan 3 Bradford Northern 15
Warrington 17 Huddersfield 5

Head-to-head form guide:
Bradford Northern 12 Warrington 0 (League)
Warrington 21 Bradford Northern 5 (League)

1949 Northern Rugby League Championship Final
HUDDERSFIELD V WARRINGTON

The 1949 Championship Final between Huddersfield and Warrington attracted a record crowd (75,194) and receipts (£11,073) for what the *Huddersfield Daily Examiner* described as 'a scintillating exhibition of football.' It was also a final with a cliff-hanger finish as Huddersfield held on for a victory that, at one stage, had looked secure, prompting the *Warrington Guardian* to say, 'No Hollywood producer has ever envisaged a more thrilling climax.' One of the many talking points occurred even before kick-off; appointed referee Frank Smith of Barrow failing to arrive and touch-judge Matt Coates taking charge at short notice. Fortunately experienced referee Paul Cowell was on hand to fill the vacant flag-waver's role, although becoming involved in another of the day's incidents. Excepting Huddersfield centre Geoff Bawden (replaced by Archie Ferguson due to fluid on a knee) both teams lined up with a full complement.

Australian wingman Lionel Cooper – scorer of Huddersfield's second try

The match began at a tremendous pace, Huddersfield winger Lionel Cooper, picking up from a play-the-ball to go flashing downfield, kicking ahead and catching the ball on the bounce, before being tackled two yards out. They continued moving the ball and skipper Pat Devery broke away but, with a try looking certain, Cooper was unable to hold the pass. Apart from a short Warrington foray into the Huddersfield 25 area, all the early pressure was from the Yorkshire side. Their winger Jock Anderson broke away, kicked and re-gathered, the ball coming loose a couple of times in the ensuing play before Mel Meek claimed it for Huddersfield. Although held, he transferred to the unmarked John Daly who strolled underneath the posts for the first score. Devery added the goal.

Warrington started opening out but without success; Brian Bevan and Jackie Fleming both

CHAMPION CAPTAIN

Pat Devery (Huddersfield 1949)

Australian international stand-off Pat Devery was a product of Tweed Heads in New South Wales and played for Fortitude Valley in the Brisbane competition before playing in the first grade for Balmain from 1944 to 1947, winning three Grand Finals (1944, 1946, 1947). Huddersfield secured his signature in September 1947 on a reported £7,000 contract. Described as a versatile and exciting all round player, he subsequently established himself in the centre at Fartown, where he won the Championship (1948/49), Rugby League Challenge Cup (1953), Yorkshire Cup (1952) and Yorkshire League (1948/49, 1949/50, 1951/52). In 1952/53, his 16 tries and 142 goals set a club record of 332 points in a season. Having represented Australia (3 times) and New South Wales (6), he gained further honours whilst at Huddersfield for Other Nationalities (11 appearances), Australasia (against Great Britain in the 'Festival of Britain' match at Headingley in 1951) and a United Kingdom XIII (versus a French XIII in Paris, 1951). He also joined the 'British Empire' party on a short tour of France in 1949. His last match for Huddersfield was in 1954, upon which he retired, returning to Australia.

Huddersfield's Welsh scrum half wizard Billy Banks

having near misses. The game was being played at a breakneck pace, the *Huddersfield Daily Examiner* saying that, 'though the tackling on both sides was grim the play was open.' Huddersfield completed the first half scoring, a length of field move involving Billy Banks and Devery saw the ball whipped out to Cooper who flew over in the corner. Devery missed the goal but the Fartowners went into the break 8–0 up.

After the restart, Huddersfield extended their lead when Anderson got a boot to a loose ball before dribbling past Les Jones, Devery – who demonstrated 'great leadership' throughout the match – appearing from nowhere to scoop up the ball and go between the posts. His goal built up a 13-point cushion. Eventually, Harold Palin got Warrington on the scoreboard with a penalty. A crucial decision then occurred after Bevan caught a ball that was kicked through by his centre Albert Pimblett, before racing clear for a certain try. Stand-in touch-judge Cowell, who was ironically from Warrington, put his flag up, claiming Bevan had stepped on to the sideline when making the catch, amidst protests from spectators and players alike. Warrington, though, was undeterred and Roy Francis eventually 'rolled over' for a try in the corner despite claims he dropped the ball. With Palin injured (he was carried off but returned despite limping badly) Bath added a tremendous touchline kick, making the score 13–7. With little time left there was a tension-filled finish, Warrington hogging possession as Huddersfield tired. But it was not until the final minutes that Bill Jackson finally found the opening for Wires' second try. Although Bath's goal made it 13–12, it was too late.

The *Warrington Guardian* said Huddersfield's players 'leapt into the air in joyous triumph' at the final whistle, adding: 'It would have been an injustice had Huddersfield lost the lead in those vital last seconds.'

STATS

Huddersfield 13 Warrington 12

Saturday 14 May at Maine Road, Manchester (3.00 pm)

Huddersfield: (white with claret and gold band) Hunter, Anderson, Ferguson, Devery (captain), Cooper, G.R. Pepperell, Banks, Maiden, Meek, Daly, Owens, Nicholson, Valentine. Coach: A. Fiddes

Warrington: (primrose and blue hoops) Jones, Bevan, Pimblett, Jackson, Francis, Fleming, Helme, Derbyshire, Fishwick, Riley, Bath, Featherstone, Palin (captain). Team manager: C. Brockbank

Half-time: 8–0 **Referee:** M. Coates
Attendance: 75,194 **Receipts**: £11,073

Weather: sunny with slight breeze

Progressive score:

Halifax	score (min)	Oldham
Huddersfield	score (min)	Warrington
Daly try, Devery goal	5–0 (-)	
Cooper try	8–0 (-)	
Devery try, Devery goal	13–0 (-)	
	13–2 (-)	Palin penalty
	13–7 (73)	Francis try, Bath goal
	13–12 (77)	Jackson try, Bath goal

League leaders	P	W	D	L	For	Agst	Pts
1 Warrington	36	31	0	5	728	247	62
2 Wigan	36	28	1	7	802	286	57
3 Huddersfield	36	27	0	9	626	290	54
4 Barrow	36	25	1	10	459	252	51

Semi-finals:
Warrington 23 Barrow 8
Wigan 5 Huddersfield 14

Head-to-head form guide:
Warrington 25 Huddersfield 2 (League)
Huddersfield 9 Warrington 11 (League)

Graham Morris

1950 Northern Rugby League Championship Final
WIGAN V HUDDERSFIELD

The *Wigan Examiner* headline declared the 1950 Championship Final as 'The finest Wigan victory of all time' and few could argue, their win being achieved without eight of their best players. The missing octet – Ernie Ashcroft, Tommy Bradshaw, Jack Cunliffe, Joe Egan, Ken Gee, Jack Hilton, Gordon Ratcliffe and Martin Ryan – who were with the Great Britain tour party in Australia, sent a telegram to their colleagues offering 'Best wishes for Saturday', asking for the result to be cabled back to them after the game. Their joy at reading the 20–2 score-line as it came off the wire later must have been mixed with feelings of astonishment. Opponents Huddersfield, on the other hand, had no players in the tour party, three of their star backs – John Hunter, Lionel Cooper and skipper Pat Devery – being Australian, their cosmopolitan side also including a South African, two Welshmen, an Irishman and three Cumbrians. Missing, though, through injury since March was centre Jim Bowden and loose forward Dave Valentine.

Brian Nordgren gave the Huddersfield defence an early warning when he beat three of them on a dazzling touchline run before being tackled. Moments later, team captain Cec Mountford cut through centres Geoff Bawden and Devery to link up with stand-in winger Nat Silcock. Normally a reserve second-row forward, Silcock powered over with only three minutes on the clock, Ted Ward adding the difficult, touchline kick. Knocked off their stride, somewhat, by the early try, the Fartowners made several handling errors. Wigan kept the pressure on, loose-forward Billy Blan – who lost five front teeth during the match – almost gaining a second touchdown before being pushed into touch at the corner. It got worse for Huddersfield when Nordgren nipped inside to intercept a pass in the Yorkshire side's half to score near the corner, another superb Ward conversion making it 10–0. Nordgren, then Blan, almost scored again before Huddersfield regained their composure as Dick Cracknell and Cooper both threatened to score, George

Winger Nat Silcock scores the opening try for Wigan within three minutes of the kick-off

CHAMPION CAPTAIN

Cec Mountford (Wigan 1950)

New Zealand stand-off Cec Mountford signed for Wigan in 1946, becoming one of the most dazzling halves seen in British rugby league. Born in Blackball, his fleet-footedness earned him the name 'The Blackball Bullet.' He went on to win the Championship (1946/47, 1949/50), Rugby League Challenge Cup (1948, 1951), Lancashire Cup (1946, 1948, 1949, 1950), and Lancashire League (1946/47, 1949/50). Having represented West Coast province and South Island in New Zealand, he appeared four times for Other Nationalities whilst with Wigan. He took over as captain at the conclusion of the 1949/50 term through Joe Egan's absence with the tourists, a role made permanent after the latter transferred to Leigh following the tour. He became Warrington coach in 1951, although it was the next year before Wigan agreed to his transfer as a player. His final match was in 1953 but he remained as their coach until 1961 before heading back to New Zealand. Apart from a spell as Blackpool Borough coach (1972–73), he continued to coach in New Zealand, including the national side (1979–82). In 1987 he received the MBE for services to New Zealand rugby league, becoming an inaugural member of New Zealand's Sports Hall of Fame in 1990.

STATS

Wigan 20 Huddersfield 2

Saturday 13 May at Maine Road, Manchester (3.00 pm)

Wigan: (cherry and white hoops) Ward, Silcock, Broome, Roughley, Nordgren, Mountford (captain), Alty, Slevin, McIntyre, Barton, Hudson, Large, W. Blan. Coach: J. Sullivan

Huddersfield: (white with claret and gold band): Hunter, Cracknell, Bawden, Devery (captain), Cooper, R. Pepperell, Banks, Daly, Mundy, Wilmot, Morrison, Nicholson, Owens. Coach: unknown

Half-time: 10–0 **Referee:** M. Coates
Attendance: 65,065 **Receipts**: £11,500

Weather: sunny and hot

Progressive score:

Wigan	score (min)	Huddersfield
Silcock try, Ward goal	5–0 (3)	
Nordgren try, Ward goal	10–0 (15)	
	10–2 (42)	Bawden penalty
Broome try, Ward goal	15–2 (68)	
W. Blan try, Ward goal	20–2 (75)	

League leaders	P	W	D	L	For	Agst	Pts
1 Wigan	36	31	1	4	853	320	63
2 Huddersfield	36	28	1	7	694	362	57
3 Swinton	36	25	4	7	516	261	54
4 Halifax	36	25	0	11	496	251	50

Semi-finals:
Wigan 5 Halifax 5
Huddersfield 9 Swinton 0
Replay: Halifax 2 Wigan 18

Head-to-head form guide:
Wigan 22 Huddersfield 12 (League)
Huddersfield 27 Wigan 8 (League)

Roughley twice producing excellent last-ditch tackles. As half-time approached, Bawden was wide with a long distance penalty attempt.

Two minutes after the interval, however, Bawden registered Huddersfield's first points with a successful penalty awarded for obstruction. But it was still Wigan that was the more forceful as Huddersfield began showing signs of tiredness. Despite dominating scrum possession Huddersfield's only route downfield was through kicking. The threat posed by their try-scoring machine Cooper was nullified by an efficient defensive display from Silcock. Wigan, almost inevitably, scored again, scrum half Johnny Alty bursting through a gap to free Jack Broome who outpaced the defence and used Silcock as a foil for a dummy pass before turning inside for a great try behind the posts. A fourth touchdown came when Ted Slevin created an opening for Blan to cross near the corner. Ward augmented both second half efforts to complete a resounding victory.

Wigan coach Jim Sullivan said after the match: 'We achieved success against what seemed impossible odds, all by first class teamwork and superior fitness and finish. I am very proud of them. What would we have felt like if Huddersfield with eight of their best players away had beaten us with a full team as we beat them today?' Tom Longworth, writing in the *News of the World* said: 'As a triumph against the odds it will become historic. I cannot recall anything to equal it.' The 65,000 attendance produced a record taking of £11,500, the highest for a match outside of Wembley.

Thirteen heroes! Wigan's make-shift line-up (from the left): Alty, McIntyre, Roughley, Slevin, Hudson, Barton, Broome, Large, Nordgren Ward, Silcock, W. Blan, Mountford

1951 Northern Rugby League Championship Final
WORKINGTON TOWN V WARRINGTON

The Championship trophy went to Cumberland for the only time following Workington Town's 'Fairy Tale' success over Warrington at Maine Road in 1951. Acclaimed in the *West Cumberland Times* as, 'this glorious chapter in the short life of the club', it climaxed six seasons of remarkable progress for Town. Founded in 1945, their rise to the summit proved a popular one amongst the rugby league fraternity, reflecting the mood of a post-war Britain seeking a new beginning. Workington put out their strongest 13, Warrington's Bill Jackson replacing centre Ron Ryder (injured in the play-off semi-final against Leigh) with Austin Heathwood preferred at loose forward to Owen Bevan (brother of winger Brian) despite the latter being 'declared fit' following injury.

Thousands of Cumbrian fans travelled southwards to Manchester to see Workington wear down a gallant Warrington, reduced to 12 players after eight minutes when Albert Johnson fell awkwardly after cutting inside, succumbing to a two man tackle. Later realised to be a broken tibia, it was a career ending leg injury. Moments earlier Bill Derbyshire tore his right shoulder ligaments, courageously remaining on the field but struggling in loose play, whilst Ally Naughton, too, became handicapped by a pulled leg muscle. But Warrington overcame their difficulties, making a match of it to lead 8–3 at half-time.

Workington, on top for the opening 10 minutes, started losing possession as Warrington, recovering from their early crisis, produced the attacking, skilful rugby that earned the League leadership. Loose forward Heathwood, at left wing in Johnson's place, put them ahead after 25 minutes with a try, disputed as not being grounded properly. There was little doubt about Jackson's touchdown seven minutes later, mesmerising Town's defence with a spectacular sidestep to score near the posts after good work from half-back's Bryn Knowelden and Gerry Helme. Harry Bath augmented for an 8–0 lead. Town reduced the arrears just before half-time, Gus Risman linking up as extra man for Tony Paskins to go racing over. Johnny Lawrenson, who missed two earlier penalties, failed with the conversion.

STATS

Workington Town 26 Warrington 11

Saturday 12 May at Maine Road, Manchester (3.00 pm)

Workington Town: (white with royal blue band) Risman (captain), Lawrenson, Paskins, Gibson, Wilson, Thomas, A. Pepperell, Hayton, McKeating, Wareing, Mudge, Thurlow, Ivison. Player-manager: A.J. Risman

Warrington: (primrose and blue narrow hoops): Frodsham, Bevan, Jackson, A. Naughton, Johnson, Knowelden (captain), Helme, Derbyshire, Fishwick, Atherton, Bath, Ryan, Heathwood. Team manager: C. Brockbank

Half-time: 3–8 **Referee:** A. Hill
Attendance: 61,618 **Receipts**: £10,993

Weather: very hot and sunny

Progressive score:

Workington Town	score (min)	Warrington
	0–3 (25)	Heathwood try
	0–8 (32)	Jackson try, Bath goal
Paskins try	3–8 (34)	
Gibson try, Risman goal	8–8 (43)	
Risman penalty	10–8 (48)	
Gibson try, Risman goal	15–8 (54)	
Lawrenson try	18–8 (59)	
Wilson try, Risman goal	23–8 (65)	
	23–11 (68)	Heathwood try
Wilson try	26–11 (71)	

League leaders	P	W	D	L	For	Agst	Pts
1 Warrington	36	30	0	6	738	250	60
2 Wigan	36	29	1	6	774	288	59
3 Workington Town	36	27	0	9	734	228	54
4 Leigh	36	24	2	10	420	288	50

Semi-finals:

Warrington 15 Leigh 9
Wigan 5 Workington Town 8

Head-to-head form guide:

Warrington 30 Workington Town 5 (League)
Workington Town 12 Warrington 8 (League)

Workington Town with the Championship trophy. Standing: J. Wilson (trainer), Ivison, Thurlow, Mudge, McKeating, Hayton, Wareing, T. Currie (secretary). Seated: Paskins, J. Graves (chairman), Risman, W. Walker (director), Gibson. On ground: Lawrenson, Pepperell, Thomas, G. Wilson

A different Workington emerged for the second half, their forwards taking control against Warrington's five-man pack. It opened the game up for some sizzling play from Town's backs. Lawrenson made a long run down the right flank before being tackled, possession from the play-the-ball switching quickly infield, Eppie Gibson bursting through near the posts. Risman goaled, adding an easy penalty after Ike Fishwick transgressed to put Town 10–8 ahead. A dazzling move involving Jacky Thomas and Gibson saw the latter grab his second try, Risman again converting. Lawrenson then claimed their third after Gibson and Paskins created the opening. Loose forward Billy Ivison, who suffered what was later confirmed as a broken jaw after 50 minutes, delivered the perfect dummy before George Wilson went through a confused defence to score in the corner, Risman landing a great touchline effort for a 23–8 lead. Warrington, although tiring, rallied gamely, Heathwood, outwitting three opponents, claiming his second score. Workington's triumph was sealed with a superb move involving Jimmy Hayton, Johnny Mudge and Wilson, the latter escaping Brian Bevan's clutches to register the ninth and concluding try of the final for a 26-11 victory.

CHAMPION CAPTAIN

Gus Risman (Salford 1937, 1939, Bradford Northern 1941, Dewsbury 1942, Workington Town 1951)

Gus Risman was one of rugby league's greatest performers, the gifted Welsh back being inducted into Rugby League's Hall of Fame in 1988. Born in Cardiff, he signed for Salford aged 17 in 1929, having played rugby union for Dinas Powis and Cardiff Scottish. With Salford, where he became captain in 1935, he won the Championship (1932/33, 1936/37, 1938/39), Rugby League Challenge Cup (1938), Lancashire Cup (1931, 1934, 1935, 1936) and Lancashire League (1932/33, 1933/34, 1934/35, 1936/37, 1938/39). He set club records that stood until the 1970s for goals (796) and points (2,021) in a career, and goals (116) and points (277) in a season (both 1933/34), twice landing 13 goals in a match (1933, 1940), a feat not exceeded until 2003. Risman toured three times (1932, 1936, 1946), the latter as captain. He made 17 Test appearances and represented Wales (18 times), England (1) and Glamorgan & Monmouthshire (3). During the Second World War, he was a guest for several clubs, winning the Championship (Bradford Northern 1940/41, Dewsbury 1941/42), Rugby League Challenge Cup (Leeds 1942), and Yorkshire Cup (Bradford Northern 1941). In 1946, he transferred to Workington Town for £750 as player-coach, leading them to success in the Championship (1950/51) and Rugby League Challenge Cup (1952). Again, he established club records for goals (716) and points (1,531) in a career, and goals (138) and points (294) in a season (both 1953/54), unchallenged until the late 1970s. He left Town in 1954, playing nine matches for Batley that year before retiring. He later coached Oldham, Bradford Northern and Salford.

Workington team manager and captain Gus Risman

1952 Northern Rugby League Championship Final
WIGAN V BRADFORD NORTHERN

The Championship Final was taken to its third soccer venue in 1952, Huddersfield Town AFC's Leeds Road ground providing the setting for the first peacetime decider in Yorkshire since 1938. It was a match that brought the curtain down on the great Wigan side of the post-Second World War period and provided the swansong for what, at the time, had been Bradford Northern's best ever team. The 48,684 attendance was considered disappointing, it being claimed the setting of a 55,000 ceiling had discouraged many from travelling.

Wigan threatened from the start, their star-studded back division being particularly potent, despite the absence of centre Ernie Ashcroft who had picked up an ankle sprain in the semi-final victory over Hull. Much of their attacking threat came through full-back Martin Ryan, linking up as the extra man to outflank the Northern defence. As expected, Bradford's pack, ably led by Barry Tyler and Ken Traill, caused most concern. Their backs, missing centre and skipper Ernest Ward – out with an injured shoulder – never got into their stride, Len Haley's lack of pace at stand-off being cited as the root cause. Although hardly pressurising Wigan's line throughout the 80 minutes, Northern did manage to take the lead on two occasions; with the first points of each half, courtesy of full-back Joe Phillips' boot, his three penalties being his side's only contribution to the score.

Wigan wingman Brian Nordgren posed the first danger when he crossed the Bradford line but was judged to have stepped in touch. It was Bradford, via the first of Phillips' penalties that took the lead after an offside decision with a quarter of the match gone. It lasted five minutes, a quick Wigan tap-penalty – awarded through Traill being pulled up for not allowing Nordgren to play the ball – catching Bradford napping, Nat Silcock putting the ball down near the posts, Ken Gee converting. Phillips' second goal, after Johnny Alty was penalised at a scrum, rang up a half-time score of 5–4 in Wigan's favour.

The break seemed to recharge Bradford's batteries for the resumption, their pack gaining

Runners-up Bradford, looking resplendent in their club blazers! Standing: Foster, Shreeve, N. Haley, Mageen, Smith, Traill, Radford, Tyler. Seated: Jenkins, Seddon, Hastings, E. Ward, Phillips, McLean, Hawes. On floor: L. Haley, Jones, Dickson, Greaves

more possession and looking more intimidating. Phillips' third penalty restored their lead but, as in the opening half, they did not retain it long. Gee failed with a penalty but then Alty got the Cherry and White's moving again with a tremendous break, after which Nordgren and Jack Large – generally considered the final's outstanding player – both came close to crossing Northern's line. Gee, making up for his earlier miss, eventually put Wigan ahead once more with a penalty. It was a lead they did not lose, adding two further tries from Jack Cunliffe (making a brilliant break to score in the left corner) and Ryan (created by a neat Alty pass in virtually the last move of the match) to assure victory, 13-6. Gee missed the extras, but Wigan fans were in a forgiving mood as they celebrated a fourth post-war title and a record ninth overall.

The final was not noted as a classic game, one journalist even describing it as 'uninspiring.' Even so, Wigan, who produced a surprise by naming George Woosey at prop instead of Frank Barton, could view it as a job well done. As *Daily Mirror* writer Joe Humphries pointed out: 'Wigan's new tactics surprised and fooled Bradford Northern. Bradford had not planned on Wigan's "get the ball and keep moving" policy – every man holding the ball and making headway instead of getting the ball to the wings.' Sidelined Bradford captain Ward, commented: 'Whenever a Wigan player got the ball he set out to make ten or twelve yards with it. That was one thing we never planned for.'

Wigan's Nat Silcock charges over the line for the opening try

CHAMPION CAPTAIN

Jack Cunliffe (Wigan 1952)

Jack Cunliffe was only 17 years old when he signed for his local club Wigan from Newtown Legion in 1939, playing his final match in 1960, over 20 years and 447 matches later. Originally a stand-off, he earned a reputation as a fine utility back, proving just as effective as a centre and, particularly, full-back, where his skilful attacking play from deep caused consternation in many defences. His honours with Wigan included the Championship (1945/46, 1946/47, 1949/50 – missing the final due to touring, 1951/52, 1959/60 – although not selected for the final), Rugby League Challenge Cup (1951, 1958), Lancashire Cup (1949, 1950, 1951), and Lancashire League (1945/46, 1946/47, 1949/50, 1951/52). He was a tourist twice (1950, 1954), appeared in four Tests for Great Britain (captain once), and selected seven times each for England and Lancashire.

STATS

Wigan 13 Bradford Northern 6

Saturday 10 May at Leeds Road, Huddersfield (3.00 pm)

Wigan: (cherry and white hoops) Ryan, Hilton, Broome, Roughley, Nordgren, Cunliffe (captain), Alty, Gee, Mather, Woosey, Silcock, Large, Street. Coach: J. Sullivan

Bradford Northern: (white with red, amber and black band) Phillips, Hawes, Mageen, Hastings, McLean, L. Haley, Jones, Shreeve, N. Haley, Radford, Tyler, Foster (captain), Traill. Team manager: D. Rees

Half-time: 5–4 **Referee:** C.F. Appleton
Attendance: 48,684 **Receipts**: £8,215

Weather: cloudy and dry, strong wind

Progressive score:

Wigan	score (min)	Bradford Northern
	0–2 (20)	Phillips penalty
Silcock try, Gee goal	5–2 (25)	
	5–4 (34)	Phillips penalty
	5–6 (52)	Phillips penalty
Gee penalty	7–6 (62)	
Cunliffe try	10–6 (68)	
Ryan try	13–6 (80)	

League leaders	P	W	D	L	For	Agst	Pts
1 Bradford Northern	36	28	1	7	758	325	57
2 Wigan	36	27	1	8	750	296	55
3 Hull	36	26	1	9	552	393	53
4 Huddersfield	36	26	0	10	785	446	52

Semi-finals:

Bradford Northern 18 Huddersfield 15

Wigan 13 Hull 9

Head-to-head form guide:

Wigan 28 Bradford Northern 12 (Challenge Cup)

1953 Northern Rugby League Championship Final
ST HELENS V HALIFAX

St Helens climaxed their best campaign to date by winning the 1953 Championship Final 24–14 against Halifax at Maine Road, having led the League table, won the Lancashire League and been runners-up in the Challenge Cup and Lancashire Cup. It ended a remarkable first season under coach Jim Sullivan who, 12 months earlier, claimed the Championship with Wigan. The *St Helens Newspaper & Advertiser* said: 'It was fast and exciting, it was tough and rugged.

Halifax winger Brian Vierod attempts to hand off his opposite number Stan McCormick

And the better team won. No quarter was asked or given, but despite this, the game was fought out in a clean and sportsmanlike manner.' Certainly Halifax, after Saints raced ahead 13–2 after 22 minutes, recovered well to play a significant part in an entertaining game. Whilst the Yorkshiremen could not match St Helens' speed, they began producing the tight, efficient rugby they were renowned for, to the point where, with less than 30 minutes remaining, there were serious thoughts on the terraces of a comeback.

St Helens struck from the beginning, Reg Blakemore getting a clear run to the line in only the 4th minute after a lightening break from Peter Metcalfe, who beat several defenders in a cross-field move before handing to Stewart Llewellyn. The winger, finding his route to the corner blocked, turned inside before delivering the scoring pass. Metcalfe added the goal and – after a similar, failed attempt by Halifax's Tyssul Griffiths, who hit the post – landed a penalty. The scoreboard kept ticking, Griffiths being more successful with his second penalty shot, before, three minutes later, Duggie Greenall raced across the whitewash for another St Helens try off a Metcalfe pass, Don Gullick having made the break. Metcalfe's kick hit the post, Saints leading 10–2. Their third touchdown was just four minutes later, a reverse pass from Gullick to Greenall enabled the latter to go charging through, passing to Metcalfe for a simple run in. The woodwork played a part once more as Metcalfe's kick hit both post and crossbar before ricocheting out.

With the score at 13–2 the Thrum Hallers rolled up their sleeves. Griffiths had two penalty attempts, the second being successful. It preceded a series of threatening raids led by their robust pack, half-backs Ken Dean and Stan Kielty looking increasingly dangerous as a result. Harry Greenwood, a replacement for knee injury victim Les White, made a great 40-yard

CHAMPION CAPTAIN

Duggie Greenall (St Helens 1953)

Douglas 'Duggie' Greenall played for the Army Training Corps, being a cadet based at Rivington Road School, prior to signing for St Helens in 1946. He developed into a hard-running centre with a tough reputation, particularly for his defensive prowess. His final match for St Helens was his 487th, during which he won the Championship (1952/53, 1958/59), Rugby League Challenge Cup (1956), Lancashire Cup (1953) and Lancashire League (1952/53). He joined Wigan in 1960 but his stay was short, moving to Bradford Northern where he was player-coach in 1960/61, appearing in the first few matches of the season. A tourist in 1954, he appeared in eight international for Great Britain (including 4 Tests) and represented England (6 times), Lancashire (3) and a Northern Rugby League XIII (twice; versus New Zealand, 1955 and France, 1958).

St Helens captain Duggie Greenall receives the Championship trophy from Lord Derby, who is assisted by Rugby Football League secretary Bill Fallowfield (right)

run but, lacking support, was tackled by Glyn Moses. The try came, though, through Tommy Lynch just before half-time, Griffiths missing the conversion.

Griffiths opened the second half scoring with his third penalty, reducing the deficit to just four points, creating immense excitement amongst the crowd. Saints, however, clawed their way back, their forwards grabbing two tries in a four-minute burst just after the hour mark; Ray Cale dropped on the ball as a scrum turned near the Halifax line, playing it quickly forward to go over and score, then Blakemore dived in from acting half-back after Metcalfe was stopped short. Metcalf appended the latter. Moses rounded off the Saints scoring nine minutes from the finish, a real scorcher that covered 75 yards of slick passing down the right channel involving Greenall, Llewellyn and himself. Halifax gained a late consolation right on time through Jack Wilkinson, Griffiths adding the extra points.

One argument the final appeared to resolve was that of best half-back combination for the Saints, a debate that had raged for several months. Metcalfe and John Dickinson displayed excellent form after getting the nod over Jimmy Honey and George Langfield, all four being named in the 17–man squad.

STATS

St Helens 24 Halifax 14

Saturday 9 May at Maine Road, Manchester (3.00 pm)

St Helens: (white with red band) Moses, Llewellyn, Greenall (captain), Gullick, McCormick, Metcalfe, Dickinson, Prescott, Blakemore, Parr, Parsons, Bretherton, Cale. Coach: J. Sullivan

Halifax: (blue and white hoops) Griffiths, Vierod, Lynch, Creeney, Cook, Dean, Kielty, Condon, Ackerley (captain), Wilkinson, Fearnley, Greenwood, Clarkson. Coach: F. Dawson

Half-time: 13–7 **Referee:** A. Hill
Attendance: 51,083 **Receipts**: £11,500

Weather: very hot and sunny

Progressive score:

St Helens	score (min)	Halifax
Blakemore try, Metcalfe goal	5–0 (4)	
Metcalfe penalty	7–0 (13)	
	7–2 (15)	Griffiths penalty
Greenall try	10–2 (18)	
Metcalfe try	13–2 (22)	
	13–4 (31)	Griffiths penalty
	13–7 (39)	Lynch try
	13–9 (51)	Griffiths penalty
Cale try	16–9 (61)	
Blakemore try, Metcalfe goal	21–9 (64)	
Moses try	24–9 (71)	
	24–14 (79)	Wilkinson try, Griffiths goal

League leaders	P	W	D	L	For	Agst	Pts
1 St Helens	36	32	2	2	769	273	66
2 Halifax	36	29	2	5	620	309	60
3 Bradford Northern	36	28	0	8	700	329	56
4 Huddersfield	36	27	2	7	747	366	56

Semi-finals:
St Helens 46 Huddersfield 0
Halifax 18 Bradford Northern 16

Head-to-head form guide:
No previous meetings during season

1954 Northern Rugby League Championship Final
WARRINGTON V HALIFAX

Three days after their historic Challenge Cup Final replay at Odsal, Warrington and Halifax met for the third time in a fortnight to decide the Championship. In contrast to their drab 4–4 Wembley draw two weeks earlier, they produced an exhilarating contest; committed attack meeting equally keen defence. Warrington played without three injured regulars; captain and centre Ally Naughton (calf) and forwards Ted White (leg) and Sid Phillips (collar bone), the latter the son of leading referee George Phillips.

Halifax took four minutes to score the only try of the final, Stan Kielty stealing from Eric Frodsham's grasp as the Warrington full-back attempted to get the ball away from his line and transferring to prop John Thorley who went over from a yard out despite defenders clinging to him. Tyssul Griffiths appended the goal for a 5–0

It took just four minutes for Halifax's prop John Thornley to register the only try of the final

lead. Warrington responded when Harry Bath, having missed a penalty from almost halfway, made amends with another effort a minute later from a 30-yard angled shot. Halifax twice failed to restore their five-point cushion; Kielty's 20-yard drop-goal attempt not getting off the ground and Griffiths' penalty from halfway being poorly struck.

The Thrum Hall side, though, was attacking with venom, coming close to a second try, Tommy Lynch and Kielty both being hauled down within touching distance of the try-line. But it was Bath that got the next score with another penalty after Derek Schofield strayed offside. Warrington was, temporarily, reduced to 12 men, hooker Frank Wright needing attention, returning in time to see Griffiths land a 40-yard

STATS

Warrington 8 Halifax 7

Saturday 8 May at Maine Road, Manchester (3.00 pm)

Warrington: (white with primrose and blue bands) Frodsham (captain), B. Bevan, Challinor, Ryder, McCormick, Price, Helme, D. Naughton, Wright, Lowe, Bath, Heathwood, Ryan. Coach: C. Mountford

Halifax: (blue and white hoops) Griffiths, Daniels, Lynch, Todd, D. Bevan, Dean, Kielty, Thorley, Ackerley (captain), Wilkinson, Schofield, Fearnley, Clarkson. Coach: F. Dawson

Half-time: 4–7 **Referee:** A. Hill
Attendance: 36,519 **Receipts**: £9,076

Weather: sunny and windy

Progressive score:

Warrington	score (min)	Halifax
	0–5 (4)	Thorley try, Griffiths goal
Bath penalty	2–5 (10)	
Bath penalty	4–5 (24)	
	4–7 (27)	Griffiths penalty
Bath penalty	6–7 (51)	
Bath penalty	8–7 (64)	

League leaders	P	W	D	L	For	Agst	Pts
1 Halifax	36	30	2	4	538	219	62
2 Warrington	36	30	1	5	663	311	61
3 St Helens	36	28	2	6	672	297	58
4 Workington Town	36	29	0	7	604	333	58

Semi-finals:
Halifax 18 Workington Town 7
Warrington 11 St Helens 0

Head-to-head form guide:
Warrington 4 Halifax 4
(Challenge Cup at Wembley Stadium, London)
Warrington 8 Halifax 4
(Challenge Cup at Odsal Stadium, Bradford)

penalty for Halifax, Bath being offside. Both teams continued to move the ball and Arthur Daniels almost scored in the corner, being tackled short, although the *Halifax Courier* later argued that photographs proved 'a mistake was made.' As the interval approached, a 40-yard penalty strike by Bath sailed wide.

After the break, Griffiths had an early penalty chance to increase Halifax's 7–4 lead, grazing the wrong side of the post from 30 yards. Bath made no mistake from the 25-yard line when Kielty was penalised for scrum feeding. Warrington worked hard at getting wing ace Brian Bevan away but namesake Dai Bevan was equal to the task, his policing of the Australian being one of the final's outstanding features. With both defences vigilant, goal attempts became a key factor as time got short. Bath was wide with a penalty just outside the 25-yard line and Halifax's Des Clarkson, with a mighty long-distance effort against the wind, hit the post. The pace was relentless, the covering and tackling of both being immaculate. Bath eventually nosed the Wires ahead for the first time, 8-7, with an easy 64th minute penalty awarded against Kielty.

The excitement mounted when Gerry Helme went on one of his will-o'-the-wisp runs beating several defenders before passing to Stan McCormick. The wingman turned infield before aiming a perfect cross-field kick to the opposite flank where Brian Bevan caught the ball on the bounce to race clear. Referee Alf Hill controversially ruled Bevan offside. It was the closest Warrington came to a try. As the tension built Kielty tried to snatch victory for Halifax with two drop-goals. The first just short, the second smothered by an alert defence. A minute from time, Griffiths had one last chance but, agonisingly for Halifax, his penalty attempt swerved wide at the crucial moment as it caught in the wind, grazing the outside of the post.

Although Warrington had greater pace amongst the backs, the *Warrington Guardian's* Jack Steel believed 'Halifax were the better side this time' crediting Wires success to the boot of 'Balmain bombshell' Harry Bath. Nonetheless, they could proudly claim the first Championship-Challenge Cup double since Swinton in 1928.

CHAMPION CAPTAIN

Eric Frodsham (Warrington 1954)

Signed by hometown club St Helens in 1947, following four years in the Royal Navy, Eric Frodsham subsequently appeared in 33 consecutive matches at full-back, before transferring in 1948. His destination was Warrington where, after two years in the reserves, he established himself as a regular first choice. Building a reputation as a sound, steady, fearless defender, he was the perfect deputy as captain for the unlucky Ally Naughton at the climax to the 1953/54 season, leading his charges to success in the Championship and Rugby League Challenge Cup. He received further winners' medals for the Championship (1954/55), plus the Lancashire League (1950/51, 1953/54, 1954/55, 1955/56). An injured wrist curtailed his career in 1956, his sole representative honour being for Lancashire against New Zealand in 1955. He had four brothers that played, two also commencing their careers at St Helens.

WARRINGTON RUGBY FOOTBALL CLUB

Back Row:—*E. White, S. Phillips, R. Ryan, G. Lowe, J. Challinor, A. Stevens, A. Humphreys, B. Bevan, H. Fishwick.*
Sitting:—*W. Sheridan, A. Heathwood, D. Naughton, S. McCormick, A. Naughton, C. Mountford, E. Frodsham, R. Ryder, H. Bath, F. Wright.*
Front:—*R. L. CHAMPIONSHIP CUP ; R. Price, R. L. CHALLENGE CUP ; G. Helme, LANCS. LEAGUE CUP.*

Warrington's success was acclaimed on this postcard

1955 Northern Rugby League Championship Final WARRINGTON V OLDHAM

Warrington – appearing at Maine Road for the fifth time in a Championship Final – retained their crown in 1955 after playing in some of the worst conditions imaginable. The exciting prospect of a Warrington-Oldham decider – the two teams having topped the League table with virtually identical records – was literally dampened by two near-tropical downpours during the morning. By noon the pitch looked unplayable and there were doubts about whether it could go ahead. Thankfully, there was a slight improvement about one hour before kick-off time although, as the *Warrington Guardian's* Jack Steel noted 'Mackintoshes and umbrellas were greatly in evidence on the open terraces.'

Oldham centre Alan Davies prepares to take evasive action against Warrington's Brian Bevan

Warrington was without stand-off Ray Price, out for several weeks with a badly sprained wrist, Jimmy Honey continuing as his deputy. Oldham selected from a full squad excepting suspended second-row Arthur Tomlinson. They also elected to continue their experiment tried in the semi-final win over Leeds; wingman Dick Cracknell moving to centre with Roland Barrow coming in on the flank, effectively costing John Etty his centre slot.

Oldham quickly justified their reputation as a dazzling ball-handling combination. Within five minutes Warrington was controversially let off the hook after Barrow had charged down the right flank from 10 yards out to dive over the line as Warrington full-back Eric Frodsham made the tackle. Referee Alf Hill signalled the try, changing his verdict after the touch-judge ruled he hit the corner flag. Barrow claimed he grounded correctly before being pushed into the flag, the *Oldham Evening Chronicle* saying the player 'emphatically stated that it was a fair and proper try.' Undeterred, the Roughyeds continued to look the 'more purposeful' side, although some doubted Oldham could continue the pace of their 'thrill-a-minute' rugby given the difficult conditions.

But it was Warrington, against the run of play that got the first try. Harry Bath retrieved the ball after a Frank Daley fumble, breaking away on a powerful diagonal run to the line and brushing off two defenders in his wake before transferring to Jim Challinor. The centre provided an inside pass for Brian Bevan who

CHAMPION CAPTAIN

Ally Naughton (Warrington 1955)

Albert (Ally) Naughton joined his hometown Widnes club in 1947, but the powerful, bustling centre soon attracted the attention of Warrington who signed him up in 1949 for a Rugby League record £4,600. He was in the Challenge Cup Final winning side of 1950 but suffered disappointment at the climax of the 1953/54 season, when a calf injury robbed him of his place for the Championship and Challenge Cup Finals successes. He made up for that setback by leading Warrington to success in the 1954/55 Championship Final, also winning the Lancashire Cup (1959) and Lancashire League (1950/51, 1953/54, 1954/55, 1955/56). He played for Great Britain in the inaugural 1954 World Cup in France, taking part in two matches, including the victorious Final against the hosts. He also appeared in two other internationals for Britain, represented England (3 times), Lancashire (8 – including 3 whilst at Widnes), a United Kingdom XIII (versus a French XIII, 1951) and a Northern Rugby League XIII (New Zealand, 1955). His last match was the 1961 Championship Final defeat by Leeds. He had two brothers who also played for Widnes, one of whom – Danny – followed him to Warrington.

STATS

Warrington 7 Oldham 3

Saturday 14 May at Maine Road, Manchester (3.00 pm)

Warrington: (white with primrose and blue bands) Frodsham, Bevan, Challinor, A. Naughton (captain), Horton, Honey, Helme, D. Naughton, McKinney, Lowe, Phillips, Bath, Ryan. Coach: C. Mountford

Oldham: (red and white hoops) Stirrup, Barrow, Cracknell, Davies (captain), O'Grady, Daley, Pitchford, Ogden, Keith, Jackson, Winslade, Little, Goldswain. Coach: G. Jenkins

Half-time: 3–3 **Referee:** A. Hill
Attendance: 49,434 **Receipts**: £11,516

Weather: heavy rain at times with strong wind; ground very muddy

Progressive score:

Warrington	score (min)	Oldham
Bevan try	3-0 (23)	
	3–3 (34)	Pitchford try
Bath penalty	5–3 (47)	
Bath penalty	7–3 (74)	

League leaders	P	W	D	L	For	Agst	Pts
1 Warrington	36	29	2	5	718	321	60
2 Oldham	36	29	2	5	633	313	60
3 Leeds	36	26	2	8	667	378	54
4 Halifax	36	26	1	9	579	269	53

Semi-finals:
Warrington 17 Halifax 9
Oldham 25 Leeds 6

Head-to-head form guide:
Oldham 8 Warrington 12 (League)
Warrington 18 Oldham 4 (League)

rebounded off several players and, although held by Frank Stirrup, forced his way over. Bath missed the goal. Oldham would not lie down, though, Cracknell and Alan Davies both coming near to scoring. Eventually Frank Pitchford got the equaliser, jinking over for a try after the ball emerged from a scrum near the Warrington line. Bryn Goldswain's goal attempt went under the bar and, with Bath missing two penalty attempts, the score remained 3–3 for the interval.

The second half was played out in a mud-bath, rain starting to fall heavily just before the interval. Under a darkened sky the players appeared wearing fresh, dry kit, to a pitch submerged in water. Warrington adapted much better to the conditions in the last 40 minutes, as both sets of players began 'skating around in the mud.' As the light improved, Bath put the Wire in front again with a superb 30-yard penalty for offside at a play-the-ball. Chances were being lost at both ends, Warrington sensibly electing to play low-risk rugby with close, conservative passing movements. Points were at a premium; Goldswain (two) and Bath (one) missing penalties, Bevan almost getting over for a try before being pushed into the corner flag by three defenders. Bath got the final score, his penalty, when captain Ally Naughton was obstructed after kicking ahead, making it 7–3. In the final minutes, Gerry Helme almost got Len Horton over, but the winger, like so many before him, slipped.

Smiling through the mud as victorious Warrington skipper Ally Naughton holds the cup up. The other players, from the left, are: Danny Naughton, Horton (almost obscured), McKinney, Helme, Ryan, Frodsham, Phillips, Bath, Challinor, Honey, Bevan, Lowe. An unidentified youngster holds the plinth

1956 Northern Rugby League Championship Final
HULL V HALIFAX

The Championship Final of 1956 ended in pure drama. A match that could have gone either way came down to one last goal kick from Hull full-back Colin Hutton. With the score 9–8 in Halifax's favour and time almost up, the Airlie Birds skipper Mick Scott handed Hutton the ball after referee Charlie Appleton awarded a penalty. But it was not an easy angle by any means, being out on the right touchline. As the hushed crowd watched with bated breath, Hutton, with one of the most vital goals of his career, sent the ball sailing through the uprights just inside the far post to claim a sensational 10–9 victory.

Halifax began as favourites having already beaten Hull in a replayed Yorkshire Cup Final, and considered to have the superior back division. But, with Tommy Harris dominating the scrums, Hull's mighty pack was generally able to dictate in a match full of incident. They looked a good bet to walk away with the trophy after bossing the opening period, although ahead only 5–0 at half-time. It was Harris on the half-hour that opened the scoring with a try under the posts, Bob Coverdale, although held, getting his pass away to Johnny Whiteley who put the Welsh hooker through. Hutton added the goal. Prior to that, there had been penalty misses by Hutton (twice – the latter touching the outside of the post) and Halifax's Billy Briers (once) whilst John Watkinson (Hull) and Johnny Freeman (Halifax) had both crossed the opposition line but prevented from getting the ball down. With half-time approaching, potential disaster hit Hull when winger Brian Darlington injured his knee when being tackled by Freeman. He left the field hobbling badly, returning before the interval barely able to walk.

CHAMPION CAPTAIN

Mick Scott (Hull 1956)

Local-born Mick Scott signed for Hull in 1948 from Boulevard Juniors, becoming the linchpin of their formidable pack of the 1950s. He was in the Championship winning sides of 1955/56 and 1957/58, but shared the frustration of losing in seven other major finals with Hull, including two for the Challenge Cup at Wembley. He was selected for England (3 times – the first when aged 19), Yorkshire (16), an Empire XIII (against a Welsh XIII, 1951) and a Northern Rugby League XIII (versus France, 1956). Having appeared in 459 matches for Hull, he joined Rochdale Hornets in 1963, playing his final game in 1964.

Eight minutes after the resumption, Halifax paid for an error after their loose forward Ken Traill broke down the blind side. He transferred to Arthur Daniels who, faced by an opponent, sent a high pass intended for Tommy Lynch but Hull's Tommy Finn intercepted to flash across the try-line at the corner. Hutton missed the goal. Halifax, 8–0 down and second-best for most of the match, woke up, taking control with a spirited rally to score three tries through Geoff Palmer (pushing Hutton aside and resisting a late double-tackle on a charge to the line off a

Hull pose for the press on the Maine Road pitch before taking on Halifax. Back: Hutton, Coverdale, J. Whiteley, W. Drake, Markham, Cooper, Watkinson, Bowman. Front: Darlington, Turner, Scott, Finn, Harris

Ken Dean pass), Daniels (from a long wide pass off Lynch who had recovered a dropped ball on the Hull line), and Freeman (after Traill had whipped the ball across). Halifax, incredibly, had turned the match round to grab a 9–8 lead. How much they missed reliable goal-kicking full-back Tyssul Griffiths (out with a broken cheekbone) when his deputy Briars missed all three conversions was apparent in the closing minutes, although, to be fair, none were particularly easy.

The fateful moment when Hutton (who grazed the outside of the post with a difficult penalty attempt prior to Halifax's last try) won the match for Hull almost never occurred. In the build-up, Darlington, still a passenger on the wing, made a brave dash down the flank being, predictably, brought down five yards from the try-line. The chance appeared lost but as he played the ball, Appleton spotted several defenders offside. Hull skipper Scott told *Daily Mirror* journalist Joe Humphreys that his first thought was to take a quick tap penalty and try to force a way over the line, adding: 'I almost had a go. But I decided to keep my word to Colin (Hutton). At Half-time he told me "Let me have any penalties in their half – we've got the wind."'

Whilst it was Hull's first Championship success in 20 years, it was Halifax's third defeat in four seasons at Maine Road, the latter two completing an unwanted double having also lost in the Challenge Cup Final.

STATS

Hull 10 Halifax 9

Saturday 12 May at Maine Road, Manchester (3.00 pm)

Hull: (black with white chevron) Hutton, Darlington, Cooper, Watkinson, Bowman, Turner, Finn, Scott (captain), Harris, Coverdale, Markham, W. Drake, J. Whiteley. Coach: R. Francis

Halifax: (white with blue chevron) Briers, Daniels, Lynch, Palmer, Freeman, Dean, Kielty, Thorley, Ackerley (captain), Wilkinson, Henderson, Schofield, Traill. Coach: F. Dawson

Half-time: 5–0
Referee: C.F. Appleton
Attendance: 36,675
Receipts: £9,179

Weather: fine and dry with strong wind

Progressive score:

Hull	score (min)	Halifax
Harris try, Hutton goal	5–0 (30)	
Finn try	8–0 (48)	
	8–3 (50)	Palmer try
	8–6 (57)	Daniels try
	8–9 (72)	Freeman try
Hutton penalty	10–9 (78)	

League leaders	P	W	D	L	For	Agst	Pts	Percent
1 Warrington	34	27	1	6	712	349	55	80.88
2 Halifax	36	28	2	6	761	306	58	80.55
3 St Helens	34	27	0	7	766	351	54	79.41
4 Hull	36	25	1	10	720	458	51	70.83

Semi-finals:
Warrington 0 Hull 17
Halifax 23 St Helens 8

Head-to-head form guide:
Hull 13 Halifax 7 (League)
Halifax 10 Hull 10 (Yorkshire Cup at Headingley, Leeds)
Halifax 7 Hull 0 (Yorkshire Cup at Odsal Stadium, Bradford)
Halifax 27 Hull 6 (League)

Halifax captain Alvin Ackerley

1957 Northern Rugby League Championship Final
OLDHAM V HULL

The classy Oldham side of the 1950s bridged a 46-year gap by lifting the Championship trophy in 1957, the club's first since 1911. In front of a 62,199 attendance that generated record Championship Final receipts of £12,054, Hull just failed to retain their title following a titanic battle that, like the previous year, produced a cliff-hanger finish.

On a firm pitch – unlike the heavy conditions that accompanied their defeat by Warrington in the 1954/55 Championship decider – League leaders Oldham, with their brilliant backs, were favoured to get the better of a Hull side whose strength lay firmly with their forwards. As he had 12 months before, hooker Tommy Harris dominated the scrum count, ensuring the Airlie Birds pack controlled much of the first half as Oldham, starved of the ball, struggled to mount a meaningful attack. A Colin Hutton penalty for offside quickly put Hull two points up and it was the 24th minute before Oldham responded. Their winger John Etty – put through by a Frank Pitchford pass after a Charlie Winslade break – escaped Harris' grip to race towards the left corner. As he reached the try-line he veered inside to place the ball closer to the posts giving Bernard Ganley an easier kick. Ganley, the ace marksman who led the team in place of out of form club captain and stand-off Frank Stirrup, duly obliged and converted the try. Etty's foresight in virtually guaranteeing the extra two

STATS

Oldham 15 Hull 14

Saturday 18 May at Odsal Stadium, Bradford (3.00 pm)

Oldham: (red and white hoops) Ganley (captain), Cracknell, Davies, Ayres, Etty, Daley, Pitchford, Jackson, Keith, Vines, Little, Winslade, D. Turner. Coach: G. Jenkins

Hull: (black and white irregular hoops) Hutton, Cowan, Dannatt, C. Turner, Watts, Moat, Finn, Scott, Harris, J. Drake, Sykes, W. Drake, J. Whiteley (captain)
Coach: R. Francis

Half-time: 5–6 **Referee:** M. Coates
Attendance: 62,199 **Receipts**: £12,054

Weather: overcast and dry at first, started raining just before half-time

Progressive score:

Oldham	score (min)	Hull
	0–2 (2)	Hutton penalty
Etty try, Ganley goal	5–2 (24)	
	5–4 (29)	Hutton penalty
	5–6 (40)	Hutton drop-goal
	5–11 (45)	C. Turner try, Hutton goal
Ganley penalty	7–11 (51)	
Ayres try, Ganley goal	12–11 (58)	
Etty try	15–11 (75)	
	15–14 (77)	Cowan try

League leaders	P	W	D	L	For	Agst	Pts
1 Oldham	38	33	0	5	893	365	66
2 Hull	38	29	2	7	764	432	60
3 Barrow	38	29	0	9	702	481	58
4 Leeds	38	28	0	10	818	490	56

Semi-finals:
Oldham 22 Leeds 12
Hull 45 Barrow 14

Head-to-head form guide:
No previous meetings during season

The ball goes wide to Hull winger Stan Cowan, despite the efforts of Oldham number '5' John Etty

CHAMPION CAPTAIN

Bernard Ganley (Oldham 1957)

Bernard Ganley joined Oldham in 1950, making his debut the following year. Signed from the Leigh Spinners amateur club, the assured, reliable full-back was to prove an ace marksman, scoring a, then, world record 219 goals in all matches during 1957/58. He also set club records – still unbeaten – of 14 goals in a match (1959), 200 goals and 412 points in a season (both 1957/58) and 1,365 goals and 2,775 points in a career. He gained winners' medals with Oldham for the Championship (1956/57), Lancashire Cup (1956, 1957, 1958), and Lancashire League (1956/57, 1957/58). Ganley, who played his final match for the club in 1961, represented Great Britain and Lancashire 3 times each. His father Bert was a half-back with Leigh, Huddersfield and Leeds during the 1910s/20s.

points would later prove crucial. Hull chipped away at the scoreboard, Hutton notching two more goals before half-time; a penalty (for a scrum offence) and drop-kick. His efforts sandwiched a missed try by Oldham when Derek Turner, following a penetrating break by winger Dick Cracknell, was frustrated in his attempt to place the ball over the line. After an uninspired opening half, Hull led 6–5.

After the restart, the Boulevard side took just five minutes to score their first try when Carl Turner, having been put through a gap by Johnny Whiteley, raced clear to score under the posts, despite attention from Dennis Ayres. Hutton added the goal and at 11–5, the signs looked ominous for Oldham. A slice of luck played a key part when referee Matt Coates awarded Oldham a penalty when Hull's Cyril Sykes did not play the ball correctly, although it became apparent that he was struggling through being injured in the tackle. As a result, Ganley, with a magnificent strike from near halfway, pulled two points back. Now only four points adrift, it positioned the Roughyeds for an all-out assault as fresh belief surged through the team. Prop Don Vines broke through Hull's ranks to send Alan Davies haring away, Ayres taking up the running to score by the posts. Ganley's goal sneaked Oldham 12–11 in front.

Oldham was now dictating play and Sid Little made another burst but his 'scoring' pass to Pitchford was judged forward. It was Pitchford, though, that was on hand minutes later when Hull's Stan Cowan lost the ball, retrieving to sprint away with Etty in support. The pair exchanged three quick passes as they drew in defenders before Etty scored by the corner flag, Ganley missing the tricky conversion attempt. The scenario was soon reversed when Pitchford threw out a long misdirected pass that Cowan recovered for a breakaway try, bringing Hull within one point at 15–14. Hutton, as at Maine Road a year earlier, took centre stage as he attempted to win the match with a kickable looking conversion. To everyone's amazement, Hutton, who racked up a club record 166 goals for the season, missed. There remained one final drama in the dying seconds, Hull's Mick Scott kicking the ball into the Oldham in-goal area, Etty just winning the race against Geoff Dannatt to clear the danger.

Oldham's Frank Pitchford and Charlie Winslade (12) get to grips with Hull centre Geoff Dannatt

1958 Northern Rugby League Championship Final
HULL V WORKINGTON TOWN

Hull made it to their third consecutive Championship Final in 1958, claiming their second title during that period, despite being without 50 percent of their regular pack. Like opponents Workington Town, their major strength lay in their forwards, the 20–3 victory they eventually achieved looking an unlikely bet before kick-off. Already short of Test hooker Tommy Harris (suspended for an alleged foul on Oldham's Frank Pitchford in the semi-final) and prop Jim Drake (knee cartilage problems), they suffered a massive blow through the late withdrawal of the latter's twin brother, second-row man Bill Drake, who stood down due to arthritic pain in an ankle.

To be fair, Workington – who had lost in the Challenge Cup Final the previous week – was also depleted, winger Bill Wookey, selected for the upcoming 1958 Great Britain tour, had a pulled leg muscle, and prop Andy Key failed a test on his ankle. Worse still for the Cumbrians was the 25th minute loss of ball-playing second-row Cec Thompson, carried off on a stretcher with torn leg ligaments, reducing them to a 12–man outfit for the remainder of the final.

As expected in a clash between two sides reliant on forward dominance, the opening half contained little flowing football, both defences being on top. Hull did attempt to give the ball some movement, Workington preferring a tighter approach with short passing amongst the pack. Having said that, Town had one of the countries finest wingmen in Ike Southward and he provided the afternoon's first threat when Thompson sent him on his way. Fortunately for Hull, their centre Brian Saville was able to haul him down from behind. Workington, using their forwards as battering rams, started to get on top. Scrum half Sol Roper scooted through a gap and almost made it to the Hull line but the chance was gone when a supporting colleague failed to take his pass.

Shortly afterwards they lost Thompson, injured making a tackle on Cyril Sykes. Although Workington battled bravely on, Hull looked more dangerous, their half-back Tommy Finn being particularly lively. They had a shock, though, when Town's Brian Edgar went charging

The Hull team on the Odsal pitch prior to the 1958 Championship Final. Back: Sykes, Holdstock, Saville, P. Whiteley, Dannatt, Bateson, Scott. Front: Cooper, Hambling, Finn, J. Whiteley, Watts, Broadhurst

through two defenders before sending Southward racing over the line. The winger failed to convert his score, the Cumbrians leading 3–0. Rather than encouraging Workington, the try lit Hull's blue touch-paper. Geoff Dannett should have scored for them but was repelled when trying to go under the posts when a run towards the flank looked a better bet. The try did come, though, Brian Cooper flying into the corner off a brilliant wide Mick Scott pass that cut out three defenders. Peter Bateson added a great goal and Hull led 5–3 at the break.

Workington fought hard to get on terms after the resumption, Southward (twice) and Ike Stamper (once – hitting the post with a massive 55-yarder) failing to land penalties. Depleted Town soon felt the strain, the Airlie Birds wrapping things up in a canter with in-form skipper Johnny Whiteley having a hand in all three of his team's second half tries. First he scored under the posts from acting half-back without hardly being touched, and then combined with younger brother, Peter, to put Scott over before, finally, sending Finn in for a brilliantly worked try. With Bateson converting all three it capped what, in the end, was a comprehensive victory.

Due to the enforced changes the Airlie Birds fielded an all Hull-born pack, coach Roy Francis saying: 'While I'm extremely sorry that the Drake twins and Tommy Harris were unable to play for various reasons, I was very, very proud of the performances of the A-team players, Alan (Holdstock) and Peter (Whiteley).'

CHAMPION CAPTAIN

Johnny Whiteley (Hull 1958)

Hull snapped up Johnny Whitely in 1950, the local born player emerging from the ranks of the Hull Boys' Club. An ability to run with the ball at pace and open up the tightest of defences with deadly accurate passing saw him develop into one of the outstanding loose forwards of his day. He toured in 1958, featured in three World Cup squads (1954, 1957, 1960 – although not called upon in the former), appeared in 15 Tests for Great Britain, represented England once and Yorkshire 11 times. He played 417 matches for Hull, the last being 1965, having twice won the Championship (1955/56, 1957/58). He did, however, suffer disappointment in seven major finals; Championship (once), Challenge Cup (twice) and Yorkshire Cup (4 times). He was Hull's player-coach from 1963, continuing as coach until 1970, whereupon he took over at Hull Kingston Rovers until 1972. At various times, he held the coaching reins of Great Britain, Great Britain under-24s, England and Yorkshire.

Mick Scott plunges over for Hull's third try

STATS

Hull 20 Workington Town 3

Saturday 17 May at Odsal Stadium, Bradford (3.00 pm)

Hull: (black and white irregular hoops) Bateson, Watts, Cooper, Saville, Dannatt, Broadhurst, Finn, Scott, Holdstock, Hambling, Sykes, P. Whiteley, J. Whiteley (captain). Coach: R. Francis

Workington Town: (white with royal blue band) McAvoy, Southward, O'Neill, Leatherbarrow, Faulder, Archer, Roper (captain), Herbert, Eden, Stamper, Edgar, Thompson, Eve. Team manager: J. Brough

Half-time: 5–3 **Referee:** R. Gelder
Attendance: 57,699 **Receipts**: £11,149

Weather: cloudy and dry; ground slippery from earlier rain

Progressive score:

Hull	score (min)	Workington Town
	0–3 (28)	Southward try
Cooper try, Bateson goal	5–3 (33)	
J. Whiteley try, Bateson goal	10–3 (51)	
Scott try, Bateson goal	15–3 (62)	
Finn try, Bateson goal	20–3 (66)	

League leaders	P	W	D	L	For	Agst	Pts
1 Oldham	38	33	1	4	803	415	67
2 St Helens	38	32	0	6	842	336	64
3 Workington Town	38	28	2	8	685	356	58
4 Hull	38	27	2	9	920	431	56

Semi-finals:
Oldham 8 Hull 20
St Helens 13 Workington Town 14

Head-to-head form guide:
No previous meetings during season

1959 Northern Rugby League Championship Final
ST HELENS V HUNSLET

Never had a player made such an impact in a Championship decider as Tom van Vollenhoven did on that May afternoon in 1959. He lifted St Helens to an incredible comeback victory against Hunslet in one of the best ever Championship Finals. As Tom Ashcroft wrote in the *St Helens Newspaper & Midweek Reporter*: 'What Saints did on the sun-baked turf of Odsal Stadium in 18 minutes of the 1959 League Championship Final will be told and re-told many years on.'

The team was trailing 12–4 to the Parksiders when, after 25 minutes, van Vollenhoven set off on, arguably, his most memorable scoring run. Taking possession some 70-odd yards from the Hunslet line, after neat passing from Wilf Smith, Duggie Greenall and Alex Murphy, very little space seemed available on the right touchline but his initial burst, having reduced speed to deceive a posse of forwards coming across to cover, took him past the first line of resistance. Shaking off full-back Billy Langton's tackle, he handed off another forward, sheer pace doing the rest before touching down near the posts. Austin Rhodes' goal left Saints 12–9 in arrears.

CHAMPION CAPTAIN

Alan Prescott (St Helens 1959)

Widnes-born Alan Prescott signed for Halifax as a winger in 1943 from his local club, St Marie's. As he matured, putting on weight, he was relocated to loose forward with some success, St Helens snapping him up for £2,275 in 1948. Saints soon moved him to prop forward, where his ability to provide precision passes to supporting colleagues came to the fore. His qualities of leadership led to the captaincy of St Helens in 1955 and, eventually, Great Britain. He gained several winners' medals with St Helens; Championship (1952/53, 1958/59), Rugby League Challenge Cup (1956), Lancashire Cup (1953) and Lancashire League (1952/53, 1959/60). He represented Great Britain in 31 Test and international fixtures, England (10 times) and Lancashire (15). He was a tourist in 1954 and captain of Britain's 1957 World Cup squad and 1958 touring side. During the latter, he famously played most of the Test against Australia in Brisbane with a broken right arm, leading his team to victory. He played his last match for St Helens in 1960, later coaching St Helens, Leigh and Workington Town. He made two guest appearances with Huddersfield during 1943/44.

By the time he completed his hat-trick in the 42nd minute, they led 27–12.

Ashcroft went on to say: 'I will not be shaken in the belief that Vollenhoven's first try was the match-winner. He took Saints from the depths of a black despair on to an overwhelming crusade to victory that must surely rank with all the great recoveries.' St Helens began poorly, two scoring opportunities being fluffed in the opening minutes. Two early penalties by their full-back Austin Rhodes, on the way to a Championship Final record 10 goals, was more than matched by tries from Jim Stockdill and Kevin Doyle. Langton converted both and added a penalty, thereby emulating the 26-year-old record of Widnes' Jimmy Hoey by playing and scoring in every match during the season.

As half-time approached van Vollenhoven got his second, cutting inside on a 30-yard run off a Greenall

Post-match changing room scenes as coach Jim Sullivan (with cup) savours the moment with Duggie Greenall (left) and Tom van Vollenhoven

STATS

St Helens 44 Hunslet 22

Saturday 16 May at Odsal Stadium, Bradford (3.00 pm)

St Helens: (white with red band) Rhodes, van Vollenhoven, Greenall, McGinn, Prinsloo, Smith, Murphy, Terry, McKinney, Prescott (captain), Briggs, Huddart, Karalius. Coach: J. Sullivan

Hunslet: (myrtle with flame and white bands) Langton, Colin, Stockdill, Preece, Walker, Gabbitas, Doyle, Hatfield, Smith, Eyre, Poole, Gunney, Shaw (captain). Coach: J. Walkington

Half-time: 24–12 **Referee:** G. Wilson
Attendance: 52,560 **Receipts**: £10,146

Weather: very hot and sunny

Progressive score:

St Helens	score (min)	Hunslet
Rhodes penalty	2–0 (3)	
	2–5 (8)	Stockdill try, Langton goal
Rhodes penalty	4–5 (11)	
	4–10 (14)	Doyle try, Langton goal
	4–12 (17)	Langton penalty
van Vollenhoven try, Rhodes goal	9–12 (25)	
Rhodes penalty	11–12 (29)	
Murphy try, Rhodes goal	16–12 (32)	
Prinsloo try	19–12 (35)	
van Vollenhoven try, Rhodes goal	24–12 (40)	
van Vollenhoven try	27–12 (42)	
Smith try, Rhodes goal	32–12 (44)	
	32–17 (58)	Gunney try, Langton goal
Rhodes penalty	34–17 (62)	
Murphy try, Rhodes goal	39–17 (67)	
	39–22 (71)	Poole penalty try, Langton goal
Huddart try, Rhodes goal	44–22 (79)	

League leaders	P	W	D	L	For	Agst	Pts
1 St Helens	38	31	1	6	1005	450	63
2 Wigan	38	29	0	9	894	491	58
3 Hunslet	38	27	3	8	819	493	57
4 Oldham	38	28	1	9	791	477	57

Semi-finals:
St Helens 42 Oldham 4
Wigan 11 Hunslet 22

Head-to-head form guide:
St Helens 31 Hunslet 15 (League)
Hunslet 19 St Helens 11 (League)

reverse pass, the third following a break by Murphy and Alan Prescott two minutes after the interval. The latter came despite a hamstring injury catching up with him, the South African flyer having been doubtful for the final after missing the semi-final win over Oldham. Daily treatment saw him declared fit, although his left thigh was heavily strapped.

The Saints garnered eight tries altogether, Murphy claiming two; from midfield (off a Vince Karalius reverse pass in the 32nd minute) and scooping up a dropped ball 70-yards out (67th minute). Another highlight was Jan Prinsloo's race into the corner five minutes before half-time, getting the ball down, despite the attentions of a defender, after a sizzling six-man move. Smith and Dick Huddart were responsible for the remaining two, both in the second half.

Hunslet contributed hugely to an entertaining match despite the adverse 44–22 score, claiming two further touchdowns through second-rowers Geoff Gunney and Harry Poole, the latter awarded for obstruction. The superior speed of St Helens was the telling factor. The Saints score was the highest in a Championship Final, their League campaign having provided a record 1,005 points surpassing Huddersfield's 996 in 1911/12. It was the last match in charge for Jim Sullivan, the coaching duties passing to triumphant skipper Prescott, recently back in action after prematurely retiring in mid-season.

St Helens supporters mob Tom van Vollenhoven after his sensational opening try

1960 Northern Rugby League Championship Final
WIGAN V WAKEFIELD TRINITY

Wigan and Wakefield Trinity clashed at the climax of the 1959/60 season, drawing the largest ever attendance to witness a Championship Final, 83,190 packing into Odsal's vast open terraces and stands. Almost 8,000 up on the previous best in 1949, it produced new record receipts of £14,482. Outside of Wembley, it stands as the second highest crowd, after the 1954 Challenge Cup Final replay, to watch a rugby league match in Britain.

On learning their team's unfamiliar back line-up, Wigan supporters must have harboured doubt about their ability to overcome Challenge Cup holders Wakefield, who had annihilated Hull 38–5 at Wembley the week before. Already forced into a reshuffle through Mick Sullivan's suspension after a squabble with St Helens' Alex Murphy in the play-off semi-final, they added more surprises when the team changes were announced before kick-off. International winger Sullivan had, unusually, played at stand-off against the Saints, regular incumbent David Bolton being at scrum half. At Odsal, Bolton unexpectedly retained that position with Terry Entwistle missing out, skipper Eric Ashton moving from centre to partner him. Billy Boston came off his familiar right flank to replace Ashton, reserve Frank Halliwell, in turn, filling in for Boston. Half-back Syd Fenton kept his

Billy Boston scored the first Wigan try just before half-time

STATS

Wigan 27 Wakefield Trinity 3

Saturday 21 May at Odsal Stadium, Bradford (3.00 pm)

Wigan: (red) Griffiths, Halliwell, Boston, Holden, Fenton, Ashton (captain), Bolton, Barton, Sayer, Collier, McTigue, Lyon, Evans. Coach: J. Egan

Wakefield Trinity: (white) Round, Smith, Skene, Fox, Etty, Rollin, Holliday, Wilkinson, Oakes, Vines, Firth, Chamberlain, Turner (captain). Coach: K. Traill

Half-time: 9–3 **Referee:** Eric Clay (Leeds)
Attendance: 83,190 **Receipts**: £14,482

Weather: cloudy, warm and dry

Progressive score:

Wigan	score (min)	Wakefield Trinity
	0–3 (2)	Smith try
Griffiths penalty	2–3 (8)	
Griffiths penalty	4–3 (22)	
Boston try, Griffiths goal	9–3 (39)	
Ashton try	12–3 (51)	
Griffiths penalty	14–3 (56)	
Sayer try, Griffiths goal	19–3 (61)	
Boston try, Griffiths goal	24–3 (67)	
Ashton try	27–3 (77)	

League leaders	P	W	D	L	For	Agst	Pts
1 St Helens	38	34	1	3	947	343	69
2 Wakefield Trinity	38	32	0	6	831	348	64
3 Hull	38	28	1	9	758	474	57
4 Wigan	38	27	2	9	828	390	56

Semi-finals:
St Helens 9 Wigan 19
Wakefield Trinity 24 Hull 4

Head-to-head form guide:
Wakefield Trinity 21 Wigan 14 (League)
Wigan 19 Wakefield Trinity 27 (League)

CHAMPION CAPTAIN

Eric Ashton (Wigan 1960)

Eric Ashton was one of rugby league's greatest ever centres, a classy player and magnificent captain and ambassador for club and country. After playing rugby league at school, he took up rugby union during his National Service with the Army, being selected for inter-services matches. Wigan was alerted, giving him a trial following his release in 1955. Signed immediately, he became club captain two years later. At Wigan his right wing partnership with Billy Boston became legendary, winning the Championship (1959/60), Rugby League Challenge Cup (1958, 1959, 1965), Lancashire Cup (1966), Lancashire League (1958/59, 1961/62), and BBC2 Floodlit Trophy (1968). Included in Great Britain's World Cup squad (1957 and 1960, captain/coach of the latter), and tour party (1958 and 1962, captain of the latter), he represented Britain in 28 internationals (captain 15 times), England (once) and Lancashire (10 times). Wigan player-coach from 1963, he remained coach until 1973 after retiring as a player in 1969 following 497 appearances. He later coached Leeds (1973–74), St Helens (1974–80), Great Britain (the 1979 tour), and England (1978–80). He received the MBE in 1966 and was elected to the Rugby League Hall of Fame in 2005.

recent place on the left wing. Another surprise was the swap round of regular prop Brian McTigue with second-row Frank Collier.

Wakefield – appearing in their first Championship Final – was missing influential stand-off Harold Poynton (shoulder injury) and upcoming forward Malcolm Sampson (motor accident), although both had able deputies in Ken Rollin and Len Chamberlain. However, Trinity suffered a massive 12th minute blow when centre and points-scoring machine Neil Fox was hurt, spending the remainder of the final limping on the left wing.

Despite being 9–3 to the good at half-time, Wigan, possibly due to their many positional changes, seemed edgy during the opening half and not at their best in the tense, excitable atmosphere generated by the huge crowd. Wakefield scored after two minutes when Fred Smith put the ball down in the right hand corner, Rollin providing the pass after a long downfield run following a Don Vines break. Fox missed the tricky conversion. Two penalties for scrum infringements from Fred Griffiths put Wigan ahead 4–3 before, almost on half-time, Boston caught Wakefield full-back Gerry Round in two minds, going round the outside to score near the corner, Griffiths kicking a wonderful goal.

Wakefield, playing with virtually a 12–man team, looked tired after the break, Wigan's forwards, ably led by the marauding runs of John Barton, Collier and McTigue, taking control. It was Ashton that scored the crucial try with almost a half-hour remaining when, kicking over Round, he retrieved the ball and dived over the whitewash. Griffiths missed the extras, adding a penalty shortly after for a comfortable 14–3 lead. Hooker Bill Sayer added a third, running it in from acting half-back despite the efforts of Trinity skipper Derek Turner. With the flood-gates open the Cherry and Whites posted two more tries before the final whistle; Boston intercepting a Chamberlain pass on halfway to scoot away practically unchallenged, and Ashton accepting a Bolton pass from a scrum 35-yards out to outmanoeuvre Round. Griffiths converted the former for a convincing 27–3 win, one report suggesting the margin could have been greater had Round not shown great courage in preventing the awesome Boston from scoring another four touchdowns!

Billy Boston, having intercepted in midfield, races away for his second try

1961 Northern Rugby League Championship Final LEEDS V WARRINGTON

Leeds finally won the Rugby League Championship in 1961 after defeating Warrington 25–10 at Odsal through a combination of irresistible power and brilliant skill. The power was supplied by their rampaging pack – aided by a favourable 29–13 scrum-count from hooker Barry Simms – that bombarded Warrington throughout the 80 minutes at a pace defying their size and weight. Much of the skill, though, came from the back division, especially stand-off and captain Lewis Jones, who produced one of his most outstanding performances in a Leeds jersey. The *Warrington Guardian's* Jack Steel gave testimony to Jones' display when describing the Welshman's last minute try, saying 'he rounded off a five-star performance with a bewildering zig-zagging run through a mass of defenders to place the ball under the crossbar in the last minute and then kick his fifth goal of the match.'

Leeds, who was missing young centre Fred Pickup due to a thigh muscle injury, opened the scoring after 16 minutes of almost constant pressure, Dennis Goodwin charging through before sending a looping pass to Jack Fairbank, who claimed the try. Jones added the goal points. The game continued as 'one way traffic' with Warrington being forced to repel one danger after another, Vince Hattee, Jones and Wilf Rosenberg all going close. The Wires, though, did have opportunities to register points, Eric Fraser missing with two penalty attempts. Three minutes before half-time, Warrington cracked again. Jones was tackled a yard short of the line after a length of field move involving Ken Thornett, Hattee and Derek Hallas, scrum half Colin Evans diving in from the play-the-ball whilst the defence was still in disarray. Jones' goal made the score 10–0 at the interval.

Any thought that Leeds would ease the tempo after the break proved unfounded, Hallas almost scoring from the first scrum of the half, but prevented from getting the ball down. He soon made amends with two tries in a five-minute salvo off passes from Thornett and Trevor Whitehead, respectively, Jones converting the first of them to make it 18-0. Warrington supporters finally had something to shout about when centre Jim Challinor raced 60 yards to score after intercepting a Leeds pass, adding a second effort three minutes from time, Laurie Gilfedder augmenting both. Jones dissected Challinor's efforts with another penalty, saving his *piece de resistance* for the 80th minute.

Referee Ron Gelder signals a try for Leeds' scrum half Colin Evans to the obvious delight of his colleagues

After the final whistle Fairbank – who himself enjoyed 'the game of his life' according to the *Yorkshire Post* – carried Jones in triumph

Leeds centre Derek Hallas dives over Warrington's Joe Pickavance to claim the first of his two tries. Wires' scrum half Jackie Edwards is on the left

around the Odsal pitch on his shoulders as Leeds finally healed the hurt of losing in five previous Championship Finals. Warrington, meanwhile was left with the task of revitalising a pack that had become destabilised after the loss of experienced prop Nat Silcock, who had emigrated to Australia two weeks earlier.

CHAMPION CAPTAIN

Lewis Jones (Leeds 1961)

Lewis Jones was hailed as 'The Golden Boy' of Welsh rugby union after making his international debut for the Principality in 1950 when 18 years old. A high profile signing for Leeds in 1952 for a record £6,000, he was a centre that possessed superb passing skills, allied to a spellbinding sidestep and acceleration. Born in Gorseinon and formerly with Neath, Devonport Services and Llanelli, he had represented Wales (10 times), Glamorgan county, and taken part in the 1950 British Isles tour of Australasia. As a rugby league player, he was picked for the 1954 tour and 1957 World Cup, playing for Great Britain (15 times – including 13 with Test status), Wales (once) and Other Nationalities (twice). With Leeds, he won the Championship (1960/61), Rugby League Challenge Cup (1957), Yorkshire Cup (1958) and Yorkshire League (1954/55, 1956/57, 1960/61), his last match being in 1964. He was a reliable marksman enabling him to set a whole range of club records at Leeds; 13 goals in a match (1957), 31 points in a match (1956), 166 goals and 431 points in a season (both 1956/57), 1,244 goals and 2,920 points in a career. His 496 points in all matches during 1956/57 are still claimed as a world record. He emigrated in 1964 to Australia to become player-coach for the Sydney-based Wentworthville club. Several years later he returned to Britain joining the coaching staff at Leeds during the mid-1970s, taking the role of Dewsbury head coach in 1977/78.

STATS

Leeds 25 Warrington 10

Saturday 20 May at Odsal Stadium, Bradford (3.00 pm)

Leeds: (blue with amber bands) Thornett, Rosenburg, Hallas, Hattee, Ratcliffe, Jones (captain), Evans, Robinson, Simms, Whitehead, Fairbank, Goodwin, Shaw. Coach: D. Prosser

Warrington: (white with primrose and blue bands) Fraser (captain), Bevan, Challinor, Pickavance, O'Grady, Greenough, Edwards, Brindle, Harper, Arkwright, Glifedder, Major, A. Naughton. Coach: C. Mountford

Half-time: 10–0 **Referee:** R. Gelder
Attendance: 52,177 **Receipts:** £10,475

Weather: cloudy and bright with strong breeze

Progressive score:

Leeds	score (min)	Warrington
Fairbank try, Jones goal	5–0 (16)	
Evans try, Jones goal	10–0 (37)	
Hallas try, Jones goal	13–0 (53)	
Hallas try	18–0 (58)	
	18–5 (70)	Challinor try, Gilfedder goal
Jones penalty	20–5 (74)	
	20–10 (77)	Challinor try, Gilfedder goal
Jones try, Jones goal	25–10 (80)	

League leaders	P	W	D	L	For	Agst	Pts
1 Leeds	36	30	0	6	620	258	60
2 Warrington	36	27	1	8	701	269	55
3 Swinton	36	27	1	8	647	271	55
4 St Helens	36	27	0	9	773	304	54

Semi-finals:
Leeds 11 St Helens 4
Warrington 13 Swinton 5

Head-to-head form guide:
No previous meetings during season

1962 Northern Rugby League Championship Final
HUDDERSFIELD V WAKEFIELD TRINITY

Huddersfield pulled off one of the major Championship Final shocks in defeating Wakefield Trinity 14-5 in the 1962 decider at Odsal, seven days after losing to the same opposition at Wembley in the Challenge Cup Final. In capturing their seventh title, Huddersfield did so without the star names that were the hallmark of previous triumphs, *Daily Herald* writer Allan Cave posed the question 'Just how did one of the most unglamorous of Huddersfield's successful sides manage it?' Huddersfield's forte was that they had gone about their business in a workmanlike, efficient manner during the campaign, earning a creditable fourth place in the League and reaching both major finals. As Cave remarked: 'They are sound and make the minimum of errors.'

One suggestion for the upset was that five Wakefield players – Neil Fox, Harold Poynton, Gerry Round, Derek Turner and Jack Wilkinson – were preoccupied with joining the Great Britain touring party, most of which had departed already for Australia. A more probable explanation is the heavy, rain-sodden Odsal pitch that suited Huddersfield's well-drilled defence more than a, normally, speedy Trinity outfit that made a lot of un-Trinity-like handling errors during the match.

CHAMPION CAPTAIN

Tommy Smales (Huddersfield 1962)

Following his senior debut with Featherstone Rovers in 1952, scrum half Tommy Smales had difficulty retaining a first team slot, the club being well covered in that position, and he transferred to Huddersfield in 1955. The move paid off, Smales being in the side that won the 1957 Yorkshire Cup. His expertise as a master tactician came to the fore in 1961/62, when, as captain, he led them to Championship success, plus runners-up slot in the Challenge Cup Final at Wembley. It brought him belated international and county recognition with appearances for Great Britain (8 – captain on one occasion), England (once) and Yorkshire (5 times). He transferred to Bradford Northern in 1964, again winning the Yorkshire Cup (1965), eventually leaving to spend the 1967 close season in Australia with North Sydney. He later coached Featherstone Rovers (1976 and 1878–79).

On paper, Wakefield began with a stronger team than at Wembley with hooker Milan Kosanovic (ankle) and robust Don Vines (thigh muscle) both returning to the pack. Huddersfield, whose prop Ken Noble was also set to join the tourists, made a few adjustments of their own from the team beaten at Wembley. Previously unfit Gwyn Davies returned at stand-off to add pace, Harry Deighton moving to centre, displacing Ray Haywood who suffered a sprained ankle at Wembley, whilst Austin Kilroy replaced Mick Clark in the pack.

Huddersfield (players only): Third row: Booth, Redfearn, Devereux, Bowman, Slevin, Dyson. Seated: Davies, Breen, Wicks, Smales, Ramsden, Deighton, Kilroy. On ground: Haywood, Close

Wakefield, with the wind and rain at their backs, made the better start, scoring a well executed 29th minute try through Fox, who, following a Brian Briggs break collected a return pass from winger Fred Smith to go over. He added the extras to push Trinity 5–2 ahead, Frank Dyson having kicked an earlier penalty for Huddersfield. Three minutes before half-time, however, the pendulum unexpectedly swung when Trinity centre Alan Skene sent a wayward pass to Round. Whilst the latter claimed he was obstructed trying to retrieve the ball, Huddersfield's Mike Wicks opportunistically steamed in to claim it, racing 25 yards for a try in the corner. Dyson added a great touchline goal, giving the men in Claret and Gold a surprise 7–5 interval lead.

The rain came down even heavier in a dourly-fought second half, Trinity struggling to get out of their own territory, Dyson, who increased the lead to 9–5 with his second penalty, continually pushing them back with long kicks downfield. In the final seconds Huddersfield fans went delirious when skipper Tommy Smales shot through a gap created by Davies for a try in the corner. It took police several minutes to clear excited fans from the pitch before Dyson's conversion, which bounced off the crossbar, added the last points of the afternoon!

STATS

Huddersfield 14 Wakefield Trinity 5

Saturday 19 May at Odsal Stadium, Bradford (3.00 pm)

Huddersfield: (claret with narrow gold hoops) Dyson, Breen, Deighton, Booth, Wicks, Davies, Smales (captain), Slevin, Close, Noble, Kilroy, Bowman, Ramsden. Coach: D. Valentine

Wakefield Trinity: (white with red and blue band) Round, Smith, Skene, Fox, Hirst, Poynton, Holliday, Wilkinson, Kosanovic, Firth, Briggs, Vines, Turner (captain). Coach: K. Traill

Half-time: 7–5 **Referee:** N.T. Railton
Attendance: 37,451 **Receipts**: £7,979

Weather: heavy rain and windy; ground muddy

Progressive score:

Huddersfield	score (min)	Wakefield Trinity
Dyson penalty	2–0 (27)	
	2–5 (29)	Fox try, Fox goal
Wicks try, Dyson goal	7–5 (37)	
Dyson penalty	9–5 (47)	
Smales try, Dyson goal	14–5 (80)	

League leaders	P	W	D	L	For	Agst	Pts
1 Wigan	36	32	1	3	885	283	65
2 Wakefield Trinity	36	32	1	3	822	288	65
3 Featherstone Rovers	36	28	1	7	621	370	57
4 Huddersfield	36	25	2	9	494	351	52

Semi-finals:
Wigan 11 Huddersfield 13
Wakefield Trinity 13 Featherstone Rovers 8

Head-to-head form guide:
Wakefield Trinity 12 Huddersfield 6
(Challenge Cup at Wembley Stadium, London)

Wakefield Trinity's Neil Fox crosses the line for the first try of the final

Post-match praise was heaped on the Fartowner's forwards, particularly Peter Ramsden, Ted Slevin and Noble, who continually opened up the middle, denying Trinity the kudos of being the fourth side to achieve 'All Four Cups', having completed a Yorkshire League and Cup double in addition to the Wembley win. Huddersfield, as fourth placed team, reached the final the hard way, eliminating leaders Wigan at Central Park 13–11 in the semi-final after losing 41–3 there a month earlier. *The Huddersfield Examiner* summed it up nicely, saying: 'Four months ago a committee member, when being congratulated on Huddersfield bidding for the top four, said he would be happy with a place in the top half!'

FIRST DIVISION CHAMPIONS

There was no Championship play-off during 1962/63 and 1963/64, when two divisions operated, Swinton being First Division Champions on both occasions.

Swinton's talented 1962/63 Championship winning side led by skipper Albert Blan (seated, centre, with ball)

1965 Northern Rugby League Championship Final
HALIFAX V ST HELENS

Halifax captain John Burnett races over near the corner flag for the opening try

Halifax captured their second Championship through winning the expanded top-16 play-off in 1965. They achieved the feat from 7th position in the League table, clearly the lowest placing by a champion team to date, given the previous system included only the leading four, a format under which, coincidentally, the Thrum Hallers had been the inaugural winners 58 years earlier. Their 15-7 success was a massive anticlimax for the defeated St Helens team after winning their opening 17 League fixtures and heading the final table four points clear of second-placed Wigan.

The Yorkshire club's biggest asset was their dominant set of forwards, although they were quite capable of rattling up points, evidenced by their 629 in the League, a figure challenged only by the leading pair. Most of the damage they inflicted on St Helens emanated from the powerful thrusts of their young second-rowers; 20-year-old Terry Fogerty – whose performance earned him the first Harry Sunderland Trophy award as the final's outstanding player – and 21-year-old Colin Dixon. With speedy Scottish loose forward Charlie Renilson, they made good use of the foraging by props Ken Roberts and Jack Scroby. Their hard graft up front enabled the half-backs to dictate, particularly livewire Paul Daley, who was integral to just about every threatening Halifax move.

St Helens had outstanding backs, including magical half-back Alex Murphy and quicksilver South African wingers Len Killeen and Tom van Vollenhoven, although the latter looked uncomfortable at centre as cover for leg injury victim Ken Williams. Their strength, though, was also built around a commanding pack. Halifax matched them on the day, although the Saints sextet was severely handicapped through the 28th minute loss of Cumbrian play-maker John Tembey due to a twisted ankle.

Two minutes before his departure, Halifax drew first blood when centre and captain John Burnett, who also had a fine game, scored the opening try. It came when Daley recovered a loose ball, knocked to ground by a Saints defender off a threatening Fogerty pass, before sending his skipper through a small gap to score. Full-back Ron James converted, two subsequent Killeen penalties cutting Halifax's lead to 5–4 at half-time.

St Helens' anticipated second half fight-back did not happen, the Knowsley Road outfit looking uncertain and spilling the ball through

CHAMPION CAPTAIN

John Burnett (Halifax 1965)

John Burnett led Halifax to the 1964/65 Championship just four months after taking over the captaincy from Ken Roberts. He signed for the Thrum Hallers from local amateurs Pellon in 1953, making his senior debut the following year. A quick, direct running centre, he also won the Yorkshire Cup (1963), Yorkshire League (1957/58) and Eastern Division Championship (1963/64) whilst with Halifax. Having adapted to the full-back role in his final 1966/67 campaign, he joined and coached Bradford Northern in 1967/68. He was selected for Yorkshire six times and played several matches on loan to Blackpool Borough during 1955.

over-anxious play at key moments. Halifax, meanwhile, was playing ruthless, efficient rugby and, with just over an hour played, Fogerty charged through a gap, the supporting Scroby getting Burnett over the whitewash to complete his brace. James tagged the extras for a 10–4 lead. Killeen gave Saints' fans hope, accepting Keith Northey's pass after a telling Murphy

LEAGUE LEADERS

	P	W	D	L	For	Agst	Pts
1 St Helens	34	28	0	6	621	226	56
2 Wigan	34	26	0	8	626	260	52
3 Castleford	34	25	1	8	555	294	51
4 Wakefield Trinity	34	24	2	8	486	228	50
5 Warrington	34	24	1	9	416	292	49
6 Workington Town	34	23	1	10	497	326	47
7 Halifax	34	22	1	11	629	335	45
8 Hull Kingston Rovers	34	22	0	12	587	377	44
9 Oldham	34	20	1	13	444	312	41
10 Leeds	34	20	0	14	469	349	40
11 Swinton	34	19	1	14	334	250	39
12 Leigh	34	19	1	14	446	349	39
13 Hull	34	19	0	15	412	381	38
14 Hunslet	34	19	0	15	477	466	38
15 Featherstone Rovers	34	18	0	16	436	463	36
16 Barrow	34	18	0	16	383	408	36

break to score an unconverted try. With the Saints defence looking increasingly vulnerable, though, the day belonged to Halifax. Four minutes from time, Fogerty broke once more, skipping out of three attempted tackles, half-backs Daley and Barry Robinson taking over to put Duncan Jackson in behind the posts, James' goal closing the scoring.

Writing in *The Sun*, Allan Cave highlighted the influence of coach Albert Fearnley, saying: 'The Fearnley formula, used by slick players backing up in great style, won the Championship for Halifax.'

STATS

Halifax 15 St Helens 7

Saturday 22 May at Station Road, Swinton (2.30 pm)

Halifax: (blue and white hoops) James, Jackson, Burnett (captain), Kellett, Freeman, Robinson, Daley, Roberts, Harrison, Scroby, Fogerty, Dixon, Renilson. Substitutes: Todd (dnp), Duffy (dnp). Coach: A. Fearnley

St Helens: (white with red chevron) F. Barrow, Harvey, van Vollenhoven, Northey, Killeen, Murphy (captain), Smith, Tembey, Dagnall, Watson, French, Mantle, Laughton. Substitutes: Coslett (dnp), Warlow. Coach: J. Coan

Half-time: 5–4 **Referee:** D.S. Brown
Attendance: 20,776 **Receipts**: £6,141

Weather: cloudy and dry with strong wind

Harry Sunderland Trophy: Fogerty (Halifax)

Progressive score:

Halifax	score (min)	St Helens
Burnett try, James goal	5–0 (26)	
	5–2 (30)	Killeen penalty
	5–4 (36)	Killeen penalty
Burnett try, James goal	10–4 (61)	
	10–7 (67)	Killeen try
Jackson try, James goal	15–7 (76)	

First round:
St Helens 23 Barrow 7
Wigan 8 Featherstone Rovers 15
Castleford 18 Hunslet 7
Wakefield Trinity 15 Hull 9
Warrington 10 Leigh 4
Workington Town 29 Swinton 2
Halifax 28 Leeds 11
Hull Kingston Rovers 26 Oldham 14

Second round:
St Helens 24 Hull Kingston Rovers 6
Castleford 11 Workington Town 3
Wakefield Trinity 17 Warrington 8
Halifax 31 Featherstone Rovers 6

Semi-finals:
St Helens 10 Wakefield Trinity 5
Castleford 18 Halifax 26

Head-to-head form guide:
No previous meetings during season

John Burnett displays the trophy in front of the main stand at Swinton

1966 Northern Rugby League Championship Final
ST HELENS V HALIFAX

St Helens extracted full revenge from Halifax in the 1966 Championship Final, erasing memories of their unexpected loss 12 months earlier. On a hot, sunny afternoon they blitzed the opposition, Len Killeen bagging a Championship Final record 21 points with three tries and six goals, and 22–year-old prop Albert Halsall also weighing in with a try hat-trick, thereby joining Killeen in equalling another record for the final. Both teams were short of key players; St Helens missing the try-scoring threat of Tom van Vollenhoven, due to a troublesome knee and ankle, Halifax minus scrum half Paul Daley through a fractured ankle.

St Helens winger Len Killeen about to place the ball over the line for one of his three touchdowns

Halifax, who surpassed last year's feat by reaching the final from a lower League placing of 10th and winning three away games to qualify, looked likely to spring another shock when they led 7–3 with almost a half-hour gone. It was Halsall who instigated St Helens' revival in the 29th minute when, taking possession from a play-the-ball, he barged over to the right of the posts. Killeen surprisingly failed to put Saints ahead when his goal attempt hit the post. But, minutes later, skipper Alex Murphy banged over a drop-goal from in front of Halifax's posts, giving them a lead they would not lose. Halsall extended the gap, racing in like an express train from 20 yards for his second try. Killeen succeeded with the conversion, adding a penalty minutes later when Barry Robinson's 25-yard line drop-out failed to travel the requisite 10 yards.

St Helens wasted little time building on their 15–7 interval lead when, five minutes into the half, good approach work by Ray French and Tony Barrow created the position for Halsall to complete his hat-trick, surging through a dishevelled defence, Killeen adding the goal. At 20–7, Saints were rampant, coming close to scoring several times as Halifax sagged in the

A female St Helens supporter wields her handbag (extreme left) as a mass brawl erupts between the two sides

STATS

St Helens 35 Halifax 12

Saturday 28 May at Station Road, Swinton (2.30 pm)

St Helens: (white with red chevron) F. Barrow, A. Barrow, Murphy (captain), Benyon, Killeen, Harvey, Bishop, Halsall, Sayer, Watson, French, Warlow, Mantle. Substitutes: Hitchen, Prosser (dnp). Coach: J. Coan

Halifax: (blue and white hoops) Cooper, Jones, Burnett (captain), Dixon, Freeman, Robinson, Baker, Roberts, Harrison, Scroby, Ramshaw, Fogerty, Renilson. Substitutes: Eastwood (dnp) Duffy. Coach: A. Fearnley

Half-time: 15–7 **Referee:** J. Manley
Attendance: 30,634 **Receipts**: £8,762

Weather: sunny and warm

Harry Sunderland Trophy: Halsall (St Helens)

Progressive score:

St Helens	score (min)	Halifax
	0–2 (6)	Cooper penalty
Killeen try	3–2 (16)	
	3–7 (22)	Fogerty try, Cooper goal
Halsall try	6–7 (29)	
Murphy drop-goal	8–7 (33)	
Halsall try, Killeen goal	13–7 (35)	
Killeen penalty	15–7 (38)	
Halsall try, Killeen goal	20–7 (45)	
A. Barrow try	23–7 (56)	
Killeen try, Killeen goal	28–7 (60)	
Killeen penalty	30–7 (67)	
Killeen try, Killeen goal	35–7 (74)	
	35–12 (79)	Baker try, Cooper goal

First round:
St Helens 35 Warrington 7
Swinton 43 Featherstone Rovers 2
Wigan 27 Widnes 10
Wakefield Trinity 36 Hull 6
Castleford 10 Hull Kingston Rovers 13
Leeds 19 Huddersfield 7
Bradford Northern 7 Halifax 21
Workington Town 6 Oldham 7

Second round:
St Helens 25 Oldham 10
Swinton 2 Halifax 33
Wigan 22 Leeds 5
Wakefield Trinity 9 Hull Kingston Rovers 10

Semi-finals:
St Helens 14 Hull Kingston Rovers 6
Wigan 12 Halifax 25

Head-to-head form guide:
St Helens 15 Halifax 4 (League)
Halifax 2 St Helens 5 (League)

heat, Tony Barrow eventually crossing the whitewash at the corner after Tommy Bishop and Murphy made the initial break. Billy Benyon then put Killeen over on the hour mark for another fine try in the corner, the winger adding a tremendous goal.

Unfortunately, many of the players then became involved in a free fight, a St Helens woman joining in and using her handbag as a weapon! Police helped restore order but, predictably, photographs of the incident dominated press coverage the next day. Killeen, having landed a 67th minute penalty, got his third try seven minutes later, appending another spectacular touchline goal. Gordon Baker, off a Terry Fogerty pass, registered a late consolation try for Halifax, Barry Cooper's goal completing the 35–12 score.

It had looked so different for Halifax at the start when Charlie Renilson looked an early try scorer until a head-on Frank Barrow tackle thwarted him. Cooper then opened the scoring with a Halifax penalty, a lead that survived 10 minutes, Peter Harvey capitalising on a gap to his left to pick out Benyon. He transferred to Killeen who shrugged off a tackle to finish with a try in the corner, missing the tricky conversion. Halifax's pack reacted positively and in the 22nd minute Fogerty, having been tackled short of the line, played the ball forward and picked it up to score. Cooper's goal put Halifax in good shape at 7–3 but St Helens had other ideas!

LEAGUE LEADERS

	P	W	D	L	For	Agst	Pts
1 St Helens	34	28	1	5	521	275	57
2 Swinton	34	27	1	6	510	283	55
3 Wigan	34	27	0	7	604	302	54
4 Wakefield Trinity	34	25	2	7	562	239	52
5 Castleford	34	23	3	8	524	233	49
6 Leeds	34	24	0	10	493	295	48
7 Bradford Northern	34	21	1	12	375	247	43
8 Workington Town	34	21	1	12	423	306	43
9 Oldham	34	20	3	11	398	347	43
10 Halifax	34	21	0	13	482	318	42
11 Huddersfield	34	20	0	14	420	267	40
12 Hull Kingston Rovers	34	20	0	14	496	321	40
13 Hull	34	20	0	14	447	346	40
14 Widnes	34	17	0	17	444	347	34
15 Featherstone Rovers	34	17	0	17	408	399	34
16 Warrington	34	16	1	17	287	339	33

1967 Northern Rugby League Championship Final
WAKEFIELD TRINITY V ST HELENS

Wakefield Trinity secured their first Championship through defeating St Helens in a replayed final at Swinton, having endured 160 minutes of thrills, drama, controversy and extreme British weather! Most of those elements accompanied their original meeting, played at Headingley in some of the foulest conditions experienced for a Championship Final, the heavens producing heavy rain, hail, thunder and lightening, the pitch, at times, being flooded.

The drama began seven minutes from time when referee George Philpott awarded a penalty-try to Wakefield scrum half Ray Owen, tying the score at 7–7, giving Neil Fox the chance of booting over the goal that could win the title. His difficult kick was hampered by hail blasting into his face, his towering effort skidding off the far post on the wrong side. With St Helens desperately hanging on, more tension unfolded in the final minute when Fox had one last chance. But his angled 20-yard penalty shot, awarded after John Mantle late-tackled Wakefield's Ken Hirst after he had kicked the ball, was just wide. Fox, struggling with a chest injury from a stray elbow early on, revealed later he had to contend with double vision in making his late bid for glory.

Wakefield scrum half Ray Owen dives over the line in the replay at Swinton to open the scoring

Owen's penalty-try came after St Helens heeled a scrum five yards from their line. In the slippery conditions, scrum half Tommy Bishop mishandled the ball, Owen kicking it over their try-line but being pulled back by Peter Douglas as he followed up. St Helens argued that full-back Frank Barrow was closer to the ball and would have saved the situation had Owen run on. It was one of two controversial incidents St Helens was vociferous about afterwards, the other – shortly after Neil Fox had put Wakefield 2–0 ahead with a penalty – being a disallowed 15th minute Saints' touchdown. It occurred when Bishop and Douglas created an opening, Brian Hogan fumbling Douglas' pass. Colleague Tony Barrow grabbed it, placing it over the line for a 'try.' The referee, however, ruled the ball hit the deck before Barrow retrieved it.

St Helens was, however, awarded a try seven minutes after that incident when Cliff Watson forced his way through near the posts after good work from Bishop, Ray French and Tom van Vollenhoven. Len Killeen landed the goal,

CHAMPION CAPTAIN

Harold Poynton (Wakefield Trinity 1967, 1968)

Harold Poynton signed for Wakefield Trinity following trials in 1958, after completing his National Service. An exciting local schoolboy talent at scrum half, he was initially lost to rugby league, showing a preference for soccer before his call-up. He established himself at Trinity as a creative stand-off, eventually becoming team captain in 1966. With Trinity, he won the Championship (1966/67, 1967/68), Rugby League Challenge Cup (1962, 1963 – missing the 1960 success through injury), Yorkshire Cup (1960, 1961, 1964) and Yorkshire League (1958/59, 1959/60, 1961/62, 1965/66). He was a Great Britain tourist in 1962, during which he made his three Test appearances, and represented Yorkshire once. He retired in 1969.

adding a 40-yard penalty, putting them 7–2 up at the break. Neil Fox responded with a penalty eight minutes after half-time. Wakefield then upped the anti by pounding St Helens throughout the second half. Saints' defence, though, excelled under the pressure, Watson standing out with his bone-crunching tackles, before capitulating for Owen's disputed try.

Four days later both teams emerged unchanged for the replay, although Joe Manley took over as referee, Philpott standing down after his wife received threatening letters due to his awarding of Owen's try. Wakefield continued where they left off, with wonderful attacking rugby, the dry, firmer conditions that evening being more conducive to their entertaining style. Ken Hirst almost scored but dropped the ball, then Harold Poynton, who had got through most of the first encounter with concussion from an early tackle, just failed with a drop-goal that came back off the crossbar, and Gert 'Oupa' Coetzer crossed the whitewash in the left corner but was recalled for an infringement. Eventually St Helens succumbed when Owen dummied his way through from acting half-back after nine minutes. Neil Fox missed the goal and also an ambitious halfway penalty attempt.

In an enthralling first half, St Helens gave as good as they got, Killeen kicking a 45-yard penalty. Don Fox then opened things up for Ian Brooke, who took the ball at speed for Trinity's second try, making it 6–2. Bishop invigorated St Helens with a neat drop-goal struck just beyond the 25-yard line, followed two minutes later by his wide pass to the right, sending van Vollenhoven racing over in the corner. Killeen missed the goal but Saints led 7–6. Wakefield remained calm, Gary Cooper almost getting

St Helens joy as Cliff Watson claims the opening try at Headingley with Peter Douglas (next to post), Ray French and Tommy Bishop (right) about to add their congratulations

STATS

Wakefield Trinity 7 St Helens 7

Saturday 6 May at Headingley, Leeds (2.30 pm)

Wakefield Trinity: (white with red and blue band) Cooper, Hirst, Brooke, N. Fox, Coetzer, Poynton (captain), Owen, Bath, Prior, Campbell, Clarkson, Haigh, D. Fox. Substitutes: Hawley (dnp), Batty (dnp). Coach: K. Traill

St Helens: (royal blue) F. Barrow, van Vollenhoven (captain), A. Barrow, Smith, Killeen, Douglas, Bishop, Warlow, Sayer, Watson, French, Hogan, Mantle. Substitutes: Houghton (dnp), Robinson. Coach: J. Coan

Half-time: 2–7 **Referee:** G. Philpott
Attendance: 20,161 **Receipts**: £6,702

Weather: heavy rain with periodic hailstone, thunder and lightening

Progressive score:

Wakefield Trinity	score (min)	St Helens
N. Fox penalty	2–0 (12)	
	2–5 (22)	Watson try, Killeen goal
	2–7 (28)	Killeen penalty
N. Fox penalty	4–7 (48)	
Owen penalty try	7–7 (73)	

Replay: Wakefield Trinity 21 St Helens 9

Wednesday 10 May at Station Road, Swinton (7.30 pm)

Wakefield Trinity: (blue with red chevron) unchanged (including substitutes, who did not play)

St Helens: (white with red chevron): unchanged (including substitutes, who did not play)

Half-time: 11–7 **Referee:** J. Manley
Attendance: 33,537 **Receipts**: £9,800

Weather: dry and mild

Harry Sunderland Trophy: Owen (Wakefield Trinity)

Progressive score:

Wakefield Trinity	score (min)	St Helens
Owen try	3–0 (9)	
	3–2 (15)	Killeen penalty
Brooke try	6–2 (19)	
	6–4 (25)	Bishop drop-goal
	6–7 (27)	van Vollenhoven try
Poynton try, N. Fox goal	11–7 (38)	
	11–9 (56)	Killeen penalty
Brooke try, N. Fox goal	16–9 (58)	
Hirst try	19–9 (61)	
N. Fox penalty	21–9 (68)	

MORE STATS

First round:
Leeds 27 Widnes 18
Hull Kingston Rovers 17 Barrow 15
Wakefield Trinity 48 Salford 8
St Helens 37 Leigh 12
Bradford Northern 12 Warrington 6
Workington Town 23 Halifax 14
Swinton 12 Oldham 12
Castleford 21 Hull 7
Replay: Oldham 7 Swinton 15

Second round:
Leeds 9 Castleford 13
Hull Kingston Rovers 36 Swinton 10
Wakefield Trinity 22 Workington Town 2
St Helens 15 Bradford Northern 8

Semi-finals:
Hull Kingston Rovers 6 Wakefield Trinity 18
St Helens 14 Castleford 3

Head-to-head form guide:
Wakefield Trinity 28 St Helens 15 (League)
St Helens 18 Wakefield Trinity 15 (League)

LEAGUE LEADERS

	P	W	D	L	For	Agst	Pts
1 1 Leeds	34	29	0	5	704	373	58
2 Hull Kingston Rovers	34	26	2	6	691	335	54
3 Wakefield Trinity	34	27	0	7	631	339	54
4 St Helens	34	22	3	9	551	344	47
5 Bradford Northern	34	22	2	10	506	346	46
6 Workington Town	34	22	1	11	517	345	45
7 Swinton	34	20	3	11	472	354	43
8 Castleford	34	21	0	13	560	409	42
9 Hull	34	18	3	13	492	430	39
10 Oldham	34	18	2	14	466	362	38
11 Halifax	34	18	2	14	567	477	38
12 Warrington	34	18	1	15	423	438	37
13 Leigh	34	17	3	14	412	433	37
14 Salford	34	18	1	15	398	424	37
15 Barrow	34	17	2	15	479	407	36
16 Widnes	34	15	5	14	366	412	35

Coetzer in, his pass being ruled forward, and Poynton's high lobbed pass to Hirst almost put the wingman over in the corner. From the resultant play-the-ball, acting half-back Owen turned the ball inside for Poynton to stroll over. Neil Fox's goal eased Trinity 11–7 ahead at the interval.

In the second period, the livewire Bishop made a tremendous break but when he kicked ahead Owen crucially managed to reach the ball first. Killeen's penalty, given for offside, reduced Saints' deficit to two points, but Wakefield was growing in confidence and finished with a flurry of points. The ever-alert Poynton sent Bob Haigh on a charge, setting up the position from which Owen's dummy prised an opening for Brooke's second try. Neil Fox added the goal. Three minutes later Hirst escaped the attentions of Watson and Frank Barrow to claim Trinity's fifth touchdown. Neil Fox missed the conversion, making amends with an excellent angled penalty as Wakefield celebrated an historic 21–9 win, achieved, according to Jack Bentley of the *Daily Express* by 'superb, slick, open football.'

It was a case of 'water, water everywhere' in the first leg at Headingley. St Helens' Tony Barrow splashes his way towards the try-line, his 'try' being subsequently disallowed for obstruction. The other Saints' player (12), who has already slid into the in-goal area, is Brian Hogan

1968 Northern Rugby League Championship Final WAKEFIELD TRINITY V HULL KINGSTON ROVERS

Wakefield Trinity retained their Championship title in 1968, after defeating Hull Kingston Rovers 17-10 at Headingley in an exciting contest where the outcome was still in doubt 10 minutes from time. It was Trinity's first win over Rovers in seven meetings that season, following three defeats and three draws. Wakefield had a slight surprise in their selection with last year's hero Ray Owen, who had hardly played all season, included at scrum half for the unfortunate Joe Bonnar who had not fully recovered from a recent ankle injury. Centre Neil Fox was also welcomed back, his only Wakefield appearance since suffering a groin injury during March being an outing in mid-April.

After a tight opening quarter, during which Don Fox (covering for his below-par brother Neil) missed two penalties for Wakefield, Trinity claimed the first try. It was down to the awareness of full-back Gary Cooper, who combined with second-row pairing Bob Haigh and Matt McLeod to send Owen over near the posts. Neil Fox – taking the kick this time – adding the goal. By half-time, though, Hull Kingston Rovers had clawed back, a Roger Millward angled 35-yard penalty goal, being followed by a fortuitous Paul Longstaff try in the left-hand corner, Phil Lowe and Colin Cooper combining to put him in after recovering a badly sliced kick from colleague Frank Foster. Millward just missed the goal, the teams going in level at the break 5–5.

Backed by a strong second half wind, Wakefield increased their lead through prop David Jeanes, whose charge for the line took three defenders over with him as he scored, Neil Fox augmenting. But Rovers, in their first Championship decider for 43 years, was determined not to collapse, putting intense pressure on the Trinity line during a 15 minute flurry. Their only reward, though, was a Roger Millward drop-goal that closed the deficit to just three points at 10–7. With the clock ticking down Neil Fox eased the tension amongst Trinity fans when he got a vital third touchdown, racing in from 30 yards as he outwitted a couple of defenders, brother Don converting. Harold Poynton weighed in with a drop-goal, opening an eight-point gap before Rovers grabbed a late consolation try through centre John Moore after some slick passing from Millward and Alan Burwell.

Wakefield Trinity 1967/68. Standing: N. Fox, Oakes, Steel, McLeod, Hawley, Haigh, Jeanes, Traill (coach). Kneeling: Coetzer, Cooper, Bonnar, Poynton, Hirst, Barry, Paley, D. Fox

Trinity skipper Harold Poynton receives the Championship trophy for the second consecutive year

Apart from Gary Cooper's constant linking up to bolster the attack, Wakefield was indebted to a workmanlike pack in which Haigh and Dave Hawley excelled. Arthur Haddock, writing in the *Yorkshire Evening Post* said: 'Those who said Hull KR would take over as Champions from Wakefield because Trinity would have their minds on Wembley, under rated the mettle of the men from Belle Vue.'

Success came at a price for Neil Fox who, in the process of scoring his try, aggravated his injury, costing him his place in the following week's Challenge Cup Final at Wembley and the forthcoming World Cup in Australia and New Zealand, where he was to captain Great Britain. Amazingly, he was asked to prove his fitness to the international selectors by taking part in Britain's warm up match against Halifax at Thrum Hall on the eve of the Championship Final, playing half of the game.

LEAGUE LEADERS

	P	W	D	L	For	Agst	Pts
1 Leeds	34	28	0	6	720	271	56
2 Wakefield Trinity	34	24	1	9	600	295	49
3 Hull Kingston Rovers	34	24	1	9	620	348	49
4 St Helens	34	24	1	9	472	334	49
5 Warrington	34	24	0	10	539	290	48
6 Bradford Northern	34	24	0	10	560	309	48
7 Leigh	34	22	1	11	426	254	45
8 Castleford	34	22	1	11	510	344	45
9 Salford	34	22	0	12	470	313	44
10 Workington Town	34	21	1	12	522	355	43
11 Wigan	34	21	0	13	602	350	42
12 Hull	34	21	0	13	530	432	42
13 Halifax	34	19	2	13	441	459	40
14 Swinton	34	18	1	15	485	448	37
15 Huddersfield	34	17	2	15	343	336	36
16 Widnes	34	17	1	16	538	420	35

STATS

Wakefield Trinity 17 Hull Kingston Rovers 10

Saturday 4 May at Headingley, Leeds (3.00 pm)

Wakefield Trinity: (white with red and blue chevron) G. Cooper, Coetzer, Brooke, N. Fox, Batty, Poynton (captain), Owen, Jeanes, Shepherd, D. Fox, Haigh, McLeod, Hawley. Substitutes: Hirst (dnp), Campbell (dnp). Coach: K. Traill

Hull Kingston Rovers: (red with white collar) Wainwright, Young, Moore, Burwell, Longstaff, Millward, C. Cooper, L. Foster, Flanagan, Mennell, Lowe, Major, F. Foster (captain). Substitutes: Coupland (dnp), Holliday (dnp). Coach: C. Hutton

Half-time: 5–5 **Referee:** D.S. Brown
Attendance: 22,586 **Receipts**: £7,823

Weather: fine and dry

Harry Sunderland Trophy: G. Cooper (Wakefield Trinity)

Progressive score:

Wakefield Trinity	score (min)	Hull Kingston Rovers
Owen try, N. Fox goal	5–0 (19)	
	5–2 (21)	Millward penalty
	5–5 (35)	Longstaff try
Jeanes try, N. Fox goal	10–5 (55)	
	10–7 (67)	Millward drop-goal
N. Fox try, D. Fox goal	15–7 (72)	
Poynton drop-goal	17–7 (78)	
	17–10 (80)	Moore try

First round:
Leeds 31 Widnes 17
Wakefield Trinity 20 Huddersfield 11
Hull Kingston Rovers 17 Swinton 2
St Helens 31 Halifax 2
Warrington 12 Hull 9
Bradford Northern 8 Wigan 28
Leigh 43 Workington Town 4
Castleford 47 Salford 15

Second round:
Leeds 7 Wigan 11
Wakefield Trinity 17 Castleford 14
Hull Kingston Rovers 22 Leigh 3
St Helens 20 Warrington 0

Semi-finals:
Wakefield Trinity 26 Wigan 9
Hull Kingston Rovers 23 St Helens 10

Head-to-head form guide:
Wakefield Trinity 12 Hull Kingston Rovers 12 (League)
Wakefield Trinity 13 Hull Kingston Rovers 13 (Yorkshire Cup)
Hull Kingston Rovers 14 Wakefield Trinity 5 (Yorkshire Cup)
Hull Kingston Rovers 25 Wakefield Trinity 7 (League)
Wakefield Trinity 5 Hull Kingston Rovers 5 (BBC2 Floodlit Trophy)
Hull Kingston Rovers 13 Wakefield Trinity 10 (BBC2 Floodlit Trophy)

1969 Northern Rugby League Championship Final
LEEDS V CASTLEFORD

The 1969 Championship Final ended dramatically, Leeds denying Castleford in the last five minutes. Ahead 14–11, Castleford's Mick Redfearn propelling a high kick deep into Leeds territory, but the ball bounced awkwardly, Leeds' Mick Shoebottom and Ken Eyre getting it away to Bev Risman. The full-back raced past Dennis Hartley and Trevor Briggs, sprinting 30 yards before taking a well aimed kick towards the corner. The ball stood up perfectly for John Atkinson, who took it in his stride to score 15 yards to the left of the posts. Risman calmly added the winning points for a last gasp 16–14 win. Apart from that thrilling finish, though, it was a match remembered for some less savoury incidents, the *Yorkshire Post's* Alf Drewry commenting 'most of what masqueraded as a football match is best forgotten.'

Risman had opened the scoring with a 30-yard penalty. Alan Hardisty responded with a drop-goal and then, at the opposite end, he charged down a similar effort from Leeds' Barry Seabourne. Castleford centre Tony Thomas, in trying to retrieve the ball, fumbled it, Leeds taking advantage to regain possession. Syd Hynes cashed in, sending Ron Cowan (a replacement for shoulder injury victim Alan Smith) into the corner for the first try. Castleford hit back when Clive Dickinson charged through to touch down near the posts, Redfearn converting. The first half scoring was completed by three penalties; two from Redfearn, encompassing a 40-yard Seabourne drop-goal that hit the post, and one from Risman.

Barry Seabourne – the Leeds skipper was forced to miss the second half after dislocating his shoulder

Redfearn missed a chance to increase Castleford's 11–7 interval lead when his penalty rebounded off the post, Risman making no mistake with a similar award shortly afterwards. In an often tense and physical encounter, several players required treatment for concussion including Castleford's Keith Hepworth and Malcolm Reilly (who did not emerge for the second half) and Leeds' Mick Clark. Unfortunately trouble also erupted amongst the crowd, the police moving in to make several arrests.

Hardisty intercepted a Mick Joyce pass, but Risman forced him to touch down in the corner, Redfearn, crucially, missing the conversion. Behind 14–9, and with Hynes limping, Leeds

CHAMPION CAPTAIN

Barry Seabourne (Leeds 1969)

Barry Seabourne – born in the Hunslet district – had a phenomenal rise to the top after signing with Leeds. Emerging through the ranks of Hunslet schools rugby league he made his blue and amber debut in 1964 when only 16 years old, becoming club captain at 21. A brilliant, tactical scrum half and team leader, he enjoyed his fair share of success with the Headingley club, winning the Championship (1968/69), League Leaders' Trophy (1966/67, 1967/68, 1968/69, 1969/70), Rugby League Challenge Cup (1968), Yorkshire Cup (1968) and Yorkshire League (1966/67, 1967/68, 1968/69, 1969/70). Midway through the 1971/72 term, he transferred to Bradford Northern for £3,000, landing the Division Two Championship (1973/74) and Players' No.6 Trophy (1974/75) before moving to Keighley as player-coach from 1977 to 1979. He subsequently coached Bradford Northern (1985–89) and Huddersfield (1990–91). He was a tourist in 1970 when he made his only Test appearance (versus New Zealand) and selected for England (twice) and Yorkshire (3 times).

STATS

Leeds 16 Castleford 14

Saturday 24 May at Odsal Stadium, Bradford (3.15 pm)

Leeds: (blue with amber bands) Risman, Cowan, Hynes, Watson, Atkinson, Shoebottom, Seabourne (captain), Clark, Crosby, K. Eyre, Joyce, Ramsey, Batten. Substitutes: Langley, Hick. Team manager: J. Warham

Castleford: (amber with black collar and cuffs) Edwards, Briggs, Howe, Thomas, Lowndes, Hardisty (captain), Hepworth, Hartley, Dickinson, Ward, Redfearn, Lockwood, Reilly. Substitutes: Bedford (dnp), Fox. Coach: D. Turner

Half-time: 7–11 **Referee:** W.H. Thompson
Attendance: 28,442 **Receipts**: £10,130

Weather: overcast and dull

Harry Sunderland Trophy: Risman (Leeds)

Progressive score:

Leeds	score (min)	Castleford
Risman penalty	2–0 (2)	
	2–2 (5)	Hardisty drop-goal
Cowan try	5–2 (12)	
	5–7 (14)	Dickinson try, Redfearn goal
	5–9 (-)	Redfearn penalty
	5–11 (-)	Redfearn penalty
Risman penalty	7–11 (-)	
Risman penalty	9–11 (45)	
	9–14 (47)	Hardisty try
Ramsey drop-goal	11–14 (51)	
Atkinson try, Risman goal	16–14 (75)	

First round:
Leeds 32 Oldham 12
St Helens 25 Keighley 7
Wigan 26 Widnes 10
Castleford 14 Hull 10
Swinton 9 Wakefield Trinity 5
Salford 13 York 7
Featherstone Rovers 16 Hull Kingston Rovers 5
Workington Town 11 Leigh 9

Second round:
Leeds 18 Workington Town 10
St Helens 47 Featherstone Rovers 4
Wigan 21 Salford 26
Castleford 50 Swinton 8

Semi-finals:
Leeds 22 Salford 12
St Helens 6 Castleford 18

Head-to-head form guide:
Leeds 22 Castleford 11 (Yorkshire Cup at Belle Vue, Wakefield)
Leeds 14 Castleford 5 (League)
Castleford 3 Leeds 18 (League)
Castleford 9 Leeds 5 (Challenge Cup)

LEAGUE LEADERS

	P	W	D	L	For	Agst	Pts
1 Leeds	34	29	2	3	775	358	60
2 St Helens	34	27	2	5	669	262	56
3 Wigan	34	25	2	7	732	368	52
4 Castleford	34	24	2	8	462	255	50
5 Swinton	34	23	0	11	503	412	46
6 Salford	34	19	5	10	573	309	43
7 Featherstone Rovers	34	21	1	12	523	346	43
8 Workington Town	34	21	0	13	512	379	42
9 Leigh	34	19	4	11	447	371	42
10 Hull Kingston Rovers	34	20	0	14	566	445	40
11 York	34	20	0	14	477	440	40
12 Wakefield Trinity	34	19	1	14	473	375	39
13 Hull	34	18	3	13	494	419	39
14 Widnes	34	19	1	14	506	434	39
15 Keighley	34	18	1	15	380	407	37
16 Oldham	34	18	0	16	479	474	36

seemed beaten. Bill Ramsey provided hope through a drop-goal but Castleford continued to threaten until fate dealt Leeds their winning hand and Castleford, close to completing a double after winning at Wembley, could only reflect on what might have been.

Victorious skipper Seabourne missed the second half after dislocating his shoulder (he did it four times in the semi-final) whilst Hartley was dismissed two minutes from time for a foul on Shoebottom. The result was a triumph out of adversity for Leeds team manager Joe Warham who took charge after coach Roy Francis unexpectedly left to take over at North Sydney in Australia and his replacement, Jack Nelson (promoted from the coaching staff to fill the void), passed away suddenly on Christmas Day.

Leeds line up for the camera before the 1969 Championship Final. Back: K. Eyre, Shoebottom, Watson, Ramsey, Atkinson, Clark. Front: Risman, Hynes, Cowan, Seabourne, Crosby, Batten, Joyce

1970 Northern Rugby League Championship Final
ST HELENS V LEEDS

St Helens confounded most predictions by defeating reigning champions Leeds in the 1970 Championship Final at Odsal with an awesome display in a memorable finale to the season. Losing 8–7 at half-time, they overwhelmed the Headingley side in the second half to win handsomely 24–12 in what was described in one newspaper as 'Saints best performance in years.' Leeds lined up without suspended centre Bernard Watson, Ron Cowan taking his place, whilst Saints provided a shock in naming Eric Prescott on the left wing, dropping Frank Wilson, who previously had missed one game all season, scoring 36 tries. Although not as fast, Prescott was considered more solid in defence, Wilson having looked vulnerable in the semi-final against Castleford.

Leeds got on the scoreboard first, Alan Smith grabbing an unconverted try out wide after accepting a long pass in the sixth minute. St Helens responded five minutes later following a tap-penalty, Frank Myler backing Eric Chisnall's break to send hooker Bill Sayer over. Kel Coslett added the goal and Saints led 5–3. Leeds regained the initiative through Cowan, his wonderful solo run taking him through a melee of defenders after fielding a drop-out 40 yards from the try-line. John Holmes converted. The score fired Leeds to greater effort but Saints kept them at bay, Coslett registering the only remaining points of the half with a penalty goal.

St Helens regained the lead six minutes after

Forwards Cliff Watson, Kel Coslett and John Mantle celebrate another Saints success

CHAMPION CAPTAIN

Cliff Watson (St Helens 1970)

The story of St Helens powerhouse prop Cliff Watson's rise to the top would make a good movie script! Born in London, he was playing for Dudley-Kingswinford Rugby Union Club in the West Midlands when he responded to a St Helens advert offering trials. Making his Saints debut at the start of the 1960/61 season, he ended the campaign as a Rugby League Challenge Cup winner at Wembley. He repeated the Challenge Cup success in 1966 and also won the Championship (1965/66, 1969/70, 1970/71 – missing the final due to a broken arm), League Leaders' Trophy (1964/65, 1965/66), Lancashire Cup (1961, 1962, 1963, 1967, 1968), Lancashire League (1964/65, 1965/66, 1966/67, 1968/69). He moved to Australia, playing for Sydney club Cronulla-Sutherland (1971–73), and Wollongong Souths in the Illawarra competition from 1974. He made 30 Test appearances for Great Britain, incorporating two tours (1966, 1970) and two World Cups (1968, 1970), and represented England (4 times).

LEAGUE LEADERS

	P	W	D	L	For	Agst	Pts
1 Leeds	34	30	0	4	674	314	60
2 Castleford	34	25	1	8	493	298	51
3 St Helens	34	23	1	10	702	292	47
4 Wigan	34	23	0	11	698	420	46
5 Hull Kingston Rovers	34	22	2	10	566	395	46
6 Salford	34	22	1	11	572	332	45
7 Leigh	34	21	3	10	554	325	45
8 Featherstone Rovers	34	22	1	11	558	385	45
9 Swinton	34	20	4	10	550	351	44
10 Widnes	34	21	2	11	473	355	44
11 Hull	34	20	2	12	420	357	42
12 Bradford Northern	34	19	0	15	511	404	38
13 Whitehaven	34	18	2	14	404	450	38
14 Warrington	34	17	2	15	559	421	36
15 Huddersfield	34	17	1	16	377	395	35
16 Halifax	34	16	0	18	395	454	32

the resumption, John Walsh hitting an excellent 25-yard drop-goal. It was a score that gave his side momentum and, just six minutes later, they scored the best try of the afternoon, the ball transferring in dazzling style through six pairs of hands before Myler's reverse pass sent Prescott over. Coslett's goal attempt hit the post. Walsh continued the pressure with a second drop-goal, pushing St Helens two scores ahead, 14–8. As rain started to fall, Coslett and Holmes grabbed two penalties each, the remaining two touchdowns coming from a St Helens hand; Walsh and Prescott being the scorers.

The result provided a wonderful send-off for Saints veteran stand-off Myler, about to lead Great Britain to what would be an Ashes victory in Australia. His incisive running and well-timed passes had provided the outstanding performance in St Helens' victory at Odsal, earning him the Harry Sunderland Trophy.

Determined St Helens full-back Frank Barrow claims the ball despite pressure from Leeds

LEAGUE LEADERS TROPHY

Presented to the team that finishes top of the Northern Rugby League.

1964/65 St Helens
1965/66 St Helens
1966/67 Leeds
1967/68 Leeds
1968/69 Leeds
1969/70 Leeds
1970/71 Wigan
1971/72 Leeds
1972/73 Warrington

STATS

St Helens 24 Leeds 12

Saturday 16 May at Odsal Stadium, Bradford (3.00 pm)

St Helens: (white with red chevron) F. Barrow, Jones, Benyon, Walsh, Prescott, Myler, Heaton, Halsall, Sayer, Watson (captain), Mantle, E. Chisnall, Coslett. Substitutes: Whittle (dnp), Rees (dnp). Coach: C. Evans

Leeds: (blue with amber bands) Holmes, A. Smith, Hynes, Cowan, Atkinson, Shoebottom, Seabourne (captain), Burke, Crosby, A. Eyre, Ramsey, Eccles, Batten. Substitutes: Langley (dnp), Hick. Coach: D. Turner

Half-time: 7–8
Referee: W.H. Thompson
Attendance: 26,358
Receipts: £9,301

Weather: fine and dry at first, heavy rainstorms later

Harry Sunderland Trophy: Myler (St Helens)

Progressive score:

St Helens	score (min)	Leeds
	0–3 (6)	A. Smith try
Sayer try, Coslett goal	5–3 (11)	
	5–8 (17)	Cowan try, Holmes goal
Coslett penalty	7–8 (24)	
Walsh drop-goal	9–8 (46)	
Prescott try	12–8 (52)	
Walsh drop-goal	14–8 (56)	
	14–10 (58)	Holmes penalty
Walsh try	17–10 (59)	
Coslett penalty	19–10 (61)	
Coslett penalty	21–10 (68)	
	21–12 (70)	Holmes penalty
Prescott try	24–12 (75)	

First round:
Leeds 24 Halifax 4
Castleford 17 Huddersfield 7
St Helens 36 Warrington 8
Wigan 20 Whitehaven 20
Hull Kingston Rovers 26 Bradford Northern 13
Salford 11 Hull 4
Leigh 21 Widnes 10
Featherstone Rovers 24 Swinton 18
Replay: Whitehaven 9 Wigan 4

Second round:
Leeds 45 Whitehaven 10
Castleford 15 Featherstone Rovers 3
St Helens 16 Leigh 5
Hull Kingston Rovers 27 Salford 16

Semi-finals:
Leeds 47 Hull Kingston Rovers 5
Castleford 9 St Helens 9
Replay:St Helens 21 Castleford 12

Head-to-head form guide:
Leeds 13 St Helens 7 (League)
St Helens 12 Leeds 5 (League)

1971 Northern Rugby League Championship Final
ST HELENS V WIGAN

Yet again, the Championship Final ended in sensational, and on this occasion, controversial circumstances, as St Helens stormed back to win 16-12 against keen rivals Wigan in the 1971 decider. Wigan led 12–6 when St Helens' forward John Mantle was sent off seven minutes from time, allegedly for kicking Bill Ashurst. The odds favoured league leaders Wigan but, perversely, it was 12–man St Helens, who had entered the fray without wingman Frank Wilson (knee dislocation) and prop Cliff Watson (broken arm), that grew in confidence. Their captain Kel Coslett said later: 'We knew we had to pull out something extra and that is when we started to play the fast, open rugby that eventually won the match for us.'

Sure enough, four minutes from time, they moved the ball quickly to the left, Bob Blackwood squeezing in at the corner, Coslett's tremendous touchline effort closing the gap to 12–11. There was a minute to go when St Helens' John Walsh attempted a drop-goal, but his contact was poor, the ball swerved to the right. The bounce deceived Wigan's Stuart Wright, but not Billy Benyon who accepted the rebound to score. Coslett added the goal amidst strong protests that Benyon, who played most of the match with an arm injury, was offside when Walsh put boot to ball.

Although trailing 6–3 at the interval, the general consensus was Wigan had been on top for much of the first half, scoring the half's only try after eight minutes when Dave Robinson was put through off a brilliant defence-splitting pass from second-row partner Ashurst. Crucially, Colin Tyrer – normally a deadly accurate marksman – missed four reasonable goal chances in the opening 40 minutes, whereas Coslett landed three; two penalties and a drop-goal. Many onlookers believed Tyrer, who appeared to have difficulty running, was not 100 percent despite passing a fitness test the previous day following a groin injury. It prompted suggestions that the goal-kicking responsibility should have been handed to Ashurst.

Backed by a strong wind in the second half, Wigan turned their superiority into points when

CHAMPION CAPTAIN

Kel Coslett (St Helens 1971, 1976)

Kel Coslett joined St Helens as a full-back from Aberavon Rugby Union Club in 1962, having represented Wales three times that year. Born in Bynea, South Wales, he proved an accomplished goal-kicker, creating club records for St Helens of 214 goals and 452 points in a season (1971/72) and 1,639 goals and 3,413 points in a career. His last match for Saints was in 1976 after establishing another club record with 519 appearances (plus 12 as substitute). In 1967, his career reached new heights when moved to loose forward, being ideally built at six feet tall and over 14 stone. In the pack his timing of a pass was put to good use, his ability to read a game leading to him taking over as captain in 1971. At St Helens he won the Championship (1965/66 – missing the final through injury, 1969/70, 1970/71, 1974/75), Premiership Trophy (1976), League Leaders' Trophy (1964/65, 1965/66), Rugby League Challenge Cup (1972, 1976), Western Division Championship (1963/64), Lancashire Cup (1962, 1963, 1967, 1968), Lancashire League (1964/65, 1965/66, 1966/67, 1968/69) and BBC2 Floodlit Trophy ((1971, 1975). In rugby league, he played for Wales (12 times, including the 1975 World Cup) and Other Nationalities (once at county level). He became Rochdale Hornets player-coach (1976–79), later coaching Wigan (1979–80), St Helens (1980–82) and Wales (1977–82).

St Helens face the photographers before the final commences. Back: Karalius, Blackwood, Stephens, Chisnall, Mantle, Rees, Wanbon, Walsh. Front: Kelly, Whittle, Heaton, Coslett, Pimblett, Jones, Benyon

STATS

St Helens 16 Wigan 12

Saturday 22 May at Station Road, Swinton (kick-off: 3.00 pm)

St Helens: (white with red chevron) Pimblett, Jones, Benyon, Walsh, Blackwood, Whittle, Heaton, Stephens, Karalius, Rees, Mantle, Chisnall, Coslett (captain). Substitutes: Kelly, Wanbon. Coach: J. Challinor

Wigan: (cherry and white hoops) Tyrer, Kevin O'Loughlin, Francis, Rowe, Wright, D. Hill, Ayres, Hogan, Clarke, Fletcher, Ashurst, Robinson, Laughton (captain). Substitutes: Gandy (dnp), Cunningham. Coach: E. Ashton

Half-time: 6–3 **Referee:** E. Lawrinson
Attendance: 21,745 **Receipts**: £10,201

Weather: sunny, warm and windy

Harry Sunderland Trophy: Ashurst (Wigan)

Progressive score:

St Helens	score (min)	Wigan
	0–3 (8)	Robinson try
Coslett penalty	2–3 (10)	
Coslett drop-goal	4–3 (-)	
Coslett penalty	6–3 (-)	
	6–8 (42)	Ashurst try, Tyrer goal
	6–10 (-)	Ashurst drop-goal
	6–12 (70)	Ashurst drop-goal
Blackwood try, Coslett goal	11–12 (76)	
Benyon try, Coslett goal	16–12 (79)	

First round:
Wigan 12 Oldham 7
St Helens 28 Huddersfield 5
Leeds 28 Batley 0
Leigh 10 Hull Kingston Rovers 5
Wakefield Trinity 10 Castleford 4
Keighley 7 Dewsbury 20
Salford 33 Halifax 3
Hull 14 Workington Town 3

Second round:
Wigan 36 Dewsbury 12
St Helens 30 Hull 5
Leeds 37 Salford 22
Leigh 5 Wakefield Trinity 8

Second round:
Wigan 49 Wakefield Trinity 15
St Helen 22 Leeds 7

Head-to-head form guide:
Wigan 0 St Helens 23 (Lancashire Cup)
Wigan 7 St Helens 7 (BBC2 Floodlit Trophy)
St Helens 16 Wigan 15 (BBC2 Floodlit Trophy)
St Helens 5 Wigan 12 (League)
Wigan 6 St Helens 9 (League)

LEAGUE LEADERS

	P	W	D	L	For	Agst	Pts
1 Wigan	34	30	0	4	662	308	60
2 St Helens	34	29	0	5	748	231	58
3 Leeds	34	28	0	6	856	352	56
4 Leigh	34	26	0	8	636	380	52
5 Wakefield Trinity	34	24	1	9	760	330	49
6 Keighley	34	21	0	13	448	375	42
7 Salford	34	20	1	13	641	432	41
8 Hull	34	20	1	13	610	444	41
9 Workington Town	34	20	1	13	504	467	41
10 Halifax	34	20	0	14	538	497	40
11 Dewsbury	34	17	3	14	474	406	37
12 Castleford	34	18	0	16	467	403	36
13 Hull Kingston Rovers	34	18	0	16	447	524	36
14 Batley	34	16	2	16	492	411	34
15 Huddersfield	34	16	2	16	440	434	34
16 Oldham	34	12	7	15	487	434	31

Ashurst, who, according to Jack McNamara in the *Manchester Evening News* 'gave one of the finest all round displays of back-row forward work seen for many a match', dived over between the uprights two minutes after the resumption. Tyrer added his elusive goal, Ashurst contributing two drop-goals, his second, with 10 minutes to go looking the match winner until Saints produced what the *St Helens Newspaper* described as 'Seven minutes of champagne football.' One blemish on the afternoon was the breakout of fighting between young rival fans, requiring police intervention.

Billy Benyon dives over the line for his dramatic, late winning try for St Helens despite the efforts of Wigan wingman Stuart Wright

1972 Northern Rugby League Championship Final
LEEDS V ST HELENS

David Barham was the unlikely hero of Leeds' 9-5 victory over St Helens in the 1972 Championship Final, his non-stop performance including a vital 'steal' off Saints' second-row John Mantle when a try looked certain. Their unexpected success, one week after losing to the Saints in the Challenge Cup Final, was all the more remarkable when it is realised Leeds was, on paper at least, forced to field a weaker line-up. Whilst Barham was thrown in at the deep end as a late replacement for scrum half Keith Hepworth, who reported ill on the morning of the game, the Loiners were also without centre Syd Hynes (recurring knee problem), and forwards Bill Ramsey (knee injury) and Bob Haigh (swollen leg). St Helens, meanwhile, took to the field without hooker Tony Karalius and back-row forward Eric Prescott, the unlucky pair failing to recover from injuries that also deprived them of a Wembley appearance.

CHAMPION CAPTAIN

Alan Hardisty (Leeds 1972)

Alan Hardisty's name is firmly rooted in Castleford folklore, the brilliant stand-off – who seemed to glide past defenders with ease – scoring a club record 206 tries in his 401 appearances for the club. A product of local Ashton Road School, his Wheldon Road career spanned 1958 until 1971 during which he notably led Castleford to Rugby League Challenge Cup glory in 1969 and 1970. Other successes included the BBC2 Floodlit Trophy (1965/66, 1966/67, 1967/68) and Yorkshire League (1964/65). His move to Leeds in 1971 – where he was joined by former Castleford half-back partner Keith Hepworth – brought a new lease of life, winning the Championship (1971/72), League Leaders' Trophy (1971/72), Players' No.6 Trophy (1972/73) and Yorkshire Cup (1972, 1973). In 1974, went to Australia as player-coach at Rockhampton in the Queensland League, returning to Britain as coach to Dewsbury (1974–75), York (1980–82) and Halifax (1989). He made 12 Test appearances, represented Yorkshire five times, and was a tourist in 1966 and 1970.

The match unfolded as a gripping, low scoring game, prop Terry Clawson placing Leeds ahead after 10 minutes with a routine looking penalty, stand-in hooker Les Greenall responding with a try for St Helens eight minutes later, pushing his way over from acting half-back. Kel Coslett missed the straightforward looking conversion, but Saints, who generally had the edge thus far, led 3–2 at half-time, Leeds duo Alan Hardisty and John Holmes having both missed drop-goal attempts.

It was in the second half, that Clawson, in a complete reversal of fortune from the last week when he blamed his side's Challenge Cup Final defeat on his poor goal kicking, showed great character, with two crucial, and difficult, match-winning strikes. His first, a penalty, 10 minutes after the restart, was a magnificent touchline effort that edged Leeds back in front. He later said: 'Once I'd put that one over all my confidence came back.' His next, from virtually the same place, was after John Atkinson had registered Leeds' only try of the match in the left-hand

David Barham was an unexpected hero in Leeds' success after being a late inclusion at scrum half

St Helens winger Frank Wilson veers inside Leeds' Alan Smith

corner. It came off two excellent long passes from Fred Pickup and Les Dyl, in what was otherwise a tightly played 'safety-first' passing game by the Yorkshire side. Just prior to that score Leeds had a penalty-try claim rejected when John Langley appeared to be brought down by John Walsh as he chased a David Ward kick. With Leeds 9–3 ahead, an upset looked on the cards, although Walsh pulled two points back for Saints with an awesome looking 45-yard drop-goal, but it proved the last score of the afternoon.

Apart from avenging their Wembley loss, it gave Leeds some retribution for going down to St Helens in the Championship Final two years earlier whilst denying the Saints a record third consecutive Championship.

LEAGUE LEADERS

	P	W	D	L	For	Agst	Pts
1 Leeds	34	28	2	4	750	325	58
2 Bradford Northern	34	26	2	6	724	357	54
3 St Helens	34	26	1	7	661	297	53
4 Wigan	34	25	0	9	702	314	50
5 Salford	34	25	0	9	720	338	50
6 Swinton	34	23	2	9	554	368	48
7 Featherstone Rovers	34	23	1	10	632	372	47
8 Rochdale Hornets	34	21	1	12	429	306	43
9 Wakefield Trinity	34	21	0	13	587	414	42
10 Castleford	34	20	1	13	488	368	41
11 Widnes	34	19	3	12	476	388	41
12 Dewsbury	34	18	2	14	431	352	38
13 Oldham	34	18	1	15	573	480	37
14 Hull Kingston Rovers	34	18	0	16	432	498	36
15 Warrington	34	16	3	15	537	397	35
16 Leigh	34	17	0	17	423	407	34

STATS

Leeds 9 St Helens 5

Saturday 20 May at Station Road, Swinton (3.00 pm)

Leeds: (blue with amber bands) Holmes, A. Smith, Langley, Dyl, Atkinson, Hardisty (captain), Barham, Clawson, Ward, Fisher, Cookson, Eccles, Batten. Substitutes: Pickup, Hick. Coach: D. Turner

St Helens: (white with red chevron) Pimblett, Jones, Benyon, Walsh, Wilson, Kelly, Heaton, Rees, Greenall, Stephens, Mantle, E. Chisnall, Coslett (captain). Substitutes: Whittle, Earl (dnp). Coach: J. Challinor

Half-time: 2–3 **Referee:** S. Shepherd
Attendance: 24,055 **Receipts**: £9,513

Weather: fine and dry

Harry Sunderland Trophy: Clawson (Leeds)

Progressive score:

Leeds	score (min)	St Helens
Clawson penalty	2–0 (10)	
	2–3 (18)	Greenall try
Clawson penalty	4–3 (50)	
Atkinson try, Clawson goal	9–3 (63)	
	9–5 (69)	Walsh drop-goal

First round:
Leeds 40 Leigh 2
Bradford Northern 37 Warrington 0
St Helens 25 Hull Kingston Rovers 5
Wigan 18 Oldham 8
Salford 23 Dewsbury 7
Swinton 11 Widnes 15
Featherstone Rovers 14 Castleford 18
Rochdale Hornets 17 Wakefield Trinity 13

Second round:
Leeds 20 Widnes 9
Bradford Northern 22 Castleford 12
St Helens 17 Rochdale Hornets 5
Wigan 9 Salford 21

Semi-finals:
Leeds 10 Salford 0
Bradford Northern 10 St Helens 14

Head-to-head form guide:
Leeds 20 St Helens 13 (League)
Leeds 0 St Helens 17 (BBC2 Floodlit Trophy)
St Helens 15 Leeds 15 (League)
St Helens 16 Leeds 13
(Challenge Cup at Wembley Stadium, London)

1973 Northern Rugby League Championship Final
DEWSBURY V LEEDS

The last staging of the Championship Final in 1973 was also one of the most sensational, underdogs Dewsbury shocking Leeds 22–13 at Odsal to claim their only peacetime title to date. It was a triumph for teamwork and well-drilled organisation over a Headingley outfit that, at times, looked out of sorts. Every man in the workmanlike Dewsbury side played his part although none caught the eye more than the two unrelated Stephenson's; Nigel in the centre and club captain Mick at hooker.

Nigel Stephenson races under the posts to virtually guarantee a shock Dewsbury victory

CHAMPION CAPTAIN

Mick Stephenson (Dewsbury 1973)

Mick Stephenson – popularly known today as Mike 'Stevo' Stevenson of Sky Television fame – was one of the fastest, most skilful hookers around in the 1970s. He signed for local side, Dewsbury, in 1965 from Shaw Cross Boys Club, becoming a central cog and influential presence in the team that won the Championship in 1972/73. A member of Great Britain's 1972 World Cup winning squad, he made a total of six Great Britain appearances overall and eight for Yorkshire. He joined Australian club Penrith in 1973 for a world record transfer of 39,000 Australian dollars (approximately £21,000), playing with them until 1978 when a jaw injury caused his retirement.

LEAGUE LEADERS

	P	W	D	L	For	Agst	Pts
1 Warrington	34	27	2	5	816	400	56
2 Featherstone Rovers	34	27	0	7	768	436	54
3 Leeds	34	26	1	7	810	324	53
4 St Helens	34	24	2	8	623	298	50
5 Wakefield Trinity	34	25	0	9	814	398	50
6 Salford	34	25	0	9	723	383	50
7 Castleford	34	25	0	9	704	404	50
8 Dewsbury	34	23	0	11	534	354	46
9 Oldham	34	20	2	12	604	349	42
10 Hull Kingston Rovers	34	20	1	13	731	522	41
11 Rochdale Hornets	34	20	1	13	438	426	41
12 Widnes	34	19	0	15	592	458	38
13 Leigh	34	18	2	14	479	390	38
14 Bramley	34	18	1	15	452	465	37
15 Whitehaven	34	18	1	15	408	512	37
16 Wigan	34	17	1	16	577	491	35

It was Mick Stephenson who, justifiably, took the Harry Sunderland man of the match award, his inspirational leadership and play-making driving his pack continually forwards as they subdued the opposition six. He also scored two very timely tries at the start of each half, giving colleagues a psychological lift at exactly the right moment. His first, after 10 minutes, was the perfect response to an early Terry Clawson penalty, taking a pass from Nigel Stephenson after John Bates had made the break. Nigel Stephenson added the conversion, following up with a drop-goal four minutes later. There was a surprise in the 25th minute when the unblemished record of Leeds skipper Alan Hardisty was shattered by his dismissal for a high tackle on John Bates. His instinctive, rather than malicious, action came after referee Harry Hunt had earlier spoken to both teams following an ugly looking flare-up. Undeterred, their centre Syd Hynes showed spirit by immediately clawing two points back with a drop-goal. However, Allan Agar notched another Dewsbury try, created by Mick Stephenson, nine minutes from the break, Nigel Stephenson's extra two points giving the Crown Flatt side a handsome 12–4 interval lead.

Mick Stephenson caused a stir with his second touchdown four minutes after the restart. His namesake added the extras as realisation dawned amongst the crowd that a major upset was taking shape. Leeds were not prepared to relinquish their crown without a fight, however, replying through two tries from second-row forwards Graham Eccles and Phil Cookson. Neither was converted, although Hynes hit the post when trying to augment the former, to make it 17–10. But, as the match headed towards three-quarter time, Nigel Stephenson chose his moment to shine, gliding over the line after a brilliant sidestep for a classic try, Joe Whittington, Jeff Grayshon and John Bates being involved in the build-up. His conversion shunted Dewsbury almost out of reach at 22–10, the remaining points coming from a late Les Dyl consolation try.

Referring to Hardisty's sending off, Mick Stephenson admitted to the *Yorkshire Post's* Alf Drewry 'We didn't want to beat 12 men. I think we had shown that we had the beating of Leeds in any case.' In winning the Championship, Dewsbury, who finished eighth became the lowest placed team to do so, joining Halifax (seventh in 1965) as the only teams outside the top four to take the title. It also avenged their 36–9 defeat to the Loiners in the Yorkshire Cup Final earlier in the season.

Leeds' centre Les Dyl is unable to prevent Dewsbury captain Mick Stephenson claiming his second try

STATS

Dewsbury 22 Leeds 13

Saturday 19 May at Odsal Stadium, Bradford (3.00 pm)

Dewsbury: (red, amber and black hoops) Rushton, Ashcroft, Clark, N. Stephenson, Day, Agar, A. Bates, Beverley, M. Stephenson (captain), Lowe, Grayshon, J. Bates, Whittington. Substitutes: Lee (dnp), Taylor. Coach: T. Smales

Leeds (blue with amber bands) Holmes, A. Smith, Hynes, Dyl, Atkinson, Hardisty (captain), Hepworth, Clawson, Fisher, Clarkson, Cookson, Eccles, Haigh. Substitutes: Langley, Ward. Coach: D. Turner

Half-time: 12–4 **Referee:** H.G. Hunt
Attendance: 18,889 **Receipts**: £9,479

Weather: sunny

Harry Sunderland Trophy: M. Stephenson (Dewsbury)

Progressive score:

Dewsbury	score (min)	Leeds
	0–2 (7)	Clawson penalty
M. Stephenson try, N. Stephenson goal	5–2 (10)	
N. Stephenson drop-goal	7–2 (14)	
	7–4 (29)	Hynes drop-goal
Agar try, N. Stephenson goal	12–4 (31)	
M. Stephenson try, N. Stephenson goal	17–4 (44)	
	17–7 (48)	Eccles try
	17–10 (51)	Cookson try
N. Stephenson try, N. Stephenson goal	22–10 (58)	
	22–13 (76)	Dyl try

First round:
Warrington 30 Wigan 15
Featherstone Rovers 14 Whitehaven 4
Leeds 45 Bramley 8
St Helens 29 Leigh 14
Wakefield Trinity 33 Widnes 6
Salford 10 Rochdale Hornets 14
Castleford 24 Hull Kingston Rovers 12
Dewsbury 29 Oldham 14

Second round:
Warrington 36 Rochdale Hornets 9
Featherstone Rovers 7 Dewsbury 26
Leeds 30 Castleford 5
St Helens 28 Wakefield Trinity 0

Semi-finals:
Warrington 7 Dewsbury 12
Leeds 7 St Helens 2

Head-to-head form guide:
Leeds 36 Dewsbury 9 (Yorkshire Cup at Odsal Stadium, Bradford)

CLUB CHAMPIONSHIP FINAL

With the re-introduction of two divisions in 1973/74 there was no longer a requirement for a Championship play-off, the team finishing top of the First Division being declared Champions. Unlike during the previous two-year experiment a decade earlier, the decision was taken to retain the tradition of an end-of-season finale by introducing what was, in effect, a separate competition. It was called the Club Championship, teams of both divisions qualifying via a merit table, compiled using possibly one of the most complex formulas devised by the sports hierarchy.

Basically, the merit table was calculated by awarding points related to final League positions and success in cup-ties. In the League, the 30 clubs (16 in the First Division, 14 in the Second Division) were given points as follows; 30 to the top team in the First Division, 29 to the second placed team, and so on, with the bottom placed team in the Second Division receiving one point. Each club also received another three points for each win in a cup-tie during the season in the following competitions: Rugby League Challenge Cup, Players' No.6 Trophy, Lancashire Cup, Yorkshire Cup, BBC2 Floodlit Trophy and Captain Morgan Trophy.

It starts to get slightly complicated through the bottom four First Division clubs (Oldham, Hull Kingston Rovers, Leigh and Whitehaven) having four points deducted from their total for being relegated, whilst the top four Second Division Clubs (Bradford Northern, York, Keighley and Halifax) were awarded four points for being promoted. In addition, although it made no difference, Warrington did not receive three points for their win in the Challenge Cup Final because that took place after the Club Championship had already started.

The Second Division clubs were guaranteed three places in the 16-club competition proper via an elimination contest between the leading 12 Second Division teams (based on the their final League table positions) that began at the end of March (before the Merit Table was finalised). The teams to emerge were Bradford Northern, Keighley and Hull. After the Merit Table was eventually compiled, the top 13 teams in the table (not including the aforementioned trio as they had already secured their places) also qualified. Therefore 14th placed Workington Town, 'eliminated' in the Second Division play-off, earned a reprieve as 13th placed Bradford had already gone through!

Warrington, who topped the Merit Table, and then went on to win the competition, received 68 points (26 for finishing fifth in the First Division, 42 for winning 14 cup-ties). Thankfully this system lasted only one season! If anyone considers the current Grand Final play-off series is complicated they should think again!

MERIT TABLE POINTS 1973/74

The 1973/74 Merit Table

1 Warrington	68°	17 Hull KR	22°
2 Leeds	64°	18 Whitehaven	20°
3 St Helens	53°	19 York	20
4 Salford	51°	20 Halifax	18
5 Featherstone Rovers	47°	21 Oldham	17°
6 Rochdale Hornets	45°	22 Swinton	17
7 Bramley	43°	23 Batley	10
8 Wakefield Trinity	42°	24 Hull	9
9 Dewsbury	40°	25 Huddersfield	8
10 Castleford	40°	26 Barrow	6
11 Widnes	39°	27 New Hunslet	4
12 Wigan	38°	28 Huyton	4
13 Bradford Northern	30	29 Blackpool Borough	3
14 Workington Town	28	30 Doncaster	2
15 Keighley	25	(° First Division team)	
16 Leigh	24°		

1974 Club Championship Final
WARRINGTON V ST HELENS

Although it survived for just one season, the 1974 Club Championship Final produced an enthralling climax to the campaign, Warrington winning a tense, tough, but always exciting match by a single point over St Helens at a rain-lashed Central Park. In a frantic finish, either side could have won, although the general consensus was that Warrington had held the edge. The major difference between the two sides was Warrington's robust pack that, with a scrum count of 13–6 in their favour thanks to influential hooker Kevin Ashcroft, always had the measure of St Helens' forwards. It also provided a platform for their imposing veteran captain and coach Alex Murphy to dictate matters at half-back.

Warrington was without several players from the Wembley triumph a week earlier; scrum half Parry Gordon (hip injury) and forwards Mike Nicholas (knee) and Dave Wright (returned to Australia). Winger Les Jones was a late withdrawal for St Helens due to a gashed hand, Dave Brown taking his place, both teams having six St Helens-born players in their ranks.

It was Murphy's quick, precision pass that set up the first try, scored by Mike Philbin after seven minutes. Although Derek Whitehead missed the kick it put Warrington 3–2 ahead,

Warrington's Alex Murphy, watched by Kevin Ashcroft (centre) and Derek Noonan, takes possession of the Club Championship cup

following an earlier Kel Coslett penalty for Saints. It took Frank Wilson just three minutes to respond for St Helens, his try near the posts following a break by prop Mick Murphy, and Coslett's subsequent goal, giving his team a 7–3 lead. Midway through the first half, though, Warrington regained the initiative when David Chisnall created the space for fellow prop Brian Brady to go charging through for a try from 15 yards out. Whitehead's goal gave his side a slender 8–7 interval lead.

Eleven minutes into the second period, Warrington stretched their lead to six points, Derek Noonan capitalising on a brilliant break

CHAMPION CAPTAIN

Alex Murphy (St Helens 1966, Warrington 1974)

Generally regarded as Britain's greatest post-Second World War scrum half, Alex Murphy was a typical cocky half-back, but one that possessed every quality; quick acceleration, superbly timed passes, and a brilliant kicking game. Born at Thatto Heath and a product of St Austins School, he signed with St Helens as a 16-year-old in 1955. With the Saints, he won the Championship (1958/59, 1965/66), League Leaders' Trophy (1964/65, 1965/66), Rugby League Challenge Cup (1961, 1966), Western Division Championship (1963/64), Lancashire Cup (1960, 1961, 1963, 1964, missing their 1962 win through injury) and Lancashire League (1959/60, 1964/65, 1965/66). A Great Britain tourist (1958, 1962) and World Cup squad member (1960), he represented Britain in 27 Tests, England (twice) and Lancashire (14 times). He took over as Leigh coach in 1966, but it was 1967 before St Helens agreed his £5,500 transfer as a player. He took Leigh to victory in the BBC2 Floodlit Trophy (1969), Lancashire Cup (1970) and Challenge Cup (1971), moving to Warrington in 1971 as player-coach. After capturing the League Leaders' Trophy in 1972/73, Warrington won four trophies in 1973/74; the Club Championship, Rugby League Challenge Cup, Players No. 6 Trophy, and Captain Morgan Trophy, although Murphy did not appear in the finals of the latter two. He stepped down from playing in 1975, continued as Warrington coach until 1978, followed by coaching appointments at Salford (1978–80), Leigh (1980–82, 1985, 1990–91), Wigan (1982–84), St Helens (1985–90), and Huddersfield (1991–94). He also coached England (1975 – including that year's World Cup) and Lancashire (1973–78, 1985–88). He was awarded the OBE in 1999, and inducted into the Rugby League Hall of Fame in 1988.

STATS

Warrington 13 St Helens 12

Saturday 18 May at Central Park, Wigan (3.00 pm)

Warrington: (royal blue with yellow collar) Whitehead, M. Philbin, Noonan, Pickup, Bevan, Whittle, A. Murphy (captain), D. Chisnall, Ashcroft, Brady, Wanbon, Mather, B. Philbin. Substitutes: Lowe, Gaskell. Player-coach: A. Murphy

St Helens: (white with red chevron) Pimblett, Brown, Wills, Wilson, Mathias, Eckersley, Heaton, Mantle, Liptrot, M. Murphy, E. Chisnall, Nicholls, Coslett (captain). Substitutes: A. Gwilliam (dnp), Warlow. Coach: J. Challinor

Half-time: 8–7 **Referee:** P. Geraghty
Attendance: 18,040 **Receipts**: £10,031

Weather: heavy rain

Harry Sunderland Trophy: B. Philbin (Warrington)

Progressive score:

Warrington	score (min)	St Helens
	0–2 (3)	Coslett penalty
M. Philbin try	3–2 (7)	
	3–7 (10)	Wilson try, Coslett goal
Brady try, Whitehead	8–7 (22)	
Noonan try, Whitehead goal	13–7 (51)	
	13–12 (64)	Wilson try, Coslett goal

Club Championship first round:
Warrington 34 Hull 12
Leeds 31 Keighley 12
St Helens 24 Workington Town 7
Salford 16 Bradford Northern 16
Featherstone Rovers 22 Wigan 14
Rochdale Hornets 5 Widnes 31
Bramley 0 Castleford 14
Wakefield Trinity 26 Dewsbury 11
Replay: Bradford Northern 17 Salford 8

Second round:
Warrington 15 Bradford Northern 9
Leeds 20 Widnes 15
St Helens 25 Castleford 9
Featherstone Rovers 16 Wakefield Trinity 19

Semi-finals:
Warrington 12 Wakefield Trinity 7
Leeds 10 St Helens 23

Head-to-head form guide:
St Helens 24 Warrington 6 (League)
Warrington 5 St Helens 11 (League)
Warrington 20 St Helens 9 (Players' No.6 Trophy)

down the middle by John Bevan, switched from wing to centre four minutes earlier due to a Billy Pickup injury, Derek Whitehead adding the extras. With around 15 minutes left, Wilson put things back into the melting pot when he raced through a gap for his second try after a break by forwards John Warlow and John Mantle. Coslett's conversion brought St Helens to within one point at 13-12. The last 15 minutes were dominated by abortive drop-goal attempts from Warrington as the tension built. In total, Alex Murphy tried six during the match and Ashcroft three. In the final seconds, Warrington hearts skipped a beat as Coslett was just wide with a towering 40-yard drop-goal effort.

Warrington's success in their 51st competitive match of the season gave them their fourth trophy of what had been a magnificent campaign, after winning the Challenge Cup, Players' No. 6 Trophy and Captain Morgan Trophy.

THE NORTHERN RUGBY FOOTBALL LEAGUE
1974 CLUB CHAMPIONSHIP FINAL
St. Helens
V
Warrington
SATURDAY
18th MAY
1974
Kick-off
3 p.m.
at
Central Park
Wigan
OFFICIAL SOUVENIR PROGRAMME — 10p

A unique event! The 1974 Club Championship Final at Central Park was to be the only one held

FIRST DIVISION LEADERS

	P	W	D	L	For	Agst	Pts
1 Salford	30	23	1	6	632	299	47
2 St Helens	30	22	2	6	595	263	36
3 Leeds	30	20	1	9	554	378	41
4 Widnes	30	18	1	11	431	329	37
5 Warrington	30	16	1	13	414	368	33

(Salford won Championship)

PREMIERSHIP TROPHY FINAL

During May 1974 it was agreed the Club Championship should be reorganised, the outcome being that a new competition for the Premiership Trophy, superseded it. The name 'Premiership' had a shiny newness about it at the time! Although Scottish football coincidently renamed its First Division as the Premier Division in 1975 (England following suit in 1992), it was probable, as with the Grand Final concept, the inspiration came from Australian rugby league. Since commencing operations in 1908, they had organised an end-of-season final to decide the 'Premiers.'

Either way, the concept was far simpler to understand than its predecessor, although in its first year, 1975, it stuck to a similar principle of 16 qualifying clubs representing both divisions (the top 12 in the First Division and the leading four in the Second Division). Unlike the Club Championship, which had rewarded teams for a good placing in the Merit Table (the top club playing at home to the bottom club and so on) the first Premiership Trophy was based on an open draw.

From 1976 it was competed for by just the leading eight First Division clubs, the draw being revised to favour the highest placed clubs (first versus eighth, etc.) providing an incentive for teams on the fringe of the Championship race to earn a good finishing slot. For a brief period (1976 to 1978 and 1980) the semi-finals took place over two legs but with the difficulty of squeezing it all into a usually busy end-of-season schedule this was discarded as being one match too many. The arrival of Super League and summer rugby in 1996 saw the competition reduced to the top four but then, in 1997 – in what was the last Premiership Trophy contest – it embraced all 12 Super League clubs!

Supporters of Wigan, with six wins out of seven appearances in the 23 Premiership Trophy Finals staged, and St Helens, with four victories from nine finals, will remember the competition with fondness. One club that can look back on that era with pride is Widnes. Having appeared in just one Championship Final in its history (in 1936) they reached eight Premiership Finals and won six.

With hindsight, it can now be judged that taking the Premiership Trophy to Old Trafford in 1987 was as important a step in the Championship series as the move to Wembley in 1929 was for the Challenge Cup Final. The Great Britain-Australia Test staged at Old Trafford in 1986 had already shown that crowds could be attracted by their thousands to watch the sport played in such a magnificent setting. The first Premiership played there was enhanced by the introduction of a preceding Second Division Premiership Final, the 'double-header' concept being a feature of every Premiership occasion at Old Trafford until the last, in 1997.

From the Rugby Football League's point of view, of course, there was the not inconsiderable bonus of the extra revenue generated in what eventually became an all-seated stadium. In 1996, in a forerunner to the Grand Final 'experience' to come, the first evening kick-off took place to accommodate Sky Television. Although many were unhappy with the arrangement at the time, which, excepting 1997, has been repeated every year since, the atmosphere generated under the Old Trafford floodlights is now seen as an integral part of the 'championship' occasion.

The Premiership Trophy served the sport well after replacing what was becoming an ailing Championship Final series. Having attracted crowds ranging from around 10,000 to 19,000 (with one exception) in the early years, the Premiership Trophy Final lifted its audience to well over 30,000, paving the way for the Grand Final revolution that followed.

1975 Premiership Trophy Final
LEEDS V ST HELENS

In the first Premiership Trophy Final, in 1975, Leeds matched the warm, sunny conditions with a sizzling performance, described by the *Yorkshire Post* as a 'display of clinical precision', to defeat St Helens 26–11. They charged into a 16–0 half-time lead, their forwards ripping apart a St Helens pack that suffered disruption through the loss of props John Warlow (rib injury in the 8th minute) and John Mantle (gashed head, 32nd minute). Second-rowers George Nicholls and Eric Chisnall took their roles, David Hull moving to the back-row from centre. Whatever the combination, they were equalled by a youthful Leeds front row of Roy Dickinson (aged 18), David Ward (21) and Steve Pitchford (23) who were at their zestful best throughout.

Leeds attacked from the start, Bob Haigh being repelled in only the third minute, before moving ahead through a John Holmes penalty. Their first try resulted from the brilliance of Mel Mason who, collecting a short Ray Batten pass, evading Mantle and Geoff Pimblett to go behind the posts. The key passage of play was a five-minute burst from Leeds before the break.

CHAMPION CAPTAIN

Syd Hynes (Leeds 1975)

Syd Hynes built a reputation as an uncompromising defender – he was dismissed in a Challenge Cup and World Cup Final – but he was also admired as a penetrative and committed player who gave his all for Leeds, Great Britain (13 Tests, including the 1970 tour and 1970 World Cup), England (4 appearances), and Yorkshire (4). He signed for Leeds in 1964 from NALGO (National and Local Government Officers' Association) Rugby Union Club, having emerged through Hunslet schools rugby league. At Leeds, he won the Premiership Trophy (1975), Championship (1968/68, 1971/72 – missing the final through injury), League Leaders' Trophy (1966/67, 1967/68, 1968/69, 1969/70, 1971/72), Rugby League Challenge Cup (1968), Players' No.6 Trophy (1972/73), BBC2 Floodlit Trophy (1970/71), Yorkshire Cup (1968, 1970, 1972, 1973, 1975, 1976) and Yorkshire League (1966/67, 1967/68, 1968/69, 1969/70). He played for Leeds until 1976, and was coach from 1975 until 1981.

Syd Hynes raises the cup aloft as Leeds revel in their success

Skipper Syd Hynes' drop-goal began it, and he following up with a try from a rehearsed move; Hepworth delaying his pass from the scrum, stand-off Mason going wide to draw the defence, Hynes racing into the gap to take the pass. John Atkinson registered their third touchdown from a perfectly timed Les Dyl off-load, handing off Pimblett as he raced down the left flank to score. The closing stages of the half saw Leeds reshuffling their ranks. Holmes departed with a shoulder injury after 34 minutes, his replacement Dave Marshall converting the Hynes effort, whilst Hynes, himself, ended his involvement after pulling a hamstring whilst scoring. Alan Smith moved inside to centre, loose-forward Bob Haigh taking over on the wing.

St Helens showed better form in the second half, scoring three tries to two. Their first, two minutes after the restart, came when Les Jones squeezed into the corner, Frank Wilson and Eddie Cunningham doing the spadework. Kel Coslett added a superb kick. It signalled a period of sustained Saints pressure as Roy Mathias (twice) and Cunningham came close to scoring.

But it was Leeds, on the hour mark, that got the next try, Alan Smith finishing an excellent bout of passing by rounding Pimblett. Marshall missed the kick, making amends with a penalty goal for a 21–5 lead after 68 minutes. Mathias and Jeff Heaton managed two late unconverted tries for St Helens before Atkinson concluded a happy day for the blue and amber contingent with a breakaway try after Pitchford switched the point of attack, Marshall adding the goal.

It was particularly poignant for Leeds coach Roy Francis, coming 17 years after his last Championship Final success with Hull.

A bitter-sweet moment for Syd Hynes. The Leeds skipper's crucial try three minutes before the interval ended his involvement after pulling a hamstring in the process

FIRST DIVISION LEADERS

	P	W	D	L	For	Agst	Pts
1 St Helens	30	26	1	3	561	229	53
2 Wigan	30	21	0	9	517	341	42
3 Leeds	30	19	1	10	581	359	39
4 Featherstone Rovers	30	19	1	10	431	339	39
5 Widnes	30	18	1	11	382	305	37
6 Warrington	30	17	1	12	428	356	35
7 Bradford Northern	30	16	1	13	393	376	33
8 Castleford	30	14	3	13	480	427	31
9 Salford	30	14	1	15	451	351	29
10 Wakefield Trinity	30	12	5	13	440	419	29
11 Keighley	30	13	0	17	300	424	26
12 Dewsbury	30	11	0	19	350	506	22

(St Helens won Championship)

SECOND DIVISION LEADERS

	P	W	D	L	For	Agst	Pts
1 Huddersfield	26	21	0	5	489	213	42
2 Hull Kingston Rovers	26	20	1	5	628	249	41
3 Oldham	26	19	0	7	406	223	38
4 Swinton	26	17	1	8	399	254	35

STATS

Leeds 26 St Helens 11

Saturday 17 May at Central Park, Wigan (3.00 pm)

Leeds: (blue with amber bands) Holmes, A. Smith, Hynes (captain), Dyl, Atkinson, Mason, Hepworth, Dickinson, Ward, Pitchford, Cookson, Batten, Haigh. Substitutes: Marshall, Eccles. Coach: R. Francis

St Helens: 11 (white with red chevron) Pimblett, Jones, Wilson, Hull, Mathias, Walsh, Heaton, Warlow, Karalius, Mantle, E. Chisnall, Nicholls, Coslett (captain). Substitutes: K. Gwilliam, Cunningham. Coach: E. Ashton

Half-time: 16–0 **Referee:** W.H. Thompson
Attendance: 14,531 **Receipts**: £8,401

Weather: sunny and warm

Harry Sunderland Trophy: Mason (Leeds)

Progressive score:

Leeds	score (min)	St Helens
Holmes penalty	2–0 (10)	
Mason try, Holmes goal	7–0 (14)	
Hynes drop-goal	8–0 (35)	
Hynes try, Marshall goal	13–0 (37)	
Atkinson try	16–0 (40)	
	16–5 (42)	Jones try, Coslett goal
A. Smith try	19–5 (60)	
Marshall penalty	21–5 (68)	
	21–8 (75)	Matthias try
	21–11 (78)	Heaton try
Atkinson try, Marshall goal	26–11 (80)	

Premiership Trophy first round:
Bradford Northern 22 Warrington 14
Castleford 37 Wakefield Trinity 7
Dewsbury 8 Keighley 9
Featherstone Rovers 8 Leeds 27
Huddersfield 18 Hull Kingston Rovers 35
St Helens 42 Oldham 5
Widnes 12 Salford 20
Wigan 19 Swinton 17

Second round:
Bradford Northern 5 St Helens 5
Hull Kingston Rovers 29 Keighley 10
Leeds 28 Castleford 8
Wigan 35 Salford 17
Replay: St Helens 14 Bradford Northern 5

Semi-finals:
Leeds 18 Hull Kingston Rovers 8
Wigan 16 St Helens 22

Head-to-head form guide:
St Helens 21 Leeds 5 (League)
St Helens 30 Leeds 2 (BBC2 Floodlit Trophy)
Leeds 11 St Helens 10 (League)

1976 Premiership Trophy Final
ST HELENS V SALFORD

The real talking points from the 1976 Premiership Trophy Final occurred during the last 12 minutes as St Helens lifted the score from 2–2 to 15–2 with a three-try salvo against Salford after a conflict mostly dominated by an unrelenting forward battle. It was a finish uncannily similar to Saints' Challenge Cup Final triumph at Wembley two weeks earlier when they had opened up Widnes with three touchdowns at the same stage.

Saints victory charge began on 68 minutes, when Peter Glynn avoided a tackle in his own 25

St Helens' Kel Coslett (left) and Salford's Chris Hesketh take hold of the Premiership Trophy in this pre-match publicity shot. The two club captains also brought along the Rugby League Challenge Cup (left) and Championship trophy, which their respective sides had already claimed that season

area to send Roy Matthias clear. David Watkins upended him, but the ball came to John Mantle and, despite Salford wing Gordon Graham knocking the ball down, the move continued. George Nicholls took over to send Glynn in with a reverse pass despite the attentions of Colin Dixon. Pimblett hit the upright with his goal attempt. The score energised St Helens who

STATS

St Helens 15 Salford 2

Saturday 22 May at Station Road, Swinton (3.00 pm)

St Helens: (white with red chevron) Pimblett, Jones, Glynn, Noonan, Mathias, Benyon, Heaton, Mantle, Karalius, James, Nicholls, E. Chisnall, Coslett (captain). Substitutes: K. Gwilliam, Pinner (dnp). Coach: E. Ashton

Salford: (red) Watkins, Fielding, Richards, Hesketh (captain), Graham, Butler, Nash, Coulman, Raistrick, Sheffield, Knighton, Dixon, Prescott. Substitutes: Turnbull, Grice (dnp). Coach: L. Bettinson

Half-time: 0–1 **Referee:** M.J. Naughton
Attendance: 18,082 **Receipts**: £13,138

Weather: overcast, warm and dry

Harry Sunderland Trophy: Nicholls (St Helens)

Progressive score:

St Helens	score (min)	Salford
	0–1 (31)	Watkins drop-goal
Pimblett penalty	2–1 (51)	
	2–2 (59)	Watkins drop-goal
Glynn try	5–2 (68)	
E. Chisnall try, Pimblett goal	10–2 (78)	
Karalius try, Pimblett goal	15–2 (80)	

Premiership Trophy first round:
Salford 21 Hull Kingston Rovers 6
Featherstone Rovers 10 Wakefield Trinity 14
Leeds 12 Widnes 2
St Helens 19 Wigan 6

Second round:
Warrington 15 Bradford Northern 9
Leeds 20 Widnes 15
St Helens 25 Castleford 9
Featherstone Rovers 16 Wakefield Trinity 19

Semi-finals (over two legs):
Salford 24 Wakefield Trinity 10 (on aggregate)
St Helens 33 Leeds 9 (on aggregate)

Head-to-head form guide:
St Helens 8 Salford 21 (Lancashire Cup)
Salford 11 St Helens 17 (Challenge Cup)
Salford 10 St Helens 9 (League)
St Helens 24 Salford 7 (League)

soon threatened again, but a Nicholls pass to Glynn was poor and the chance was lost. Undeterred, they roared downfield once more, Watkins again having to halt Matthias, but it was in vain, Nicholls sending Eric Chisnall racing across the line near posts. Pimblett added the goal. In the dying seconds, the rampant Knowsley Road side was back in Salford territory, a quick, decisive passing movement ending with hooker Tony Karalius going over behind the posts, Pimblett's conversion completing the score.

St Helens had started the match without Eddie Cunningham, whose place in the centre went to Glynn, and loose forward David Hull, both due to hamstring injuries, whilst Salford was minus stand-off and play-maker Ken Gill who had been staying away for several weeks following a dispute. It was Salford who had the first chance to trouble the scoreboard when Watkins' 7th minute touchline penalty strike was just wide, Kel Coslett suffering a similar fate with a 40-yard effort five minutes later. In the 26th minute the Red Devils almost took the lead, Watkins hitting the post with a drop-goal attempt, Pimblett responding with a similar effort that went wide. On the half-hour Salford spurned their best chance of a try when John Butler – Bill Sheffield and Knighton having sucked in the opposition – raced through a gap but failed to provide speedster Keith Fielding with the ball, succumbing to the tackle of lone defender Pimblett instead. A minute later, Watkins' spectacular 40-yard drop-goal provided the only first half score, Pimblett missing with his second attempt before the break.

St Helens looked a more resolute outfit at the start of the second half as their forwards started to make inroads, Nicholls being carried back from the Salford try-line. They eventually took a 2–1 lead when Pimblett landed a penalty goal 11 minutes after the restart, Watkins having fouled Derek Noonan. Eight minutes later, Watkins made amends, levelling the score after beating an opponent and straightening up for another drop-goal, but it was the last real threat from Salford.

St Helens coach Eric Ashton said afterwards: 'We had to make Salford work. We could not afford to let them run with the ball. If anything they had us beaten for pace, so we had to keep up our tackling.' Prior to St Helens' late burst, the match was considered a dour encounter that had provided few chances for the backs to shine, rather than the classic anticipated. As a confrontation between First Division Championship winners Salford and Challenge Cup victors St Helens it had been billed the 'Clash of the Champions', the only occasion in 23 Premiership Trophy Finals that such an occurrence took place.

St Helens' Peter Glynn evades Chris Hesketh to score the opening try 12 minutes from full time

FIRST DIVISION LEADERS

	P	W	D	L	For	Agst	Pts
1 Salford	30	22	1	7	555	350	45
2 Featherstone Rovers	30	21	2	7	526	348	44
3 Leeds	30	21	0	9	571	395	42
4 St Helens	30	19	1	10	513	315	39
5 Wigan	30	18	3	9	514	399	39
6 Widnes	30	18	1	11	448	369	37
7 Wakefield Trinity	30	17	0	13	496	410	34
8 Hull Kingston Rovers	30	17	0	13	446	472	34

(Salford won Championship)

1977 Premiership Trophy Final
ST HELENS V WARRINGTON

St Helens kept hold of the Premiership Trophy in 1977, their 32–20 victory over Warrington on a blisteringly hot afternoon being a personal triumph for Geoff Pimblett, his 17 points being a record haul for the final. His reward was the Harry Sunderland Trophy, thereby becoming the first to achieve the double of being voted man of the match in both major British rugby league finals, having won the Lance Todd Trophy at Wembley the previous year.

Of the 10 tries scored, nine came during a free-flowing second half, partly due to the dismissal of Harry Pinner (St Helens) and Alan Gwilliam (Warrington) following a touchline punch-up in front of the main stand three minutes after the break. The incident changed the course of the match, the consequent 12-a-side encounter in the stifling heat taking its toll on the remaining players. John Bevan took over stand-off Gwilliam's role, but the adjustment was more disruptive to Warrington's pattern than Pinner's loss to St Helens. It was also Alan Gwilliam that scored the only try of a lack-lustre first half, accepting Tommy Martyn inside pass just inside Saints' 25 area to race in unopposed down the right. Steve Hesford's conversion tipped the scales Warrington's way 5–4 at the interval, Pimblett having notched two St Helens penalties.

Concentration is etched on the face of Warrington skipper Parry Gordon as he attempts to set up an attack

Moments after the dismissals St Helens took a 9–5 lead when Billy Benyon shrugged off a tackle to go over, Pimblett, who provided the pass, adding the goal. Hesford landed a penalty two minutes later before St Helens opened up with two more tries, five minutes apart, from Pimblett (racing into the corner after a move initiated by Eric Chisnall's break) and Roy Mathias (taking a pass from Eddie Cunningham after superb passing to score near the corner flag). Pimblett converted the former with a magnificent touchline goal, St Helens leading 17–7 with just over 20 minutes remaining.

As the depleted sides tired during the final quarter, defenders fell away, both conceding three more tries. Warrington's Barry Philbin got the first, in the corner, Hesford being unable to add the extras. St Helens' trio, all converted by Pimblett, followed in a seven-minute spell placing the game well beyond Warrington's

CHAMPION CAPTAIN

Billy Benyon (St Helens 1977)

Former local junior Billy Benyon achieved incredible success with St Helens following his capture as a 16-year-old in 1962. A centre that showed as much determination in defence as attack, he took over the club captaincy in 1976 after Kel Coslett moved to Rochdale Hornets. His list of winners' medals covered the Premiership Trophy (1976, 1977), Championship (1965/66, 1969/70, 1970/71, 1974/75), League Leaders' Trophy (1964/65. 1965/66), Rugby League Challenge Cup (1966, 1972, 1976), BBC2 Floodlit Trophy (1971/72, 1975/76), Lancashire Cup (1962, 1964, 1967, 1968) and Lancashire League (1964/65, 1965/66, 1966/67, 1968/69). He appeared in five Test matches, and represented England (twice) and Lancashire (13 times). After 514 St Helens appearances, he joined Warrington in 1977, winning the Players' No.6 Trophy (1977/78). He was appointed their player-coach in 1978 and, after playing his last match in 1981, continued in charge until 1982. He later coached St Helens (1982–85) and Leigh (1986–90). During the 1974 close season he played in Australia for Cronulla-Sutherland.

STATS

St Helens 32 Warrington 20

Saturday 28 May at Station Road, Swinton (3.00 pm)

St Helens: (white with red chevron): Pimblett, Jones, Benyon (captain), Cunningham, Mathias, Glynn, K. Gwilliam, D. Chisnall, Liptrot, James, Nicholls, E. Chisnall, Pinner. Substitutes: Ashton, Karalius. Coach: E. Ashton

Warrington: (blue with primrose trim): Finningan, Curling, Bevan, Hesford, M. Kelly, A. Gwilliam, Gordon (captain), Weavill, Price, Case, Lester, Martyn, B. Philbin. Substitutes: Cunliffe, Peers. Coach: A. Murphy

Half-time: 4–5 **Referee:** G.F. Lindop
Attendance: 11,178 **Receipts**: £11,626

Weather: sunny and hot

Harry Sunderland Trophy: Pimblett (St Helens)

Progressive score:

St Helens	score (min)	Warrington
Pimblett penalty	2–0 (12)	
	2–5 (29)	A. Gwilliam try, Hesford goal
Pimblett penalty	4–5 (36)	
Benyon try, Pimblett goal	9–5 (45)	
	9–7 (47)	Hesford penalty
Pimblett try, Pimblett goal	14–7 (53)	
Matthias try	17–7 (58)	
	17–10 (65)	B. Philbin try
Cunningham try, Pimblett goal	22–10 (68)	
K. Gwilliam try, Pimblett goal	27–10 (70)	
James try, Pimblett goal	32–10 (75)	
	32–15 (78)	Gordon try, Hesford goal
	32–20 (80)	Weavill try, Hesford goal

Premiership Trophy first round:
Featherstone Rovers 13 Bradford Northern 2
St Helens 10 Wigan 10
Castleford 25 Salford 17
Hull Kingston Rovers 18 Warrington 13
(Hull KR later disqualified for using ineligible player)
Replay:Wigan 3 St Helens 8

Semi-finals (over two legs):
Warrington 24 Featherstone Rovers 18 (on aggregate)
St Helens 61 Castleford 25 (on aggregate)

Head-to-head form guide:
St Helens 23 Warrington 9 (League)
Warrington 12 St Helens 13 (Challenge Cup)
Warrington 12 St Helens 11 (League)

FIRST DIVISION LEADERS

	P	W	D	L	For	Agst	Pts
1 Featherstone Rovers	30	21	2	7	568	334	44
2 St Helens	30	19	1	10	547	345	39
3 Castleford	30	19	1	10	519	350	39
4 Hull Kingston Rovers	30	18	1	11	496	415	37
5 Warrington	30	18	0	12	532	406	36
6 Salford *	29	17	1	11	560	402	35
7 Wigan	30	15	2	13	463	416	32
8 Bradford Northern	30	15	2	13	488	470	32

(*Salford v Leeds abandoned due to tragic death of Chris Sanderson of Leeds and match declared void)

(Featherstone Rovers won Championship)

Post-match changing room smiles from St Helens' Geoff Pimblett (left, holding his Harry Sunderland man of the match award) and captain Billy Benyon (with the Premiership Trophy)

reach, through Cunningham (a 40-yard charge to the line), Ken Gwilliam (Pimblett shaking off a tackle to put him over) and Mel James (breaking through a wilting defence). Warrington finished it off with two late consolations from Parry Gordon and David Weavill, both goaled by Hesford.

Warrington, who played without stand-off Ken Kelly (broken arm) and forward Mike Nicholas (knee injury), had initially lost in the play-offs at Hull Kingston Rovers. They were reinstated after Rovers were disqualified for including second-rower Phil Lowe, having been instructed by the Rugby Football League not to play him pending resolution of a contract dispute with his Australian club, Manly. One sour note during the final was the arrest of 12 people and the ejection of 19 others following crowd trouble.

1978 Premiership Trophy Final
BRADFORD NORTHERN V WIDNES

Having never won a peacetime Championship Final, Bradford Northern finally succeeded in its end-of-season successor, taking the 1978 Premiership Trophy by beating favourites Widnes 17–8 in an enthralling encounter at Swinton. The match marked the climax to a remarkable comeback from their veteran skipper Bob Haigh, who retired after quitting Leeds in 1976. Tempting him back in 1977, Bradford paid Leeds £750 for his transfer, his inspirational performance earning him the Harry Sunderland Trophy. It was also a special day for Bradford veteran Neil Fox – rugby league's most prolific point scorer and brother of club coach Peter – who came on as a second half substitute to earn a winners' medal over 22 years after his senior debut with Wakefield Trinity.

Widnes went into an early 5–0 lead when centre Mal Aspey ran on to a high pass from Reg Bowden, Paul Woods – having missed a relatively easy penalty before Bradford had touched the ball – augmenting. Haigh restored Northern's confidence 11 minutes later, squeezing in by the posts off a perfect Alan Redfearn pass, Keith Mumby's goal tying the scores. On the half-hour the Odsal outfit recorded the go-ahead score when Peter Roe sprinted over from 30-yards out after an Ian van Bellen-Haigh combination worked the opening, Mumby missing the goal. Widnes began to look uncomfortable after John Wolford's drop-goal

FIRST DIVISION LEADERS

	P	W	D	L	For	Agst	Pts	Percent
1 Widnes	30	24	2	4	613	241	50	
2 Bradford Northern°	29	21	2	6	500	291	44	75.86
3 St Helens	30	22	1	7	678	384	45	75.00
4 Hull Kingston R	30	16	3	11	495	419	35	
5 Wigan	30	17	1	12	482	435	35	
6 Salford	30	16	0	14	470	446	32	
7 Featherstone R°	29	15	2	12	443	452	32	
8 Leeds	30	15	1	14	512	460	31	
9 Warrington	30	15	0	15	561	367	30	

(°Featherstone v Bradford fixture not played due to Featherstone players' strike; Bradford awarded second place over St Helens on percentage basis, Featherstone excluded from Premiership as disciplinary measure and replaced by Warrington)

(Widnes won Championship)

STATS

Bradford Northern 17 Widnes 8

Saturday 20 May at Station Road, Swinton (3.00 pm)

Bradford Northern: (white with red, amber and black band) Mumby, Barends, Roe, Austin, D. Redfearn, Wolford, A. Redfearn, I. van Bellen, Raistrick, Thompson, Joyce, Trotter, Haigh (captain). Substitutes: Forsyth, N. Fox. Coach: P. Fox

Widnes: (white with black trim) Eckersley, Wright, Hughes, Aspey, Woods, Gill, Bowden (captain), Mills, Elwell, Shaw, Adams, Hull, Laughton. Substitutes: George, Ramsey. Coach: F. Myler

Half-time: 9–5 **Referee:** J.E. Jackson
Attendance: 16,813 **Receipts**: £18,677

Weather: fine and dry

Harry Sunderland Trophy: Haigh (Bradford Northern)

Progressive score:

Bradford Northern	score (min)	Widnes
	0–5 (11)	Aspey try, Woods goal
Haigh try, Mumby goal	5–5 (22)	
Roe try	8–5 (30)	
Wolford drop-goal	9–5 (35)	
	9–8 (54)	Aspey try
D. Redfearn try, Mumby goal	14–8 (62)	
Barends try	17–8 (80)	

Premiership Trophy first round:
Widnes 33 Warrington 8
Bradford Northern 18 Leeds 10
St Helens 29 Salford 11
Hull Kingston Rovers 17 Wigan 0

Semi-finals (over two legs):
Widnes 35 Hull Kingston Rovers 31 (on aggregate)
Bradford Northern 29 St Helens 26 (on aggregate)

Head-to-head form guide:
Widnes 14 Bradford Northern 10 (Players' No.6 Trophy)
Bradford Northern 5 Widnes 5 (League)
Widnes 19 Bradford Northern 2 (League)

Bradford's David Barends dives over the line in the final minute to seal victory

CHAMPION CAPTAIN

Bob Haigh (Bradford Northern 1978)

Bob Haigh signed for hometown club Wakefield Trinity in 1962 after progressing through their junior ranks. At Trinity, where he developed into a back-row forward noted for his powerful running and excellent cover tackling, he won the Championship (1966/67, 1967/68), Yorkshire Cup (1964) and Yorkshire League (1965/66). Transferring to Leeds for £6,000 in 1970, he gained further success in the Championship (1971/72, although missing the final through injury), Premiership Trophy (1975), League Leaders' Trophy (1971/72), Players' No.6 Trophy (1972/73), and BBC2 Floodlit Trophy (1970/71). During the 1970/71 campaign he scored 40 tries, a new Rugby League record for a forward. After finishing at Leeds in 1976, he made a comeback with Bradford Northern the following year, adding the Premiership Trophy (1978) and Yorkshire Cup (1978) to his medal collection. He concluded his playing career with Dewsbury (1979–80), returning to Wakefield for a brief coaching spell in 1984. He appeared for Great Britain (6 times, being a member of the 1968 and 1970 World Cup squads), England (3) and Yorkshire (2).

increased the Yorkshire sides lead to 9–5 shortly before half-time.

Having played second fiddle to Bradford's forwards for most of the first period, Widnes' task became harder in the second half, their pack suffering the loss, due to injury, of prop Glyn Shaw (midway through the first half) and subsequent replacement Bill Ramsey (at half-time). Widnes, though, fought bravely and, following a period of sustained pressure, Aspey – who excelled as a stand-in second-row forward – crossed the line off Doug Laughton's pass for his second try, although Woods' kick, that would have put Widnes ahead, missed, leaving them trailing 9–8. Bradford responded with a brilliant piece of teamwork that began when Alan Redfearn made a blind-side break from 10 yards inside his own half. David Barends, Haigh, Wolford, Dennis Trotter and Jack Austin carried on the move, which ended with David Redfearn placing the ball down in the left corner. Mumby added an excellent conversion to put Northern two scores in front at 14–8. The final action of the afternoon saw Barends dive over from acting half-back after second-row forward Graham Joyce had been held on the line. The field had to be cleared of excited Bradford fans to allow Mumby – who missed – to attempt the conversion.

Brian Smith of the *Bradford Telegraph and Argus* commented that Bradford had 'finally fulfilled years of promise', going on to suggest the victory 'raises real hopes that Northern are at last on the verge of a major breakthrough.' The receipts of £18,677 created a new Premiership Trophy Final record, exceeding the Championship Final's best, set in 1960.

Bradford Northern skipper Bob Haigh, having just received the Premiership and Harry Sunderland trophies, is captured in a frivolous mood with his delighted coach Peter Fox

1979 Premiership Trophy Final
LEEDS V BRADFORD NORTHERN

The fifth Premiership Trophy Final, between Leeds and holders Bradford Northern in 1979, was the first to take place east of the Pennines, Huddersfield's ex-Fartown home being host for the only time. It drew a new attendance record for the final of 19,486, the receipts of £21,291 also being the highest so far. Another record was Leeds' winning margin of 22 points, as they convincingly disposed of Bradford 24–2 in a disappointingly one-sided affair. The Odsalites made it through to the final despite finishing eighth in the League, the lowest placing of any club in the history of the Premiership Trophy competition to do so.

Both teams were bereft of key backs through injury. Leeds being without centre Tim Wilby and stand-off John Holmes, himself scheduled to relocate to Wilby's slot but failing a late test on an ankle problem. They resolved their centre problem by bringing David Smith inside off the wing, veteran winger Alan Smith replacing his namesake on the flank. Meanwhile, Holmes' intended move from half-back had opened the way up for the reintroduction of Kevin Dick. Leeds' plans were slightly undone eight minutes into the match when their other centre Les Dyl had to be substituted, due to an ankle strain, by Paul Fletcher. Bradford was short of wingman David Barends (a late withdrawal through a stomach complaint) and stand-off David Redfearn (thigh injury) and, although Derek Parker and Steve Ferres were worthy replacements, the Leeds back division retained a much stronger look.

Leeds' Kevin Dick looks for a gap in the Bradford defence

Overall, the Leeds forwards outplayed Bradford's formidable looking pack, allowing space and time for half-backs Dick and John 'Sammy' Sanderson to pin them down in their own backyard with a supreme display in the arts of tactical kicking. In spite of Leeds' domination up front, Bradford was still in with a shout at the interval, trailing by just 7–2, having taken an early lead through a Ferres penalty. In the 31st minute, Leeds' full-back Neil Hague made a 50-yard break that resulted in Alan Smith being brought down just short of the line but, moments later, David Smith went over at the corner following a long pass from Mick Harrison. Dick converted, adding a penalty to

FIRST DIVISION LEADERS

	P	W	D	L	For	Agst	Pts
1 Hull Kingston Rovers	30	23	0	7	616	344	46
2 Warrington	30	22	0	8	521	340	44
3 Widnes	30	21	2	7	480	322	44
4 Leeds	30	19	1	10	555	370	39
5 St Helens	30	16	2	12	485	379	34
6 Wigan	30	16	1	13	484	411	33
7 Castleford	30	16	1	13	498	469	33
8 Bradford Northern	30	16	0	14	523	416	32

(Hull Kingston Rovers won Championship)

CHAMPION CAPTAIN

David Ward (Leeds 1979)

David Ward was born in Morley, signing for Leeds from Shaw Cross Boys' Club of Dewsbury during 1971. He was a workmanlike, skilful hooker, being just 23 years old when he led Leeds to Wembley success in 1977, subsequently being the first recipient of the prestigious Man of Steel Award the same year. His list of successes with the Headingley club include the Premiership Trophy (1975, 1979), Championship (1971/72), League Leaders' Trophy (1971/72), Challenge Cup (1977, 1978), Players' No.6 Trophy (1973), John Player Trophy (1984) and Yorkshire Cup (1972, 1973, 1976, 1979 and 1980). He represented Great Britain in 12 Tests, being a member of the 1977 World Cup squad and 1979 touring party, appearing for England and Yorkshire six times each. After finishing his playing career in 1986, he coached Hunslet (1986–88), Leeds (1989–91), Batley (1991–94, 1997–2000, 2001) and Featherstone Rovers (1994–97).

the Loiners account prior to half-time.

Dick, in fine kicking form, added three more goals – two penalties and a drop – after the break, his interception with ten minutes remaining, enabling him to send winger David Smith sprinting 50 yards for the line. Although tackled by Les Gant, a quick play-the-ball resulted in acting-half Alan Smith going over, Dick's conversion opening up a 17–2 lead to virtually seal victory. Dick continued to keep the scoreboard operator busy with another penalty before tagging on the extras to a late try from skipper David Ward.

Harry Sunderland Trophy winner Dick had a massive influence on the result claiming a new Premiership Trophy Final record of eight goals, the *Yorkshire Post's* Peter Snape commenting: 'Dick proved the perfect foil to the quicksilver Sanderson at scrum half.' He played at stand-off although wearing the '7' of a scrum half on his back, coach Syd Hynes later admitting 'He wore the number seven shirt to kid them a bit!'

STATS

Leeds 24 Bradford Northern 2

Sunday 27 May at Fartown, Huddersfield (3.00 pm)

Leeds: (blue with amber bands) Hague, A. Smith, D. Smith, Dyl, Atkinson, Dick, Sanderson, Harrison, Ward (captain), Pitchford, Joyce, Eccles, Cookson. Substitutes: Fletcher, Adams. Coach: S. Hynes

Bradford Northern: (white with red, amber and black band) Mumby, Parker, Okulicz, Gant, Spencer, Ferres, A. Redfearn, Thompson (captain), Bridges, Forsyth, Trotter, Grayshon, Casey. Substitutes: Mordue, I. van Bellen. Coach: P. Fox

Half-time: 7–2 **Referee:** W.H. Thompson
Attendance: 19,486 **Receipts**: £21,291

Weather: sunny and warm

Harry Sunderland Trophy: Dick (Leeds)

Progressive score:

Leeds	score (min)	Bradford Northern
	0–2 (5)	Ferres penalty
D. Smith try, Dick goal	5–2 (31)	
Dick penalty	7–2 (-)	
Dick penalty	9–2 (-)	
Dick penalty	11–2 (-)	
Dick drop-goal	12–2 (60)	
A. Smith try, Dick goal	17–2 (70)	
Dick penalty	19–2 (-)	
Ward try, Dick goal	24–2 (80)	

Premiership Trophy first round:
Hull Kingston Rovers 17 Bradford Northern 18
Warrington 17 Castleford 10
Widnes 8 Wigan 12
Leeds 21 St Helens 10

Semi-finals:
Warrington 11 Bradford Northern 14
Leeds 20 Wigan 10

Head-to-head form guide:
Bradford Northern 24 Leeds 23 (Yorkshire Cup)
Leeds 5 Bradford Northern 10 (League)
Bradford Northern 10 Leeds 13 (League)

Four of the classy Leeds backs that inflicted so much damaged during this era (from the left); John Atkinson, Alan Smith, Les Dyl and John Holmes. Holmes missed out on the 1979 Premiership triumph after failing a late fitness test

1980 Premiership Trophy Final
WIDNES V BRADFORD NORTHERN

Mal Aspey created one of the most outstanding tries witnessed in a Premiership Trophy Final as Widnes stormed to their first ever success in the competition in 1980. It was an exceptional piece of play that inevitably led to him becoming the first three-quarter to receive the Harry Sunderland Trophy. Bradford Northern, beaten 19–5, and with a try count of five to one against, disappointed in the final for the second consecutive year. Having claimed the First Division Championship and John Player Trophy – Widnes being runners-up in both – Bradford was tipped to add to their silverware haul but was guilty of losing possession in good positions. On a hot, sunny afternoon at Swinton, Northern was outgunned by a competent Widnes outfit that, according to one report, 'won in style casting off their usual professional caution to make the ball do the work.'

Widnes captain Reg Bowden lifts the Premiership Trophy

Aspey's moment of glory came just two minutes before the break when Bradford, 6–5 down and pressing the Widnes line, lost the ball. Widnes scrum half Reg Bowden quickly pounced, passing to Aspey who set off down the outside channel in an arcing run towards the sideline before executing a dummy scissors move with his wingman Keith Bentley. Appearing to transfer to Bentley with a one-handed inside pass, he retained possession to race clear of a confused Bradford defence. Reaching the halfway line, Aspey was held by Northern full-back Keith Mumby but, sensing an opportunity, somehow managed to kick the ball towards the Bradford line. An alert Bentley outpaced two defenders in pursuit of the ball for a great touchdown, described in the *Bradford Telegraph & Argus* by Brian Smith as 'a glorious

STATS

Widnes 19 Bradford Northern 5

Saturday 17 May at Station Road, Swinton (2.45 pm)

Widnes: (white with black trim) Burke, Wright, George, Aspey, Bentley, Eckersley, Bowden (captain), Shaw, Elwell, M. O'Neill, Gorley, Hull, Adams. Substitutes: Moran (dnp), Hogan. Coach: D Laughton

Bradford Northern: (white with red, amber and black band) Mumby, MacLean, D. Redfearn, Parker, Gant, Stephenson, A. Redfearn, Thompson (captain), Bridges, Forsyth, Clarkson, Grayshon, Hale. Substitutes: Ferres, G. van Bellen. Coach: P. Fox

Half-time: 9–5 **Referee:** W.H. Thompson
Attendance: 10,215 **Receipts**: £13,665

Weather: sunny and hot

Harry Sunderland Trophy: Aspey (Widnes)

Progressive score:

Widnes	score (min)	Bradford Northern
	0–5 (3)	D. Redfearn try, Mumby goal
Elwell try, Burke goal	5–5 (16)	
Elwell drop-goal	6–5 (28)	
Bentley try	9–5 (38)	
Wright try	12–5 (62)	
Aspey try	15–5 (64)	
Eckersley drop-goal	16–5 (75)	
Gorley try	19–5 (78)	

Premiership Trophy first round:
Bradford Northern 30 St Helens 0
Widnes 20 Hull Kingston Rovers 10
Hull 0 Leigh 8
Salford 13 Leeds 27

Semi-finals (over two legs):
Bradford Northern 31 Leigh 16 (on aggregate)
Widnes 18 Leeds 17 (on aggregate)

Head-to-head form guide:
Bradford Northern 6 Widnes 0
(John Player Trophy at Headingley, Leeds)
Widnes 10 Bradford Northern 11 (League)
Bradford Northern 5 Widnes 21 (League)

try which will be treasured for years.' It placed Widnes 9–5 ahead as the teams returned to the changing rooms.

In a repeat of the previous year, Bradford – who was without injured winger David Barends – recorded their only points of the match before the opposition managed to score. It followed one of their few worthwhile moves, David Redfearn crossing for a third minute try before Widnes, apart from kicking off, had touched the ball. Keith Mumby's goal made it 5–0. Widnes, though, remained calm and, with Keith Elwell leading the way, had forged ahead by the 28th minute. It was Elwell that chased after his own speculative kick in the 16th minute, collecting what was described as a 'fortunate' bounce to touch the ball down, Mick Burke adding the goal to level the scores. Elwell then coolly added a drop-goal 12 minutes later to edge Widnes 6–5 ahead, setting the stage for Aspey's inspirational run.

CHAMPION CAPTAIN

Reg Bowden (Widnes 1980)

Wily, competitive scrum half Reg Bowden was signed from local amateur ranks in 1968, making his Widnes debut in 1969. With Bowden – who took over as captain in 1975 – dictating play in the middle, Widnes built a reputation as the 'Cup Kings' of the 1970s winning the Premiership Trophy (1980), Championship (1977/78), Rugby League Challenge Cup (1975, 1979), Players' No.6 Trophy/John Player Trophy (1975/76, 1978/79), BBC2 Floodlit Trophy (1978/79) and Lancashire Cup (1974, 1975, 1976, 1978, 1979). He left in 1980 to take over as player-coach of the new London-based Fulham (which has now evolved into the Harlequins RL club), capturing the Second Division Championship with them in 1982/83. He returned north in 1984 as player-coach of Warrington, competing in his final matches later that year but continuing as coach until 1986. Considered by many as unfortunate not to receive international recognition, he represented Lancashire 10 times.

Widnes' 1980 squad. Standing: Mills, Shaw, M. O'Neill, Hogan, Dearden, Aspey, George, Gorley. Seated: J. Myler, Hull, Burke, Wright, Laughton, Bowden, Elwell, Bentley, Adams, Moran

Widnes continued the momentum in the second half, their flowing passing movements keeping Bradford's defence busy. The Chemics added three more tries without response, through Stuart Wright (placing the ball near the corner flag amidst claims he appeared to lose possession in the tackle as he went over), Aspey (rubber-stamping his man of the match claim) and Les Gorley (tearing through after a glorious dummy from Mick Adams). Burke failed to augment any of them in an unusual off day for the normally competent marksman, landing just one of five attempts, David Eckersley being more successful with a drop-goal, shortly before Gorley's score.

FIRST DIVISION LEADERS

	P	W	D	L	For	Agst	Pts
1 Bradford Northern	30	23	0	7	448	272	46
2 Widnes	30	22	1	7	546	293	45
3 Hull	30	18	3	9	454	326	39
4 Salford	30	19	1	10	495	374	39
5 Leeds	30	19	0	11	590	390	38
6 Leigh	30	16	1	13	451	354	33
7 Hull Kingston Rovers	30	16	1	13	539	445	33
8 St Helens	30	15	2	13	505	410	32

(Bradford Northern won Championship)

1981 Premiership Trophy Final
HULL KINGSTON ROVERS V HULL

For the third time in two seasons, and the sixth overall, the two Hull clubs clashed in a major rugby league final, on this occasion to settle the destination of the 1981 Premiership Trophy. Although the close 11–7 score-line in Hull Kingston Rovers' favour represents a fair reflection of their tense, keenly fought struggle, the Rovers held sway over Hull for much of the 80 minutes, their extra pace producing three tries to the one gained by the Airlie Birds. As with three of their previous finals, it took place at Headingley, Leeds, the possibility of using Hull City Football Club's Boothferry Park being discounted. Although the choice of a West Yorkshire venue put extra miles on the clock for many supporters, it attracted new Premiership Final records for attendance (29,448 – almost 10,000 up on the 1979 high) and receipts (£47,529 – the highest outside Wembley).

CHAMPION CAPTAIN

Len Casey (Hull Kingston Rovers 1981)

Len Casey was born in Hull and represented both of the city's senior clubs. A fiercely competitive second-row or loose forward with excellent ball-distribution skills, he joined Hull from the Beverley amateur club in 1968, transferring to rivals Hull Kingston Rovers in 1975 for £6,000. With Rovers, he won the BBC2 Floodlit Trophy (1977) leaving midway through their 1978/79 Championship campaign to join Bradford Northern for £25,000. Having won the John Player Trophy (1979/80) with Northern, he returned to Hull Kingston Rovers during 1980 for a Rugby League record £38,000. Success followed in the Rugby League Challenge Cup (1980), Premiership Trophy (1981) and Championship (1983/84). He played in 14 Tests for Great Britain (3 as captain), being a member of the 1977 World Cup squad and 1979 tour party (withdrawing from the 1984 tour due to suspension), and represented England (5 times) and Yorkshire (once). Joining Wakefield Trinity as player-coach in 1985, he played his final match that year, continuing as coach until 1986. He subsequently coached Hull (1986–88) and Scarborough Pirates (1991).

Mike Smith breaks through the Hull defence on his way to scoring Rovers' third touchdown

Hull, unexpected qualifiers through two excellent play-off wins at Warrington and Castleford, received a shock transfer request from scrum half Clive Pickerill three days before the final. He backed it up by withdrawing from the squad, resulting in him not taking his anticipated place on the bench. The Airlie Birds were also missing suspended centre Graham Walters, his replacement David Elliott making only his second first team appearance. Rovers, meanwhile, were short of full-back Ian Robinson and forward Steve Crooks, both sidelined during the final month of the campaign.

The first points came on 13 minutes following a powerful break from Rovers' prop Roy Holdstock that took play to the Hull 25 area. Centre Phil Hogan gained possession, dummying a pass to a colleague before charging towards the corner flag for the touchdown. Steve Hubbard, despite losing balance as he made the kick, managed to land the difficult conversion. Hull full-back Paul Woods, having

Steve Hartley races towards the try-line to claim Hull Kingston Rovers vital second try five minutes before the interval

been off-target with a 4th minute penalty, then hit the post with a second opportunity. The Robins lead increased to eight points when, with arguably the best try of the match, stand-off Steve Hartley accepted a pass at speed from veteran international second-row Phil Lowe to sprint 65 yards for the corner, avoiding Tim Wilby and Woods on the way. Hubbard missed the goal. As half-time approached Woods pulled two points back with a penalty given for offside.

Four minutes into the second half, Hubbard missed with a 45-yard penalty but Rovers soon increased their lead with a third try seven minutes later, scorer Mike Smith, from a Len Casey pass, evading three defenders in the process. Hubbard failed to add the extras but at 11–2 the Rovers were looking confident. Thirteen minutes later, that comfort looked decidedly prickly when Hull second-row Mick Crane went over, team captain Charlie Stone having dispersed several defenders before supplying the scoring pass. Woods goal made it 11–7 ensuring a plentiful supply of fireworks in the remaining minutes as Hull, with Steve Norton in brilliant form, endeavoured to snatch victory. Both defences held out, though, in a nail-biting finale, Rovers fans breathing a sigh of relief at the end of an absorbing contest, their team winning the Premiership Trophy for the first time.

STATS

Hull Kingston Rovers 11 Hull 7

Saturday 16 May at Headingley, Leeds (2.45 pm)

Hull Kingston Rovers: (white with red band) Proctor, Hubbard, M. Smith, Hogan, Muscroft, Hartley, Harkin, Holdstock, Watkinson, Millington, Lowe, Casey (captain), Hall. Substitutes: Burton, Watson (dnp). Coach: R. Millward

Hull: (black and white irregular hoops) Woods, Peacham, Elliott, Wilby, Prendiville, Banks, Dean, Tindall, Wileman, Stone (captain), Skerrett, Crane, Norton. Substitute: Madley, Chester (dnp). Team manager: A. Bunting

Half-time: 8–2 **Referee:** J. Holdsworth
Attendance: 29,448 **Receipts**: £47,529

Weather: fine and dry, some sunshine

Harry Sunderland Trophy: Casey (Hull Kingston Rovers)

Progressive score:

Hull Kingston Rovers	score (min)	Hull
Hogan try, Hubbard goal	5–0 (13)	
Hartley try	8–0 (35)	
	8–2 (38)	Woods penalty
M. Smith try	11–2 (51)	
	11–7 (64)	Crane try, Woods goal

Premiership Trophy first round:
Bradford Northern 12 St Helens 14
Warrington 7 Hull 19
Hull Kingston Rovers 14 Widnes 12
Wakefield Trinity 8 Castleford 25

Semi-finals:
Hull Kingston Rovers 30 St Helens 17
Castleford 11 Hull 12

Head-to-head form guide:
Hull Kingston Rovers 25 Hull 10 (League)
Hull 16 Hull Kingston Rovers 17 (League)

FIRST DIVISION LEADERS

	P	W	D	L	For	Agst	Pts
1 Bradford Northern	30	20	1	9	447	345	41
2 Warrington	30	19	1	10	459	330	39
3 Hull Kingston Rovers	30	18	2	10	509	408	38
4 Wakefield Trinity	30	18	2	10	544	454	38
5 Castleford	30	18	2	10	526	459	38
6 Widnes	30	16	2	12	428	356	34
7 Hull	30	17	0	13	442	450	34
8 St Helens	30	15	1	14	465	370	31

(Bradford Northern won Championship)

1982 Premiership Trophy Final
WIDNES V HULL

Widnes full-back Mick Burke celebrated an amazing turn around in fortune to inspire his colleagues to a convincing 23–8 Premiership Trophy Final win over Hull in 1982. In only his fourth start after being absent for three months with a back injury, he returned looking overweight and out of condition through his enforced inactivity. His vintage performance was described in the *Widnes Weekly* News as 'real Roy of the Rovers stuff!' Hull, who already boasted a formidable set of forwards, paraded a different and stronger looking back division than in recent seasons, their impressive list of recruits including Test stars Gary Kemble, Dane O'Hara and James Leuluai (all from New Zealand), David Topliss (Wakefield Trinity – who was appointed club captain), and Steve Evans (Featherstone Rovers).

Widnes captain Mick Adams proudly displays the Premiership Trophy watched by colleague Eric Hughes (right)

Burke put Widnes ahead with a 4th minute penalty. Hull's 18-year-old second-row forward Lee Crooks then took the game to the Chemics with a drop-goal on the half-hour, followed by a try near the posts when he burst through two defenders four minutes later, adding the conversion to put the Airlie Birds 6–2 up. Three minutes before the break, Burke pulled Widnes back into the contest when he broke through the middle, off-loading to left-winger John Basnett who kept two defenders at bay for a great try.

STATS

Widnes 23 Hull 8

Saturday 15 May at Headingley, Leeds (2.15 pm)

Widnes: (white with black trim) Burke, Wright, O'Loughlin, Cunningham, Basnett, Hughes, Gregory, M. O'Neill, Elwell, Lockwood, Gorley, Prescott, Adams (captain). Substitutes: Myler, Whitfield. Coach: D. Laughton

Hull: (black and white irregular hoops) Kemble, O'Hara, Leuluai, Evans, Prendiville, Topliss (captain), Harkin, Tindall, Wileman, Stone, Skerrett, Crooks, Norton. Substitutes: Day, Lloyd. Team manager: A .Bunting

Half-time: 5–6
Referee: S. Wall
Attendance: 12,100
Receipts: £23,749

Weather: fine and dry

Harry Sunderland Trophy: Burke (Widnes)

Progressive score:

Widnes	score (min)	Hull
Burke penalty	2–0 (4)	
	2–1 (30)	Crooks drop-goal
	2–6 (34)	Crooks try, Crooks goal
Basnett try	5–6 (37)	
Wright try, Burke goal	10–6 (48)	
	10–8 (60)	Crooks penalty
Hughes try, Burke goal	13–8 (65)	
Burke try	18–8 (68)	
Adams try, Burke goal	23–8 (78)	

Premiership Trophy first round:
Leigh 1 Warrington 1
Hull 23 St Helens 8
Widnes 39 Leeds 11
Hull Kingston Rovers 17 Bradford Northern 8
(Abandoned after 56 minutes when Bradford walked off – match awarded to Hull KR)
Replay: Warrington 10 Leigh 9

Semi-finals:
Hull 27 Warrington 7
Widnes 16 Hull Kingston Rovers 15

Head-to-head form guide:
Widnes 16 Hull 2 (League)
Hull 21 Widnes 3 (League)
Hull 14 Widnes 14
(Challenge Cup at Wembley Stadium, London)

CHAMPION CAPTAIN

Mick Adams (Widnes 1982)

Mick Adams signed for hometown Widnes in 1971 from the club's 'B' team having previously played for the Blackbrook (St Helens) amateur club. Initially used as a reserve full-back, he began establishing himself in the back-row of the pack in 1973. A shrewd passer, noted for his style of running with the ball held to his chest, he took over as loose-forward in 1979 when Doug Laughton retired, replacing the departed Reg Bowden as team captain in 1980. At Widnes, he won the Premiership Trophy (1980, 1982, 1983), Championship (1977/78), Rugby League Challenge Cup (1975, 1979, 1981, 1984), Players' No.6 Trophy/John Player Trophy (1975/76, 1978/79), BBC2 Floodlit Trophy (1978/79) and Lancashire Cup (1974, 1975, 1976, 1978, 1979). He was a tourist twice (1979, 1984), appeared in 13 Test matches, represented England (6 times – including the 1975 World Cup) and Lancashire (12). He retired after 416 matches for Widnes in 1984, later emigrating to Australia. He spent the 1975 and 1976 close seasons in Australia playing for Canterbury-Bankstown.

Burke missed the goal, Widnes going in at the interval one point down.

Eight minutes after the restart Burke became Widnes' hero once more when he punched another hole through Hull's defensive line. This time he attacked down the right, his perfect pass to Stuart Wright sending him racing in from 10 yards out to dive over in spectacular fashion. Burke added the goal and Widnes led 10–6. Crooks landed a penalty for Hull, but it was their last points of the day as Hull's forwards, who had lost hooker Ron Wileman after 30 minutes with a back injury, began to look jaded. Widnes homed in with three touchdowns in the last 15 minutes. First, Eric Hughes crossed in the corner after a brilliant 40-yard arcing run. Then Burke scored under the posts after moving quickly into the line to charge through three defenders (completing a well-executed move after Andy Gregory, from a scrum, transferred to Hughes, who delivered the final short pass). Finally, skipper Mick Adams added an easy looking try off a Fred Whitfield off-load. Burke added the extra points to two of them to round off the scoring. Hull gained revenge four days later, defeating Widnes 18–9 in the Challenge Cup Final replay at Elland Road, Leeds.

FIRST DIVISION LEADERS

	P	W	D	L	For	Agst	Pts
1 Leigh	30	24	1	5	572	343	49
2 Hull	30	23	1	6	611	273	47
3 Widnes	30	23	1	6	551	317	47
4 Hull Kingston Rovers	30	22	1	7	565	319	45
5 Bradford Northern	30	20	1	9	425	332	41
6 Leeds	30	17	1	12	514	418	35
7 St Helens	30	17	1	12	465	415	35
8 Warrington	30	14	2	14	403	468	30

(Leigh won Championship)

The opening round of the Premiership play-off was eventful. Bradford Northern, losing 17–8 at Hull Kingston Rovers, controversially walked off the field in the 56th minute, the club chairman saying they would take no further part in the match. Amongst several 'punishments' meted out to them, Bradford (who had four players sent off) was excluded from the competition, the tie being awarded to Rovers (two sent off). Another talking point was when the soccer-like score of 1–1 between Leigh and visitors Warrington meant a replay at Wigan, Warrington's Wilderspool ground being unavailable following severe fire damage to the main stand.

Man of the match Mick Burke races over for Widnes' fourth try

1983 Premiership Trophy Final
WIDNES V HULL

In a rerun of the previous year's Premiership Trophy Final, Widnes again defeated Hull in the 1983 event, this time by 22–10. Widnes – the first to win three Premierships and the first to appear in four finals – became the only side ever to succeed in the competition from outside the top four, finishing fifth in the League table. Most of the credit was accorded to their 21-year-old stand-off Tony Myler, who dominated the match, having a hand in two tries and scoring another. The Chemics' had prop Kevin Tamati unavailable, whilst Hull were short of winger Paul Prendiville (tonsillitis) and scrum half Paul Harkin (after-effects of concussion)

Pre-match favourites Hull had an early scare when Myler, starting from inside his own 25 area, twice kicked the ball ahead after Paul Rose had lost possession. In an exciting chase Dane O'Hara just got back to dive over the try-line and get the touch ahead of him. Joe Lydon put Widnes two points up with an 8th minute penalty from in front of the posts for offside. After their nervous opening the Airlie Birds began to look the stronger side, tearing into their opposition with some sizzling rugby, skipper David Topliss scoring a try between the posts after recovering a loose ball. With Lee Crooks adding the extras plus a penalty six minutes later, following a high tackle by Myler on Topliss, they led 7–2 after 18 minutes. Crooks just missed another penalty chance from 35-yards before Myler brought Widnes back into the frame 11 minutes before half-time, taking a long pass from loose forward Mick Adams before rounding Gary Kemble to go under the posts. Lydon's goal levelled the scores at 7–7. A few minutes later, John Basnett put Widnes in front, going over in the corner despite O'Hara's tackle after Mick Burke and Lydon had worked an overlap. Lydon missed the goal. The Boulevarders then took advantage of the five-minute sin-binning of Adams for dissent,

Tony Myler proved to be the Widnes hero

Widnes' Cumbrian prop Les Gorley was appearing in his third Premiership Trophy Final with Widnes

CHAMPION CAPTAIN

Eric Hughes (Widnes 1983)

Eric Hughes played 488 times for Widnes in a playing career that stretched from 1969 to 1984. Signed from Widnes Rugby Union Club, having been selected for England and Lancashire at various age levels, the speedy stand-off enjoyed his fair share of honours at Naughton Park, including the Premiership Trophy (1982, 1983), Championship (1977/78), Rugby League Challenge Cup (1975, 1979, 1981, 1984), Players' No.6 Trophy/John Player Trophy (1975/76, 1978/79), BBC2 Floodlit Trophy (1978/79) and Lancashire Cup (1974, 1975, 1978, 1979). He was a tourist in 1979, played in 8 Tests, and represented England (10 times – including 1975 World Cup) and Lancashire (11). During the 1976 close season he played in Australia with Canterbury-Bankstown. After retiring as a player, he held several coaching appointments; Widnes (1984–86), Rochdale Hornets (1987–88), St Helens (1994–96), Leigh (1996) and Wigan (1997). His elder brother Arthur was in the Widnes pack at Wembley in 1964.

O'Hara squaring the match with a try in the corner after quick passing from Terry Day and Crooks, the latter missing the conversion.

The Chemics came alive in the second half, scoring 12 points without reply, Hull's pack – as they had 12 months earlier – tiring as Adams and Myler started to run the show with some mesmerising ball distribution. Another Lydon penalty, following a scrum infringement, restored their lead before Myler went on a brilliant run down the left side enabling Lydon to put Basnett in at the corner for his second try, Lydon missing the goal. It was then the turn of captain Eric Hughes to be the instigator, releasing Myler on another powerful burst. The stand-off, despite being held, flipped the ball up for half-back partner Andy Gregory, who raced unopposed to dive over the whitewash. Lydon converted, adding a penalty, after Tony Dean was judged to have kicked out at Gregory, to complete the scoring.

The *Widnes Weekly News* described their team's performance as 'arguably the(ir) best display of the last decade' with Myler the 'chief assassin.' Hull, meanwhile, was left to ponder the disappointment of three consecutive Premiership Trophy Final defeats, all of them at Headingley.

FIRST DIVISION LEADERS

	P	W	D	L	For	Agst	Pts
1 Hull	30	23	1	6	572	293	47
2 Hull Kingston Rovers	30	21	1	8	496	276	43
3 Wigan	30	20	3	7	482	270	43
4 St Helens	30	19	1	10	516	395	39
5 Widnes	30	18	2	10	534	357	38
6 Leeds	30	18	2	10	480	443	38
7 Castleford	30	18	1	11	629	458	37
8 Oldham	30	15	2	13	346	320	32

(Hull won Championship)

STATS

Widnes 22 Hull 10

Saturday 14 May at Headingley, Leeds (2.15 pm)

Widnes: (red with white trim) Burke, Linton, Hughes (captain), Lydon, Basnett, Myler, Gregory, M. O'Neill, Elwell, Gorley, Whitfield, Prescott, Adams. Substitutes: D. Hulme, S. O'Neill. Coaches: H. Dawson and C. Tyrer

Hull: (black and white irregular hoops) Kemble, O'Hara, Day, Leuluai, Evans, Topliss (captain), Dean, Skerrett, Bridges, Stone, Rose, Crooks, Norton. Substitutes: Solal, Crane. Team manager: A. Bunting

Half-time: 10–10 **Referee:** G.F. Lindop
Attendance: 17,813 **Receipts**: £34,145

Weather: overcast with heavy rain at times

Harry Sunderland Trophy: Myler (Widnes)

Progressive score:

Widnes	score (min)	Hull
Lydon penalty	2–0 (8)	
	2–5 (12)	Topliss try, Crooks goal
	2–7 (18)	Crooks penalty
Myler try, Lydon goal	7–7 (29)	
Basnett try	10–7 (33)	
	10–10 (37)	O'Hara try
Lydon penalty	12–10 (45)	
Basnett try	15–10 (57)	
Gregory try, Lydon goal	20–10 (63)	
Lydon penalty	22–10 (74)	

Premiership Trophy first round:
Hull 24 Oldham 21
Hull Kingston Rovers 35 Castleford 14
Wigan 9 Leeds 12
St Helens 7 Widnes 11

Semi-finals:
Hull 19 Leeds 5
Hull Kingston Rovers 10 Widnes 21

Head-to-head form guide:
Hull 13 Widnes 4 (League)
Widnes 18 Hull 21 (League)

1984 Premiership Trophy Final
HULL KINGSTON ROVERS V CASTLEFORD

Hull Kingston Rovers coach Roger Millward did some astute pack reshuffling during the interval of the 1984 Premiership Trophy Final at Headingley, ensuring his club became the first to complete the double of Championship and Premiership. In what was a fast, entertaining final, a rejuvenated Rovers side mounted a spirited second half revival against Castleford, overturning an 8–0 deficit to triumph 18-10. The Robins were without inspirational forward and team captain Len Casey, who had been suspended for six months after allegedly pushing a touch-judge during the Good Friday derby with Hull, his previous day's appeal at Leeds County Court being unsuccessful. Also missing was their New Zealand scrum half Gordon Smith (broken jaw), Castleford hooker Kevin Beardmore being ruled out with a chest injury.

Rovers had a couple of early 30-yard drop-goal attempts, John Dorahy being wide on both occasions, before Castleford, on six minutes, registered their only try, winger John Kear – destined to build his reputation as a leading Super League coach – scoring near the posts after a scintillating five-man attacking move. Bob Beardmore added the extras. The Rovers almost claimed a try through Garry Clark but the winger brushed the corner flag. Castleford had similar misfortune when Gary Connell knocked on as he went over the line. Beardmore, after a failed drop-goal and penalty attempt, was given a further opportunity when George Fairbairn's drop-out, following the latter, sailed directly into touch. This time,

Australian stand-off John Dorahy was an influential figure in the Hull Kingston Rovers side

CHAMPION CAPTAIN

David Hall (Hull Kingston Rovers 1984)

Locally-born David Hall rose from the ranks of Hull Kingston Rovers Juniors to sign for the senior club, making his debut as a 17-year-old in 1971. Originally a centre, he also had spells at full-back before making an impact as a robust, all-action loose forward in the latter stages of his career, when he also took over the role of club captain. He gained winners' medals for the Premiership Trophy (1981, 1984), Championship (1978/79, 1983/84, 1984/85), Rugby League Challenge Cup (1980) and BBC2 Floodlit Trophy (1977/78). His last first team match for Rovers was the 1985 Premiership Trophy Final loss to St Helens, although he subsequently made three appearances during a loan spell with Wakefield Trinity in 1986. In 1984, he twice represented Great Britain against France.

FIRST DIVISION LEADERS

	P	W	D	L	For	Agst	Pts
1 Hull Kingston Rovers	30	22	2	6	795	421	46
2 Hull	30	22	1	7	831	401	45
3 Warrington	30	19	2	9	622	528	40
4 Castleford	30	18	3	9	686	438	39
5 Widnes	30	19	1	10	656	457	39
6 St Helens	30	18	1	11	649	507	37
7 Bradford Northern	30	17	2	11	519	379	36
8 Leeds	30	15	3	12	553	514	33

(Hull Kingston Rovers won Championship)

Beardmore's penalty flew over, creating a new Castleford club record of 332 points in a season (extended to 334 during the second half).

Although Rovers were showing signs of getting on top as the interval approached, Millward – who used three props in his starting line up to subdue the faster Castleford forwards – made some telling changes during the break. In an effort to speed up the pack, centre Mike Smith went to loose-forward, captain David Hall moved up to the second-row, Mark Broadhurst going to prop in place of the sacrificed John Millington. The changes paid off instantly with Dorahy breaking through the Castleford defence within a minute of the resumption to put Gary Prohm in for a converted try. Beardmore again missed with a drop-goal attempt before Smith got Rovers' second try after Hall created the gap in the 54th minute, putting his team ahead for the first time at 10–8. Dorahy sprinted clear to slide over the line three minutes later for the next, Hall again supplying the pass. Eleven minutes from time Dorahy missed another drop-goal attempt, Beardmore – a minute later – landing a penalty following an offence at a play-the-ball. At 14–10 it set up a dramatic finish, David Laws making it safe a few minutes from time, racing 30 yards to the corner after receiving a perfectly weighted pass from Prohm. With four of the Robins tries being scored in or near the left corner, it made goal-kicking life difficult for their classy Australian stand-off Dorahy, who was only able to append the first. His overall contribution, however, was sufficiently impressive for him to become the first overseas winner of the Harry Sunderland Trophy.

STATS

Hull Kingston Rovers 18 Castleford 10

Saturday 12 May at Headingley, Leeds (2.15 pm)

Hull Kingston Rovers: (red with blue band) Fairbairn, Clark, M. Smith, Prohm, Laws, Dorahy, Harkin, Holdstock, Rudd, Millington, Burton, Broadhurst, Hall (captain). Substitutes: Lydiat, I. Robinson. Coach: R. Millward

Castleford: (amber with black trim) Rookley, Coen, Marchant, Hyde, Kear, S. Robinson, R. Beardmore (captain), Ward, Horton, Connell, Crampton, Atkins, Joyner. Substitutes: Orum (dnp), Mountain (dnp). Coach: M. Reilly

Half-time: 0–8 **Referee:** R. Campbell
Attendance: 12,515 **Receipts**: £31,769

Weather: sunny

Harry Sunderland Trophy: Dorahy (Hull Kingston Rovers)

Progressive score:

Hull Kingston Rovers	score (min)	Castleford
	0–6 (6)	Kear try, Beardmore goal
	0–8 (20)	Beardmore penalty
Prohm try, Dorahy goal	6–8 (41)	
M. Smith try	10–8 (54)	
Dorahy try	14–8 (57)	
	14–10 (70)	Beardmore penalty
Laws try	18–10 (77)	

Premiership Trophy first round:
Hull Kingston Rovers 54 Leeds 0
Hull 42 Bradford Northern 12
Warrington 13 St Helens 19
Castleford 36 Widnes 4

Semi-finals:
Hull Kingston Rovers 21 St Helens 16
Hull 12 Castleford 22

Head-to-head form guide:
Hull Kingston Rovers 14 Castleford 26 (League)
Castleford 8 Hull Kingston Rovers 18 (League)

Hull Kingston Rovers' coach Roger Millward who made some telling changes during the interval

1985 Premiership Trophy Final
ST HELENS V HULL KINGSTON ROVERS

The 1985 Premiership Trophy Final continued the recent trend of producing a high quality, exciting finale to the season, St Helens equalling the Widnes record of three wins and four appearances in overwhelming holders Hull Kingston Rovers 36–16. The first of two Premiership Finals staged at Elland Road, Leeds, the 10-try spectacular is especially remembered for the marauding charges of Saints' giant Australian centre Mal Meninga, signing off his only season in Britain with two interception tries at vital moments. Their loose forward and captain Harry Pinner also made a massive contribution, being involved in each of his side's five other strikes as he orchestrated the attack.

It was St Helens' hooker Gary Ainsworth who got the opening touchdown after two minutes, Pinner's perfectly timed pass having sent Peter Gorley through a gap for the initial break, Sean Day augmenting. Rovers' full-back George Fairbairn responded, scoring a try after racing on to a pass from Gordon Smith after his side won a scrum against the head 15 yards out. Fairbairn added the goal to level matters. Pinner was again a thorn in the side of the Humberside club as he carved open their defence, his pass to full-back Phil Veivers, who came up in support, resulting in the Saints' second try, Day's goal making it 12–6 after only 12 minutes. Two unconverted tries followed; Barry Ledger for St Helens in the 21st minute (scoring in the corner following a sharp passing move instigated by a spectacular Meninga burst), David Laws replying for Rovers six minutes later (another try in the corner after quick passing by Phil Hogan and Gary Prohm). With the score standing at 16–10 in Saints' favour, Meninga claimed his first timely interception try, recovering a wayward pass from Rovers' loose forward David Hall to race 25 yards virtually unopposed, Day adding a simple goal. Pinner was then wide with a 30-yard drop-goal. The first half scoring concluded three minutes before the break when Hull Kingston centre Ian Robinson dived over in the corner after a Mark Broadhurst dummy created the opening. Fairbairn just missed the goal giving St Helens a 22–14 lead.

The pace eased off a little

CHAMPION CAPTAIN

Harry Pinner (St Helens 1985)

Born in St Helens, Harry Pinner signed for his hometown club from their Colts team in 1974. Although not the biggest loose forward around, his industrious play and subtle handling ability made him a formidable opponent. He was a tourist in 1984 and represented Great Britain in seven Tests (4 as captain), England (3 times) and Lancashire (7). With St Helens he won the Premiership Trophy (1977, 1985) and Lancashire Cup (1984). He joined Widnes in 1986, subsequently playing for Leigh (1988), Bradford Northern (1988–89) and Carlisle (1989).

Harry Pinner (with cup) and his St Helens team celebrate their victory over Hull Kingston Rovers. Mal Meninga – scorer of two crucial tries – is at the back, extreme right

St Helens captain Harry Pinner exploits a gap in the Rovers' defence

after the interval, as did the scoring despite a drop-goal attempt from Gordon Smith and penalty strikes from Fairbairn and Day. Eventually Fairbairn succeeded in reducing the arrears to six points with a penalty for offside before Saints slipped back into gear with three tries in the last 16 minutes. The first was another breakaway from Meninga, his interception, again off the unfortunate Hall, preceding his 80-yard charge down the field. It put his team two scores ahead, killing off any hope of a Rovers fight back. Pinner got the next, breaking down the right channel after a big hole appeared in a tired Rovers defence, Day adding the goal. In the final minute Ledger finished it off with one of the afternoon's most exciting tries, the move being started by Pinner in his own half and continued with aplomb by Neil Holding and Shaun Allen.

Following their impressive display over Championship winners Hull Kingston Rovers, the *St Helens Reporter's* Steve Nicholson suggested that, after a lean spell for the club, their performance 'has re-instated Saints as a leading force in Rugby League.' Their 36 points was a new Premiership Trophy Final record, surpassing the 32 they scored in the 1977 decider.

FIRST DIVISION LEADERS

	P	W	D	L	For	Agst	Pts
1 Hull Kingston Rovers	30	24	0	6	778	391	48
2 St Helens	30	22	1	7	920	508	45
3 Wigan	30	21	1	8	720	459	43
4 Leeds	30	20	1	9	650	377	41
5 Oldham	30	18	1	11	563	439	37
6 Hull	30	17	1	12	733	550	35
7 Widnes	30	17	0	13	580	517	34
8 Bradford Northern	30	16	1	13	600	500	33

(Hull Kingston Rovers won Championship)

STATS

St Helens 36 Hull Kingston Rovers 16

Saturday 11 May at Elland Road, Leeds (2.15 pm)

St Helens: (light blue with navy blue chevron and sleeves) Veivers, Ledger, Peters, Meninga, Day, Arkwright, Holding, Burke, Ainsworth, Gorley, Platt, Haggerty, Pinner (captain). Substitutes: Allen, Forber. Coach: W. Benyon

Hull Kingston Rovers: (red with blue band) Fairbairn, Clark, Robinson, Prohm, Laws, M. Smith, G. Smith, Broadhurst, Watkinson (captain), Ema, Kelly, Hogan, Hall. Substitutes: Harkin, Lydiat. Coach: R. Millward

Half-time: 22–14 **Referee:** S. Wall
Attendance: 15,518 **Receipts**: £46,950

Weather: overcast and dry

Harry Sunderland Trophy: Pinner (St Helens)

Progressive score:

St Helens	score (min)	Hull Kingston Rovers
Ainsworth try, Day goal	6–0 (2)	
	6–6 (8)	Fairbairn try, Fairbairn goal
Veivers try, Day goal	12–6 (12)	
Ledger try	16–6 (21)	
	16–10 (27)	Laws try
Meninga try, Day goal	22–10 (29)	
	22–14 (37)	Robinson try
	22–16 (54)	Fairbairn penalty
Meninga try	26–16 (64)	
Pinner try, Day goal	32–16 (70)	
Ledger try	36–16 (80)	

Premiership Trophy first round:
Hull Kingston Rovers 42 Bradford Northern 18
St Helens 26 Widnes 2
Wigan 46 Hull 12
Leeds 36 Oldham 18

Semi-finals:
Hull Kingston Rovers 15 Leeds 14
St Helens 37 Wigan 14

Head-to-head form guide:
Hull Kingston Rovers 32 St Helens 6 (League)
St Helens 3 Hull Kingston Rovers 8 (Challenge Cup)
St Helens 30 Hull Kingston Rovers 14 (League)

1986 Premiership Trophy Final
WARRINGTON V HALIFAX

Warrington won their only Premiership Trophy in 1986, creating new records for the finale of the competition, scoring 38 points and producing a winning margin of 28. Played at Elland Road, Leeds, it also brought in record Premiership Final receipts of £50,879. Although opponents Halifax had clinched the League Championship with some sterling performances from their forwards throughout the season, they had to settle for second best against Warrington's awesome pack, superbly led by an Antipodean front row of Australians Les Boyd and Bob Jackson and New Zealander Kevin Tamati, who all registered tries on the day.

CHAMPION CAPTAIN

Les Boyd (Warrington 1986)

Australian prop or second-row forward Les Boyd was born in Nyngan, New South Wales. Emerging from junior rugby league in Cootamundra, he played for Sydney clubs Western Suburbs (1976–79) and Manly-Warringah (1980–84). He toured Great Britain with the Kangaroos (1978, 1982), made 17 Test appearances and represented New South Wales seven times. Renowned for his explosive running and fierce tackling, he was twice suspended in Australia for long periods. He joined Warrington in 1985 where, as team captain, his led them to success in the 1986 Premiership Trophy. His last Warrington match was in 1989, after which he returned home to become captain-coach of Cootamundra.

Boyd opened the scoring with a touchdown after only two minutes, forcing his way over the try-line after being put through by Tamati. Halifax, though, overcame that early setback, captain-coach Chris Anderson finishing a wonderfully executed move after accepting a pass from Paul Dixon, who had raced clear on the back of a neat dummy. Colin Whitfield added the points, his earlier penalty putting the Thrum Hallers four points up. Half-back Paul Bishop soon levelled the scores when he pushed his way over the line in the 13th minute. Having failed to convert both Warrington tries, Bishop was on target with a penalty 11 minutes later to regain the lead. Whitfield, however, managed a long-range penalty before half-time, the two sides going in all-square at 10–10.

Warrington's jubilant players hoist skipper Les Boyd as they celebrate victory on the Elland Road pitch

The second half was far less competitive as Warrington's pack bulldozed a Halifax set severely depleted through the loss of prop Neil James, who had dislocated his shoulder in the 29th minute, to score 28 points without reply. They shot into a commanding 12-point lead within five minutes of the restart, Tamati (from a play-the-ball under the posts) and Jackson (following confusion in the Halifax ranks when Bishop's failed drop-goal landed on the left side of the posts) crossing for a try each. Bishop enhanced both

A thoughtful looking Halifax team line up for the pre-match presentations

touchdowns. Next on the score-sheet was winger Mark Forster, bursting clear off Paul Cullen's pass after the centre had recovered Andy Gregory's neat kick amidst Halifax protests of offside. Four minutes from time, Brian Johnson – who had replaced Paul Ford as full-back after 22 minutes – caught a Halifax drop-out (taken after Bishop missed with a penalty) near his own 25 area and sprinted down the centre of the field. His neat dummy and sidestep put him into the clear and he raced under the posts to send Warrington fans into a frenzy, Bishop adding the extra points. Halifax almost earned a late consolation but Seamus McCallion was unable to ground the ball. It was left to Wires captain Boyd to score the last try, crossing near the posts after dummying his way through from 20 yards out. Bishop was again on target with the kick.

Warrington's post-match celebration was particularly rewarding for their caretaker-coach Tony Barrow who took up the batten from departed coach Reg Bowden two months earlier, his position being ratified by euphoric club officials in the changing room. After the match Barrow divulged that his plan had been to nullify Halifax's main strength by matching their forward threat down the middle, something he succeeded with admirably.

FIRST DIVISION LEADERS

	P	W	D	L	For	Agst	Pts
1 Halifax	30	19	6	5	499	365	44
2 Wigan	30	20	3	7	776	300	43
3 St Helens	30	20	2	8	730	503	42
4 Warrington	30	20	1	9	665	393	41
5 Widnes	30	19	3	8	520	454	41
6 Leeds	30	15	3	12	554	518	33
7 Hull Kingston Rovers	30	16	1	13	507	498	33
8 Hull	30	15	2	13	616	508	32

(Halifax won Championship)

STATS

Warrington 38 Halifax 10

Sunday 18 May at Elland Road, Leeds (3.00 pm)

Warrington: (white with primrose and blue band) Ford, Forster, Cullen, R. Duane, Carbert, Bishop, A. Gregory, Boyd (captain), Tamati, Jackson, Sanderson, Roberts, M. Gregory. Substitutes: Johnson, McGinty. Coach: A. Barrow

Halifax: (blue and white hoops) Whitfield, Riddlesden, T. Anderson, C. Anderson (captain), Wilson, Crossley, Stephens, Robinson, McCallion, Scott, Juliff, James, Dixon. Substitutes: Smith, Bond. Player-coach: C. Anderson

Half-time: 10–10 **Referee:** G.F. Lindop
Attendance: 13,683 **Receipts**: £50,879

Weather: fine and dry

Harry Sunderland Trophy: Boyd (Warrington)

Progressive score:

Warrington	score (min)	Halifax
Boyd try	4–0 (2)	
	4–2 (6)	Whitfield penalty
	4–8 (8)	C. Anderson try, Whitfield goal
Bishop try	8–8 (13)	
Bishop penalty	10–8 (24)	
	10–10 (40)	Whitfield penalty
Tamati try, Bishop goal	16–10 (42)	
Jackson try, Bishop goal	22–10 (45)	
Forster try	26–10 (63)	
Johnson try, Bishop goal	32–10 (76)	
Boyd try, Bishop goal	38–10 (80)	

Premiership Trophy first round:
Halifax 32 Hull 20
Wigan 47 Hull Kingston Rovers 0
St Helens 22 Leeds 38
Warrington 10 Widnes 8

Semi-finals:
Halifax 16 Leeds 13
Wigan 12 Warrington 23

Head-to-head form guide:
Warrington 12 Halifax 14 (League)
Halifax 18 Warrington 6 (League)

1987 Premiership Trophy Final
WIGAN V WARRINGTON

The 1987 Premiership Trophy Final between Wigan and Warrington remains in the consciousness of most people present that afternoon because it was the first held at Manchester United's world famous Old Trafford ground. The decision to take the Premiership to the so-called 'Theatre of Dreams' – as a double header coupled with the newly-instigated Second Division Premiership Final – was a huge success commercially, setting impressive new records for the competition with an attendance of 38,752 (exceeding the 1981 high by over 9,000) and receipts of £165,166 (more than treble the previous year's figure). The atmosphere and excitement of the event itself was possibly its saving grace. In truth the main contest, won 8–0 by Wigan, was probably the dourest Premiership Final since the competition began with both defences on top. Certainly the miserable, wet conditions did not help, and the pitch had cut up badly during the preceding game – Hunslet and Swinton providing an entertaining Second Division clash – and perhaps the sense of occasion generated by the impressive stadium inhibited the players to a degree.

FIRST DIVISION LEADERS

	P	W	D	L	For	Agst	Pts
1 Wigan	30	28	0	2	941	193	56
2 St Helens	30	20	1	9	835	465	41
3 Warrington	30	20	1	9	728	464	41
4 Castleford	30	20	0	10	631	429	40
5 Halifax	30	17	1	12	553	487	35
6 Hull Kingston Rovers	30	16	0	14	446	531	32
7 Bradford Northern	30	15	1	14	555	550	31
8 Widnes	30	14	0	16	598	613	28

(Wigan won Championship)

CHAMPION CAPTAIN

Ellery Hanley (Wigan 1987)

Ellery Hanley was, arguably, the most outstanding player to emerge in British rugby league during the 1980s, his power and pace creating an imposing on-field presence. He first signed with Bradford Northern as a 17-year-old in 1978 from the Corpus Christi club of Leeds, playing mostly at stand-off. His reputation grew and during the 1984/85 season he scored 55 tries, the highest in Britain since 1960/61. He moved to Wigan in 1985 for a Rugby League record £85,000, taking over as club captain during the 1986/87 campaign, relocating to loose forward that season and scoring 63 tries. With Wigan he won the Premiership Trophy (1987), Championship (1986/87, 1989/90, 1990/91), Rugby League Challenge Cup (1988, 1989, 1990, 1991), World Club Challenge (1987), John Player Trophy (1985/86, 1986/87, 1988/89), Regal Trophy (1989/90) and Lancashire Cup (1985, 1986, 1987, 1988). A £250,000 transfer to Leeds in 1991 set another Rugby League record, his final match being in 1995. He had several short-term spells in Australia with Balmain (1988, 1996, 1997) and Western Suburbs (1989). A tourist in 1984, 1988 and 1992, the latter two as captain (injury costing him a third tour captaincy in 1990), he made 36 Test appearances (19 as captain), played for England (twice) and Yorkshire (5 times). He coached Great Britain (1994–95), England (1994–95) and St Helens (1998–2000), later moving to rugby union, being on the coaching staff for England, Bristol and Bath. He received the MBE in 1990 and was elected to the Rugby League Hall of Fame in 2005.

Wigan's Joe Lydon breaks through the Warrington defence on his way to scoring the only try of the match

STATS

Wigan 8 Warrington 0

Sunday 17 May at Old Trafford, Manchester (3.30 pm)

Wigan: (cherry and white hoops) Hampson, Gill, Stephenson, Bell, Lydon, Edwards, A. Gregory, Case, Kiss, Wane, Goodway, Potter, Hanley (captain). Substitutes: Russell, West. Coach: G. Lowe

Warrington: (white with primrose and blue chevron) Johnson, Drummond, Ropati, Peters, Forster, Cullen, Bishop, Tamati, Roberts, Jackson (captain), Humphries, Sanderson, R. Duane. Substitutes: M. Gregory, Eccles. Coach: A. Barrow

Half-time: 6–0 **Referee:** K. Allatt
Attendance: 38,756 **Receipts**: £165,166

Weather: heavy rain, cold

Harry Sunderland Trophy: Lydon (Wigan)

Progressive score:

Wigan	score (min)	Warrington
Stephenson penalty	2–0 (2)	
Lydon try	4–0 (35)	
Gill penalty	4–6 (75)	

Premiership Trophy first round:
Wigan 22 Widnes 18
St Helens 46 Bradford Northern 14
Warrington 24 Hull Kingston Rovers 12
Castleford 6 Halifax 18

Semi-finals:
Wigan 18 Halifax 10
St Helens 8 Warrington 18

Head-to-head form guide:
Warrington 23 Wigan 12 (League)
Wigan 4 Warrington 6 (League)
Wigan 18 Warrington 4
(John Player Trophy at Burnden Park, Bolton)

Wigan coach Graham Lowe with his clubs 1986/87 silverware haul; Lancashire Cup and First Division Championship (back), Premiership Trophy (centre), Colts Championship and John Player Trophy (front)

Wigan's Joe Lydon gave the crowd their only real moment of excitement five minutes before the interval with a stunning try. Scrum half Andy Gregory was the provider, booting the ball up the field from inside his own 25 area. Although Gregory appeared to be impeded, referee Kevin Allatt allowed advantage as Lydon gave chase, the speedy winger three times getting his foot to the ball as he propelled it towards the Warrington try-line. Despite the presence of opposite number and equally quick Des Drummond, Lydon managed to pick up the slippery ball and dive over, staving off desperate late tackles by two more defenders for the only try of the match. David Stephenson missed the conversion. But that was not Lydon's only contribution to Wigan's success, coming up with some excellent tactical kicking, including a 70-yard effort to touch, on a day when running with the ball was always less effective. The other scores came from two Wigan penalties; Stephenson in the 2nd minute (a 30 yard effort after alleged use of the elbow in a tackle), and Henderson Gill five minutes from time (Ronnie Duane being pulled up for a high tackle).

Warrington – missing hooker Mark Roskell, stand-off Keith Holden and captain and prop Les Boyd due to injuries – came closest to a touchdown when second-row man Gary Sanderson had one disallowed three minutes after the break for 'accidental' offside. Their scrum half Paul Bishop was also off-target with the boot, missing penalties in the 4th and 26th minutes followed by a misfired drop-goal.

For Wigan, the result justified their 'gamble' of playing half-backs Shaun Edwards (torn knee ligaments – although still below par by his own high standard) and Andy Gregory (sprung shoulder). In achieving their first Premiership Trophy win, Wigan completed an impressive haul for the season, having won the Championship, John Player Special Trophy (beating Warrington in the final) and Lancashire Cup.

1988 Premiership Trophy Final
WIDNES V ST HELENS

Widnes claimed a record fourth Premiership Trophy success on a sun-drenched, baking hot afternoon at Old Trafford, with the weather, according to David Candler in the *Widnes Weekly News*, being matched by a 'white hot display' from Widnes. Certainly their brilliant, breathtaking performance against St Helens entertained the 35,000 plus crowd, who generated new record receipts for the final of £202,616, their 38 points equalling the record set by Warrington two years earlier. They also shared with the Saints the distinction of appearing in a record fifth Premiership final.

St Helens, without loose forward Andy Platt who chipped a bone in his leg during the semi-final, was looking comfortable in the opening stages, containing early Widnes pressure and claiming a 5th minute lead through Paul Loughlin's 45-yard penalty after Joe Grima allegedly punched Paul Forber. From then on, though, it was Widnes' day, skipper Kurt Sorenson charging through Neil Holding a minute later for the first try, Duncan Platt adding the goal. Eighteen minutes elapsed before their next score, Darren Wright, using winger Martin Offiah as a foil and producing an exquisite dummy pass to cross in the left corner. Andy Currier converted with a towering kick. Five minutes later St Helens came closest to a first half try, Stuart Evans being turned on his back in the Widnes in-goal area. With 30 minutes gone, Offiah made his first threatening run, his 40-yard sprint ending near halfway when Barry Ledger forced him out. Eight minutes from the interval David Hulme scored the final points of the half, racing over after supporting a Richie Eyres break for a 16–2 lead.

Loughlin opened the second half scoring with a penalty one minute after the resumption. David Hulme, though, completed his brace just five minutes later after a tremendous move,

CHAMPION CAPTAIN

Kurt Sorenson (Widnes 1988, 1989, 1990)

Kurt Sorenson has the distinction of being the only player to captain three Premiership Trophy winning sides, achieving his treble with Widnes in consecutive years (1988, 1989, 1990). A fearsome defender with a fair turn of speed, the prop or second-row forward was born in Auckland, being just 17 years old when he first represented Auckland province, making an impressive 27 appearances for New Zealand (including four World Cups). He played for local club Mount Wellington before Wigan brought him to England for the 1976/77 season. He was unattached during 1978 whilst living in Australia prior to joining Sydney clubs Cronulla-Sutherland (1979–83) and Eastern Suburbs (1984). He joined Widnes a few months into the start of the 1984/85 campaign, remaining until 1993, although having a final stint with Cronulla-Sutherland during the 1985 British close-season. Other honours at Widnes include the World Club Challenge (1989), Championship (1987/88, 1988/89), Regal Trophy (1991/92), Lancashire Cup (1990) and Charity Shield (1988, 1989, 1990). He transferred to Whitehaven as player-coach (1993–95) and later coached Workington Town (1995–96) and was also the joint-Cumbria coach (1994–95).

David Hulme – scorer of two Widnes touchdowns

Widnes' Kurt Sorenson with the Premiership Trophy. He was destined to be the first captain to lead a team to three consecutive wins

Eyres again being the provider, lobbing the ball across despite being apprehended by Mark Bailey. Currier added the goal and Widnes looked well in control at 22–4 with over a half-hour left. Roy Haggerty gave St Helens hope when he charged through a complacent defence for his team's first try, Loughlin adding the two points. Widnes soon recovered, Offiah racing towards the try-line in the 59th minute, only for referee John Holdsworth to bring him back for a knock-on, a decision subsequently shown as incorrect. Four minutes later Alan Tait scored his first try for Widnes on the opposite flank, receiving the ball from Currier. Recently signed from Scottish rugby union, Tait came off the bench in the 7th minute replacing unlucky winger Rick Thackray who injured his hip when he tripped. Ledger shot over for a second Saints try but at 26–14 and a little over 10 minutes remaining it was mere consolation. Two more Widnes tries wrapped things up nicely for the winners; Wright taking David Hulme's pass on the burst, and Phil McKenzie crossing from 40 yards out, after Wright intercepted Holding's pass, before sending him clear. Currier tagged on both goals to clinch an emphatic 38–14 win claimed by the *Widnes Weekly* News correspondent as 'one of the most memorable triumphs in the club's history.'

FIRST DIVISION LEADERS

	P	W	D	L	For	Agst	Pts
1 Widnes	26	20	0	6	641	311	40
2 St Helens	26	18	0	8	672	337	36
3 Wigan	26	17	2	7	621	327	36
4 Bradford Northern	26	18	0	8	528	304	36
5 Leeds	26	15	3	8	577	450	33
6 Warrington	26	14	2	10	531	416	30
7 Castleford	26	13	0	13	505	559	26
8 Halifax	26	12	0	14	499	437	24

(Widnes won Championship)

STATS

Widnes 38 St Helens 14

Sunday 15 May at Old Trafford, Manchester (3.30 pm)

Widnes: (white with black trim) Platt, Thackray, Currier, Wright, Offiah, Dowd, D. Hulme, Sorenson (captain), McKenzie, Grima, M. O'Neill, P Hulme, R. Eyres. Substitutes: Tait, S. O'Neill. Coach: D. Laughton

St Helens: (white with red chevron) Loughlin, Ledger, Tanner, Elia, Quirk, Bailey, Holding, Burke, Groves (captain), Evans, Forber, Fieldhouse, Haggerty. Substitutes: Dwyer, Allen. Coach: A. Murphy

Half-time: 16–2 **Referee:** J. Holdsworth
Attendance: 35,252 **Receipts**: £232,298

Weather: very hot and sunny, slight breeze

Harry Sunderland Trophy: D. Hulme (Widnes)

Progressive score:

Widnes	score (min)	St Helens
	0–2 (5)	Loughlin penalty
Sorenson try, Platt goal	6–2 (6)	
Wright try, Currier goal	12–2 (24)	
D. Hulme try	16–2 (32)	
	16–4 (41)	Loughlin penalty
D. Hulme try, Currier goal	22–4 (46)	
	22–10 (56)	Haggerty try, Loughlin goal
Tait try	26–10 (63)	
	26–14 (69)	Ledger try
Wright try, Currier goal	32–14 (72)	
McKenzie try, Currier goal	38–14 (76)	

Premiership Trophy first round:
Widnes 36 Halifax 26
St Helens 40 Castleford 8
Wigan 12 Warrington 24
Bradford Northern 32 Leeds 18

Semi-finals:
Widnes 20 Warrington 10
St Helens 24 Bradford Northern 10

Head-to-head form guide:
St Helens 12 Widnes 10 (John Player Trophy)
St Helens 25 Widnes 0 (League)
Widnes 16 St Helens 6 (League)

1989 Premiership Trophy Final
WIDNES V HULL

The Premiership Trophy seemed to come of age when Widnes met Hull in the 1989 final, the double decider – Sheffield Eagles defeated Swinton in the Second Division Final – drawing in excess of 40,000 for the first time with receipts rising significantly to a new high of £264,242. Widnes again proved to be a team for the big occasion, the First Division Champions producing three spectacular tries in seeing off a determined Hull combination, 18-10.

Shortly after having a try claim from David Hulme ruled out for a forward pass, Widnes scored the first of their magnificent trio in the 11th minute, second-row forward Emosi Koloto breaking through Hull's defence to send centre Darren Wright racing from near halfway to finish behind the uprights. Jonathan Davies, the former Wales rugby union star, appearing in his first final after transferring from Llanelli the previous January, added the conversion. Hull, however, was not ready to throw in the towel so early in the contest, their forwards exerting great pressure to crack the Widnes resistance just five minutes later, loose forward Gary Divorty evading a would-be tackler before sending Paul Welham over with a defence-splitting pass. Stand-off Gary Pearce added the goal. Widnes became temporarily reduced to 12 men when Joe Grima was sin-binned in the 21st minute after being accused of punching Pearce.

Widnes captain Kurt Sorenson charges through the Hull defence

He was back by the time that Pearce slotted over a penalty three minutes before the break, Paul Hulme having been pulled up for scrum-feeding, conceding further yardage through dissent. It gave Hull what looked like being an interval lead of 8–6. Widnes, though, had other ideas, centre Andy Currier almost scoring moments later following a brilliant Alan Tait run before being hauled down by a desperate last-ditch Paul Fletcher tackle. Fate then took a

STATS

Widnes 18 Hull 10

Sunday 14 May at Old Trafford, Manchester (3.30 pm)

Widnes: (white with black trim) Tait, Davies, Currier, Wright, Offiah, D. Hulme, P. Hulme, Sorenson (captain), McKenzie, Grima, M. O'Neill, Koloto, R. Eyres. Substitutes: Myler, Pyke. Coach: D. Laughton

Hull: (black and white irregular hoops) Fletcher, Eastwood, Blacker, Price, O'Hara (captain), Pearce, Windley, Dannatt, Jackson, S. Crooks, Welham, Sharp, Divorty. Substitutes: R. Nolan, Wilby. Coach: B. Smith

Half-time: 10–8 **Referee:** J. Holdsworth
Attendance: 40,194 **Receipts**: £264,242

Weather: fine and dry

Harry Sunderland Trophy: Tait (Widnes)

Progressive score:

Widnes	score (min)	Hull
Wright try, Davies goal	6–0 (11)	
	6–6 (16)	Welham try, Pearce goal
	6–8 (37)	Pearce penalty
Currier try	10–8 (40)	
Offiah try, Davies goal	16–8 (42)	
Davies penalty	18–8 (55)	
	18–10 (60)	Pearce penalty

Premiership Trophy first round:
Widnes 30 Bradford Northern 18
Wigan 2 St Helens 4
Leeds 12 Featherstone Rovers 15
Hull 32 Castleford 6

Semi-finals:
Widnes 38 St Helens 14
Hull 23 Featherstone Rovers 0

Head-to-head form guide:
Widnes 38 Hull 6 (League)
Hull 23 Widnes 16 (League)

FIRST DIVISION LEADERS

	P	W	D	L	For	Agst	Pts
1 Widnes	26	20	1	5	726	345	41
2 Wigan	26	19	0	7	543	434	38
3 Leeds	26	18	0	8	530	380	36
4 Hull	26	17	0	9	427	355	34
5 Castleford	26	15	2	9	601	480	32
6 Featherstone Rovers	26	13	1	12	482	545	27
7 St Helens	26	12	1	13	513	529	25
8 Bradford Northern	26	11	1	14	545	518	23

(Widnes won Championship)

hand when, with a minute left to the break and Hull pressing the Widnes line, centre Richard Price attempted a kick on the last tackle. In what was a pivotal moment in the game, he misdirected the ball into the waiting arms of Currier, who ran almost the full length of the field for a dramatic touchdown that had Widnes fans jumping out of their seats. Davies missed the goal but Widnes had an uplifting 10–8 half-time lead they had not expected moments before. There was a dark cloud on their silver lining, however, David Hulme – who had passed a late fitness check on a bruised ankle tendon incurred three weeks earlier – having to be helped off the pitch and out of the match, Tony Myler replacing him.

Just two minutes into the second period, Widnes scored their third try after winning a scrum on Hull's 25-yard line. Try-scoring machine Martin Offiah drifted in from the wing to accept Tait's pass at speed, cutting through for a crucial score. Davies appended the goal to make it 16–8. Three minutes later Dane O'Hara appeared to have scored a try in the corner despite being tackled by Tait and Currier in the process. The touch-judge ruled O'Hara had gone in touch, although the New Zealander later said 'I've no doubts whatsoever that I scored.' Ten minutes afterwards Davies kicked over a penalty following a foul on Paul Hulme, stretching the lead to 10 points. The only remaining score came from the boot of Pearce, registering his second penalty after one hour's play.

Whilst Widnes could rejoice, having repeated their previous season's feat of winning a Championship-Premiership double, Hull were left to lament that they had lost all four of their Premiership Final appearances to date, three at the hands of Widnes.

Alan Tait – the Scottish full-back produced a man of the match display for Widnes

1990 Premiership Trophy Final
WIDNES V BRADFORD NORTHERN

Cup Kings Widnes became the first club to win three consecutive Premiership Trophy Finals – an accomplishment not achieved in the days of the Championship Final – disposing of off colour Bradford Northern 28–6 in the 1990 finale. It was a proud moment for their New Zealand captain Kurt Sorenson who had the distinction of leading the team to all three victories. Widnes had to complete their treble the hard way playing the entire second half a man short after the 39th minute dismissal of scrum half Paul Hulme for allegedly gouging Northern's Paul Medley. Such was their display after the interval it was difficult to detect the handicap.

Rival hookers Phil McKenzie of Widnes (left) and Bradford's Brian Noble await developments as Chemics' loose forward Les Holliday weighs the options

The outstanding performer in most eyes was Widnes' full-back Alan Tait who repeated his feat of the previous year by being awarded the Harry Sunderland Trophy, the first player to win it twice. His excellent support play led to the opening four Widnes tries, two of which he scored himself. The first came in the 2nd minute when loose forward Les Holliday broke down the middle from halfway, Tait racing up to accept his pass, returning the favour to enable Holliday to go between the posts. Jonathan Davies added the simple goal. Keith Mumby missed two penalty attempts for Bradford Northern before the Scot again linked up. A Widnes attack in the 26th minute appeared to falter when the ball went loose but Davies recovered it, passing to the supporting Tait who sprinted between two defenders for the score. Davies missed the conversion. Mumby then failed with another penalty opportunity awarded on the back of Paul Hulme's dismissal, the score being 10–0 at half-time.

The third Widnes try arrived shortly after the interval when Tony Myler (the stand-off being introduced off the bench for the second half in place of skipper Sorenson in a reshuffle to cover Paul Hulme's loss) broke out from Widnes

STATS

Widnes 28 Bradford Northern 6

Sunday 13 May at Old Trafford, Manchester (3.30 pm)

Widnes: (white with black trim) Tait, Davies, Currier, Wright, Offiah, D. Hulme, P. Hulme, Sorenson (captain), McKenzie, M. O'Neill, Koloto, R. Eyres, Holliday. Substitutes: Myler, Grima. Coach: D. Laughton

Bradford Northern: (white with red, amber and black chevron) Wilkinson, Cordle, McGowan, Marchant, Francis, Simpson, Harkin, Skerrett, Noble, Hobbs (captain), Medley, Fairbank, Mumby. Substitutes: Cooper, Richards. Player-coach: D. Hobbs

Half-time: 10–0 **Referee:** C. Morris
Attendance: 40,796 **Receipts**: £273,877

Weather: sunny and warm

Harry Sunderland Trophy: Tait (Widnes)

Progressive score:

Widnes	score (min)	Bradford Northern
Holiday try, Davies goal	6–0 (2)	
Tait try	10–0 (26)	
Tait try	14–0 (43)	
Currier try, Davies goal	20–0 (50)	
Currier try, Davies goal	26–0 (53)	
	26–6 (63)	Marchant try, Mumby goal
Davies penalty	28–6 (70)	

Premiership Trophy first round:
Wigan 28 Warrington 26
Leeds 24 Castleford 18
Widnes 18 Hull 8
Bradford Northern 25 St Helens 8

Semi-finals:
Wigan 0 Bradford Northern 9
Leeds 7 Widnes 27

Head-to-head form guide:
Bradford Northern 16 Widnes 6 (League)
Widnes 14 Bradford Northern 40 (League)

FIRST DIVISION LEADERS

	P	W	D	L	For	Agst	Pts
1 Wigan	26	20	0	6	699	349	40
2 Leeds	26	18	0	8	704	383	36
3 Widnes	26	16	2	8	659	423	34
4 Bradford Northern	26	17	0	9	614	416	34
5 St Helens	26	17	0	9	714	544	34
6 Hull	26	16	1	9	577	400	33
7 Castleford	26	16	0	10	703	448	32
8 Warrington	26	13	1	12	424	451	27

(Wigan won Championship)

territory. It put his side deep into Hull's half, setting up Tait for his second try, Davies being unable to add the extras, his touchline kick falling just short. Two minutes later Darren Wright almost got Martin Offiah away, following a Mike O'Neill break, but the flying wingman was unable to hold the pass. Ian Wilkinson of Bradford provided the next piece of excitement, the full-back beating seven defenders on a mesmerising 80-yard break from his own territory but, lacking support, he was eventually stalled by Tait. Widnes returned the ball up the field with interest, Andy Currier dummied his way over for another try and struck again for his second off a pass from hooker Phil McKenzie.

Widnes' Paul Hulme shrugs off a Roger Simpson tackle

Davies converted both to put Widnes 26–0 ahead after 13 minutes of the second half.

Centre Tony Marchant eventually scored for Northern, racing around Tait in the 63rd minute after good approach work from scrum half Paul Harkin and second-rower Karl Fairbank, Mumby providing the additional points. Davies hit a penalty 10 minutes from time, given for holding down after a tackle, Offiah and Mike O'Neill almost adding further tries in the closing minutes.

Whilst the *Bradford Telegraph & Argus* felt that Northern had 'arguably' given their worst showing of the campaign, triumphant Widnes coach Doug Laughton said of his team afterwards: 'That's by far our best performance out of four at Old Trafford including the one against Canberra Raiders in the (1989) World Club championship.' The occasion again produced a record Premiership Final crowd (40,796) and receipts (£273,877), Widnes being able to boast, with some justification, of a record sixth win in a record seventh appearance.

1991 Premiership Trophy Final
HULL V WIDNES

Hull won the Premiership Trophy Final in 1991 at the fifth time of asking, producing a ruthlessly efficient performance to defeat strongly fancied favourites Widnes 14–4, thereby gaining revenge over the club that had defeated them in three of their four previous finals.

With Hull's forwards taking a firm grip on proceedings, it allowed half-backs – Australian Greg Mackey and Frenchman Patrick Entat – the room to orchestrate play. It was skipper Mackey's craftiness that set up the opening try in the 12th minute, kidding the Widnes defence into believing he was about to kick the ball skywards but, instead, slipping a perfect pass to Richard Gay who avoided Kurt Sorenson's tackle to dive over the line. Paul Eastwood, who missed with an earlier penalty attempt, was also wide with the conversion. The Hull pack, led by an awesome front row of Karl Harrison, Lee Jackson and Andy Dannatt, took an iron grip, continually testing the Widnes resistance.

French half-back Patrick Entat in full flow for Hull

Midway through the first half Eastwood almost got their second touchdown after a break by Entat, Jonathan Davies making the vital saving tackle. But, 14 minutes before half-time, the pressure told; Entat evaded several would-be tacklers on a brilliant cross-field run, Eastwood taking his pass and cutting inside to send Russ Walker crashing over from two yards out. Eastwood again missed the kick, Hull leading 8–0.

Widnes stepped up their efforts after the break and must have thought the match was set to turn their way when Martin Offiah crossed the Hull try-line almost on the hour. It came after Sorenson had broken free with a neat step on the halfway line before aiming a short pass to David Hulme. The Widnes scrum half drew Hull full-back Gay before delivering the scoring pass. Although Davies missed the kick, they were encouraged at registering their first score and, with just four points in it, the Chemics looked a more motivated outfit. But a great chance was lost after Sorenson again made an opening, Emosi Koloto taking the wrong option, ignoring unmarked Darren Wright on the inside in favour of hemmed in John Devereux on the flank, the pass being ruled forward. With Hull showing determination to deny Widnes' star-studded back division any opportunity to shine, that was their last real glimmer. Ten minutes from full time the Airlie Birds sewed the game up with a try that contained a story straight off the pages of *Boy's Own*. The scorer, Gary Nolan,

CHAMPION CAPTAIN

Greg Mackey (Hull 1991)

Sydney-born Australian half-back Greg Mackey played for the Mascot Juniors club before joining South Sydney (1981–83), Illawarra Steelers (1984–88) and Canterbury-Bankstown (1989). He also turned out for Paris-based Chatillon during the 1983/84 French season. In 1989 he came to England and joined Warrington, winning the Lancashire Cup the same year, unexpectedly moving to Hull a few months later. At Hull, his slick passing, kicking game, and ability to control a match led to him becoming team captain. After helping Hull lift the Premiership Trophy in 1991, he rejoined Warrington the following year, where he was also made captain. After the 1995/96 season, he returned to Australia where he coached at country club level.

had come off the bench nine minutes after the interval to replace injured centre Damien McGarry. It was only his fourth senior appearance – all but one as a substitute – since signing the previous month from the National Dock Labour Board amateur club in Hull. His try came after Mackey shoved the ball out to him a few yards from the corner flag, Nolan reaching through a melee of bodies with an outstretched arm to earn his moment of glory. Eastwood finally got his elusive goal with a great touchline effort for the only two-pointer of the afternoon to complete the scoring.

Hull coach Noel Cleal received post-match acclaim for the effectiveness of his game plan but any resolve Widnes may have had must have been severely shaken by pre-match stories that coach Doug Laughton was set to take over at Leeds and wing star Offiah had requested a transfer. Both reports proved true, Offiah joining Wigan for a record £440,000 the following season. The Premiership Final, meanwhile, continued its trend for setting records with an attendance of 42,043 and receipts of £384,300.

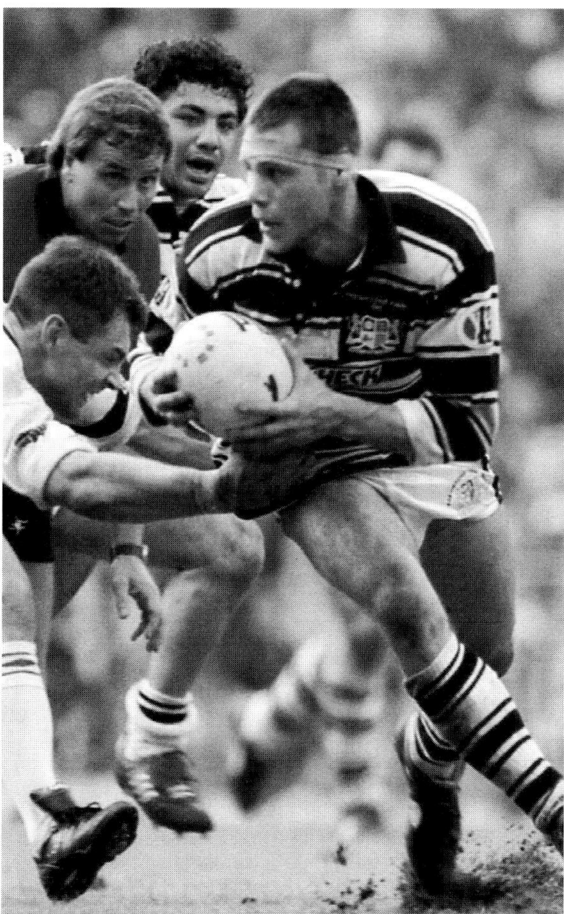

Referee John Holdsworth gets caught up in the action as Hull's Les Jackson takes evasive action

FIRST DIVISION LEADERS

	P	W	D	L	For	Agst	Pts
1 Wigan	26	20	2	4	652	313	42
2 Widnes	26	20	0	6	635	340	40
3 Hull	26	17	0	9	513	367	34
4 Castleford	26	17	0	9	578	442	34
5 Leeds	26	14	2	10	602	448	30
6 St Helens	26	14	1	11	628	533	29
7 Bradford Northern	26	13	1	12	434	492	27
8 Featherstone Rovers	26	12	1	13	533	592	25

(Wigan won Championship)

STATS

Hull 14 Widnes 4

Sunday 12 May at Old Trafford, Manchester (3.30 pm)

Hull: (black and white irregular hoops) Gay, Eastwood, McGarry, Webb, Turner, Mackey (captain), Entat, Harrison, Jackson, Dannatt, Marlow, Walker, Sharp. Substitutes: G. Nolan, Busby. Coach: N. Cleal

Widnes: (white with black and red chevron) Tait, Devereux, Currier, Davies (captain), Offiah, Dowd, D. Hulme, Sorenson, McKenzie, Grima, P. Hulme, Koloto, McCurrie. Substitutes: Wright, Howard. Coach: D. Laughton

Half-time: 8–0 **Referee:** J. Holdsworth
Attendance: 42,043 **Receipts:** £384,300

Weather: hazy sunshine and warm

Harry Sunderland Trophy: Mackey (Hull)

Progressive score:

Hull	score (min)	Widnes
Gay try	4–0 (12)	
Walker try	8–0 (26)	
	8–4 (59)	Offiah try
Nolan try, Eastwood goal	14–4 (70)	

Premiership Trophy first round:
Wigan 26 Featherstone Rovers 31
Widnes 46 Bradford Northern 10
Hull 28 St Helens 12
Castleford 20 Leeds 24

Semi-finals:
Widnes 42 Featherstone Rovers 28
Hull 10 Leeds 7

Head-to-head form guide:
Hull 32 Widnes 6 (League)
Widnes 24 Hull 16 (Regal Trophy)
Widnes 28 Hull 2 (League)

1992 Premiership Trophy Final
WIGAN V ST HELENS

On a roasting hot afternoon, Wigan, having already secured a League and Challenge Cup double, rounded off their 1991/92 term with a convincing 48–16 victory over St Helens in the Premiership Trophy Final. Looking at that score-line it is difficult to believe the Saints held a 12–10 lead prior to the 52nd minute before Wigan defied the sapping heat to run in six tries, registering their 25th consecutive victory in the process.

St Helens started strongest but, after a penalty apiece from Saints' Paul Loughlin and Wigan's Frano Botica, they briefly lost their way, going behind 10–2 after an 18th minute sin-bin for captain Shane Cooper for allegedly kicking Shaun Edwards. Botica, on his way to Premiership records of 10 tries and 20 points, put Wigan ahead from the resultant penalty. The Cherry and Whites notched the opening try five minutes later, Andy Platt dummying his way through, Botica augmenting. Although still down to 12 men, St Helens retaliated, Paul Bishop and George Mann sending Loughlin over by the corner flag, to which he added a great touchline kick. Cooper was back for Saints' next try, seven minutes before the break, Loughlin creating space for Anthony Sullivan to leave Edwards trailing in a 30-yard sprint for the line. Loughlin missed the kick, St Helens leading 12–10 at half-time.

Twelve minutes after the resumption the outcome altered on the back of a stunning Wigan try. Deep inside his own territory,

A powerful burst by Wigan second-row forward Denis Betts leaves the St Helens defence trailing

CHAMPION CAPTAIN

Dean Bell (Wigan 1992)

New Zealand centre Dean Bell was born in Otara, Auckland, and played for Manukau. He came to England for the 1982/83 season with Carlisle, returning the following campaign with the New Zealand Maoris touring side that played several games against amateur opposition. After the tour, he concluded the season with Leeds, winning the John Player Trophy. He rejoined Manukau, transferring to Australian club Eastern Suburbs for their 1985 and 1986 terms (he returned there on loan in 1988). Wigan signed him during September 1986, the talented, but tough opponent – known as 'Mean Dean' – taking over the captaincy in 1991/92. His medal tally covers success in the Championship (1986/87, 1989/90, 1990/91, 1991/92, 1992/93, 1993/94), Premiership Trophy (1987, 1992), Rugby League Challenge Cup (1988, 1989, 1990, 1991, 1992, 1993, 1994), John Player Trophy (1986/87, 1988/89), Regal Trophy (1989/90, 1992/93), Lancashire Cup (1986, 1987, 1988, 1992) and Charity Shield (1987, 1991), missing the 1987 and 1991 World Club Challenge wins through injury. His final Wigan match was in 1994, joining Auckland Warriors as skipper for their inaugural 1995 season, after which he retired. He returned to England to coach Leeds (1995–97), later concentrating on youth development at the club, followed by a similar role at Wigan from 1999 until 2007. He made 26 Test appearances for New Zealand (four as captain) and was a Kiwi tourist three times, being captain of the 1987 squad to Australia and Papua New Guinea.

FIRST DIVISION LEADERS

	P	W	D	L	For	Agst	Pts
1 Wigan	26	22	0	4	645	307	44
2 St Helens	26	17	2	7	550	388	36
3 Castleford	26	15	2	9	558	365	32
4 Warrington	26	15	0	11	507	431	30
5 Leeds	26	14	1	11	515	406	29
6 Wakefield Trinity	26	13	1	12	400	435	27
7 Halifax	26	12	0	14	618	566	24
8 Widnes	26	12	0	14	511	477	24

(Wigan won Championship)

Edwards sent Gene Miles on a blistering run, his perfectly executed off-load to Martin Offiah (scorer of a Premiership record 10 tries in the 74–6 semi-final annihilation of Leeds) sending the winger on a 45-yard dash to the posts. Botica added the goal plus a penalty six minutes later to lead 18–12. Suddenly, Wigan rediscovered their electric form, running in five more tries in a magical 20-minute spell; Denis Betts (an inside pass off Botica ending a five-man move), David Myers (almost strolling past Loughlin barely a minute after coming on as substitute), Miles (latching on to Phil Clarke's pass to score in the corner), Offiah (taking Edwards' pass at speed and 'goose stepping' over the line), Betts again (a typical charge over the line by the second-rower). All five tries were converted by Botica, Sullivan grabbing a late consolation try for the runners-up.

Wigan set new Premiership Final records for points (48 – a figure that also exceeded St Helens' Championship Final high of 44 in 1959) and winning margin (32). The £389,988 receipts from a 'sell out' crowd were also a Premiership Final record, despite reduced capacity due to rebuilding work at the Stretford End. Dynamic scrum half Andy Gregory missed out due to a leg injury sustained in the Challenge Cup Final two weeks earlier, his last appearance before transferring to Leeds.

A great moment for New Zealander Dean Bell as the Wigan captain lifts the trophy to the obvious delight of his colleagues

STATS

Wigan 48 St Helens 16

Sunday 17 May at Old Trafford, Manchester (3.30 pm)

Wigan: (cherry and white irregular hoops) Hampson, Lydon, Bell (captain), Miles, Offiah, Botica, Edwards, Cowie, Dermott, Platt, Betts, McGinty, Clarke. Substitutes: Panapa, Myers. Coach: J. Monie

St Helens: (white with blue zig-zag design, armbands and trim) Veivers, Hunte, Connolly, Loughlin, Sullivan, Ropati, Bishop, Neil, Dwyer, Ward, Nickle, Mann, Cooper (captain). Substitutes: Griffiths, Groves. Coach: M. McClennan

Half-time: 10–12 **Referee:** J. Holdsworth
Attendance: 33,157 **Receipts**: £389,988

Weather: hot and sunny

Harry Sunderland Trophy: Platt (Wigan)

Progressive score:

Wigan	score (min)	St Helens
	0–2 (5)	Loughlin penalty
Botica penalty	2–2 (10)	
Botica penalty	4–2 (18)	
Platt try, Botica goal	10–2 (23)	
	10–8 (27)	Loughlin try, Loughlin goal
	10–12 (33)	Sullivan try
Offiah try, Botica goal	16–12 (52)	
Botica penalty	18–12 (58)	
Betts try, Botica goal	24–12 (59)	
Myers try, Botica goal	30–12 (64)	
Miles try, Botica goal	36–12 (69)	
Offiah try, Botica goal	42–12 (73)	
Betts try, Botica goal	48–12 (77)	
	48–16 (79)	Sullivan try

Premiership Trophy first round:
Wigan 42 Widnes 16
St Helens 52 Halifax 16
Castleford 28 Wakefield Trinity 18
Warrington 18 Leeds 18
Replay: Leeds 22 Warrington 8

Semi-finals:
Wigan 74 Leeds 6
St Helens 30 Castleford 14

Head-to-head form guide:
St Helens 28 Wigan 16 (Lancashire Cup)
Wigan 16 St Helens 6 (League)
St Helens 6 Wigan 13 (Challenge Cup)
St Helens 6 Wigan 16 (League)

1993 Premiership Trophy Final
ST HELENS V WIGAN

It was almost impossible to predict the outcome of the 1993 Premiership Trophy Final between St Helens and Wigan. Although Wigan had won the previous year's Old Trafford date between the two by some distance and could proudly point to having won a phenomenal 19 consecutive finals across various competitions, the Saints had proved a very competitive outfit during 1992/93. Wigan had continued to gather silverware, winning the Challenge Cup and Regal Trophy, but their two other successes that term had been close run affairs, taking the Championship on scoring difference over St Helens after tying on points, and the Lancashire Cup by beating St Helens 5–4 at Knowsley Road in the decider.

Bernard Dwyer attempts to get the ball moving for St Helens

The Premiership Trophy encounter was to be just as tight as the experts anticipated, the two sides level 4–4 with only 20 minutes remaining. Unlike their 1992 Old Trafford clash, it was St Helens who proved the stronger combination in the final quarter. Two drop-goals from ex-Wigan half-back Gus O'Donnell, who had struggled to get fit during the week after a knee injury, gave St Helens a slender 6–4 lead, setting the stage for a knife-edge finish over the remaining 12 minutes. Frano Botica missed an opportunity to tie the scores with an abortive penalty attempt

STATS

St Helens 10 Wigan 4

Sunday 16 May at Old Trafford, Manchester (3.30 pm)

St Helens: (white with blue zigzag design, armbands and trim) Lyon, Riley, Connolly, Loughlin, Hunte, Ropati, O'Donnell, Neill, Dwyer, Mann, Joynt, Nickle, Cooper (captain). Substitute: Griffiths, Veivers (dnp). Coach: M. McClennan

Wigan: (cherry and white hoops) Atcheson, Robinson, Panapa, Farrar, Offiah, Botica, Edwards (captain), Cowie, Dermott, Skerrett, Cassidy, Farrell, Clarke. Substitutes: Forshaw, Gildart. Coach: J. Monie

Half-time: 4–0 **Referee:** J. Holdsworth
Attendance: 36,598 **Receipts:** £454,013

Weather: cloudy and dry

Harry Sunderland Trophy: Joynt (St Helens)

Progressive score:

St Helens	score (min)	Wigan
Connolly try	4–0 (38)	
	4–4 (60)	Forshaw try
O'Donnell drop-goal	5–4 (63)	
O'Donnell drop-goal	6–4 (68)	
Loughlin try	10–4 (76)	

Premiership Trophy first round:
Wigan 40 Warrington 5
St Helens 34 Halifax 25
Bradford Northern 6 Castleford 19
Widnes 10 Leeds 22

Semi-finals:
Wigan 25 Castleford 8
St Helens 15 Leeds 2

Head-to-head form guide:
St Helens 17 Wigan 0
(Charity Shield at Gateshead International Stadium)
St Helens 4 Wigan 5 (Lancashire Cup)
St Helens 41 Wigan 6 (League)
Wigan 23 St Helens 3 (Challenge Cup)
Wigan 8 St Helens 8 (League)

and it was left to St Helens centre Paul Loughlin to grab the headlines a minute later. He raced over the try-line after a high-speed move involving David Lyon, Teo Ropati, and Shane Cooper although unable to land the conversion that would have put Saints two scores ahead. It left his side 10-4 up with an anxious last few minutes remaining before acclaiming victory.

St Helens, after missing two early first half penalty chances (both by Loughlin) and a drop-goal (O'Donnell), had opened the scoring just before half-time. Gary Connolly crossed the whitewash after recovering the ball from a probing kick by skipper Cooper that rebounded off the legs of Andrew Farrar, Loughlin missing the goal. Wigan's best chance in the opening half was lost when Martin Offiah – who missed a drop-goal attempt shortly afterwards – looked to have an opportunity to make the line but passed to Shaun Edwards, who was subsequently tackled.

Midway through the second half, Mike Forshaw set off alarm bells in the Saints' camp, warning of a potential Wigan fight back when he levelled the scores with a try in the right corner. He got over the line by diving through Lyon's tackle after quick passing from Kelvin Skerrett, Edwards, Martin Dermott and Botica. The goal attempt by Botica struck the upright. St Helens, who enjoyed greater possession after the break, remained calm – Alan Hunte and Jonathan Griffiths both coming close to a try – to thwart Wigan's valiant attempt to lift all five major trophies open to them that season.

Both teams entered the final with depleted ranks. Wigan was missing injury victims Steve Hampson (calf – he did not play for Wigan again), Joe Lydon (leg), Andy Platt (pain from previously dislocated shoulder), Denis Betts (torn ankle ligaments) and skipper Dean Bell (knee ligaments), all of whom had played in the narrow 20–14 victory over Widnes at Wembley two weeks earlier. Although less affected in terms of numbers, St Helens was short of two key performers in winger Anthony Sullivan (his attack of tonsillitis bringing a late call-up for Mark Riley) and prop Kevin Ward, who had shattered his left ankle and lower leg in the traditional Good Friday meeting between Saints and Wigan, and was destined not to play again.

CHAMPION CAPTAIN

Shane Cooper (St Helens 1993)

Scheming, gutsy New Zealand stand-off or loose forward Shane Cooper made a big impact with St Helens, where his playing career covered 1987 to 1995. Born in Auckland, he played for local clubs Mount Albert and Mangere East prior to joining the Saints, where his trophy haul included the Premiership Trophy (1993), John Player Trophy (1987/88), Lancashire Cup (1991) and Charity Shield (1992). Representative honours included New Zealand (12 times), and Auckland province. He later played for Widnes (1995–97).

St Helens prop George Mann succumbs to some keen Wigan tackling

FIRST DIVISION LEADERS

	P	W	D	L	For	Agst	Pts
1 Wigan	26	20	1	5	744	327	41
2 St Helens	26	20	1	5	632	345	41
3 Bradford Northern	26	15	0	11	553	434	30
4 Widnes	26	15	0	11	549	446	30
5 Leeds	26	14	2	10	595	522	30
6 Castleford	26	14	1	11	544	401	29
7 Halifax	26	13	0	13	557	505	26
8 Warrington	26	12	1	13	487	450	25

(Wigan won Championship)

1994 Premiership Trophy Final
WIGAN V CASTLEFORD

Wigan ended a season tinged with controversy in fine style, defeating Castleford in the 1994 Premiership Trophy Final. It replicated their treble of two years earlier having already won the Championship and Challenge Cup. The latter contest had had an unsavoury finish with club coach John Dorahy being dismissed four days after their triumph over Leeds amidst rumours of a post-match altercation with a club official. Former player Graeme West stepped up from looking after the reserves to take temporary charge for the Premiership series.

Wigan nearly went ahead after four minutes when a pass from Castleford's Andy Hay found its way to Wigan's Martin Offiah, the wingman almost getting Kelvin Skerrett in at the corner before being forced into touch. Instead, it was Castleford that got away to a quick start, leading 8–0 after 19 minutes; Lee Crooks landing a penalty after Skerrett was penalised and adding

Sheer joy for Wigan skipper Shaun Edwards after receiving the Premiership Trophy following the defeat of Castleford

CHAMPION CAPTAIN

Shaun Edwards (Wigan 1994, 1995)

Shaun Edwards signed for Wigan in a blaze of publicity in 1983. A brilliant half-back, he was destined to win more honours than any player in the history of rugby league, the former Wigan St Patrick's starlet becoming one of the most influential and committed players the game has seen. His penchant for supportive play brought him 274 tries for Wigan including a club record-equalling 10 tries in one match during 1992. He was 17 years old when he appeared in the 1984 Challenge Cup Final at Wembley and still only 21 when he captained Wigan there in 1988. His trophy haul with Wigan covers the Premiership Trophy (1987, 1992, 1994, 1995, 1996), Championship (1986/87, 1989/90, 1990/91, 1991/92, 1992/93, 1993/94, 1994/95, 1995/96), Rugby League Challenge Cup (1985, 1988, 1989, 1990, 1991, 1992, 1993, 1994, 1995), World Club Challenge (1987, 1991, 1994), John Player Trophy (1985/86, 1986/87, 1988/89), Regal Trophy (1989/90, 1992/93, 1994/95, 1995/96), Lancashire Cup (1985, 1986, 1987, 1988, 1992) and Charity Shield (1985, 1987, 1991). He represented Great Britain in 36 Tests, England (3 times, including the 1995 World Cup), Ireland (1), Lancashire (4), and was a tourist in 1988 and 1992. London Broncos signed him for £60,000 in 1997, although he moved to Bradford Bulls later that year for £40,000. Returning to the Broncos in 1998, he ended his playing career there in 2000. During 1989, he played for Balmain in Australia. He later became head coach at London Wasps Rugby Union Club. In 1996, he received the OBE.

FIRST DIVISION LEADERS

	P	W	D	L	For	Agst	Pts
1 Wigan	30	23	0	7	780	403	46
2 Bradford Northern	30	23	0	7	784	555	46
3 Warrington	30	23	0	7	628	430	46
4 Castleford	30	19	1	10	787	466	39
5 Halifax	30	17	2	11	682	581	36
6 Sheffield Eagles	30	16	2	12	704	671	34
7 Leeds	30	15	2	13	673	680	32
8 St Helens	30	15	1	14	704	537	31

(Wigan won Championship)

the extras to a try created by a brilliant sidestepping run from stand-off Graham Steadman before passing to Dean Sampson, who forced his way through, despite three defenders. Wigan, encouraged by fine tactical kicking from skipper Shaun Edwards, soon asserted themselves, their dominance eventually opening up Castleford. It led to a 16-8 lead before the break with three tries from Andrew Farrell (barging over off a pass from Frano Botica), Sam Panapa (racing clear off an Edwards pass after St John Ellis lost the ball moments earlier) and Botica (getting over after Farrell had charged through the defence). Botica converted the first two.

Wigan slowed the tempo in the second period, but still looked superior for much of the half. Castleford was, temporarily, reduced to 12 men when Steadman found himself in the sin-bin for time wasting. In the 68th minute Botica increased the Wigan lead with a penalty and then converted a Denis Betts touchdown a few minutes later, created by a Mick Cassidy run from midfield, drawing Ellis before parting. Castleford got two late tries from Nathan Sykes (the ball initially rebounding off his head from Sampson's pass) and Streadman (who burst past the cover after Hay and Richie Blackmore had set up the position). With Steadman converting both, it gave the score a more flattering appearance for Castleford, Wigan just winning 24–20. The match ended with Edwards in the sin-bin after obstructing Mike Ford in the build up to Sykes' try.

The day was tarnished for Skerrett, who received a double-fracture of the jaw after a 55th minute incident with Sampson. Subsequently cited by Wigan, Sampson was suspended for four matches for alleged use of the elbow, based on video evidence. It cost Skerrett a trip with the Wigan team to Australia where they achieved one of their greatest triumphs in beating the Brisbane Broncos in the World Club Challenge 10 days later, a success that rubber-stamped West's permanent appointment as senior coach.

Wigan club captain Dean Bell missed the triumph, knee ligament problems dictating that, with his imminent move to join Auckland Warriors, he had already played his last match for the club. Meanwhile, prop Andy Platt, also due to join Auckland, had been unceremoniously dropped for, apparently, declaring he was unavailable for the World Club Challenge. Also missing for the Cherry and Whites was mid-season signing Va'aiga Tuigamala (ankle strain) and Barrie-Jon Mather (dislocated finger and a shoulder injury).

STATS

Wigan 24 Castleford 20

Sunday 22 May at Old Trafford, Manchester (3.30 pm)

Wigan: (cherry and white design) Atcheson, Robinson, Panapa, Connolly, Offiah, Botica, Edwards (captain), Skerrett, Hall, Cowie, Betts, Farrell, Clarke. Substitutes: Lydon, Cassidy. Coach: G. West

Castleford: (amber, black and white design) Ellis, C. Smith, Blackmore, T. Smith, Middleton, Steadman, Ford, Crooks (captain), Russell, Sampson, Ketteridge, Hay, Nikau. Substitutes: Smales, Sykes. Coach: J. Joyner

Half-time: 16–8 **Referee:** S. Cummings
Attendance: 35,644 **Receipts**: £475,000

Weather: fine and dry

Harry Sunderland Trophy: Panapa (Wigan)

Progressive score:

Wigan	score (min)	Castleford
	0–2 (9)	Crooks penalty
	0–8 (19)	Sampson try, Crooks goal
Farrell try, Botica goal	6–8 (23)	
Panapa try, Botica goal	12–8 (27)	
Botica try	16–8 (35)	
Botica penalty	18–8 (68)	
Betts try, Botica goal	24–8 (70)	
	15–14 (76)	Sykes try, Steadman goal
	16–20 (80)	Steadman try, Steadman goal

Premiership Trophy first round:
Wigan 34 St Helens 16
Bradford Northern 42 Leeds 16
Warrington 16 Sheffield Eagles 32
Castleford 28 Halifax 23

Semi-finals:
Wigan 52 Sheffield Eagles 18
Bradford Northern 16 Castleford 24

Head-to-head form guide:
Castleford 46 Wigan 0 (League)
Castleford 33 Wigan 2 (Regal Trophy at Headingley, Leeds)
Wigan 20 Castleford 6
(Challenge Cup at Headingley, Leeds)
Wigan 21 Castleford 12 (League)

1995 Premiership Trophy Final
WIGAN V LEEDS

Wigan produced a near-flawless performance in a devastating and emphatic 69–12 victory over Leeds in the 1995 Premiership Trophy Final. It was the highest score registered in a rugby league final in any competition and completed a full set of honours that season for Wigan who had already won the Championship, Challenge Cup and Regal Trophy, Leeds being runner-up in the former two. Old Trafford sold out for the Premiership event, limited to 30,160 due to redevelopment work.

Fate took a hand before the final when Wigan's giant three-quarter Va'aiga Tuigamala withdrew to attend a family funeral in New Zealand, opening the way for 19-year-old Kris Radlinski to replace him in the centre. Radlinski, whose performance would earn him the Harry Sunderland Trophy as the youngest recipient to date, became the first player, along with co-centre Gary Connolly, to score three tries in the Premiership Final. Leeds was also depleted, missing their two most influential players in skipper Ellery Hanley (his Wembley appearance three weeks earlier when he aggravated a shoulder injury would be his last match) and Garry Schofield (suspended after alleged verbal abuse of the referee in the Premiership semi-final).

No way through the Wigan line for Leeds winger Francis Cummins

Radlinski began the rout in the 8th minute after a brilliant seven-man move, Frano Botica adding the conversion on his way to equalling his 1992 record of 10 goals and 20 points in a Premiership Final. Richie Eyres responded with a try for Leeds six minutes later, Graham Holroyd adding the goal to level the scores, but that was the last act from the Headingley side as a competitive force. Wigan quickly responded, Kelvin Skerrett charging over the line three minutes later after good work from Andrew Farrell, Botica's goal placing them 12–6 in front. The unlucky Skerrett, badly injured in the previous Premiership Final, had to quit minutes later with broken ribs. The match was as good as won after the Cherry and Whites hit Leeds with four tries in a 15-minute period before half-time, all augmented by Botica for a 36–6 interval lead; Radlinski claimed his second (set up by Shaun Edwards), Connolly chipped in with two (the first after a four-to-one overlap left Alan Tait helpless, the second being acclaimed the try of the match, Jason Robinson racing from Wigan's try-line, transferring via Botica and Henry Paul to Connolly), and Edwards (after Martin Hall broke clear).

Within three minutes of the restart Radlinski (recovering a Paul grubber-kick towards the

Wigan's Henry Paul – as he did so often during the final – shows a clean pair of heels to the Leeds defence

corner) completed his trio, Botica missing the goal for once, but having no trouble adding points to further tries from Denis Betts (who powered his way over) and Paul (linking up from his full-back berth). It gave Wigan an unassailable 52–6 lead with still 30 minutes left on the clock. Connolly completed his hat-trick on the hour off an astute Botica pass, followed two minutes later with a try from Hall, capping an all-action display from the hooker. Botica converted the latter, Wigan being ahead 62–6 when centre Craig Innes got Leeds' second try, Holroyd adding the goal. With five minutes left, Farrell added a drop-goal before Simon Haughton registered the concluding try after a 50-yard charge for the line, Botica's goal ending the scoring.

In addition to claiming the most points in a Premiership Trophy Final, Wigan did so with a record winning margin of 57, adding to their achievement of scoring a record 1,148 points in League fixtures, the previous best (excepting lower divisions) being St Helens' 1,005 in 1958/59. Their triumph bade a fond-farewell to three players who were heading for a new playing career in Australasia; Betts (who returned to Wigan three years later) and Botica joining Auckland Warriors, Phil Clarke moving to Sydney club, Eastern Suburbs.

FIRST DIVISION LEADERS

	P	W	D	L	For	Agst	Pts
1 Wigan	30	28	0	2	1148	386	56
2 Leeds	30	24	1	5	863	526	49
3 Castleford	30	20	2	8	872	564	42
4 St Helens	30	20	1	9	893	640	41
5 Halifax	30	18	2	10	782	566	38
6 Warrington	30	18	2	10	753	570	38
7 Bradford Northern	30	17	1	12	811	650	35
8 Sheffield Eagles	30	15	0	15	646	699	30

(Wigan won Championship)

STATS

Wigan 69 Leeds 12

Sunday 21 May at Old Trafford, Manchester (4.00 pm)

Wigan: (cherry and white design) Paul, Robinson, Radlinski, Connolly, Offiah, Botica, Edwards (captain), Skerrett, Hall, Cowie, Betts, Farrell, Clarke. Substitutes: Cassidy, Haughton. Coach: G. West

Leeds: (blue with amber band and sleeves) Tait, Fallon, Iro (captain), Hassan, Cummins, Innes, Holroyd, Howard, Lowes, Faimalo, Mann, Eyres, Mercer. Substitutes: Harmon, Vassilakopoulos. Coach: D. Laughton

Half-time: 36–6 **Referee:** S. Cummings
Attendance: 30,160 **Receipts**: £351,038

Weather: overcast, warm and dry

Harry Sunderland Trophy: Radlinski (Wigan)

Progressive score:

Wigan	score (min)	Leeds
Radlinski try, Botica goal	6–0 (8)	
	6–6 (14)	Eyres try, Holroyd goal
Skerrett try, Botica goal	12–6 (17)	
Radlinski try, Botica goal	18–6 (24)	
Connolly try, Botica goal	24–6 (28)	
Connolly try, Botica goal	30–6 (32)	
Edwards try, Botica goal	36–6 (39)	
Radlinski try	40–6 (43)	
Betts try, Botica goal	46–6 (47)	
Paul try, Botica goal	52–6 (50)	
Connolly try	56–6 (60)	
Hall try, Botica goal	62–6 (62)	
	62–12 (68)	Innes try, Holroyd goal
Farrell drop-goal	63–12 (75)	
Haughton try, Botica goal	69–12 (76)l	

Premiership Trophy first round:
Wigan 48 Sheffield Eagles 16
Leeds 50 Bradford Northern 30
Castleford 22 Warrington 30
St Helens 32 Halifax 16

Semi-finals:
Wigan 50 Warrington 20
Leeds 30 St Helens 26

Head-to-head form guide:
Wigan 38 Leeds 6 (League)
Leeds 33 Wigan 28 (League)
Wigan 30 Leeds 10
(Challenge Cup at Wembley Stadium, London)

1996 Premiership Trophy Final
WIGAN V ST HELENS

The first Premiership Trophy Final of the summer era saw Wigan earn an unexpectedly convincing win over pre-match favourites and great rivals St Helens by 44–14. Wigan's success denied the Saints a clean-sweep of the silverware on offer having already won the Rugby League Challenge Cup and the new Super League Championship. It also averted the Cherry and Whites from being trophy-less for the first time since the 1983/84 season. St Helens took part without injured forwards Chris Joynt and Vila Matautia.

The game had a blistering start when, after 10 minutes play, Wigan centre Gary Connolly raced 30-yards from a play-the-ball to outwit Saints full-back Steve Prescott for the opening try, Andrew Farrell missing the kick. Paul Newlove replied four minutes later, taking a Derek McVey pass before charging past two would-be tacklers. Skipper Bobbie Goulding's conversion put his Saints side 6–4 up. Tommy Martyn failed to increase the gap with a 40-yard drop-goal attempt, before Jason Robinson re-ignited Wigan by racing through a gap from acting half-back 15 yards out to put Shaun Edwards in. Farrell added the goal, restoring the lead at 10–6. Danny Ellison kept the momentum with Wigan, racing down the right flank to claim two further tries. His first when Farrell and Edwards combined to send him away, whilst the latter was considered the best of the match; Kris Radlinski broke through from well inside his own half before transferring to Farrell, the ball travelling through the hands of Robinson and Edwards before the wingman touched down. Ellison's efforts – which Farrell was unable to augment – sandwiched a penalty from Goulding, the teams returning to the changing rooms with Wigan 18–8 ahead.

Jason Robinson – instigated Wigan's vital second try for Shaun Edwards in the 22nd minute

Gary Connolly – who scored the opening try for Wigan – races through a gap in the St Helens defence

St Helens opened the second half determined to bounce back into contention and, during what was probably their best period of the game, Newlove shrugged off two defenders to send Martyn over for a touchdown eight minutes after the restart. Despite claims of a double-movement, the video referee sanctioned the score, Goulding's goal narrowing the deficit to four points. Saints, though, were unable to build on that break-through and looked tired as the Central Park side began firing on all cylinders. The last half-hour belonged exclusively to Wigan as the side produced five brilliant tries; Simon Haughton (charging into the corner from 40 yards off a Farrell pass), Henry Paul (under the posts after receiving a delayed pass from Edwards following Farrell's break from a midfield scrum), Robinson (after one of his bewildering runs), Craig Murdock (created by Connolly and Ellison), and Ellison (squeezing in from acting half-back after Kelvin Skerrett was held in the corner, his hat-trick equalling the Premiership Final record).

Farrell converted three of those second half tries in an evening of personal triumph, having been appointed Wigan skipper earlier that season at only 21 years of age. Apart from lifting the Premiership Trophy, he also received the Harry Sunderland Trophy as the outstanding player, adding to his Man of Steel Award of a few days earlier. Reflecting changes that were introduced during the season, it was the first Premiership Trophy Final to allow four substitutes per team and the first to employ video referees to resolve debatable tries.

STATS

Wigan 44 St Helens 14

Sunday 8 September at Old Trafford, Manchester (7.00 pm)

Wigan: (blue and white chequered) Radlinski, Ellison, Connolly, Tuigamala, Robinson, Paul, Edwards, Skerrett, Hall, O'Connor, Haughton, Cassidy, Farrell (captain). Substitutes: A. Johnson, Murdock, Barrow, Cowie. Coach: G. West

St Helens: (red with broad white bands and chevron) Prescott, Hayes, Hunte, Newlove, Sullivan, Martyn, Goulding (captain), Perelini, Cunningham, Fogerty, McVey, Morley, Hammond. Substitutes: Pickavance, Arnold, Haigh, Booth. Coach: S. McRae

Half-time: 18–8 **Referee:** D. Campbell
Attendance: 35,013 **Receipts**: £404,000

Weather: warm and dry

Harry Sunderland Trophy: Farrell (Wigan)

Progressive score:

Wigan	score (min)	St Helens
Connolly try	4–0 (10)	
	4–6 (14)	Newlove try, Goulding goal
Edwards try, Farrell goal	10–6 (22)	
Ellison try	14–6 (26)	
	14–8 (30)	Goulding penalty
Ellison try	18–8 (36)	
	18–14 (48)	Martyn try, Goulding goal
Haughton try	22–14 (51)	
Paul try, Farrell goal	28–14 (63)	
Robinson try, Farrell goal	34–14 (67)	
Murdock try, Farrell goal	40–14 (77)	
Ellison try	44–14 (79)	

Super League leaders	P	W	D	L	For	Agst	Pts
1 St Helens	22	20	0	2	950	455	40
2 Wigan	22	19	1	2	902	326	39
3 Bradford Bulls	22	17	0	5	767	409	34
4 London Broncos	22	12	1	9	611	462	25

(St Helens won Super League Championship)

Premiership Trophy semi-finals:
St Helens 25 London Broncos 14
Wigan 42 Bradford Bulls 36

Head-to-head form guide:
St Helens 41 Wigan 26 (League)
Wigan 35 St Helens 19 (League)

Tommy Martyn's try eight minutes after the break gave St Helens hope

1997 Premiership Trophy Final
WIGAN WARRIORS V ST HELENS

After 116 years as 'Wigan', it was the Wigan Warriors that met St Helens in the 1997 Premiership Trophy Final, reflecting the summer revolution that saw most clubs 'glamorise' their names. For the second successive year it proved a special occasion for Wigan skipper Andrew Farrell, emulating Widnes' Alan Tait in receiving the Harry Sunderland Trophy in successive finals. Farrell had a hand – or boot – in most Wigan scoring efforts, claiming a try and being involved in the other four, and landing six goals in a repeat of last year's victory over St Helens, this time by 33–20. The Saints – who had pre-match injury concerns for Anthony Sullivan, Andy Leathem and Apollo Perelini after their semi-final win over Castleford although all passed fit – was missing scrum half Bobbie Goulding, serving a four-match ban for an alleged high tackle against Leeds Rhinos the previous month.

The first half saw both teams register two tries each, Farrell being the instigator of the Wigan efforts, his two perfectly directed kicks sending Andy Johnson over in the corner during the 4th minute and Jason Robinson diving in on the 31st minute. Farrell failed with his touchline kick after the former, making amends with two penalties and tagging the extras to Robinson's try. St Helens' response was through Derek McVey's 23rd minute try, created by Sean Long – which left Saints trailing 6–4 at that point – and Paul Newlove with a 40-yard charge in the 34th minute off a beautifully timed Keiron Cunningham pass. Wigan's 14–8 interval lead could have been greater, three potential tries from Henry Paul, Danny Ellison and Gary Connolly – who quit after 26 minutes through an Achilles tendon injury – all being disallowed midway through the first half.

But St Helens had courageously held on, a penalty from Long two minutes into the second period bringing them within four points. As in previous Premiership finals, though, the Warriors slipped into a higher gear, 19 points

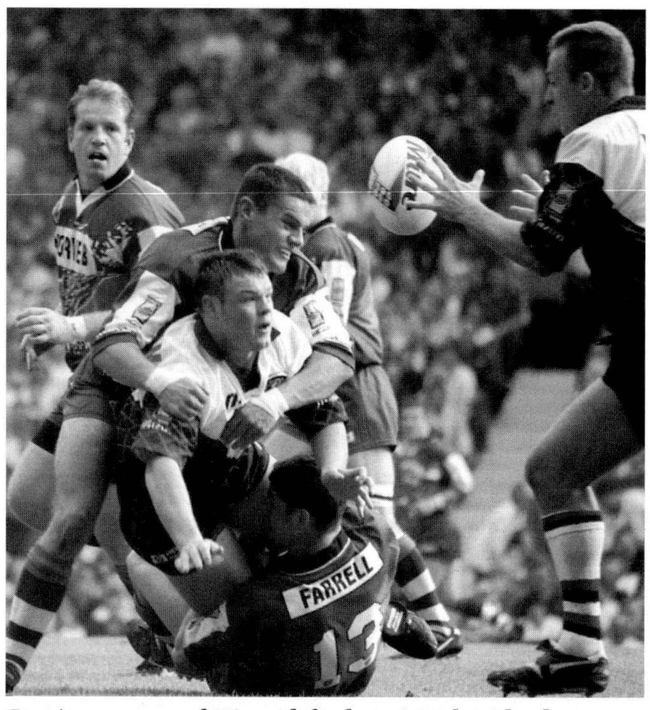

Despite a swarm of Wigan defenders, St Helens' hooker Keiron Cunningham gets the ball away to Paul Newlove

being added during a 20-minute blitz. Farrell began it with a 44th minute penalty, Nigel Wright contributing a crucial drop-goal three minutes later, placing Wigan two scores ahead at 17–10. Robinson then brought off a vital, superb tackle on St Helens' winger Sullivan, who looked

SUPER LEAGUE

	P	W	D	L	For	Agst	Pts
1 Bradford Bulls	22	20	0	2	769	397	40
2 London Broncos	22	15	3	4	616	418	33
3 St Helens	22	14	1	7	592	506	29
4 Wigan Warriors	22	14	0	8	683	398	28
5 Leeds Rhinos	22	13	1	8	544	463	27
6 Salford Reds	22	11	0	11	428	495	22
7 Halifax Blue Sox	22	8	2	12	524	549	18
8 Sheffield Eagles	22	9	0	13	415	574	18
9 Warrington Wolves	22	8	0	14	437	647	16
10 Castleford Tigers	22	5	2	15	334	515	12
11 Paris St Germain	22	6	0	16	362	572	12
12 Oldham Bears	22	4	1	17	461	631	9

(Bradford Bulls won Super League Championship)

set to resurrect his team after racing half the length of the field. With that danger averted, Wigan pushed on to claim three more tries, each the result of a combination of passing between Kris Radlinski, Farrell, and Simon Haughton, the trio claiming a try apiece in that sequence. Farrell added two of the goals, failing to augment his own effort, elevating Wigan into a 33–10 lead with a quarter-hour left. St Helens, though, plugged the gaps in their defence whilst making their own tally more respectable with two touchdowns in the closing minutes through Paul Anderson (after exchanging passes with Sullivan) and Karle Hammond (off a Chris Morley off-load), Long converting the former.

Despite a try count of only 5–4 in their favour, Wigan was a comfortable and deserving winner. The last of 23 Premiership Trophy Finals, several records were established. Wigan claimed three; sixth win overall (tied with Widnes), fourth consecutive win, and sixth consecutive final. St Helens could boast a record nine Premiership Final appearances, their 20 points equalling the highest from a losing side.

Wigan captain Andrew Farrell – who was awarded the Harry Sunderland Trophy as the outstanding player - prepares to hand off a St Helens defender

STATS

Wigan Warriors 33 St Helens 20

Sunday 28 September at Old Trafford, Manchester (3.00 pm)

Wigan: Warriors (blue with pale blue and white patterned band) Robinson, A. Johnson, Radlinski, Connolly, Ellison, Paul, Smith, Cowie, Clarke, Hansen, Haughton, Cassidy, Farrell (captain). Substitutes: O'Connor, Holgate, Wright, Tallec. Coach: E. Hughes

St Helens: (black covered with red web design and full white chevron) Arnold, Stewart, Hunte, Newlove, Sullivan, Hammond, Long, Leathem, Cunningham, O'Neill, Perelini, McVey, Joynt (captain). Substitutes: Pickavance, Booth, Morley, Anderson. Coach: S. McRae

Half-time: 14–8 **Referee:** S. Cummings
Attendance: 33,389 **Receipts**: £359,303

Weather: sunny and mild

Harry Sunderland Trophy: Farrell (Wigan Warriors)

Progressive score:

Wigan Warriors	score (min)	St Helens
Johnson try	4–0 (4)	
Farrell penalty	6–0 (8)	
	6–4 (23)	McVey try
Farrell penalty	8–4 (26)	
Robinson try, Farrell goal	14–4 (31)	
	14–8 (34)	Newlove try
	14–10 (42)	Long penalty
Farrell penalty	16–10 (44)	
Wright drop-goal	17–10 (47)	
Radlinski try, Farrell goal	23–10 (52)	
Farrell try	27–10 (59)	
Haughton try, Farrell goal	33–10 (64)	
	33–16 (76)	Anderson try, Long goal
	33–20 (79)	Hammond try

Premiership Trophy preliminary round:
Leeds Rhinos 42 Oldham Bears 16
Salford Reds 48 Paris St Germain 6
Halifax Blue Sox 18 Castleford Tigers 23
Sheffield Eagles 26 Warrington Wolves 16

Quarter-finals:
Bradford Bulls 12 Castleford Tigers 25
London Broncos 16 Sheffield Eagles 58
St Helens 26 Salford Reds 12
Wigan Warriors 38 Leeds Rhinos 22

Semi-finals:
St Helens 32 Castleford Tigers 18
Wigan Warriors 22 Sheffield Eagles 10

Head-to-head form guide:
St Helens 26 Wigan Warriors 12 (Challenge Cup)
Wigan Warriors 10 St Helens 22 (League)
St Helens 12 Wigan Warriors 65 (League)

SUPER LEAGUE GRAND FINAL

The Grand Final – since its introduction in 1998 – has consistently provided an evening of excitement, tension and high drama under the Old Trafford floodlights. It has created a finale that contrasts sharply with the, often sunny, Spring Saturday or Sunday afternoon Championship and Premiership clashes that climaxed the conclusion of past seasons.

It is undoubtedly one of the modern success stories in British sport, attendances having grown dramatically year-on-year from an initial 43,553 – itself in excess of any of the Premiership Final attendances – to a massive 72,582 by 2006, when it was the third largest crowd to see a rugby league 'championship' final in England. It was also the first time since 1960 that it exceeded the Challenge Cup Final attendance.

Australian rugby league had held a Grand Final since 1930, having introduced a play-off at the end of their first competitive season of 1908. The initial top-5 format used by Super League (expanded to a top-6 in 2002) was a direct copy from Australia, who had first used the idea in 1973. Heavily weighted towards the clubs who finished highest in the League it also provided the previously alien concept of the top teams having a 'second chance' after initially losing a play-off tie. When it was first suggested, there was a lot of scepticism about the system. Whilst the many Australians involved in British rugby league fully endorsed the idea, based on their own homeland experience, most Brits felt it looked too complicated. In fact there was quite a bit of humour generated as tongue-tied broadcasters tried to explain the idea to the public on television and radio after it was first announced. Nobody was laughing though once the play-off series took place, as all the ties up to and including the final proved to be compelling viewing either in the flesh or on television.

It helped promote the developing image of the sport as summer rugby league was more aggressively marketed to attract family audiences. Part of that strategy included a whole host of new names as virtually every club, inside and outside of Super League, added a moniker to their title, the Wigan 'Warriors' meeting the Leeds 'Rhinos' in the first Grand Final. The Grand Final evening took on its own personality, 'Jerusalem' being sung instead of the National Anthem that accompanies the Challenge Cup Final. And, right from the first event, winners' rings were awarded to players instead of medals, copying the Australian Rugby League who, in turn, probably took the idea from American football's National Football League who do the same at their Super Bowl.

There had been discussions of the top clubs breaking away to form a 'Super League' in the past, and as recently as 1986, ten of the leading clubs met to explore such a move, before it became reality in 1996. Super League's biggest criticism has been that the power base created has squeezed out the majority of the sport's traditional clubs, a debate that rages on endlessly. Even within Super League itself, there has been a tendency towards a pecking order with the more affluent clubs dominating. A 'salary cap' was introduced in 1998 to help spread playing talent more evenly, clubs being fined and deducted competition points for breaches. This has led, on two occasions, to clubs that won the Grand Final (St Helens in 2002, Bradford Bulls in 2005) subsequently having points deducted.

There is no doubt Super League has become more competitive in recent years but, until Hull bucked the trend in 2006, the Grand Final had been the domain of just four clubs. For the welfare of the competition as a whole, the gap in capability needs to be closed even further.

LEAGUE LEADERS' SHIELD WINNERS

Presented to the team that finishes top of the Super League;

2003 Bradford Bulls
2004 Leeds Rhinos
2005 St Helens
2006 St Helens
2007 St Helens

1998 Super League Grand Final
WIGAN WARRIORS V LEEDS RHINOS

The first Super League Grand Final, staged at Old Trafford, proved a tremendous success. The match itself, contested by Wigan Warriors and Leeds Rhinos was a thrilling, edge-of-your-seat, tense encounter, and commercially it exceeded most expectations. The attendance of 43,553, on a very wet and windy but atmospheric evening, was the best for an end-of-season play-off decider since the 1961 Championship Final whilst the receipts, at £637,105 were the highest outside Wembley. In a very physical, bruising affair, there was little to pick between the sides whose joint-defensive effort coughed up just two tries. Both were virtually at full strength, the major absences being Wigan's Denis Betts who, in his second spell with the club sustained a season-ending leg injury during August, and Leeds winger Paul Sterling, dropped after the qualifying semi-final play-off defeat to the Warriors.

Leeds captain Iestyn Harris – whose inspirational performance was not quite enough to avert defeat – puts the Wigan defence in two minds

For much of the first half, Leeds, who had completed a League 'double' over Wigan, looked the most likely victors, Iestyn Harris particularly making a menace of himself to Wigan's defence with his probing kicks and deft handling. Leeds' only reward, though, was a try from centre Richie Blackmore, accepting a well-timed Ryan Sheridan pass and evading two defenders close to the line. Harris, who missed an earlier penalty attempt, failed with the conversion, Leeds deservedly winning 4–0 with just over a quarter of the match gone. As the interval approached, Jason Robinson

CHAMPION CAPTAIN

Andrew Farrell
(Wigan/Wigan Warriors 1996, 1997, 1998)

Andrew Farrell first played in Wigan's senior side as a 16-year-old during 1991, being formally signed from local club, Orrell St James, in January 1992. He was to make 370 appearances for the Cherry and Whites, including 21 as substitute, becoming captain in 1996 at the age of only 21. His list of club honours covers the Championship (1993/94, 1994/95, 1995/96), Super League Grand Final (1998), Rugby League Challenge Cup (1993, 1994, 1995, 2002), World Club Challenge (1994), Premiership Trophy (1994, 1995, 1996, 1997) and Charity Shield (1995). He became Wigan's regular goal-kicker in 1995 and, in 2001, created a new club record for the season of 429 points (183 goals including five drop-goals, 17 tries). His final haul of 1,355 goals and 3,135 points places him in second place on both counts behind Jim Sullivan in the club's all-time list. Acknowledged as one of Great Britain's most outstanding back-row forwards, he displayed pace, power, wonderful distribution and solid defence, becoming his country's youngest Test forward at 18 years, 5 months, against New Zealand in November 1993. For the remainder of his rugby league career, he never missed a Test match, setting a record run of 34 appearances. He created another milestone as skipper for the latter 29 of those Tests, having begun his run as Britain's youngest tour captain in 1996. He also represented England (11 times, including the World Cups of 1995 – when in the team beaten by Australia in the final – and 2000) and Lancashire (3). He was awarded the OBE in the 2005 New Years Honours, which was followed in March 2005, by the announcement of his departure for rugby union, joining Saracens and making his England debut in 2007.

unexpectedly conjured up the key moment of the evening with a tremendous solo effort. Running from acting half-back at a play-the-ball, he avoided several defenders as he shot away to cross the whitewash, Andrew Farrell putting the Warriors 6–4 in front against the run of play. It was a crucial score that would ultimately settle the outcome of the match.

Robinson's strike lifted Wigan, and they were in the ascendancy for most of the second half as the Rhinos' composure began to wane, several uncharacteristic handling errors being made in the watery conditions. The only second half points came from the boot of Farrell, with two successful penalties, awarded for foul play by Marc Glanville and Graham Holroyd, respectively. The latter, a minute from the end, effectively made the game safe, Wigan winning 10–4 after a clash that had been a real old-fashioned battle of attrition.

The victory gave the Cherry and Whites their only silverware of the term, extending their enviable record of trophy collecting to 15 consecutive seasons. Including the former Premiership Trophy competition, it was Wigan's seventh consecutive appearance at Old Trafford and their fifth win there on the trot, the last three with Farrell as captain. Commenting on the new Grand Final experience, Farrell said afterwards: 'That was as tough a game as I have played in. it was just like Test football.'

STATS

Wigan Warriors 10 Leeds Rhinos 4

Saturday 24 October at Old Trafford, Manchester (6.30 pm)

Wigan Warriors: (cherry with white bands) Radlinski, Robinson, Moore, Connolly, M. Bell, Paul, Smith, O'Connor, McCormack, Mestrov, Gilmour, Holgate, Andrew Farrell (captain). Substitutes: Cowie, Haughton, Cassidy, P. Johnson. Coach: J. Monie

Leeds Rhinos: (blue with large amber 'Rhinos' logo and amber sleeve bands): Harris (captain), Rivett, Blackmore, Godden, Cummins, Powell, Sheridan, Masella, Newton, Fleary, Morley, Anthony Farrell, Glanville. Substitutes: Mathiou, Holroyd, Hay, St Hilaire. Coach: G. Murray

Half-time: 6–4 **Referee:** R. Smith
Attendance: 43,553 **Receipts**: £637,105

Weather: heavy rain, blustery winds

Harry Sunderland Trophy: Robinson (Wigan Warriors)

Progressive score:

Wigan Warriors	score (min)	Leeds Rhinos
	0–4 (21)	Blackmore try
Robinson try, Farrell goal	6–4 (38)	
Farrell penalty	8–4 (47)	
Farrell penalty	10–4 (79)	

Super League leaders	P	W	D	L	For	Agst	Pts
1 Wigan Warriors	23	21	0	2	762	222	42
2 Leeds Rhinos	23	19	0	4	662	369	38
3 Halifax Blue Sox	23	18	0	5	658	390	36
4 St Helens	23	14	1	8	673	459	29
5 Bradford Bulls	23	12	0	11	498	450	24

Super League play-offs:
Elimination play-off: St Helens 46 Bradford Bulls 24
Qualifying play-off: Leeds Rhinos 13 Halifax Blue Sox 6
Elimination semi-final: Halifax Blue Sox 30 St Helens 37
Qualifying semi-final: Wigan Warriors 17 Leeds Rhinos 4
Final eliminator: Leeds Rhinos 44 St Helens 16

Head-to-head form guide:
Leeds Rhinos 16 Wigan Warriors 8 (League)
Wigan Warriors 8 Leeds Rhinos 15 (League)
Wigan Warriors 17 Leeds Rhinos 4 (play-off)

Wigan's Andrew Farrell - the first captain to receive the Super League trophy at a Grand Final

1999 Super League Grand Final
ST HELENS V BRADFORD BULLS

St Helens came up with an unexpected victory over Bradford Bulls in the 1999 Super League Grand Final. Like the 1998 event it was a tense, low-scoring affair played out in miserable wet conditions. The weather, though, did not dampen the ardour of the supporters, the attendance topping 50,000 in a play-off final for the first time in 38 years.

It was a final that embraced controversy. Bradford, leading 6–2 at the break, continued to press in the second half but was twice denied tries after referee Stuart Cummings passed the decisions to David Campbell for video analysis. Whilst the second effort when James Lowes was held under the posts was clear cut, the first, two minutes into the half was contentious and, ultimately, crucial to the outcome of the match. That Leon Pryce had raced in by the side of the posts and placed the ball over the line was not in dispute, but the way Michael Withers obtained possession prior to feeding him was. He appeared to go for the interception when Saints' full-back Paul Atcheson attempted a pass to Kevin Iro, recovering the ball as it bounced. Had Withers made early contact and propelled the ball forward when he intervened? It was a difficult decision, Campbell eventually ruling a knock-on, although the contact could have been little more than a fingernail's width.

The match had begun at a ferocious pace, the two packs tearing into each other. The Bulls had the early edge, a tremendous Stuart Spruce break leading to nought after the supporting Tevita Vaikona had his pass intercepted by Saints' Tommy Martyn. Shortly after, Martyn's attempted drop-goal barely rose above the slippery surface. Henry Paul finally put points on the board in the 19th minute, speeding away on a 65-yard dash, avoiding two defenders to slide across the wet turf under the posts, losing a boot on the way. He then added the extras for a 6–0 lead. Sean Long was introduced off the bench for St Helens in the 24th minute, his inventiveness lifting the team, posting his side's only first half points with a penalty after Bradford was deemed offside.

The St Helens players punch the air with delight as their captain Chris Joynt lifts the Super League trophy

The Bulls worked hard at the start of the second half and, apart from the aforementioned video decisions going against them, came close several times. St Helens then inched their way towards victory and, when Bradford's Paul Anderson was penalised for not being square at a play-the-ball, they saw their chance to go for the jugular. In typical Saints style, the ball transferred quickly as Keiron Cunningham, Long and Atcheson combined to send Iro haring away, sliding in at the right corner, despite the efforts of Pryce and Mike Forshaw. The video referee confirmed the score, making it 6–6. Long became the St Helens hero by coolly slotting the difficult touchline kick, putting his team ahead for the first time. In a frantic last 15 minutes both sides came close to increasing their score, particularly when Iro had his second 'try' scrubbed out, the video replay ruling a Freddie Tuilagi knock-on in the lead up, Saints holding on for an 8–6 triumph after a game full of passion.

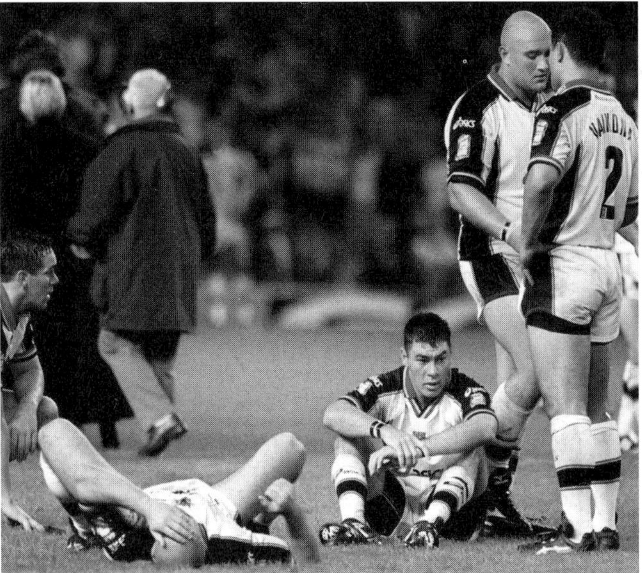

Every picture tells a story! Michael Withers (seated on ground) stares into space as he and his dejected Bradford Bulls colleagues contemplate their narrow defeat

CHAMPION CAPTAIN

Chris Joynt (St Helens 1999, 2000, 2002)

Chris Joynt signed for Oldham in 1989 from his local amateur club, Wigan St Patrick's, joining St Helens in 1992. The following year, the skilful, all-action second-row forward made his Great Britain debut, the first of 25 Tests. A member of the 1996 touring side to New Zealand and the South Pacific, he also represented England (6 times including the 1995 World Cup), Ireland (4 – in the 2000 World Cup) and Lancashire (1). At St Helens, where he took over as captain in 1997, he won the Super League Grand Final (1999, 2000, 2002), Rugby League Challenge Cup (1996, 1997, 2001, 2004), World Club Challenge (2001), Super League Championship (1996) and Premiership Trophy (1993). He played in Australia for Newcastle Knights during 1995. Following the 2004 season, he decided to retire.

STATS

St Helens 8 Bradford Bulls 6

Saturday 9 October at Old Trafford, Manchester (6.30 pm)

St Helens: (teal with broad orange side panels) Atcheson, Smith, Iro, Newlove, Sullivan, Sculthorpe, Martyn, Perelini, Cunningham, O'Neill, Tuilagi, Nickle, Joynt (captain). Substitutes: Long, Hoppe, Matautia, Wellens. Coach: E. Hanley

Bradford Bulls: (white with black, red and amber trim) Spruce, Vaikona, Naylor, Withers, Pryce, H. Paul, R. Paul (captain), Anderson, Lowes, Fielden, Boyle, Dwyer, McNamara. Substitutes: Deacon, McAvoy (dnp), Forshaw, McDermott. Coach: M. Elliott

Half-time: 2–6 **Referee:** S. Cummings
Attendance: 50,717

Weather: heavy rain; ground slippery

Harry Sunderland Trophy: H. Paul (Bradford Bulls)

Progressive score:

St Helens	score (min)	Bradford Bulls
	0–6 (19)	H. Paul try, H. Paul goal
Long penalty	2–6 (32)	
Iro try, Long goal	8–6 (65)	

Super League leaders	P	W	D	L	For	Agst	Pts
1 Bradford Bulls	30	25	1	4	897	445	51
2 St Helens	30	23	0	7	1034	561	46
3 Leeds Rhinos	30	22	1	7	910	558	45
4 Wigan Warriors	30	21	1	8	877	390	43
5 Castleford Tigers	30	19	3	8	712	451	41

Super League play-offs:
Elimination play-off: Wigan Warriors 10 Castleford Tigers 14
Qualifying play-off: St Helens 38 Leeds Rhinos 14
Elimination semi-final: Leeds Rhinos 16 Castleford Tigers 23
Qualifying semi-final: Bradford Bulls 40 St Helens 4
Final eliminator: St Helens 36 Castleford Tigers 6

Head-to-head form guide:
St Helens 58 Bradford Bulls 14 (League)
Bradford Bulls 46 St Helens 22 (League)
St Helens 25 Bradford Bulls 16 (League)
Bradford Bulls 40 St Helens 4 (play-off)

2000 Super League Grand Final
ST HELENS V WIGAN WARRIORS

The 2000 Super League Grand Final was the most exciting of the three to date, Wigan staging an unexpected and dramatic second half comeback that, effectively, meant St Helens had to win the match twice! With just 30 minutes to go, it was already the highest scoring Grand Final to date, although most of the points had gone the way of a rampant St Helens who looked good value for their 17–4 lead. Wigan then put everyone in the stadium on tenterhooks as they courageously fought back.

The Warriors conjured up two tries out of the hat in a three-minute burst that, temporarily at least, turned the final on its head. The first came from winger David Hodgson in the 58th minute, outpacing Sean Hoppe after a Chris Chester blind-side run had created space, Tony Smith following up with the second touchdown after cashing in on Andrew Farrell's break. Farrell added both goals and St Helens' lead was suddenly cut to 17–16 and it was 'game on.' But, with just over 10 minutes remaining, under-pressure Saints was awarded two quick penalties which took them downfield deep into Wigan territory. St Helens, never a side to duck an opportunity, made their next set of six count with Freddie Tuilagi scoring in the corner off Tommy Martyn's long pass. It was a decision referred to and subsequently endorsed by video referee Ray Tennant due to a suspicion of a Chris Joynt knock-on in the build up. Shaun Long delivered the important goal from the touchline to put Saints two scores in front at 23–16.

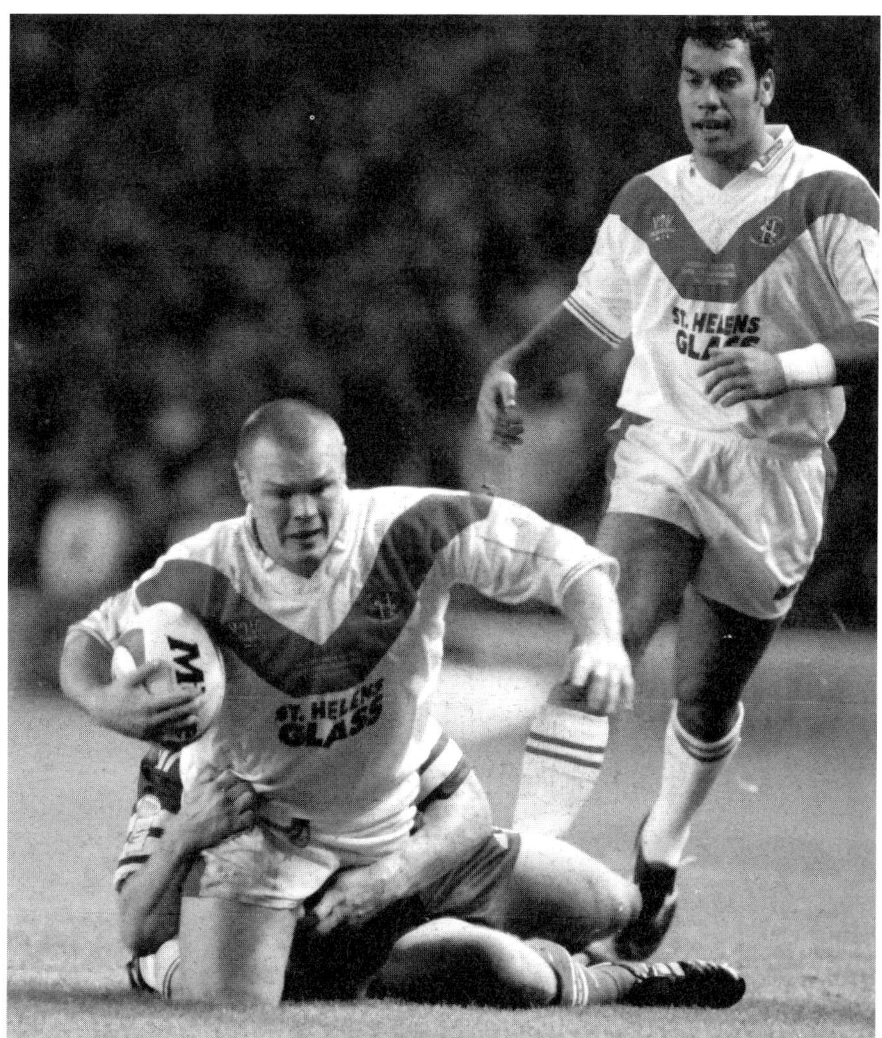

St Helens hooker Keiron Cunningham is grounded by a Wigan defender as his team-mate Kevin Iro prepares to lend support

With time running out, Wigan attempted another fight back, St Helens resisting five consecutive sets of tackles, Warriors' centre Steve Renouf being held on the line. Saints produced the 'sucker punch' in the final minute when forward Tim Jonkers burst through off John Stankevitch's pass after a searing break by Anthony Sullivan. Long added the goal to seal a 29–16 victory.

Brilliantly led by their skipper Joynt, who played with a fractured thumb, St Helens looked to have the measure of Wigan in the early stages of the match as they set about retaining their Super League prize. It took just seven minutes before Hoppe burst through for their opening try, Joynt holding off a defender before squeezing the ball out to him. Surprisingly Long missed the relatively straight-forward kick. Farrell brought Wigan level with a touchdown six minutes later, latching on to a Smith pass before scattering several Saints defenders to score. Joynt claimed the next score after breaking three tackles, Long adding the goal to make it 10–4. Paul Sculthorpe chipped in with a vital drop-goal, sending Saints back to their changing room 11–4 up. Ten minutes into the second half Joynt struck again, being on hand to support a superb break from Long, who tagged on the extra points, opening up a 17–4 lead. Many thought it was all over by the shouting, but Wigan earned full marks for a gritty rearguard action that kept the contest alive.

Both sides were missing experienced centres. For St Helens, Paul Newlove was unfit, Wigan being without Gary Connolly. Another change, although positional, occurred when Warriors' coach Frank Endacott raised a few eyebrows by switching full-back Kris Radlinski to centre, Jason Robinson, in his final match before defecting to rugby union, relocating from the wing to fill the void. After the comparative modest scoring of the first two finals, the 45 points aggregate produced a new Grand Final record score (29) and winning margin (13). The attendance record, meanwhile, continued its upward spiral, 58,132 being present.

Delight on the face of Tim Jonkers as he scores St Helens' final try in the last minute

STATS

St Helens 29 Wigan Warriors 16

Saturday 14 October at Old Trafford, Manchester (6.30 pm)

St Helens: (white with red chevron) Wellens, Hall, Iro, Hoppe, Sullivan, Martyn, Long, Perelini, Cunningham, O'Neill, Joynt (captain), Jonkers, Sculthorpe. Substitutes: Barrow (dnp), Nickle, Stankevich, Tuilagi. Coach: I. Millward

Wigan Warriors: (blue with white bands) Robinson, Dallas, Radlinski, Renouf, Hodgson, Smith, Peters, O'Connor, Newton, Cowie, Cassidy, Betts, Farrell (captain). Substitutes: Gilmour, Mestrov, Chester, Malam. Coach: F. Endacott

Half-time: 11–4 **Referee:** R. Smith
Attendance: 58,132

Weather: rain

Harry Sunderland Trophy: Joynt (St Helens)

Progressive score:

St Helens	score (min)	Wigan Warriors
Hoppe try	4–0 (7)	
	4–4 (13)	Farrell try
Joynt try, Long goal	10–4 (28)	
Sculthorpe drop-goal	11–4 (31)	
Joynt try, Long goal	17–4 (50)	
	17–10 (58)	Hodgson try, Farrell goal
	17–16 (61)	Smith try, Farrell goal
Tuilagi try, Long goal	23–16 (69)	
Jonkers try, Long goal	29–16 (80)	

Super League leaders	P	W	D	L	For	Agst	Pts
1 Wigan Warriors	28	24	1	3	960	405	49
2 St Helens	28	23	0	5	988	627	46
3 Bradford Bulls	28	20	3	5	1004	408	43
4 Leeds Rhinos	28	17	0	11	692	626	34
5 Castleford Tigers	28	17	0	11	585	571	34

Super League play-offs:
Elimination play-off: Leeds Rhinos 22 Castleford Tigers 14
Qualifying play-off: St Helens 16 Bradford Bulls 11
Elimination semi-final: Bradford Bulls 46 Leeds Rhinos 12
Qualifying semi-final: Wigan Warriors 16 St Helens 54
Final eliminator: Wigan Warriors 40 Bradford Bulls 12

Head-to-head form guide:
St Helens 38 Wigan Warriors 14 (League)
Wigan Warriors 28 St Helens 30 (League)
St Helens 4 Wigan Warriors 42 (League)
Wigan Warriors 16 St Helens 54 (play-off)

2001 Super League Grand Final
BRADFORD BULLS V WIGAN WARRIORS

Bradford Bulls finally came of age in 2001, inflicting a resounding 37–6 defeat on Wigan Warriors in the most one-sided Super League Grand Final so far. Despite being one of the forerunners since the birth of summer rugby league, the Bulls had tended to flounder in big finals under the new era, losing all three Challenge Cup Finals and their only previous Grand Final.

Whilst the Bulls' score (37) and winning margin (31) broke St Helens' 12-month old records, their full-back Michael Withers was who had one of his best ever games in Bulls colours, dived over from acting half-back, Henry Paul obtaining his second goal. Withers' first effort quickly followed, avoiding the reach of two defenders to race over from acting half-back five yards out. Henry Paul added the conversion, having created the position with a tremendous run that covered half the length of the field. Following another Henry Paul penalty (after interference at the play-the-ball by Neil Cowie), Withers got his second in the 27th minute, placing the ball beneath the posts after

Bradford's Mike Forshaw, surrounded by Wigan defenders, attempts to break free

creating his own piece of history as the first player to score three tries in a Grand Final. He succeeded in doing so during a 20-minute period midway through the first half as Bradford racked up a 26–0 lead before half-time. At that stage, even the most optimistic Wigan supporters knew their side was hardly likely to stage a revival to match their previous year's effort.

Bradford got off to a quick start, Henry Paul knocking over a penalty from halfway after 97 seconds when Wigan's Harvey Howard was judged not square at a play-the-ball. Seven minutes later, ever-alert hooker James Lowes, supporting a fine break from halfway by right wing pair Scott Naylor and Tevita Vaikona. There were protests that the final pass from Vaikona was forward but the try stood, Henry Paul again adding the goal. Withers' quick-fire hat-trick was completed four minutes later, this time backing up a move by Henry Paul, Robbie Paul and Stuart Fielden. Henry Paul, for once, missed the goal and then failed with a penalty from halfway two minutes later.

Wigan did manage to stem the Bradford tide after that opening half-hour salvo and there was no further scoring until just after the hour mark. This time, though, the points went the way of the Warriors who had battled manfully through the third quarter in an effort to regain some pride, scrum half Adrian Lam reaping the reward, bypassing three defenders for a 63rd minute try. David Furner augmented, usual marksman Andrew Farrell having retired from the game with a thigh injury four minutes earlier. It gave a glimmer of hope to the Wigan faithful but with just over a quarter-hour left to play and a 20-point deficit still showing on the scoreboard it was hardly more than that. Within two minutes even that slender thread had snapped when Fielden scored after Naylor and Daniel Gartner had made the initial running. Henry Paul missed the kick but then added a soaring long-range drop-goal. Bradford completed their perfect day when centre Graham Mackay latched on to a beautifully judged kick from Paul Deacon eight minutes from time, celebrating his farewell appearance by converting it himself.

Withers' outstanding performance earned him the Harry Sunderland Trophy, getting the verdict just ahead of Henry Paul, playing his final match for the Bulls before switching to rugby union with Gloucester. It was also a great occasion for head coach Brian Noble, being his first season in charge, having stepped out of the shadows of predecessors Brian Smith and Matthew Elliott. Once again, the Old Trafford attendance showed an increase, over 60,000 passing through the turnstiles.

STATS

Bradford Bulls 37 Wigan Warriors 6

Saturday 13 October at Old Trafford, Manchester (6.30 pm)

Bradford Bulls: (white with red, amber and black chevron) Withers, Vaikona, Naylor, Mackay, Pryce, H. Paul, R. Paul (captain), Vagana, Lowes, McDermott, Gartner, Peacock, Forshaw. Substitutes: Deacon, Anderson, Rigon, Fielden. Coach: B. Noble

Wigan Warriors: (cherry and white hoops) Radlinski, Dallas, Connolly, Renouf, Carney, Johns, Lam, O'Connor, Newton, Howard, Cassidy, Furner, Farrell (captain). Substitutes: Cowie, Betts, P. Johnson, Chester. Coach: S. Raper

Half-time: 26–0 **Referee:** S. Cummings
Attendance: 60,164

Weather: fine and dry

Harry Sunderland Trophy: Withers (Bradford Bulls)

Progressive score:

Bradford Bulls	score (min)	Wigan Warriors
H. Paul penalty	2–0 (2)	
Lowes try, H. Paul goal	8–0 (9)	
Withers try, H. Paul goal	14–0 (11)	
H. Paul penalty	16–0 (23)	
Withers try, H. Paul goal	22–0 (27)	
Withers try	26–0 (31)	
	26–6 (63)	Lam try, Furner goal
Fielden try	30–6 (65)	
H. Paul drop-goal	31–6 (70)	
Mackay try, Mackay goal	37–6 (72)	

Super League leaders	P	W	D	L	For	Agst	Pts
1 Bradford Bulls	28	22	1	5	1120	474	45
2 Wigan Warriors	28	22	1	5	989	494	45
3 Hull FC	28	20	2	6	772	630	42
4 St Helens	28	17	2	9	924	732	36
5 Leeds Rhinos	28	16	1	11	774	721	33

Super League play-offs:
Elimination play-off: St Helens 38 Leeds Rhinos 30
Qualifying play-off: Wigan Warriors 27 Hull FC 24
Elimination semi-final: Hull FC 20 St Helens 24
Qualifying semi-final: Bradford Bulls 24 Wigan Warriors 18
Final eliminator: Wigan Warriors 44 St Helens 10

Head-to-head form guide:
Bradford Bulls 35 Wigan Warriors 24 (League)
Wigan Warriors 44 Bradford Bulls 30 (League)
Wigan Warriors 16 Bradford Bulls 10 (League)
Bradford Bulls 24 Wigan Warriors 18 (play-off)

Henry Paul – who landed six goals for Bradford – flies through an opening

2002 Super League Grand Final
ST HELENS V BRADFORD BULLS

The Super League Grand Final of 2002 was the closest, most thrilling to date, St Helens defeating Bradford Bulls by a single point in a match that could have gone either way. It also courted controversy in the dying seconds. With Saints leading 19–18 and the klaxon about to signal the end, their loose forward Chris Joynt – on his way to becoming the only player, to date, to captain a team to three Grand Final wins – appeared to deliberately fall at the feet of two Bulls' defenders. Referee Russell Smith dismissed vociferous Bradford appeals of a voluntary tackle that, if recognised, would have given Paul Deacon, from 40 yards out towards the touchline, a difficult, but kickable, chance to claim victory. Bulls' hooker James Lowes continued to debate the issue vehemently with the official after the match was finished, whilst coach Brian Noble, at the post-match interview, also expressed disappointment at the referee's interpretation. It was a sour note to end the contest, but could not detract from what had been a brilliant advertisement for rugby league and the Super League competition in particular.

Sean Long outflanks Bradford's Paul Deacon to put St Helens ahead for the first time

With just over a quarter of the match played, Bradford led 8–0, hitting St Helens with a morale-boosting try in the 2nd minute from Scott Naylor who took a defender over with him as he touched down, having threaded his way through off Michael Withers' inside pass. Paul Deacon added the kick, followed by a 45-yard penalty 19 minutes later. The margin could have been greater, Deacon missed a 10th minute penalty and then had a 'try' under the posts disallowed two minutes later. The video referee ruled a knock on by Bulls' Jamie Peacock in the build-up, another decision hotly disputed by the Yorkshire side. St Helens fought back, sparking the match into life with two well taken tries, both converted by Sean Long, to lead 12–8 at half-time. The first, two minutes after Deacon's penalty, was scored by Mike Bennett, finishing off a frenetic bout of

Leon Pryce looks virtually unstoppable as he makes an awesome looking break for the Bulls

passing after Martin Gleeson had somehow recovered an up-and-under from Long, the try being given by the video referee. Nine minutes later, Keiron Cunningham made the running after Brandon Costin had spilled the ball, beating two defenders and drawing Withers before sending Long racing over. As the interval approached, Bradford's chagrin increased when Smith disregarded Deacon's obstruction plea whilst pursuing Robbie Paul's kick.

Bradford started strongly after the interval, Deacon's inside pass sending Paul Anderson rampaging downfield before Brian McDermott despatched Paul over the whitewash from 30 yards out. Deacon converted and the Bulls were back in front, 14–12. Shortly after, Deacon's pass sent Naylor scything through on the left, Withers supporting to score in the corner after confirmation by the video referee. This time Deacon missed the goal and it was 18–12. The see-saw nature of the match continued as Gleeson shot over for the Saints in the 56th minute, Cunningham and Long having transferred to him at speed. Long's kick from a wide angle dropped beneath the crossbar, but he tied the score at 18–18 nine minutes later with a penalty in front of the posts, Bradford's Stuart Fielden having been placed offside by an unfortunate bounce. With a quarter-hour remaining, there was, inevitably, a flurry of late drop-goal attempts; Deacon (twice – including an ambitious halfway effort), Long (twice – his second effort being charged down) and Paul Sculthorpe all failing. Then in the final minute, from 20 yards, Long succeeded, giving St Helens a sensational victory, although Joynt's near-misdemeanour just moments later stopped a few hearts beating!

For Saints' full-back Paul Wellens, it was a less than perfect experience, departing the final after two minutes through a fractured cheekbone. The club also had half-back Tommy Martyn indisposed through an arm injury. Their victory marked the fifth time in five major finals that Saints had defeated Bradford during the Super League era.

STATS

St Helens 19 Bradford Bulls 18

Saturday 19 October at Old Trafford, Manchester (6.30 pm)

St Helens: (blue with green bands) Wellens, Albert, Gleeson, Newlove, Stewart, Sculthorpe, Long, Britt, Cunningham, Ward, Bennett, Jonkers, Joynt (captain). Substitutes: Hoppe, Shiels, Stankevitch, Higham. Coach: I. Millward

Bradford Bulls: (white with black, amber and red shoulders and sleeves): Withers, Vaikona, Naylor, Costin, Vainikolo, R. Paul (captain), Deacon, Vagana, Lowes, Fielden, Gartner, Peacock, Forshaw. Substitutes: Pryce, Anderson, Gilmour, McDermott. Coach: B. Noble

Half-time: 12–8 **Referee:** R. Smith
Attendance: 61,138

Weather: clear, cold evening

Harry Sunderland Trophy: Deacon (Bradford Bulls)

Progressive score:

St Helens	score (min)	Bradford Bulls
	0–6 (2)	Naylor try, Deacon goal
	0–8 (21)	Deacon penalty
Bennett try, Long goal	6–8 (23)	
Long try, Long goal	12–8 (32)	
	12–14 (44)	Paul try, Deacon goal
	12–18 (47)	Withers try
Gleeson try	16–18 (56)	
Long penalty	18–18 (65)	
Long drop-goal	19–18 (80)	

Super League leaders	P	W	D	L	For	Agst	Pts
1 St Helens	28	23	0	5	927	522	46
2 Bradford Bulls	28	23	0	5	910	519	46
3 Wigan Warriors	28	19	1	8	817	475	39
4 Leeds Rhinos	28	17	0	11	865	700	34
5 Hull FC	28	16	0	12	742	674	32
6 Castleford Tigers	28	14	2	12	736	615	30

Super League play-offs:
Elimination play-off: Wigan Warriors 26 Castleford Tigers 14
Elimination play-off: Leeds Rhinos 36 Hull FC 22
Elimination semi-final: Wigan Warriors 41 Leeds Rhinos 18
Qualifying semi-final: St Helens 26 Bradford Bulls 28
Final eliminator: St Helens 24 Wigan Warriors 8

Head-to-head form guide:
Bradford Bulls 54 St Helens 22 (League)
St Helens 34 Bradford Bulls 26 (League)
Bradford Bulls 22 St Helens 50 (League)
St Helens 26 Bradford Bulls 28 (play-off)

2003 Super League Grand Final
BRADFORD BULLS V WIGAN WARRIORS

Bradford Bulls defeated Wigan Warriors, 25-12, in the 2003 Grand Final in a repeat of 2001, although this time it was a more competitive affair, the Bulls not establishing authority until the last half-hour after breaking a 6–6 tie.

Wigan took a deserved 6–0 lead with a 16th minute Danny Tickle try after he made a 40-yard break down the right, avoiding two defenders. Andrew Farrell added the goal. In the preceding five minutes, the Warriors had twice come close to opening their account; David Hodgson being halted by Stuart Reardon after a 40-yard run, and Farrell hitting the post with a penalty. Wigan continued to press but the momentum turned after Paul Deacon slotted over the first of his three penalties that would eventually level the scores. It came in the 25th minute from 30-yards, Wigan's Gareth Hock inadvertently being placed offside by a rebounding ball. The Bulls then had a 'try' discounted by the video referee after Lesley Vainikolo was judged to have knocked-on recovering Deacon's towering kick into the corner. Deacon's remaining two penalties – for a

Bradford Bulls' loose forward Mike Forshaw bursts through a Mark Smith tackle

CHAMPION CAPTAIN

Robbie Paul (Bradford Bulls 2001, 2003)

Robbie Paul was 18 when he joined Bradford Bulls (then 'Bradford Northern') in 1994, becoming club captain in the 1995/96 season. A powerful, inspirational scrum half, he won the Challenge Cup (2000, 2003), Super League Grand Final (2001, 2003, 2005), Super League Championship (1997), World Club Challenge (2002 – missing the 2004 success through injury) and League Leaders' Shield (2003) with the Bulls. Born in Tokoroa, New Zealand, he played for Waitakere, representing his country 27 times, including the 2000 World Cup. He transferred to Huddersfield Giants for 2006, being a runner-up in that year's Challenge Cup Final, moving to Salford for 2008. During the 1995/96 close season, he played rugby union for Harlequins.

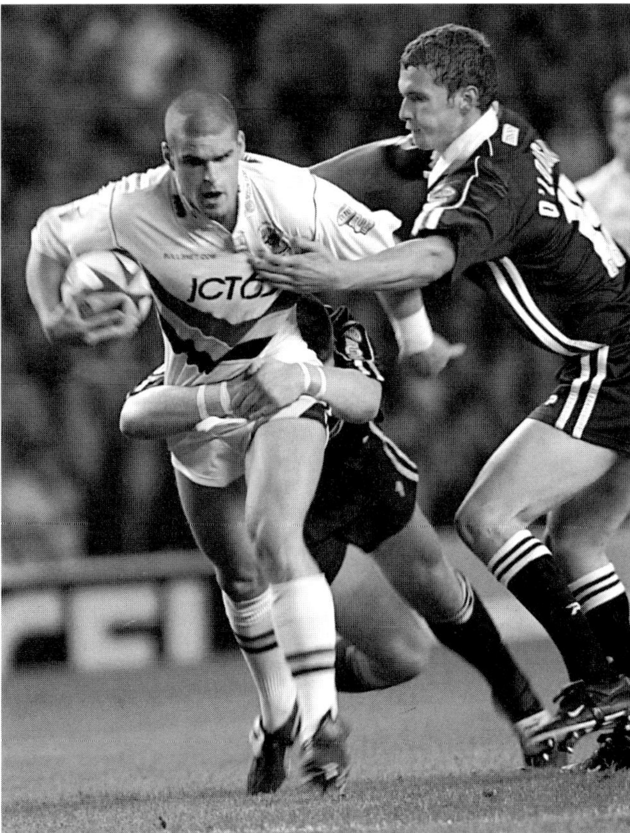

Bradford full-back Stuart Reardon – the winner of the Harry Sunderland Trophy - is detained by Wigan's Sean O'Loughlin (right) and an unidentified colleague

STATS

Bradford Bulls 25 Wigan Warriors 12

Saturday 18 October at Old Trafford, Manchester (6.30 pm)

Bradford Bulls: (white with red, amber and black chevron) Reardon, Vaikona, Withers, Hape, Vainikolo, Pratt, Deacon, Vagana, Lowes, Fielden, Gartner, Peacock, Forshaw. Substitutes: R. Paul (captain), L. Pryce, Anderson, Radford. Coach: B. Noble

Wigan Warriors: (black with white trim) Radlinski, Carney, Aspinwall, Hodgson, Dallas, O'Loughlin, Robinson, Pongia, Newton, C. Smith, Cassidy, Tickle, Farrell (captain). Substitutes: P. Johnson, O'Connor, M. Smith, Hock. Coach: M. Gregory

Half-time: 4–6 **Referee:** K. Kirkpatrick
Attendance: 65,537

Weather: cold and damp with light breeze

Harry Sunderland Trophy: Reardon (Bradford Bulls)

Progressive score:

Bradford Bulls	score (min)	Wigan Warriors
	0–6 (16)	Tickle try, Farrell goal
Deacon penalty	2–6 (25)	
Deacon penalty	4–6 (34)	
Deacon penalty	6–6 (48)	
Reardon try, Deacon goal	12–6 (53)	
Hape try, Deacon goal	18–6 (61)	
Deacon drop-goal	19–6 (70)	
	19–12 (71)	Radlinski try, Farrell goal
Lowes try, Deacon goal	25–12 (75)	

Super League leaders	P	W	D	L	For	Agst	Pts
1 Bradford Bulls	28	22	0	6	878	529	44
2 Leeds Rhinos	28	19	3	6	751	555	41
3 Wigan Warriors	28	19	2	7	776	512	40
4 St Helens*	28	16	1	11	845	535	31
5 London Broncos	28	14	2	12	643	696	30
6 Warrington Wolves	28	14	1	13	748	619	29

(* two points deducted for exceeding salary cap in 2002)

Super League play-offs:
Elimination play-off: Wigan Warriors 25 Warrington Wolves 12
Elimination play-off: St Helens 24 London Broncos 6
Elimination semi-final: Wigan Warriors 40 St Helens 24
Qualifying semi-final: Bradford Bulls 30 Leeds Rhinos 14
Final eliminator: Leeds Rhinos 22 Wigan Warriors 23

Head-to-head form guide:
Bradford Bulls 36 Wigan Warriors 22
(Challenge Cup at McAlpine Stadium, Huddersfield)
Wigan Warriors 8 Bradford Bulls 14 (League)
Bradford Bulls 22 Wigan Warriors 35 (League)
Wigan Warriors 26 Bradford Bulls 12 (League)

stray-hand by Paul Johnson in a tackle and obstruction by Luke Robinson (deputising at scrum half for Adrian Lam who suffered a knee injury in the play-off win over St Helens) – tying the scores 6–6 eight minutes into the second half.

Moments later – in the 53rd minute – disaster struck Wigan when Irish winger Brian Carney was injured in a double-tackle, leaving the field on a stretcher. The Warriors lost possession in the incident, the ensuing play seeing the Bulls go ahead for the first time. The scorer was Reardon who supported a Joe Vagana break, accepting his pass to dive over the line despite almost tripping as he evaded several defenders. Paul Deacon's goal made it 12–6. The power of the raging Bulls pack began to take its toll on Wigan's spirited resistance and eight minutes later Shontayne Hape raced over for Bradford's second try, Leon Pryce and Deacon having moved the ball out to the left. Deacon popped over the extras, adding a 20-yard drop-goal to put the Bulls into a commanding 19–6 lead with 10 minutes left.

Wigan was not finished, however, Martin Aspinwall making a terrific break after receiving from Robinson following a scrum 15 yards from their own line. He avoided two defenders before going around Vainikolo and sending Kris Radlinski in from 20 yards, Farrell converting. Wigan comeback hopes faded when Tickle dropped Deacon's deep restarting kick, returning possession to Bradford. The Yorkshire side did not waste it, Mike Forshaw and Stuart Fielden both going close before James Lowes went over from acting half-back, the hooker grabbing a trademark try in his final match before retiring, Deacon augmenting.

The first Grand Final to sell out in advance, a record 65,537 attendance watched Bradford become the first club to complete a Grand Final and Challenge Cup double, as well as being the inaugural winners of the League Leaders' Shield for heading the Super League table. The match also marked a triumphant return for Bradford skipper Robbie Paul, out for three months with a broken arm.

2004 Super League Grand Final
LEEDS RHINOS V BRADFORD BULLS

In 2004, Leeds Rhinos turned back the clock 32 years by claiming their first Championship title since 1972, defeating Bradford Bulls in the first all-Yorkshire Super League Grand Final. It was a success Leeds thoroughly merited after yet another, tense, enthralling evening at Old Trafford, having led the League table throughout the season. They were in the driving seat for most of the match but, leading only 10–8 shortly after the break there was always an element of self-doubt in the minds of the Headingley faithful, until Danny McGuire exploded into action late in the match for his 39th try of the season.

CHAMPION CAPTAIN

Kevin Sinfield (Leeds Rhinos 2004, 2007)

Kevin Sinfield was only 22 years old when he took over as Leeds Rhinos skipper in 2003, the Oldham born loose forward – equally adept at stand-off – having been signed from the Waterhead amateur club in 1997. A superb ball distributor who reads the game well, he has, so far, led Leeds to success in the Super League Grand Final (2004, 2007), League Leaders' Shield (2004) and World Club Challenge (2005). His representative honours, to date, cover appearances for Great Britain (12), England (4, including the 2000 World Cup) and Lancashire (4).

McGuire was also to the fore in Leeds' plan to keep the powerhouse Bradford side as far down the field as possible with a persistent kicking game. Potential match-winner Lesley Vainikolo was a particular target, the ball being continually kicked behind the giant winger to keep him on the defensive, rather than the offensive. The Bulls started the final without speedy Leon Pryce, who had a dislocated shoulder, being further depleted after kick-off through the loss of full-back Michael Withers with a quad injury and the first half departure of heavyweight forward Paul Anderson, limping just 10 minutes after coming off the bench.

A promising opening few minutes for Bradford went without reward and, when their prop Joe Vagana was penalised for stripping the ball in a tackle, Leeds captain Kevin Sinfield knocked over the resultant penalty from in front of the posts. The Bulls responded quickly, a sky-high kick from Iestyn Harris being well taken by Rhinos' full-back Richie Mathers, but the tackle on him behind the line forced a drop-out from which Bradford took possession to score the first try of the evening in the 8th minute. It went the way of Vainikolo, receiving the ball from Shontayne Hape after brilliant work by their elusive skipper Robbie Paul who set it up after performing a run-around move with Lee Radford. Paul Deacon missed the goal, the Bulls leading 4–2.

Six minutes later, Matt Diskin put Leeds back in front with a superb solo break from acting half-back 20 yards out, his angled run and dummy-pass taking him between two Bulls defenders to score to the left of the posts. Sinfield added the extras to widen the gap to four points. A stunned Bradford struggled to get their act together until, in the 25th minute,

The entry of the gladiators! Bradford Bulls' (left) and Leeds Rhinos' players emerge into the famous Old Trafford arena

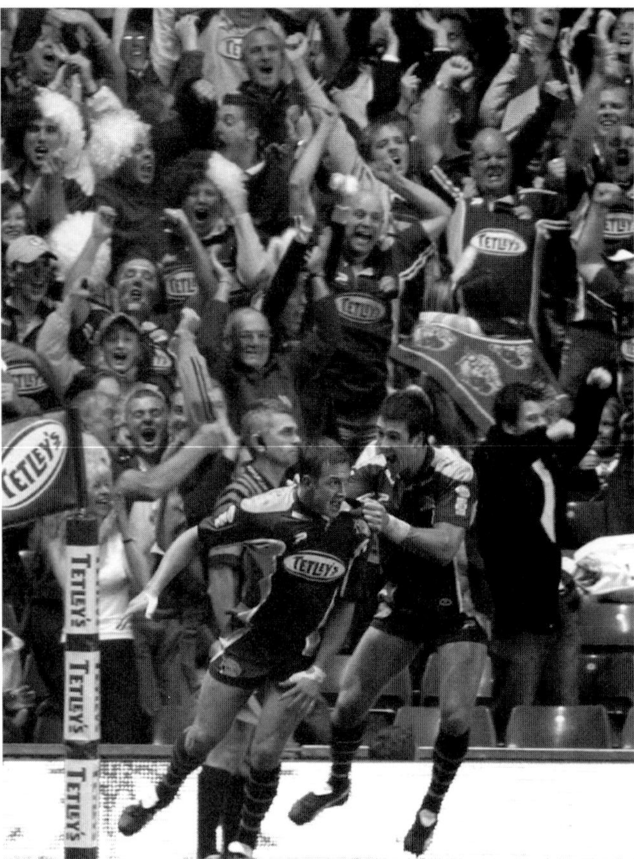

Elation in the stands and on the pitch after Danny McGuire had crossed the whitewash for his match-winning try six minutes from the end

Hape went over near the left corner flag. Video referee David Campbell wiped out the 'score', however, judging an earlier tackle attempt on Radford had been completed when his ball-carrying arm hit the ground. Sinfield concluded the first half scoring through a penalty after Harris was penalised for stealing the ball from Willie Poching.

Just four minutes after the interval, the match was back in the melting pot when Hape gave Bradford supporters hope of a second half revival, crossing the whitewash after being put into a gap by Logan Swann. Deacon just missed the goal, leaving the Bulls trailing by two points. For the next 30 minutes, the game rested on a knife-edge as the teams cancelled each other out, both missing half-chances. Then, with six minutes remaining, McGuire settled matters after Paul spilled the ball 10 yards from his own line, his pass to Keith Senior being returned with interest for him to slide over the line. Sinfield was again on target, completing the scoring at 16–8 in Leeds' favour.

STATS

Leeds Rhinos 16 Bradford Bulls 8

Saturday 16 October at Old Trafford, Manchester (6.00 pm)

Leeds Rhinos: (blue with amber shoulders and trim) Mathers, Calderwood, Walker, Senior, Bai, Sinfield (captain), McGuire, Ward, Diskin, Bailey, McKenna, Lauitiiti, Furner. Substitutes: Burrow, McDermott, Poching, Jones-Buchanan. Coach: T. Smith

Bradford Bulls: (white with black, amber and red shoulders and sleeves) Withers, Reardon, Johnson, Hape, Vainikolo, Harris, Deacon, Vagana, R. Paul (captain), Fielden, Peacock, Swann, Radford. Substitutes: Anderson, Pratt, Langley, Parker. Coach: B. Noble

Half-time: 10–4 **Referee:** S. Ganson
Attendance: 65,547

Weather: overcast and damp; ground slippery

Harry Sunderland Trophy: Diskin (Leeds Rhinos)

Progressive score:

Leeds Rhinos	score (min)	Bradford Bulls
Sinfield penalty	2–0 (2)	
	2–4 (8)	Vainikolo try
Diskin try, Sinfield goal	8–4 (14)	
Sinfield penalty	10–4 (33)	
	10–8 (44)	Hape try
McGuire try, Sinfield goal	16–8 (74)	

Super League leaders	P	W	D	L	For	Agst	Pts
1 Leeds Rhinos	28	24	2	2	1037	443	50
2 Bradford Bulls	28	20	1	7	918	565	41
3 Hull FC	28	19	2	7	843	478	40
4 Wigan Warriors	28	17	4	7	736	558	38
5 St Helens	28	17	1	10	821	662	35
6 Wakefield T Wildcats	28	15	0	13	788	662	30

Super League play-offs:
Elimination play-off: Hull FC 18 Wakefield Trinity Wildcats 28
Elimination play-off: Wigan Warriors 18 St Helens 12
Elimination semi-final:
Wigan Warriors 18 Wakefield Trinity Wildcats 14
Qualifying semi-final: Leeds Rhinos 12 Bradford Bulls 26
Final eliminator: Leeds Rhinos 40 Wigan Warriors 12

Head-to-head form guide:
Leeds Rhinos 26 Bradford Bulls 18 (League)
Bradford Bulls 12 Leeds Rhinos 26 (League)
Leeds Rhinos 40 Bradford Bulls 12 (League)
Leeds Rhinos 12 Bradford Bulls 26 (play-off)

2005 Super League Grand Final
BRADFORD BULLS V LEEDS RHINOS

Bradford Bulls gained revenge over Leeds Rhinos in the 2005 Grand Final, reversing the previous year's result in defeating them 15–6. It was an unlikely outcome two months earlier, the Bulls lying fifth after their worst ever Super League start. Their late 12-match winning run, including the play-offs, pulled them up to third place to become the first winners from outside the top two.

Bradford included Adrian Morley in their side, his sixth and last appearance for the club. The Great Britain Test forward was one of several players permitted to fly to England on short-term end-of-season deals after their Australian clubs, Sydney Roosters in Morley's case, had been eliminated from their own

Bradford Bulls scrum half Paul Deacon dodges his way through the Leeds defence

STATS

Bradford Bulls 15 Leeds Rhinos 6

Saturday 15 October at Old Trafford, Manchester (6.00 pm)

Bradford Bulls: (white with red, black and amber chevron) Withers, L. Pryce, B. Harris, Hape, Vainikolo, I. Harris, Deacon, Peacock (captain), Henderson, Fielden, Johnson, Meyers, Radford. Substitutes: R. Paul, Vagana, Langley, Morley. Coach: B. Noble

Leeds Rhinos: (blue with amber bands) Mathers, Calderwood, Walker, McKenna, Bai, McGuire, Burrow, Bailey, Dunemann, Ward, Ellis, Poching, Sinfield (captain). Substitutes: Diskin, McDermott, Lauitiiti, Jones-Buchanan. Coach: T. Smith

Half-time: 8–6 **Referee:** A. Klein
Attendance: 65,537

Weather: mild and dry

Harry Sunderland Trophy: L. Pryce (Bradford Bulls)

Progressive score:

Bradford Bulls	score (min)	Leeds Rhinos
Deacon penalty	2–0 (19)	
	2–4 (22)	McGuire try
Deacon penalty	4–4 (23)	
L. Pryce try	8–4 (29)	
	8–6 (32)	Sinfield penalty
Vainikolo try, Deacon goal	14–6 (52)	
I. Harris drop-goal	15–6 (75)	

Super League leaders	P	W	D	L	For	Agst	Pts
1 St Helens	28	23	1	4	1028	537	47
2 Leeds Rhinos	28	22	0	6	1152	505	44
3 Bradford Bulls	28	18	1	9	1038	684	37
4 Warrington Wolves	28	18	0	10	792	702	36
5 Hull FC	28	15	2	11	756	670	32
6 London Broncos	28	13	2	13	800	718	28

Super League play-offs:
Elimination play-off: Bradford Bulls 44 London Broncos 22
Elimination play-off: Warrington Wolves 6 Hull FC 40
Elimination semi-final: Bradford Bulls 71 Hull FC 0
Qualifying semi-final: St Helens 16 Leeds Rhinos 19
Final eliminator: St Helens 18 Bradford Bulls 23

Head-to-head form guide:
Bradford Bulls 12 Leeds Rhinos 42 (League)
Leeds Rhinos 36 Bradford Bulls 26 (League)
Leeds Rhinos 10 Bradford Bulls 42 (League)

Perfect poise and assurance from Bradford skipper Jamie Peacock as he finds an opening in the Leeds ranks

domestic competition. His inclusion was undoubtedly an asset to the Bulls, although it meant previously ever-present Andy Lynch had to stand down. Leeds, meanwhile, entered the fray without centre Keith Senior after he sustained an ankle injury during August. Whilst interest in the match was maintained well into the second half due to the closeness of the score, the general feeling was it was the least impressive of the eight Grand Final's to date, Andy Wilson in the *The Guardian*, summing it up as 'Astonishingly tough, yet distinctly unmemorable.'

Paul Deacon opened the scoring midway through the first period with a 20-yard goal after Barrie McDermott was penalised for a high tackle on Morley. The Bulls threw away their advantage by coughing up possession at the restart. Within minutes Leeds struck when acting half-back Andrew Dunemann, from close in, kicked the ball neatly across Bradford's line at the corner, Danny McGuire pouncing for the opening try. Kevin Sinfield missed the difficult kick. Bradford drew level at 4–4 when Deacon hit his second penalty, Dunemann being guilty of stripping the ball from Ian Henderson. Six minutes later Bradford got their first touchdown when Leon Pryce, accepting a long Iestyn Harris pass, gave a dummy before racing through two defenders on a 20-yard burst that took him over the line. Deacon surprisingly missed the goal. Eight minutes before the break Morley was pulled up for alleged use of the elbow on McDermott, Sinfield being on target with the resulting penalty, the Bulls leading 8–6 at half-time.

The second half opened with two debatable video decisions, ruling out tries for each side; Bradford's Shontayne Hape in the 45th minute (Lesley Vainikolo impeding Mark Calderwood) and Leeds' Chev Walker in the 50th (fumbling the ball as he made a one-handed touchdown in the corner). In the 52nd minute a try was awarded, Vainikolo being the scorer, his dummy pass being a prelude to him brushing off three defenders to go over. Deacon's conversion opened an eight-point lead, having a chance to extend it 13 minutes later, but slicing his penalty attempt. It was left to Iestyn Harris to ignite the Bradford celebrations with a neat drop-goal five minutes from time. Leeds attempted to rescue matters, recovering the short kick-off at the restart but when Rob Burrow mishandled the game was up.

It was a record fifth consecutive Grand Final for Bradford who equalled St Helens' feat of three wins, the pair also claiming the Super League title once each before the play-offs were introduced in 1998.

CHAMPION CAPTAIN

Jamie Peacock (Bradford Bulls 2005)

Leeds-born Jamie Peacock joined Bradford Bulls in 1997. The powerhouse second-row forward, signed from Stanningley in Leeds, gained early experience in Australia with Wollongong University, near Sydney, where he was studying, and a New South Wales country club. Returning to England, he was loaned to Featherstone Rovers for several matches during 1998, making his Bradford debut in 1999 when he was 21 years old. With the Bulls, he enjoyed success in the Super League Grand Final (2001, 2003, 2005), League Leaders' Shield (2003), Rugby League Challenge Cup (2000, 2003), and World Club Challenge (2002, 2004). He transferred to Leeds Rhinos for the 2006 season winning the Super League Grand Final in 2007. To date, he has represented Great Britain (23 times, including the 2005 and 2006 Tri-Nations when he was captain for both), England (5, including the 2000 World Cup) and Yorkshire (4).

2006 Super League Grand Final
ST HELENS V HULL FC

St Helens crowned a magnificent 2006 season, winning the Super League Grand Final 26–4 after a brilliant all-round performance against Hull FC. Watched by a massive 72,582 attendance at the recently expanded Old Trafford – the third largest after 1960 and 1949 to witness a rugby league 'championship' final in Britain – the Saints made it a record four Grand Final wins. They also claimed a treble having won the Challenge Cup and League Leaders' Shield, emulating Bradford Bulls' feat of 2003. Although losing by a 22-point margin, Hull could take credit from an excellent display in what was their Grand Final debut.

With the sides tied 4–4 just before half-time and little to choose between them up to that point, the pivotal moment went St Helens' way via a Leon Pryce try. There was, however, an element of controversy in the build up. Hull, attacking inside the Saints half, was penalised for 'shepherding', a debatable decision that did not go down well with their coach, Peter Sharp. St Helens regained possession as a consequence and, moments later, Pryce 'sold' a dummy pass before scorching between two defenders on a 45-yard sprint to score in the corner, reminiscent of his Bradford try in the previous Grand Final. Jamie Lyon, in his farewell match before returning to Australia after two spellbinding seasons with the Saints, added an excellent touchline kick for a crucial 10–4 interval lead.

CHAMPION CAPTAIN

Sean Long (St Helens 2006)

Sean Long was signed by St Helens from Widnes in 1997 for £80,000, having joined the latter just two months earlier from his local club Wigan. An inventive scrum half, whose quicksilver breaks and tremendous kicking ability make him one of the game's most dangerous attackers, he joined Wigan in 1993 from the local St Judes club. With St Helens he has won the World Club Challenge (2001, 2007), Super League Grand Final (1999, 2000, 2002, 2006), League Leaders' Shield (2005, 2006, 2007) and Challenge Cup (2001, 2004, 2006, 2007). To date, he has played in 15 Tests for Great Britain and represented England five times (all in the 2000 World Cup).

Sid Domic crosses in the corner for Hull's only points of the final

Sean Long – deputising as the St Helens captain in the absence of knee injury victim Paul Sculthorpe – had created the opening try of the night in the 17th minute with a perfect kick into the left corner from 20 yards out after the 4th tackle, Francis Meli diving onto the ball for the touchdown. Lyon's kick was just wide of the far upright. Hull responded quickly and it took an excellent tackle from Saints' Jon Wilkin to save a certain looking Shaun Briscoe try after Richard Horne had put him in the clear. By the 24th minute, though, Hull was deservedly level, Paul Cooke, from 15 yards out just in front of the Saints posts, hoisting a kick towards the right corner. In the mayhem that followed Motu Tony retrieved the ball, turning it inside for Shayne McMenemy who quickly fired it out again to Sid Domic, the centre getting the ball down to the absolute delight of the large Hull following. Cooke's towering conversion attempt frustratingly bounced back off the far post. Briscoe and Richard Swain both came close to giving Hull the lead but it was Pryce's telling break that broke the first half deadlock.

The contest was as good as settled in the opening 12 minutes of the second half, St Helens scoring two tries through Willie Talau (wide on the left off Jason Hooper's pass) and Ade Gardner (near the right touchline after leaping above Gareth Raynor to recover Long's high kick – video referee Steve Presley confirming the score). Long was wide with the first kick but the latter succeeded for a 20–4 lead. Hull tried hard to resurrect their chances but was frustrated by an excellent defence, particularly from St Helens' full-back Paul Wellens. The only remaining points, though, went to the Saints 18 minutes from the end when Keiron Cunningham ran across the face of the Hull posts from acting half-back before feeding Maurie Fa'asavalu. The hooker accepted the return pass to go over the line, Lyon adding the goal.

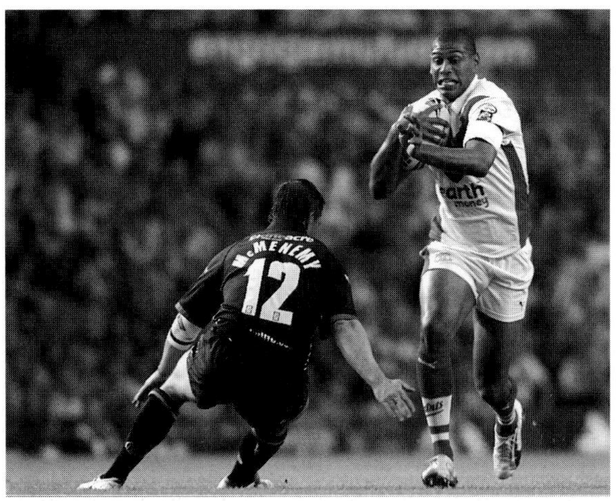

St Helens' stand-off Leon Pryce surges past Hull's Shayne McMenemy

STATS

St Helens 26 Hull FC 4

Saturday 14 October at Old Trafford, Manchester (6.00 pm)

St Helens: (white with red chevron) Wellens, Gardner, Lyon, Talau, Meli, Pryce, Long (captain), P. Anderson, Cunningham, Cayless, Gilmour, Wilkin, Hooper. Substitutes: Roby, Bennett, Graham, Fa'asavalu. Coach: D. Anderson

Hull FC: (black with white trim) Briscoe, Tony, Domic, Yeaman, Raynor, Cooke, R. Horne, Dowes, Swain (captain), Carvell, Radford, McMenemy, Washbrook. Substitutes: Whiting, King, G Horne, Wheeldon. Coach: P. Sharp

Half-time: 10–4 **Referee:** K. Kirkpatrick
Attendance: 72,582

Weather: fine and warm

Harry Sunderland Trophy: Wellens (St Helens)

Progressive score:

St Helens	score (min)	Hull FC
Meli try	4–0 (17)	
	4–4 (24)	Domic try
Pryce try, Lyon goal	10–4 (39)	
Talau try	14–4 (49)	
Gardner try, Lyon goal	20–4 (52)	
Cunningham try, Lyon goal	26–4 (62)	

Super League leaders	P	W	D	L	For	Agst	Pts
1 St Helens	28	24	0	4	939	430	48
2 Hull FC	28	20	0	8	720	578	40
3 Leeds Rhinos	28	19	0	9	869	543	38
4 Bradford Bulls*	28	16	2	10	802	568	32
5 Salford City Reds	28	13	0	15	600	539	26
6 Warrington Wolves	28	13	0	15	743	721	26

(*two points deducted for exceeding salary cap in 2005)

Super League play-offs:
Elimination play-off: Leeds Rhinos 17 Warrington Wolves 18
Elimination play-off: Bradford Bulls 52 Salford City Reds 16
Elimination semi-final: Bradford Bulls 40 Warrington Wolves 24
Qualifying semi-final: St Helens 12 Hull FC 8
Final eliminator: Hull FC 19 Bradford Bulls 12

Head-to-head form guide:
Hull FC 0 St Helens 46 (League)
St Helens 26 Hull FC 27 (League)
St Helens 12 Hull FC 8 (play-off)

2007 Super League Grand Final
LEEDS RHINOS V ST HELENS

Leeds Rhinos gave departing coach Tony Smith the perfect send-off with an unexpectedly one-sided score-line over St Helens in the 2007 Grand Final. Smith – set to focus on his new role as Great Britain's mentor – saw his sides miserly defence limit the Saints attacking machine to one converted try, taking the second half spoils with 25 unanswered points. Super League leaders St Helens, who beat second-placed Leeds 10-8 two weeks earlier in the qualifying semi-final, were without skipper Paul Sculthorpe for the second successive year, an Achilles tendon injury in June curtailing his season, although Sean Long and Maurie F'asavalu returned following hamstring setbacks.

St Helens dominated the first 15 minutes but were unable to breach a well-organised Leeds outfit, their opportunity to open the scoring denied when Long missed a kickable 3rd minute penalty 20 yards out after he was obstructed by Matt Diskin when following up his own kick. Rhinos' captain Kevin Sinfield made no mistake 12 minutes later, his angled penalty goal – after Saints' Chris Flannery was ruled offside – placing him in the record book as the first player to score in every Leeds match during a season. Just four minutes later the gap was extended to 8-0 when Brent Webb went over in the left corner off Scott Donald's inside pass following a sizzling six-man move, Sinfield adding an excellent conversion.

Saints, though, hit back with a fabulously worked try. Long's break, from just inside his own half after executing a run around with halfback partner Leon Pryce, was continued by Lee Gilmour who transferred to the supporting James Roby, the latter outpacing Leeds' remaining cover to race in from 20 yards to the right of the posts. Long, from a slightly more acute angle than his earlier penalty miss, augmented. It remained 8-6 for Leeds until the break although a piece of Danny McGuire magic in the 30th minute almost increased the margin. Chipping the ball over the Saints' defence, he recovered possession, directing another kick to the left corner, but it bounced agonisingly out of play as Donald tried to capitalise.

After the interval, St Helens again bossed the opening exchanges. Leeds, though, held firm

Kevin Sinfield hoists the Super League Trophy for the second time in four seasons

before turning the game on its head with a blistering five-minute scoring burst. It began in the 50th minute when Ali Lauitiiti's arcing 15-yard charge took him through a melee of defenders to score in the left corner. Two minutes later Donald registered a classic winger's try. Accepting Keith Senior's pass 70 yards out, he flew down the left flank, moving in from the touchline before veering outside Paul Wellens for a try that brought the Leeds contingent to its feet. Sinfield appended the latter effort, Rob Burrow's drop-goal three minutes later crucially shunting the Rhinos' three scores ahead at 19-6. The closest St Helens came to increasing their tally was when stand-in captain Keiron Cunningham was held up over the Leeds try-line in the 59th minute. But it was Leeds that finished strongest adding two further tries through Lee Smith (successfully competing with Francis Meli to claim McGuire's high kick towards the right corner) and Jamie Jones-Buchanan (his last-minute try being confirmed by video referee Ben Thaler after a hint of a double movement although Weller appeared to temporarily lose his grip on the player). Sinfield added both goals, plus a 73rd minute penalty when Pryce was deemed to have made a high tackle on Jones-Buchanan.

Whilst acknowledging St Helens as 'the stand out (team) for the last two years', Sinfield said 'the guts, determination, spirit and will to win was evident from our guys.'

Rob Burrow, whose display earned him the Harry Sunderland Trophy, probes for an opening in the Saints' defence

STATS

Leeds Rhinos 33 St Helens 6

Saturday 13 October at Old Trafford, Manchester (6.00 pm)

Leeds Rhinos: (black with amber trim) Webb, Smith, Toopi, Senior, Donald, McGuire, Burrow, Leuluai, Diskin, Peacock, Jones-Buchanan, Ellis, Sinfield (captain). Substitutes: Lauitiiti, Bailey, Kirke, Ablett. Coach: T Smith

St Helens: (white with red chevron and trim) Wellens, Gardner, Gidley, Talau, Meli, Pryce, Long, Fozzard, Cunningham (captain), Cayless, Gilmour, Flannery, Wilkin. Substitutes: Roby, Bennett, Graham, Fa'asavalu. Coach: D Anderson

Half-time: 8-6 **Referee:** A Klein
Attendance: 71,352

Weather: overcast and mild with some drizzle

Harry Sunderland Trophy: Burrow (Leeds Rhinos)

Progressive score:

Leeds Rhinos	score (min)	St Helens
Sinfield penalty	2-0 (15)	
Webb try, Sinfield goal	8-0 (19)	
	8-6 (27)	Roby try, Long goal
Lauitiiti try	12-6 (50)	
Donald try, Sinfield goal	18-6 (52)	
Burrow drop-goal	19-6 (55)	
Smith try, Sinfield goal	25-6 (68)	
Sinfield penalty	27-6 (73)	
Jones-Buchanan try, Sinfield goal	33-6 (80)	

Super League leaders	P	W	D	L	For	Agst	Pts
1 St Helens	27	19	0	8	783	442	38
2 Leeds Rhinos	27	18	1	8	747	487	37
3 Bradford Bulls*	27	17	1	9	778	560	33
4 Hull FC	27	14	2	11	573	553	30
5 Huddersfield Giants	27	13	1	13	638	543	27
6 Wigan Warriors**	27	15	1	11	621	527	27

(* two points deducted for exceeding salary cap in 2006
** four points deducted for exceeding salary cap in 2006)

Super League play-offs:
Elimination play-off: Bradford Bulls 30 Wigan Warriors 31
Elimination play-off: Hull FC 22 Huddersfield Giants 16
Elimination semi-final: Hull FC 18 Wigan Warriors 21
Qualifying semi-final: St Helens 10 Leeds Rhinos 8
Final eliminator: Leeds 36 Wigan 6

Head-to-head form guide:
Leeds 38 St Helens 19 (League)
St Helens 10 Leeds 22 (League)
St Helens 10 Leeds 8 (play-off)

SUMMARY OF RESULTS

Northern Rugby League Championship Final:

Year	Winner	Runner-up	Venue
1907	Halifax 18	Oldham 3	Huddersfield
1908	Hunslet 7	Oldham 7	Salford
Replay	Hunslet 12	Oldham 2	Wakefield
1909	Wigan 7	Oldham 3	Salford
1910	Oldham 13	Wigan 7	Broughton
1911	Oldham 20	Wigan 7	Broughton
1912	Huddersfield 13	Wigan 5	Halifax
1913	Huddersfield 29	Wigan 2	Wakefield
1914	Salford 5	Huddersfield 3	Headingley
1915	Huddersfield 35	Leeds 2	Wakefield
1916 to 1919 – no competition due to First World War			
1920	Hull 3	Huddersfield 2	Headingley
1921	Hull 16	Hull KR 14	Headingley
1922	Wigan 13	Oldham 2	Broughton
1923	Hull KR 15	Huddersfield 5	Headingley
1924	Batley 13	Wigan 7	Broughton
1925	Hull KR 9	Swinton 5	Rochdale
1926	Wigan 22	Warrington 10	St Helens
1927	Swinton 13	St Helens Recs 8	Warrington
1928	Swinton 11	Featherstone R 0	Oldham
1929	Huddersfield 2	Leeds 0	Halifax
1930	Huddersfield 2	Leeds 2	Wakefield
Replay	Huddersfield 10	Leeds 0	Halifax
1931	Swinton 14	Leeds 7	Wigan
1932	St Helens 9	Huddersfield 5	Wakefield
1933	Salford 15	Swinton 5	Wigan
1934	Wigan 15	Salford 3	Warrington
1935	Swinton 14	Warrington 3	Wigan
1936	Hull 21	Widnes 2	Huddersfield
1937	Salford 13	Warrington 11	Wigan
1938	Hunslet 8	Leeds 2	Elland Rd, Leeds
1939	Salford 8	Castleford 6	Maine Rd, M/cr

War Emergency League Championship Final:

Year	Winner	Runner-up	Venue
1940	Bradford N 37	Swinton 22	Over two legs
1941	Bradford N 45	Wigan 15	Over two legs
1942	Dewsbury 13	Bradford N 0	Headingley
1943	Dewsbury 33	Halifax 16	Over two legs
(1943 later declared null and void as Dewsbury fielded ineligible player)			
1944	Wigan 25	Dewsbury 14	Over two legs
1945	Bradford N 26	Halifax 20	Over two legs

Northern Rugby League Championship Final:

Year	Winner	Runner-up	Venue
1946	Wigan 13	Huddersfield 4	Maine Rd, M/cr
1947	Wigan 13	Dewsbury 4	Maine Rd, M/cr
1948	Warrington 15	Bradford N 5	Maine Rd, M/cr
1949	Huddersfield 13	Warrington 12	Maine Rd, M/cr
1950	Wigan 20	Huddersfield 2	Maine Rd, M/cr
1951	Workington T 26	Warrington 11	Maine Rd, M/cr
1952	Wigan 13	Bradford N 6	Leeds Rd, Hudd'sf'ld
1953	St Helens 24	Halifax 14	Maine Rd, M/cr
1954	Warrington 8	Halifax 7	Maine Rd, M/cr
1955	Warrington 7	Oldham 3	Maine Rd, M/cr
1956	Hull 10	Halifax 9	Maine Rd, M/cr
1957	Oldham 15	Hull 14	Bradford
1958	Hull 20	Workington T 3	Bradford
1959	St Helens 44	Hunslet 22	Bradford
1960	Wigan 27	Wakefield T 3	Bradford
1961	Leeds 25	Warrington 10	Bradford
1962	Huddersfield 14	Wakefield T 5	Bradford
1963 to 1964 – no play-offs; two divisions in operation			
1965	Halifax 15	St Helens 7	Swinton
1966	St Helens 35	Halifax 12	Swinton
1967	Wakefield T 7	St Helens 7	Headingley
Replay	Wakefield T 21	St Helens 9	Swinton
1968	Wakefield T 17	Hull KR 10	Headingley
1969	Leeds 16	Castleford 14	Bradford
1970	St Helens 24	Leeds 12	Bradford
1971	St Helens 16	Wigan 12	Swinton
1972	Leeds 9	St Helens 5	Swinton
1973	Dewsbury 22	Leeds 13	Bradford

Club Championship Final:

Year	Winner	Runner-up	Venue
1974	Warrington 13	St Helens 12	Wigan

Premiership Trophy Final:

Year	Winner	Runner-up	Venue
1975	Leeds 26	St Helens 11	Wigan
1976	St Helens 15	Salford 2	Swinton
1977	St Helens 32	Warrington 20	Swinton
1978	Bradford N 17	Widnes 8	Swinton
1979	Leeds 24	Bradford N 2	Huddersfield
1980	Widnes 19	Bradford N 5	Swinton
1981	Hull KR 11	Hull 7	Headingley
1982	Widnes 23	Hull 8	Headingley
1983	Widnes 22	Hull 10	Headingley
1984	Hull KR 18	Castleford 10	Headingley
1985	St Helens 36	Hull KR 16	Eland Rd, Leeds
1986	Warrington 38	Halifax 10	Elland Rd, Leeds
1987	Wigan 8	Warrington 0	Old Trafford
1988	Widnes 38	St Helens 14	Old Trafford
1989	Widnes 18	Hull 10	Old Trafford
1990	Widnes 28	Bradford N 6	Old Trafford
1991	Hull 14	Widnes 4	Old Trafford
1992	Wigan 48	St Helens 16	Old Trafford
1993	St Helens 10	Wigan 4	Old Trafford
1994	Wigan 24	Castleford 20	Old Trafford
1995	Wigan 69	Leeds 12	Old Trafford
1996	Wigan 44	St Helens 14	Old Trafford
1997	Wigan W 33	St Helens 20	Old Trafford

Super League Grand Final:

Year	Winner	Runner-up	Venue
1998	Wigan W 10	Leeds R 4	Old Trafford
1999	St Helens 8	Bradford B 6	Old Trafford
2000	St Helens 29	Wigan W 16	Old Trafford
2001	Bradford B 37	Wigan W 6	Old Trafford
2002	St Helens 19	Bradford B 18	Old Trafford
2003	Bradford B 25	Wigan W 12	Old Trafford
2004	Leeds R 16	Bradford B 8	Old Trafford
2005	Bradford B 15	Leeds R 6	Old Trafford
2006	St Helens 26	Hull FC 4	Old Trafford
2007	Leeds R 33	St Helens 6	Old Trafford

CLUB RECORDS

Championship Finals (1907–73):

(Excluding War Emergency League Finals 1940–45)

Most wins: 9 by Wigan

Most appearances: 15 by Wigan

Most consecutive wins: 2 by Oldham (1910, 1911), Huddersfield (1912, 1913), Hull (1920, 1921), Swinton (1927, 1928), Huddersfield (1929, 1930), Wigan (1946, 1947), Warrington (1954, 1955), Wakefield T (1967, 1968) and St Helens (1970, 1971)

Most consecutive appearances: 5 by Oldham (1907, 1908, 1909, 1910, 1911), Wigan (1909, 1910, 1911, 1912, 1913) and Huddersfield (1912, 1913, 1914, 1915, 1920)

Highest score: 44 by St Helens (1959)

Highest score by losing team: 22 by Hunslet (1959)

Widest marginal win: 33 – Huddersfield 35 Leeds 2 (1915)

Highest aggregate score: 66 – St Helens 44 Hunslet 22 (1959)

Lowest aggregate score: 2 – Huddersfield 2 Leeds 0 (1929)

Premiership Trophy Finals (1975–97):

Most wins: 6 by Widnes and Wigan/Wigan Warriors

Most appearances: 9 by St Helens

Most consecutive wins: 4 by Wigan/Wigan Warriors (1994, 1995, 1996, 1997)

Most consecutive appearances: 6 by Wigan/Wigan Warriors (1992, 1993, 1994, 1995, 1996, 1997)

Highest score: 69 by Wigan (1995)

Highest score by losing team: 20 by Warrington (1977), Castleford (1994) and St Helens (1997)

Widest marginal win: 57 – Wigan 69 Leeds 12 (1995)

Highest aggregate score: 81 – Wigan 69 Leeds 12 (1995)

Lowest aggregate score: 8 – Wigan 8 Warrington 0 (1987)

Super League Grand Finals (1998–2007):

Most wins: 4 by St Helens

Most appearances: 6 by Bradford B

Most consecutive wins: 2 by St Helens (1999, 2000)

Most consecutive appearances: 5 by Bradford B (2001, 2002, 2003, 2004, 2005)

Highest score: 37 by Bradford B (2001)

Highest score by losing team: 18 by Bradford B (2002)

Widest marginal win: 31 – Bradford B 37 Wigan W 6 (2001)

Highest aggregate score: 45 – St Helens 29 Wigan W 16 (2000)

Lowest aggregate score: 14 – Wigan W 10 Leeds R 4 (1998) and St Helens 8 Bradford B 6 (1999)

Attendance and receipt records

Championship Finals (1907–1973):

Highest attendance: 83,190 – Wigan 27 Wakefield T 3 (at Bradford, 1960)

Highest receipts: £14,482 – Wigan 27 Wakefield T 3 (at Bradford, 1960)

Premiership Trophy Finals (1975–1997):

Highest attendance: 42,043 – Hull 14 Widnes 4 (at Old Trafford, 1991)

Highest receipts: £475,000 – Wigan 24 Castleford 20 (at Old Trafford, 1994)

Super League Grand Finals (1998–2007):

Highest attendance: 72,582 – St Helens 26 Hull FC 4 (at Old Trafford, 2006)

Highest receipts: No receipts have been reported from 1999. The receipts of £737,105 for the first Super League Grand Final in 1998 were reported, at the time, as the highest outside of Wembley

Breakdown of wins by League position

Championship Finals (1907–1973):

The total number of peacetime finals held is 55

The team finishing first won 27, second won 17, third won 4, fourth won 5, seventh won 1, eighth won 1

Premiership Trophy Finals (1975–1997):

The total number of finals held is 23

The team finishing first won 7, second won 6, third won 5, fourth won 4, fifth won 1

Super League Grand Finals (1998–2007):

The total number of finals held to date is 10

The team finishing first has won 6, second won 3, third won 1

PLAYERS RECORDS

Championship Finals (1907–73):

(Excluding War Emergency League Finals 1940-45)

Most wins: 4 by John Higson (Hunslet 1908, Huddersfield 1912, 1913, 1915), Fred Beswick (Swinton 1927, 1928, 1931, 1935), Gus Risman (Salford 1933, 1937, 1939, Workington T 1951) and Brian Nordgren (Wigan 1946, 1947, 1950, 1952)

Most appearances: 6 by John Higson (Hunslet 1908*, Huddersfield 1912, 1913, 1914, 1915, 1920), Fred Beswick (Swinton 1925, 1927, 1928, 1931, 1933, 1935), Brian Bevan (Warrington 1948, 1949, 1951, 1954, 1955, 1961) and John Mantle (St Helens 1965, 1966, 1967*, 1970, 1971, 1972) (*Also appeared in replay for year indicated)

Most consecutive wins: 2 by 79 players!

Most consecutive appearances: 5 by Bert Avery, Billy Dixon, Joe Ferguson, Arthur Smith (all Oldham 1907, 1908*, 1909, 1910, 1911), Johnny Thomas (Wigan 1909, 1910, 1911, 1912, 1913), John Higson, Major Holland and Albert Rosenfeld (all Huddersfield 1912, 1913, 1914, 1915, 1920) (*Also appeared in replay for year indicated)

Most tries: 3 by Duggie Clark (Huddersfield 1913), Johnny Ring (Wigan 1926), Tom van Vollenhoven (St Helens 1959), Albert Halsall (St Helens 1966) and Len Killeen (St Helens 1966)

Most goals: 10 by Austin Rhodes (St Helens 1959)

Most points: 21 by Len Killeen (St Helens 1966)

Premiership Trophy Finals (1975–97):

Most wins: 6 by Mike O'Neill (Widnes 1980, 1982, 1983, 1988, 1989, 1990) and Martin Offiah (Widnes 1988, 1989, 1990, Wigan 1992, 1994, 1995)

Most appearances: 8 by Martin Offiah (Widnes 1988, 1989, 1990, 1991, Wigan 1992, 1993, 1994, 1995)

Most consecutive wins: 5 by Gary Connolly (St Helens 1993, Wigan 1994, 1995, 1996, 1997)

Most consecutive appearances: 8 by Martin Offiah (Widnes 1988, 1989, 1990, 1991, Wigan 1992, 1993, 1994, 1995)

Most tries: 3 by Kris Radlinski (Wigan 1995), Gary Connolly (Wigan 1995) and Danny Ellison (St Helens 1996)

Most goals: 10 by Frano Botica, twice (Wigan 1992, 1995)

Most points: 20 by Frano Botica, twice (Wigan 1992, 1995)

Super League Grand Finals (1998–2007):

Most wins: 4 by Keiron Cunningham, Sean Long, Paul Wellens (all St Helens 1999, 2000, 2002, 2006), Leon Pryce (Bradford B 2001, 2003, 2005, St Helens 2006) and Jamie Peacock (Bradford B 2001, 2003, 2005, Leeeds R 2007)

Most appearances: 7 by Leon Pryce (Bradford B 1999, 2001, 2002, 2003, 2005, St Helens 2006, 2007)

Most consecutive wins: 2 by Keiron Cunningham, Sean Hoppe, Kevin Iro, Chris Joynt, Sean Long, Tommy Martyn, Sonny Nickle, Julian O'Neill, Apollo Perelini, Paul Sculthorpe, Anthony Sullivan, Freddie Tuilagi, Paul Wellens (all St Helens 1999, 2000) and Leon Pryce (Bradford B 2005, St Helens 2006)

Most consecutive appearances: 5 by Paul Deacon, Stuart Fielden, Robbie Paul, Jamie Peacock, Joe Vagana and Michael Withers (all Bradford B 2001, 2002, 2003, 2004, 2005)

Most tries: 3 by Michael Withers (Bradford B 2001)

Most goals: 7 by Paul Deacon (Bradford B 2003)

Most points: 13 by Paul Deacon (Bradford B 2003)

Player that missed the Final

Tourists:

(Players on the sea voyage to Australia before air travel was used)

1910: Tom Helm (Oldham), Dick Ramsdale (Wigan)

1920: Billy Stone (Hull), Duggie Clark, Ben Gronow, Johnny Rogers, Gwyn Thomas, Harold Wagstaff (all Huddersfield)

1924: Frank Gallagher (Batley), Tommy Howley, Danny Hurcombe, Jack Price, Johnny Ring, Jim Sullivan (all Wigan)

1928: Bryn Evans, Jack Evans, Billo Rees (all Swinton), Tommy Askin (Featherstone R).

1932: Alf Ellaby, Albert Fildes (both St Helens), Stanley Brogden (Huddersfield)

1936: Harold Ellerington (Hull), Tommy McCue, Nat Silcock (both Widnes)

1946: Joe Egan, Ken Gee, Martin Ryan, Ted Ward (all Wigan), Bob Nicholson (Huddersfield)

1950: Ernie Ashcroft, Tommy Bradshaw, Jack Cunliffe, Joe Egan, Ken Gee, Jack Hilton, Gordon Ratcliffe, Martin Ryan (all Wigan)

Suspended:

(Players not available due to suspension)

1920: Jack Beasty, Tom Herridge, Fred Newsome (all Hull)

1925: Bert Morris (Swinton)

1938: Ken Jubb (Leeds)

1955: Arthur Tomlinson (Oldham)

1958: Tommy Harris (Hull)

1960: Mick Sullivan (Wigan)

1970: Bernard Watson (Leeds)

1981: Graham Walters (Hull)

1984: Len Casey (Hull KR)

1995: Garry Schofield (Leeds)

1997: Bobbie Goulding (St Helens)

Players sent off

Red cards:

(Players dismissed from the game during final)

1909: Walter Cheetham (Wigan), Arthur Smith (Oldham)

1920: Alf Grice (Hull)

1922: Rod Marlor (Oldham)

1930: Tom Banks (Huddersfield)

1935: Nat Bentham (Warrington)

1940 (2nd leg): Emlyn Jenkins (Bradford N), Frank Bowyer (Swinton)

1941 (2nd leg): Cliff Carter (Bradford N), Joe Egan (Wigan)

1969: Dennis Hartley (Castleford)

1971: John Mantle (St Helens)

1973: Alan Hardisty (Leeds)

1977: Harry Pinner (St Helens), Alan Gwilliam (Warrington)

1990: Paul Hulme (Widnes)

Yellow cards:

(Players sent to the 'sin bin' – introduced in 1983 initially for 5 or 10 minutes and later standardised at 10)

1983: Mick Adams (Widnes)*

1989: Joe Grima (Widnes)

1992: Shane Cooper (St Helens)

1994: Graham Steadman (Castleford), Shaun Edwards (Wigan)

(*5 minutes duration – the remainder are for 10 minutes)

COACHES/REFEREES RECORDS

Coaches records

Championship Finals (1907–73):
(Excluding War Emergency League Finals 1940–45)
Most wins: 7 by Jim Sullivan (Wigan 1934, 1946, 1947, 1950, 1052, St Helens 1953, 1959)
Most appearances: 7 by Jim Sullivan (Wigan 1934, 1946, 1947, 1950, 1952, St Helens 1953, 1959)
Most consecutive wins: 2 by Arthur Bennett (Huddersfield 1912, 1913), Sid Melville (Hull 1920, 1921), Billy Kearns (Swinton 1927, 1928), Joe Withers (Huddersfield 1929, 1930), Jim Sullivan on two occasions (Wigan 1946, 1947 and Wigan 1952, St Helens 1953), Cec Mountford (Warrington 1954, 1955) and Ken Traill (Wakefield T 1967, 1968) (Note: Oldham won in 1911 under trainer Jim Mallalieu but it has not been possible to confirm the trainer when they won in 1910)
Most consecutive appearances: 4 by Arthur Bennett (Huddersfield 1912, 1913, 1914, 1915) (Note: It has not been possible to confirm the Oldham trainer in 1907, 1908, 1909 and 1910)

Premiership Trophy Finals (1975–97):
Most wins: 5 by Doug Laughton (Widnes 1980, 1982, 1988, 1989, 1990)
Most appearances: 7 by Doug Laughton (Widnes 1980, 1982, 1988, 1989, 1990, 1991, Leeds 1995)
Most consecutive wins: 3 by Doug Laughton (Widnes 1988, 1989, 1990)
Most consecutive appearances: 4 by Doug Laughton (Widnes 1988, 1989, 1990, 1991)

Super League Grand Finals (1998–2007):
Most wins: 3 by Brian Noble (Bradford B 2001, 2003, 2005)
Most appearances: 5 by Brian Noble (Bradford B 2001, 2002, 2003, 2004, 2005)
Most consecutive wins: no coach has won consecutive finals
Most consecutive appearances: 5 by Brian Noble (Bradford B 2001, 2002, 2003, 2004, 2005)

Referees records

Championship Finals (1907–1973):
(Excluding War Emergency League Finals 1940–45)
Most finals: 4 by Albert Dobson (1934, 1946, 1947, 1948), Frank Fairhurst (1923, 1929, 1932, 1938) and Alf Hill (1951, 1953, 1954, 1955)
Most consecutive finals: 3 by Albert Dobson (1946, 1947, 1948) and Alf Hill (1953, 1954, 1955)

Premiership Trophy Finals (1975–1997):
Most finals: 6 by John Holdsworth (1981, 1988, 1989, 1991, 1992, 1993)
Most consecutive finals: 3 by John Holdsworth (1991, 1992, 1993)

Super League Grand Finals (1998–2007):
Most finals: 3 by Russell Smith (1998, 2000, 2002)
Most consecutive finals: no referee has controlled consecutive finals

INDEX OF PLAYERS

Includes Northern Rugby League Championship Finals 1907–73 (incorporating War Emergency League Finals 1940–45), Club Championship Final 1974, Premiership Trophy Finals 1975–97, Super League Grand Finals 1998-2007

(Abbreviations: Bat – Batley, Bra – Bradford Northern/Bradford Bulls, Cas – Castleford, Dew – Dewsbury, Fea – Featherstone Rovers, Hfx – Halifax, HKR – Hull Kingston Rovers, Hud – Huddersfield, Hull – Hull/Hull FC, Hun – Hunslet, Lee – Leeds/Leeds Rhinos, Old – Oldham, Sfd – Salford, SHR – St Helens Recreation, StH – St Helens, Swi – Swinton, Wak – Wakefield Trinity, War – Warrington, Wid – Widnes, Wig – Wigan/Wigan Warriors, Work – Workington Town, r – replay, 1 – 1st leg only, 2 – 2nd leg only, 1+2 – played in both legs, s – substitute played, * - substitute did not play, W – won, L – lost)

INDEX OF PLAYERS

INDEX OF PLAYERS

INDEX OF PLAYERS

Jim Finnerty: Old 1922L
Derek Finnigan: War 1977L
Albert Firth: Wak 1960L, 1962L
Tony Fisher: Lee 1972W, 1973L
Harold 'Ike' Fishwick: War 1949L, 1951L
Peter 'Flash' Flanagan: HKR 1968L
Chris Flannery: StH 2007L
Darren Fleary: Lee 1998L
Jackie Fleming: Wig 1944(1+2)W, War 1948W, 1949L
Geoff Fletcher: Wig 1971L
Paul Fletcher: Lee 1979sW
Paul Fletcher: Hull 1989L
Tommy Flynn: War 1926L
Adam Fogerty: StH 1996L
Terry Fogerty: Hfx 1965W, 1966L
Paul Forber: StH 1985sW, 1988L
Mike Ford: Cas 1994L
Paul Ford: War 1986W
Mike Forshaw: Wig 1993sL, Bra 1999sL, 2001W, 2002L, 2003W
Mark Forster: War 1986W, 1987L
Colin Forsyth: Bra 1978sW, 1979L, 1980L
Frank Foster: HKR 1968L
Les Foster: HKR 1968L
Trevor Foster: Bra 1940(1+2)W, 1941(1+2)W, 1942L, 1948L, 1952L
Ike Fowler: Bat 1924W
Don Fox: Wak 1967D, 1967rW, 1968W
Frank Fox: Cas 1969sL
Neil Fox: Wak 1960L, 1962L, 1967D, 1967rW, 1968W, Bra 1978sW
Nick Fozzard: StH 2007L
Alf Francis: Hull 1920W
Arthur Francis: Wig 1913L
Bill Francis: Wig 1971L
Richard Francis: Bra 1990L
Roy Francis: Dew 1942W, 1943(1)W, 1944(1+2)L, War 1949L
Eric Fraser: War 1961L
Johnny Freeman: Hfx 1956L, 1965W, 1966L
Ray French: StH 1965L, 1966W, 1967D, 1967rL
Eric Frodsham: War 1951L, 1954W, 1955W
Harry Frodsham: StH 1932W
Arthur Frowen: War 1926L
David Furner: Wig 2001L, Lee 2004W

Brian Gabbitas: Hun 1959L
Frank Gallagher: Lee 1929L
Alf Gallimore: Wid 1936L
David Gandy: Wig 1971°L
Bernard Ganley: Old 1957W
Bert Ganley: Hud 1915W
Les Gant: Bra 1979L, 1980L
Ade Gardner: StH 2006W, 2007L
Joe Gardner: Dew 1942W, 1943(1+2)W, 1944(1+2)L
Fred Garner: Swi 1940(1+2)L
Harold 'Pete' Garrett: Hull 1920W, 1921W
Jack Garrett: War 1935L
Daniel Gartner: Bra 2001W, 2002L, 2003W
Jack Garvey: StH 1932W
Wayne Gaskell: War 1974sW
Richard Gay: Hull 1991W
Albert Gear: Sfd 1937W, 1939W
Hector Gee: Wig 1934W, 1944(1)W
Ken Gee: Wig 1941(1+2)L, 1944(1+2)W, 1947W, 1952W
S. Gee: Hud 1929W, 1930D, 1930rW
Derek 'Mick' George: Wid 1978sL, 1980W
Edward 'Eppie' Gibson: Work 1951W
Frank 'Sandy' Gibson: HKR 1921L
Matt Gidley: StH 2007L
Cyril Gilbertson: Dew 1947L
Ian Gildart: Wig 1993sL
Laurie Gilfedder: War 1961L
Henderson Gill: Wig 1987W
James Gill: Lee 1930D, 1931L
Ken Gill: Wid 1978L
Lee Gilmour: Wig 1998W, 2000sL, Bra 2002sL, StH 2006W, 2007L
Marc Glanville: Lee 1998L
Fred Gleave: Wig 1911l, 1912L, 1913L
Martin Gleeson: StH 2002W
Tommy Gleeson: Hud 1913W, 1914L, 1915W, 1920L
Peter Glynn: StH 1976W, 1977W
Brad Godden: Lee 1998L
Fred Godward: Lee 1915L
Joe Golby: Wig 1934W
J.W. 'George' Goldie: Lee 1930rL
Harry Goldsmith: Sfd 1914W
Bryn Goldswain: Old 1955L
Albert Goldthorpe: Hun 1908D, 1908rW
Walter Goldthorpe: Hun 1908D, 1908rW
Jack Goodall: War 1935L, 1937L
Andy Goodway: Wig 1987W
Dennis Goodwin: Lee 1961W
Parry Gordon: War 1977L
Les Gorley: Wid 1980W, 1982W, 1983W
Peter Gorley: StH 1985W
Bobbie Goulding: StH 1996L
Gordon Graham: Sfd 1976L
James Graham: StH 2006sW, 2007sL
Tommy Grahame: Hud 1946L
Les Grainge: Lee 1931L
Jeff Grayshon: Dew 1973W, Bra 1979L, 1980L
Dick Green: Swi 1935W
Douglas 'Duggie' Greenall: StH 1953W, 1959W
Johnny Greenall: STH 1927L
Les Greenall; StH 1972L
Bobby Greenough: War 1961L
Harry Greenwood: Hfx 1953L
Andy Gregory: Wid 1982W, 1983W, War 1986W, Wig 1987W
Mike Gregory: War 1986W, 1987sL
Tommy Grey: Hfx 1907W, Hud 1912W, 1913W
Alan Grice: Sfd 1976°L
Alf Grice: Hull 1920W
Fred Griffiths: Wig 1960W
Jonathan Griffiths: StH 1992sL, 1993sW
Ossie Griffiths: Wig 1934W
Tyssul Griffiths: Hfx 1953L, 1954L
Joe Grima: Wid 1988W, 1989W, 1990sW, 1991L
Ben Gronow: Hud 1912W, 1913W, 1914L, 1915W, 1923L
Paul Groves, StH 1988L, 1992sL
Walter Groves: StH 1932W
Don Gullick: StH 1953W
Geoff Gunney: Hun 1959L
Alan Gwilliam: StH 1974°L, War 1977L
Ken Gwilliam: StH 1975sL, 1976sW, 1977W

Robert Habron: Hud 1920L
Roy Haggerty: StH 1985W, 1988L
Neil Hague: Lee 1979W
Andy Haigh: StH 1996sL
Arthur Haigh: Fea 1928L
Bob Haigh: Wak 1967D, 1967rW, 1968W, Lee 1973L, 1975W, Bra 1978W
Gary Hale: Bra 1980L
Harold Haley: Cas 1939L
Len Haley: Bra 1952L
Norman Haley: Bra 1952L
Ben Halfpenny: StH 1932W
Billy Hall: Old 1922L
David Hall: HKR 1981W, 1984W, 1985L
Joe Hall: Fea 1928L
Martin Hall: Wig 1994W, 1995W, 1996W
Steve Hall: StH 2000W
Derek Hallas: Lee 1961W
Cyril Halliday: Hud 1929W, 1930D, 1930rW, 1932L
Frank Halliwell: Wig 1960W
Tom Halliwell: Swi 1925L, 1927W
Albert Halsall: StH 1966W, 1970W
Hector Halsall: Swi 1927W, 1928W
Brian Hambling: Hull 1958W
Harry Hammond: Dew 1942W, 1943(1+2)W, 1944(1+2)L, 1947L
Karle Hammond: StH 1996L, 1997L
Steve Hampson: Wig 1987W, 1992W
Ellery Hanley: Wig 1987W
Lee Hansen: Wig 1997W
Shontayne Hape: Bra 2003W, 2004L, 2005W
Roy Hardgrave: StH 1932W
Alan Hardisty: Cas 1969L, Lee 1972W, 1973L
Sam Hardman: War 1935L
Tommy Hardy: Cas 1939L
Kevin Harkin: Hull 1982L
Paul Harkin: HKR 1981W, 1984W, 1985sL, Bra 1990L
Neil Harmon: Lee 1995sL
Bill Harper: War 1961L
Ben Harris: Bra 2005W
Eric Harris: Lee 1938L

INDEX OF PLAYERS

INDEX OF PLAYERS

John Joyner: Cas 1984L
Chris Joynt: StH 1993W, 1997L, 1999W, 2000W, 2002W
Bill Jukes: Hun 1908d, 1908rW
Brian Juliff: Hfx 1986L

Tony Karalius: StH 1971W, 1975L, 1976W, 1977sW
Vince Karalius: StH 1959W
John Kear: Cas 1984L
Jack Keith: Old 1955L, 1957W
Alan Kellett: Hfx 1965W
Andy Kelly: HKR 1985L
Ken Kelly: StH 1971sW, 1972L
Mike Kelly: War 1977L
Gary Kemble: Hull 1982L, 1983L
Jim Kennedy: Hull 1920W, 1921W
Jack Kenny: Swi 1931W, 1933L
Tom Kenny: Sfd 1939W, Dew 1942W, 1943(1+2)W
George Kershaw: Dew 1942W, 1943(1+2)W, 1944(1+2)L
Martin Ketteridge: Cas 1994L
Stan Kielty: Hfx 1953L, 1954L, 1956L
Len Killeen: StH 1965L, 1966W, 1967D, 1967rL
Austin Kilroy: Hud 1962W
Harry King: SHR 1927L
Rex King: War 1935L
Paul King: Hull 2006sL
Ian Kirke: Lee 2007sW
Nicky Kiss: Wig 1987W
Billy Kitchin: Hud 1912W
Jack Kitching: Bra 1945(1+2)W
Ernie Knapman: Old 1922L
John Knighton: Sfd 1976L
Bryn Knowelden: War 1948W, 1951L
Emosi Koloto: Wid 1989W, 1990W, 1991L
Milan Kosanovic: Wak 1962L

Adrian Lam: Wig 2001L
Norman Lambert: Bra 1940(2)W
George Langhorn: Hfx 1907W
Jamie Langley: Bra 2004sL, 2005sW
John Langley: Lee 1969sW, 1970°L, 1972W, 1973sL
Billy Langton: Hun 1959L
Jack Large: Wig 1950W, 1952W
Doug Laughton: StH 1965L, Wig 1971L, Wid 1978L
Ali Lauitiiti: Lee 2004W, 2005sL, 2007sW
Harry Launce: Sfd 1914W
Johnny Lawrenson: Wig 1941(1+2)L, 1944(1+2)W, 1947W, Work 1951W
David Laws: HKR: 1984W, 1985L
Bill Leake: Hud 1946L
Andy Leathem: StH 1997L
Danny Leatherbarrow: Work 1958L
Jimmy Ledgard: Dew 1947L
Barry Ledger: StH 1985W, 1988L
Aaron Lee: Hud 1913W, 1914L, 1915W
Steve Lee: Dew 1973°W
Jack Leeming: Bat 1924W

Arthur Lees: Old 1907L
Elwyn Leigh: Swi 1927W
Roy Lester: War 1977L
James Leuluai: Hull 1982L, 1983L
Kylie Leuluai: Lee 2007W
Dan Lewis: Lee 1915L
George Lewis: StH 1932W
George Lewis: Cas 1939L
Randall Lewis: Swi 1940(1+2)L
Jimmy Leytham: Wig 1909W, 1910L, 1911L
Ralph Linton: Wid 1983W
Graham Liptrot: StH 1974L, 1977W
Billy Little: Hfx 1907W
Sid Little: Old 1955L, 1957W
Fred Littlewood: Hfx 1907W
Stewart Llewellyn: StH 1953W
Tom Llewellyn: Old 1908D, 1908rL, 1909L
Arthur Lloyd: Lee 1929L
Geoff 'Sammy' Lloyd: Cas 1982sL
Reg Lloyd: Cas 1939L
Brian Lockwood: Cas 1969L, Wid 1982W
Hubert Lockwood: Hfx 1943(1+2)L, 1945(1+2)L
James Lomas: Old 1911W
Sean Long: StH 1997L, 1999sW, 2000W, 2002W, 2006W, 2007L
Fred Longstaff: Hud 1912W, 1913W, 1914L, 1915W
Paul Longstaff: HKR 1968L
Billy Longworth: Old 1907L, 1908D, 1908rL
Paul Loughlin: StH 1988L, 1992L, 1993W
Arthur Loveluck: Sfd 1914W
Gerry Lowe: War 1954W, War 1955W
Jimmy Lowe: Dew 1944(1+2)L
Johnny Lowe: War 1974sW
Phil Lowe: HKR 1968L, 1981W
Trevor Lowe: Dew 1973W
James Lowes: Lee 1995L, Bra 1999L, 2001W, 2002L, 2003W
Alan Lowndes: Cas 1969L
Reg Lowrey: Wig 1946W
John Lydiat: HKR 1984sW, 1985sL
Joe Lydon: Wid 1983W, Wig 1987W, 1992W, 1994sW
Tommy Lynch: Hfx 1953L, 1954L, 1956L
David Lyon: StH: 1993W
Geoff Lyon: Wig 1960W
Jamie Lyon: StH 2006W

John 'Jock' McAvoy: Work 1958L
Nathan McAvoy: Bra 1999°L
Tom McCabe: Old 1910W, 1911W
Seamus McCallion: Hfx 1986L
Joe McComas: SHR 1927L
Robbie McCormack: Wig 1998W
Stan McCormick: StH 1953W, War 1954W
Tommy McCue: Hfx 1943(1+2)L, 1945(1+2)L
Steve McCurrie: Wid 1991L

Barrie McDermott: Lee 2004sW, 2005sL
Brian McDermott: Bra 1999sL, 2001W, 2002sL
Hughie McDowell: Wid 1936L, Hfx 1943(1+2)L
Damien McGarry: Hull 1991W
Tommy McGiever: HKR 1921L
Brian McGinn: StH 1959W
Billy McGinty: War 1986sW, Wig 1992W
Steve McGowan: Bra 1990L
Jim McGregor: Swi 1935L
Danny McGuire: Lee 2004W, 2005L, 2007W
Jack McGurk: Swi 1940(1+2)L
Harold McIntyre: Wig 1950W
John 'Paddy' McIntyre: HKR 1923W, 1925W
Graham Mackay: Bra 2001W
Vince McKeating: Dew 1947L, Work 1951W
Chris McKenna: Lee 2004W, 2005L
Phil McKenzie: Wid 1988W, 1989W, 1990W, 1991L
Greg Mackey: Hull 1991W
Tom McKinney: War 1955W, StH 1959W
Ian MacLean: Bra 1980L
Jack McLean: Bra 1952L
Tom McLean: Old 1910W
Matt McLeod: Wak 1968W
Shayne McMenemy: Hull 2006L
Steve McNamara: Bra 1999L
Brian McTigue: Wig 1960W
Derek McVey: StH 1996L, StH 1997L

Ian Madley: Hull 1981sL
Joe Mageen: Bra 1952L
John Maiden: Hud 1949W
Harry Major: War 1961L
Terry Major: HKR 1968L
Brady Malam: Wig 2000sL
Ken Mallinson: Hud 1946L
Jack Maloney: Wig 1941(1+2)L
George Mann: StH 1992L, 1993W, Lee 1995L
John Mantle: StH 1965L, 1966W, 1967D, 1967rL, 1970W, 1971W, 1972L, 1974L, 1975L, 1976W
Tony Marchant: Cas 1984L, Bra 1990L
J.W. Markham: Hull 1920W
Harry Markham: Hull 1956W
Alf Marklew: Bra 1945(1+2)W
Rothwell 'Rod' Marlor: Old 1922L
Ian Marlow: Hull 1991W
C. Marsden: Hud 1920L
Dave Marshall: Lee 1975sW
Tommy Martyn: War 1977L
Tommy Martyn: StH 1996L, 1999W, 2000W
Martin Masella: Lee 1998L
Len Mason: Wig 1934W
Mel Mason: Lee 1975W
Vila Matautia: StH 1999sW
Ian Mather: War 1974W

INDEX OF PLAYERS

INDEX OF PLAYERS

INDEX OF PLAYERS

Ryan Sheridan: Lee 1998L
Ernie Sherratt: Wid 1936L
Arthur Sherwood Hud 1920L, 1923L
Herbert 'Con' Sherwood: Hud 1912W
Herbert Sherwood: Hud 1932L
Edwin Shield: Hull 1920W
Paul Shiels: StH 2002sW
Mick Shoebottom: Lee 1969W, 1970L
Bill Shreeve: Bra 1952L
Dick Silcock: Wig 1909W, 1910L, 1912L, 1913L
Nat Silcock: Wig 1950W, 1952W
Barry Simms: Lee 1961W
Jack Simpson: Wig 1941(1+2)L
Roger Simpson: Bra 1990L
Kevin Sinfield: Lee 2004W, 2005L, 2007W
Alan Skene: Wak 1960L, 1962L
Kelvin Skerrett: Bra 1990L, Wig 1993L, 1994W, 1995W, 1996W
Trevor Skerrett: Hull 1981L, 1982L, 1983L
Ted Slevin: Wig 1950W, Hud 1962W
Bob Sloman: Old 1922L
Ian Smales: Cas 1994sL
John Smales: Hun 1908rW
Tommy Smales: Hud 1962W
Freddy Smart: Hud 1929W
Alan Smith: Lee 1970L, 1972W, 1973L, 1975W, 1979W
Arthur Smith: Old 1907L, 1908D, 1908rL, 1909L, 1910W, 1911W
Bert Smith: Bra 1940(1+2)W, 1941(1+2), 1942L, 1948L
R. 'Bob' Smith: Lee 1931L
Charlie Smith: Hfx 1943 (1+2)L
Chris Smith: Cas 1994L, StH 1999W
Craig Smith: Wig 2003L
David Smith: Lee 1979W
Fred Smith: Hun 1908D, 1908rW
Fred Smith: Wak 1960L, 1962L
George Smith: Old 1908D, 1909L, 1910W, 1911W
Gordon Smith: HKR 1985L
Jack Smith: Bat 1924W
J.W. Smith: Fea 1928L
Lee Smith: Lee 2007W
Mark Smith: Wig 2003sL
Mike Smith: HKR 1981W, 1984W, 1985L
Sam Smith: Hun 1959L
Stanley Smith: Lee 1930D, 1930rL, 1931L, 1938L
Steve Smith: Hfx 1986sL
Ted Smith: Wig 1922W
Tommy Smith: SHR 1927L
Tony Smith: Cas 1994L, Wig 1997W, 1998W, 2000L
Wilf Smith: StH 1959W, 1965L, 1967D, 1967rL
Patrick Solal: Hull 1983sL
Kurt Sorenson: Wid 1988W, 1989W, 1990W, 1991L
Ike Southward: Work 1958L
Alan Spencer: Bra 1979L
Stanley Spencer: Hud 1929W, 1930D, 1930rW
Stuart Spruce: Bra 1999L
Farragher Stamper: Hud 1923L
Tom Stamper: Work 1958L
John Stankevitch: StH 2000sW, 2002sW
Colin Stansfield: Hun 1938W
Billy Stead: Hull 1936W, Cas 1939W
Graham Steadman: Cas 1994L
Frank Stephens: Wig 1926W
Gary Stephens: Hfx 1986L
John Stephens: StH: 1971W, 1972L
David Stephenson: Wig 1987W
Mike 'Mick' Stephenson: Dew 1973W
Nigel Stephenson: Dew 1973W, Bra 1980L
Anthony Stewart: StH 1997L
Frank Stirrup: Old 1955L
Jim Stockdill: Hun 1959L
John Stocks: Hud 1930D, 1930rW
Jack Stoddart: Swi 1940(1+2)L
Billy Stone: Hull 1921W
Richard 'Charlie' Stone: Hull 1981L, 1982L, 1983L
Arthur Street: Dew 1947L
Harry Street: Wig 1952W
Miller Strong: Swi 1925L, 1927W, 1928W, 1933L
Anthony Sullivan: StH 1992L, 1996L, 1997L, 1999W, 2000W, 2002W
Jim Sullivan: Wig 1922W, 1926W, 1934W, 1944(2)W
Joe Sullivan: Swi 1935W
Wilf Sulway: Swi 1925L, 1928W
H. Sutcliffe: Hud 1920L
Richard Swain: Hull 2006L
Logan Swann: Bra 2004L
Walter Swift: Lee 1929L
Arthur Swinden: Hud 1920L, 1923L
Cyril Sykes: Hull 1957L, 1958W
Nathan Sykes: Cas 1994sL

Alan Tait: Wid 1988sW, 1989W, 1990W, 1991L, Lee 1995L
Willie Talau: StH 2006W, 2007L
Gael Tallec: Wig 1997sW
Kevin Tamati: War 1986W, 1987L
David Tanner: StH 1988L
Bill Targett: Wig 1934W
Ted Tattersfield: Lee 1938L
Bob Taylor: Hull 1920W, 1921W
Brian Taylor: Dew 1973sW
Friend Taylor: Hfx 1945(1+2)L
George Taylor: Fea 1928L
Tommy Taylor: Cas 1939L
John Tembey: StH 1965L
Abe Terry: StH 1959W
Laurie Thacker: Hull 1936W
Rick Thackray: Wid 1988W
Arthur 'Ginger' Thomas: Lee 1929L, 1930rL, 1931L
Evan Thomas: Sfd 1914W
Gwyn Thomas: Hud 1923L
Harold Thomas: Sfd 1939W
Jacky Thomas: Work 1951W
Johnny Thomas: Wig 1909W, 1910L, 1911L, 1912L, 1913L
R.L. 'Dicky' Thomas: Old 1907L, 1908D, 1908rL
Tony Thomas: Cas 1969L
WS 'Willie' Thomas: Sfd 1914W
Cec Thompson: Work 1958L
Ernie 'Cherry' Thompson: Hud 1930D, 1930rW, 1932L
Jimmy Thompson: Bra 1978W, 1979L, 1980L
Joe Thompson: Lee 1929L, 1930D, 1930rL, 1931L
John Thorley: Hfx 1954L, 1956L
Ken Thornett: Lee 1961W
Willie Thornton: Hun 1938W
Steve Thurlow: Work 1951W
Danny Tickle: Wig 2003L
Henry Tiffany: Hud 1930D, 1930rW, 1932L
Maurice Tighe: Old 1922L
Keith Tindall: Hull 1981L, 1982L
Brian Todd: Hfx 1965°W
George Todd: Hud 1920L
George Todd: Hfx 1943(1+2)L, 1945(1+2)L
Lance Todd: Wig 1909W, 1910L, 1911L, 1913L
Peter Todd: Hfx 1954L
Mark Tolson: Hun 1938W
Alf Tomkins: Old 1922L
Motu Tony: Hull 2006L
Clinton Toopi: Lee 2007W
Harry Topham: Old 1907L, 1909L
David Topliss: Hull 1982L, 1983L
Joe Topping: Wig 1910L
Peter Topping: Wid 1936L
Ken Traill: Bra 1948L, 1952L, Hfx 1956L
Jimmy Tranter: War 1926L
Dennis Trotter: Bra 1978W, 1979L
Va'aiga Tuigamala: Wig 1996W
Fereti 'Freddie' Tuilagi: StH 1999W, 2000sW
Sam Turnbull: Sfd 1976sL
Carl Turner: Hull 1956W, 1957L
Derek Turner: Old 1957W, Wak 1960L, 1962L
Neil Turner: Hull 1991W
Albert 'Dicky' Twose: Wig 1934W
Barry Tyler: Bra 1948L, 1952L
Colin Tyrer: Wig 1971L
George Tyson: Old 1907L, 1908D, 1908rL, 1909L

Joe Vagana: Bra 2001W, 2002L, 2003W, 2004L, 2005sW
Tevita Vaikona: Bra 1999L, 2001W, 2002L, 2003W
Lesley Vainikolo: Bra 2002L, 2003W, 2004L, 2005W

INDEX OF PLAYERS

INDEX OF COACHES

Includes Northern Rugby League Championship Finals 1907–73 (incorporating War Emergency League Finals 1940–45), Club Championship Final 1974, Premiership Trophy Finals 1975–97, Super League Grand Finals 1998–2007

(Abbreviations: W – won, L – lost)

Chris Anderson: Halifax 1986L

Daniel Anderson: St Helens 2006W, 2007L

A. Armitage: Batley 1924W

Eric Ashton: Wigan 1971L, 1975L, St Helens 1976W, 1977W

A. 'Tony' Barrow: Warrington 1986W, 1987L

Arthur Bennett: Huddersfield 1912W, 1913W, 1914L, 1915W

W. 'Billy' Bennett: Warrington 1935L, Halifax 1943L, 1945L

W. 'Billy' Benyon: St Helens 1985W

Les Bettinson: Salford 1976L

Chris Brockbank: Warrington 1937L, 1948W, 1949L, 1951L

Jim Brough: Workington Town 1958L

Arthur Bunting: Hull 1981L, 1982L, 1983L

Eddie Caswell: Hull 1936W

Jim Challinor: St Helens 1971W, 1972L, 1974L

Noel Cleal: Hull 1991W

Joe Coan: St Helens 1965L, 1966W, 1967L

Frank 'Dolly' Dawson: Halifax 1953L, 1954L, 1956L

Harry Dawson & Colin Tyrer: Widnes 1983W

Joe Egan: Wigan 1960W

Matthew Elliott: Bradford Bulls 1999L

Frank Endacott: Wigan Warriors 2000L

Cliff Evans: St Helens 1970W

Albert Fearnley: Halifax 1965W, 1966L

Alex Fiddes: Huddersfield 1949W

Jack Fish: Warrington 1926L

E 'Ted' Forber: St Helens Recreation 1927L

Peter Fox: Bradford Northern 1978W, 1979L, 1980L

Roy Francis: Hull 1956W, 1957L, 1958W, Leeds 1975W

Mike Gregory: Wigan Warriors 2003W

Ellery Hanley: St Helens 1999W

W. 'Billy' Hannah: Hunslet 1908W, 1938W

Jack Hesketh: Wigan 1909W, 1910L, 1911L, 1912L, 1913L

Vic Hey: Dewsbury 1947L

B. Heyhirst: Leeds 1929L, 1939L, 1931L

David Hobbs: Bradford Northern 1990L

Eric Hughes: Wigan Warriors 1997W

Colin Hutton: Hull Kingston Rovers 1968L

Syd Hynes: Leeds 1979W

W 'Billy' Jacques: Hull Kingston Rovers 1921L, 1923W, 1926W

Griff Jenkins: Oldham 1955L, 1957W

John Joyner: Castleford 1994L

W. 'Billy' Kearns: Swinton 1925L, 1927W, 1928W, 1931W, 1933L, 1935W, 1940L

Doug Laughton: Widnes 1980W, 1982W, 1988W, 1989W, 1990W, 1991L, Leeds 1995L

Graham Lowe: Wigan 1987W

Peter Lyons: Widnes 1936L

Tommy McCarty: Wigan 1922W, 1924L, 1926W

Mike McClennan: St Helens 1992L, 1993W

Shaun McRae: St Helens 1996L, 1997L

Jim Mallalieu: Oldham 1911W

Charles Marsden: Oldham 1922L

Sid Melville: Hull 1920W, 1921W

Joe Midgley: Halifax 1907W

Ian Millward: St Helens 2000W, 2002W

Roger Millward: Hull Kingston Rovers 1981W, 1984W, 1985L

John Monie: Wigan/Wigan Warriors 1992W, 1993L, 1998W

W. Morn: Leeds 1915L

Cec Mountford: Warrington 1954W, 1955W, 1961L

Alex Murphy: Warrington 1974W, 1977L, St Helens 1988L

Graham Murray Leeds Rhinos 1998L

Frank Myler: Widnes 1978L

Brian Noble: Bradford Bulls 2001W, 2002L, 2003W, 2004L, 2005W

E. 'Teddy' Parkes: Wigan 1941L, 1944W

Dai Prosser: Leeds 1961W

Stuart Raper Wigan Warriors 2001L

Dai Rees: Bradford Northern 1940W, 1941W, 1942L, 1945W, 1948L, 1952L

Malcolm Reilly: Castleford 1984L

W. 'Billy' Rhodes: Castleford 1939L

A.J. 'Gus' Risman: Workington Town 1951W

Peter Sharp: Hull FC 2006L

Tommy Smales: Dewsbury 1973W

Brian Smith: Hull 1989L

E. 'Ted' Smith: St Helens 1932W

Tony Smith: Leeds Rhinos 2004W, 2005L, 2007W

W. 'Billy' Smith: Leeds 1938L

Jim Sullivan: Wigan 1934W, 1946W, 1947W, 1950W, 1952W, St Helens 1953W, 1959W

L.B. 'Lance' Todd: Salford 1933W, 1934L, 1937W, 1939W

Ken Traill: Wakefield Trinity 1960L, 1962L, 1967W, 1968W

Derek Turner: Castleford 1969L, Leeds 1970L, 1972W, 1973L

Dave Valentine: Huddersfield 1962W

Jack Walkington: Hunslet 1959L

Joe Warham: Leeds 1969W*

Eddie Waring: Dewsbury 1942W, 1943W**, 1944L

Graeme West: Wigan 1994W, 1995W, 1996W

Joe White: Salford 1914W

J.T. 'Joe' Withers: Huddersfield 1929W, 1930W, 1932L

* Joe Warham had temporary charge of Leeds in 1969 after Jack Nelson died on Christmas Day

** Dewsbury's 'win' in 1943 later declared null and void

(Note: The above list includes whoever is deemed responsible for the team, whether coach, trainer or team manager. Trainers, who were responsible for players' fitness rather than tactics, gave way to coaches and team managers during the 1930s/1940s)

(Note: The author regrets he has been unable to confirm the coach, trainer or team manager for the following teams: Featherstone R 1928, Huddersfield 1920, 1923, 1946, 1950, Oldham 1907, 1908, 1909, 1910)

INDEX OF REFEREES

Includes Northern Rugby League Championship Finals 1907–73 (incorporating War Emergency League Finals 1940–45), Club Championship Final 1974, Premiership Trophy Finals 1975–97, Super League Grand Finals 1998–2007

(Abbreviations: Bat – Batley, Bra – Bradford Northern/Bradford Bulls, Cas – Castleford, Dew – Dewsbury, Fea – Featherstone Rovers, Hfx – Halifax, HKR – Hull Kingston Rovers, Hud - Huddersfield, Hull – Hull/Hull FC, Hun – Hunslet, Lee – Leeds/Leeds Rhinos, Old – Oldham, Sfd – Salford, SHR - St Helens Recreation, StH – St Helens, Swi – Swinton, Wak - Wakefield Trinity, War – Warrington, Wid – Widnes, Wig – Wigan/Wigan Warriors, Work – Workington Town, r – replay, 1 – 1st leg, 2 – 2nd leg)

Stan Adams (Hull): 1939 Cas v Sfd

Kevin Allatt (Southport): 1987 War v Wig

C.F. 'Charlie' Appleton (Warrington): 1952 Bra v Wig, 1956 Hfx v Hull

Arthur Brown (Wakefield): 1921 Hull v HKR, 1925 HKR v Swi

D.S. 'Deryk' Brown (Dewsbury): 1965 Hfx v StH; (Preston): 1968 HKR v Wak

David Campbell (Widnes): 1996 StH v Wig

Ron Campbell (Widnes): 1984 Cas v HKR

Reverend F.H. 'Frank' Chambers (Huddersfield): 1928 Fea v Swi

Eric Clay (Leeds): 1960 Wak v Wig

Matt Coates (Pudsey): 1949 Hud v War*, 1950 Hud v Wig, 1957 Hull v Old

Paul Cowell (Warrington): 1936 Hull v Wid, 1940(2) Bra v Swi, 1941(2) Bra v Wig

Stuart Cummings (Widnes): 1994 Cas v Wig, 1995 Lee v Wig, 1997 StH v Wig, 1999 Bra v StH, 2001 Bra v Wig

A.S. 'Albert' Dobson (Featherstone): 1934 Sfd v Wig, 1941(1) Wig v Bra, 1943(1) Dew v Hfx, 1943(2) Hfx v Dew, 1944(1) Wig v Dew, 1945(2) Bra v Hfx, 1946 Hud v Wig, 1947 Dew v Wig, 1948 Bra v War

Frank Fairhurst (Wigan): 1923 Hud v HKR, 1929 Hud v Lee, 1932 Hud v StH, 1938 Hun v Lee

Steve Ganson (St Helens): 2004 Bra v Lee

Ron Gelder (Wakefield): 1958 Hull v Work; (Wilmslow): 1961 Lee v War

Peter Geraghty (York): 1974 StH v War

A.E. 'Albert' Harding (Manchester): 1930 Hud v Lee, 1930(r) Hud v Lee

Albert Hestford (Broughton): 1920 Hud v Hull

Alf Hill (Dewsbury): 1951 War v Work, 1953 Hfx v StH, 1954 Hfx v War, 1955 Old v War

Andy Holbrook (Warrington): 1944(2) Dew v Wig

John Holdsworth (Kippax): 1981 Hull v HKR, 1988 StH v Wid, 1989 Hull v Wid, 1991 Hull v Wid, 1992 StH v Wig, 1993 StH v Wig

Harry Horsfall (Batley): 1927 SHR v Swi

H.G. 'Harry' Hunt (Prestbury): 1973 Dew v Lee

J.E. 'Joe' Jackson (Pudsey): 1978 Bra v Wid

Karl Kirkpatrick (Warrington): 2003 Bra v Wig, 2006 Hull v StH

Ashley Klein (Keighley): 2005 Bra v Lee, 2007 Lee v StH

Eric Lawrinson (Warrington): 1971 StH v Wig

G.F. 'Fred' Lindop (Wakefield): 1977 StH v War, 1983 Hull v Wid, 1986 Hfx v War

J.C. 'Jimmy' Lumley (Leeds): 1909 Old v Wig

W. 'Billy' McCutcheon (Oldham): 1913 Hud v Wig, 1914 Hud v Sfd

Joe Manley (Warrington): 1966 Hfx v StH, 1967(r) StH v Wak

J.F. 'Jimmy' May (St Helens): 1912 Hud v Wig, 1915 Hud v Lee

Frank Mills (Oldham): 1924 Bat v Wig

Colin Morris (Huddersfield): 1990 Bra v Wid

M.J. 'Mick' Naughton (Widnes): 1976 StH v Sfd

Frank Peel (Bradford): 1931 Lee v Swi, 1935 Swi v War, 1937 Sfd v War

G.S. 'George' Phillips (Widnes): 1942 Bra v Dew

George Philpott (Leeds): 1967 StH v Wak

Joseph Priestley (Salford): 1907 Hfx v Old

N.T. 'Norman' Railton (Wigan): 1962 Hud v Wak

R. 'Bob' Robinson (Bradford): 1908 Hun v Old, 1922 Old v Wig, 1926 War v Wig

Sam Shepherd (Oldham): 1972 Lee v StH

J.H. 'Jack' Smith (Widnes): 1910 Old v Wig

Russell Smith (Castleford): 1998 Lee v Wig, 2000 StH v Wig, 2002 Bra v StH

Harold Swift (Halifax): 1933 Sfd v Swi

J.E. 'Jack' Taylor (Wakefield): 1940(1) Swi v Bra, 1945(1) Hfx v Bra

W.H. 'Billy' Thompson (Huddersfield): 1969 Cas v Lee, 1970 Lee v StH, 1975 Lee v StH, 1979 Bra v Lee, 1980 Bra v Wid

Ernest Tonge (Swinton): 1908(r) Hun v Old

Stan Wall (Leigh): 1982 Hull v Wid, 1985 HKR v StH

J.W. Whiteley (Wakefield): 1911 Old v Wig

George Wilson (Dewsbury): 1959 Hun v StH

* In 1949 Matt Coates was originally a touch judge, being a late replacement for referee Frank Smith of Barrow, who did not arrive, subsequently claiming he had not received 'official notification' of his appointment.

(Note: Excepting the earlier years, when referees place names were listed according to the clubs they were attached to, the city/town name is based on their place of residence, hence Deryk Brown and Ron Gelder, who changed addresses, are each associated with two place names)